Ian Williams was a foreign correspondent for Channel 4 News, based in Russia (1992–95), and Asia (1995–2006). He then joined NBC News as Asia Correspondent (2006–2015), working from bureaus in Bangkok and Beijing. As well as reporting from China and across the region, he covered conflicts in the Balkans, the Middle East and Ukraine, and won an Emmy and BAFTA awards for his discovery and reporting on the Serb detention camps during the war in Bosnia. His previous book. *Every Breath You Take: China's New Tyranny*, was published to critical acclaim in 2021.

'Absolutely fascinating'
Andrew Marr, LBC

'An essential read for anybody who wants to understand the foreign policy of modern-day China, and in particular the role and goals of China's leader Xi Jinping ... A fascinating book, a really good read'
Phil Harding, journalist and broadcaster

'A fascinating, accessible guide to our new geopolitical reality'
James Wilson, Tortoise Media

'[A] superb book... I recommend it very highly'
Benedict Rogers, chief executive of Hong Kong Watch

'The most important book I've read this year . . . Eye opening'
Matt Ridley, author of *Viral: The Search for the Origin of Covid-19*

Praise for *Every Breath You Take: China's New Tyranny*

'Superb and deeply informed . . . a chilling reminder to all who believe in the rule of law and an open society of China's present threats to our way of life'
Chris Patten, Governor of Hong Kong, 1992–97

'Williams knows his stuff. This is an accessible, valuable, troubling, timely book'
Iain Martin, Reaction

'A persuasive, alarming wake-up call'
*Irish Times*

'A superb book'
Benedict Rogers, chief executive, Hong Kong Watch

'Fascinating . . . a really interesting book'
Stig Abell, Times Radio

IAN WILLIAMS

# THE FIRE OF THE DRAGON

## CHINA'S NEW COLD WAR

BIRLINN

This edition first published in 2024 by
Birlinn Limited
West Newington House
10 Newington Road
Edinburgh
EH9 1QS

*www.birlinn.co.uk*



ISBN: 978 1 78027 875 9

British Library Cataloguing-in-Publication Data

A catalogue record for this book is available from the British Library

Typeset by Initial Typesetting Services, Edinburgh

Papers used by Birlinn are from well-managed forests and other responsible sources

Printed and bound by Clays Ltd, Elcograf S.p.A.

# *Contents*

# *Acknowledgements*

The ambition of the Chinese Communist Party is broad and growing, and that is reflected in the scope of this book. Much of it is drawn from many years travelling and reporting from China and across Asia, bearing witness as Beijing flexed its muscles overseas and increased its repression at home. I am indebted to the many people who have shared their insights and been so generous with their time. They are too numerous to name individually, and many anyway prefer anonymity. It is safer that way. The Party is a capricious and vengeful organisation – increasingly so under Xi Jinping. It is intolerant of criticism, wherever that comes from. Speaking up can incur considerable cost – and this book is dedicated to those with the courage to do so.

In many ways the themes of this book build upon those of *Every Breath You Take: China's New Tyranny*, my earlier study of the surveillance state. Understanding China and the threat it poses is more important than ever – and special thanks are due to Hugh Andrew of Birlinn, who immediately recognised this. Many thanks also to my editor, Andrew Simmons, for his deft touch and expertise; and to my agent, Andrew Lownie, for his enthusiasm and encouragement throughout. Lastly, a big thank you to my family for their support and feedback as this manuscript took shape.

Ian Williams
June 2022

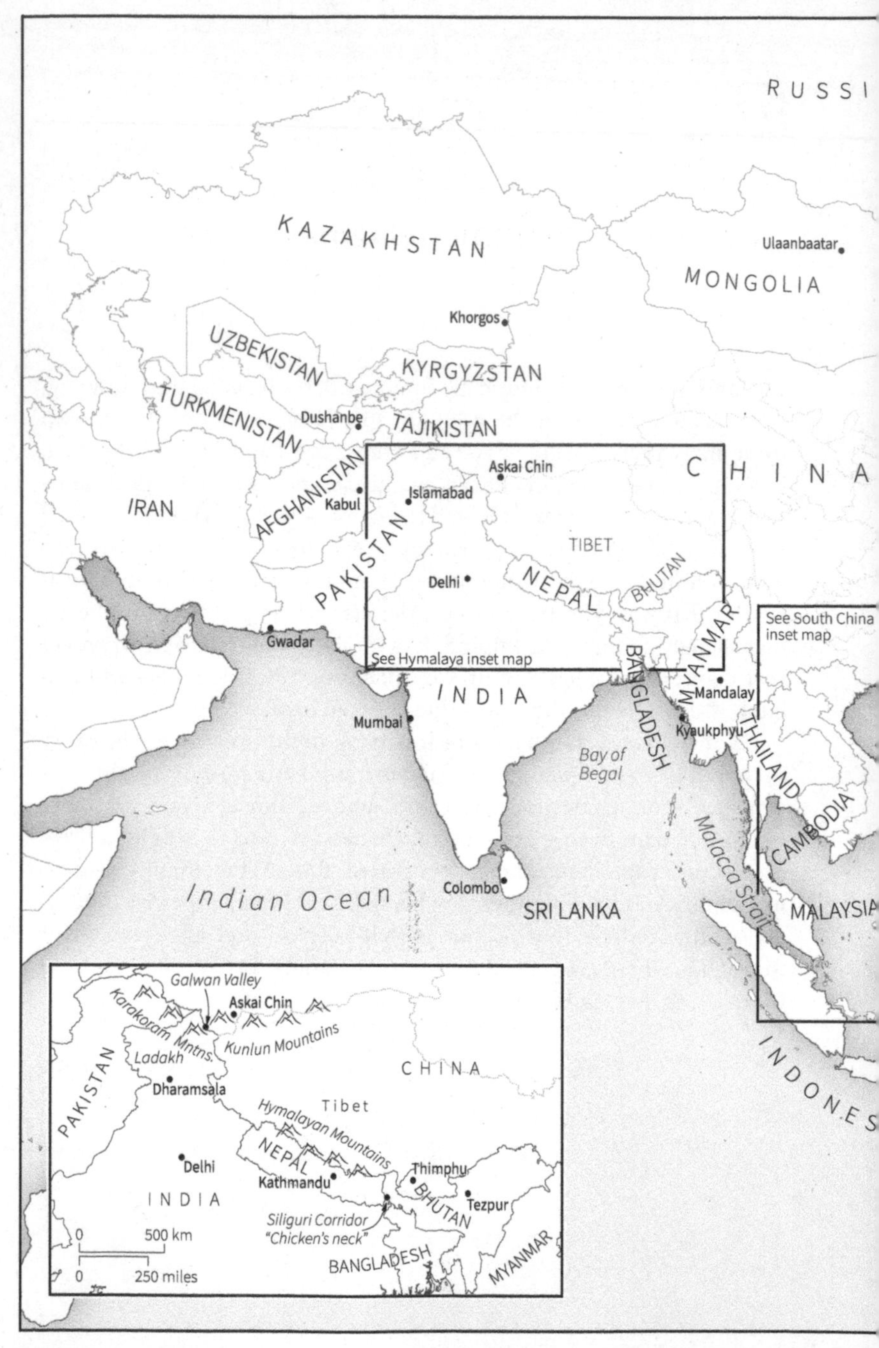
RUSSI
KAZAKHSTAN
MONGOLIA
Ulaanbaatar
Khorgos
UZBEKISTAN
KYRGYZSTAN
TURKMENISTAN
Dushanbe
TAJIKISTAN
AFGHANISTAN
Kabul
Askai Chin
Islamabad
C H I N A
IRAN
TIBET
PAKISTAN
Delhi
NEPAL
BHUTAN
Gwadar
See Hymalaya inset map
BANGLADESH
MYANMAR
See South China inset map
INDIA
Mandalay
Mumbai
Kyaukphyu
THAILAND
Bay of Begal
CAMBODIA
Malacca Strait
Indian Ocean
Colombo
SRI LANKA
MALAYSIA
INDONES
Galwan Valley
Askai Chin
Karakoram Mntns.
Kunlun Mountains
Ladakh
PAKISTAN
CHINA
Dharamsala
Tibet
Hymalayan Mountains
NEPAL
Delhi
Thimphu
Kathmandu
BHUTAN
Tezpur
INDIA
Siliguri Corridor
"Chicken's neck"
0 500 km
0 250 miles
BANGLADESH
MYANMAR

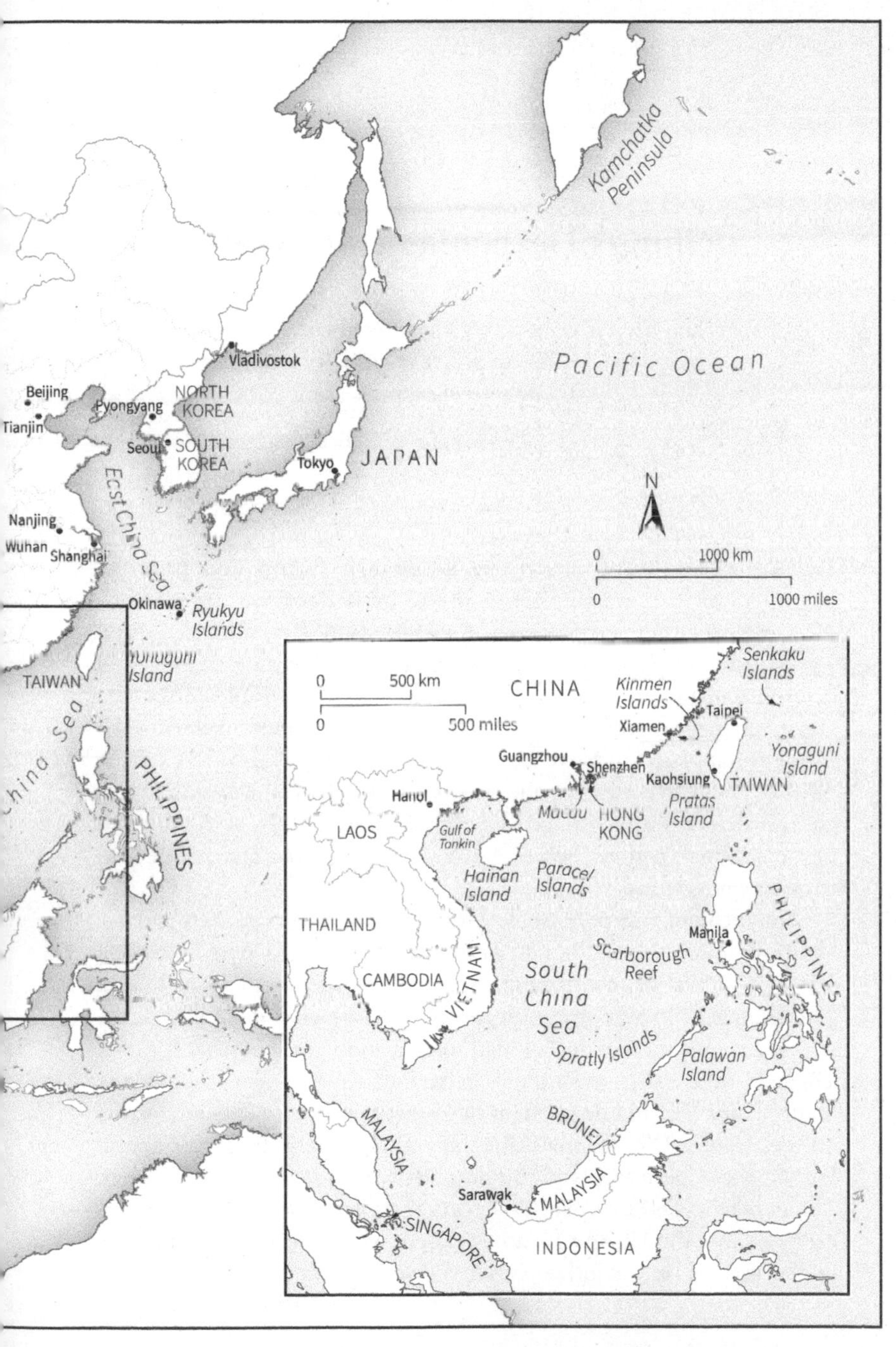
Kamchatka Peninsula
Pacific Ocean
Vladivostok
Beijing
Tianjin
Pyongyang
NORTH KOREA
Seoul
SOUTH KOREA
Tokyo
JAPAN
East China Sea
Nanjing
Wuhan
Shanghai
N
0
1000 km
0
1000 miles
Okinawa
Ryukyu Islands
Yonaguni Island
TAIWAN
China Sea
PHILIPPINES
0
500 km
0
500 miles
CHINA
Kinmen Islands
Senkaku Islands
Taipei
Xiamen
Yonaguni Island
Guangzhou
Shenzhen
Kaohsiung
TAIWAN
Hanoi
Macau
HONG KONG
Pratas Island
LAOS
Gulf of Tonkin
Hainan Island
Paracel Islands
THAILAND
Manila
PHILIPPINES
Scarborough Reef
CAMBODIA
VIETNAM
South China Sea
Spratly Islands
Palawan Island
BRUNEI
MALAYSIA
Sarawak
MALAYSIA
SINGAPORE
INDONESIA

# Preface to the 2024 Edition

## *China's Deepening Cold War*

'When friends visit us, we welcome them with fine wine. When jackals or wolves come, we will face them with shotguns'

*Li Shangfu, China's defence minister, June 2023*

The Australian divers were trying to untangle fishing nets from the propellers of their warship when the Chinese destroyer approached, directing powerful sonar pulses towards them. The intense sound waves, used to detect and track submarines, can cause dizziness and hearing damage, and the Australians were quickly pulled from the water having suffered what were described as 'minor injuries'. The incident happened in November 2023 in international waters off the coast of Japan, even though the Australian ship had signalled the presence of divers. Canberra accused the Chinese miliary of 'unsafe and unprofessional' actions, while Beijing attacked Australia's 'rude and irresponsible claims'.

The incident was only the latest in a series of increasingly intense confrontations around the East and South China Seas since this book was first published, confirming the area as a dangerous front line in China's new Cold War. A month earlier, the US Department of Defense released a collection of declassified images and videos of what it called 'coercive and risky operational behaviour' in the skies above the South China Sea. In one incident, a Chinese jet fighter flew as close as 10 feet from a US reconnaissance aircraft in international air space, forcing the American plane to take evasive action to avoid collision. The Pentagon said that over two years there had been 300 such intercepts against the US and its allies. There were also close encounters in the sea below – another video showed a Chinese guided-missile destroyer cutting dangerously across the bow of a US warship transiting the Taiwan Strait. China claims almost the entire South China Sea as its sovereign territory, a claim ruled to have no legal basis under the UN Convention on the Law of the Sea, to which Beijing is a signatory. However, China ignores the ruling, asserting its claim with increasing aggression. For their part, the US and its allies have stepped up 'freedom of navigation' missions. During the last Cold War, Soviet warships and fighter jets regularly sparred with Western forces; such 'intercepts' are now a part of the playbook of the People's Liberation Army.

Second Thomas Shoal, a lonely outpost of the Philippines in the Spratly Islands in the South China Sea, is fast becoming another dangerous flashpoint. In late 2023, swarms of ships from China's coast guard sought to prevent vessels from the Philippines re-supplying marines on board a marooned transport ship, the *Sierra Madre*, which serves as a military base on the shoal and is a symbol of Manila's sovereignty. The Chinese ships, superior in numbers and firepower, circled, jostled and cut-up their rivals, firing water cannon at them and colliding with two. When one Philippine ship made it through with Christmas presents donated by the public, it was celebrated in Manila as a victory of sorts over China's marine militia. In response, the US navy stepped up patrols off the coast of the Philippines, with the re-supply of the *Sierra Madre* seen as a key test of the re-invigorated US–Philippines defence treaty.

Vital sub-sea data cables have become another source of tension in the region, with projects for laying and upgrading data cables across the floor of the South China Sea facing delays because of Chinese obstruction. The vulnerability of this vital digital infrastructure to sabotage was highlighted by the repeated severing of cables linking the Taiwanese-controlled island of Matsu, which sits just 10 miles off the Chinese coast, to the outside world. The cables were snapped 27 times in the five years to 2023. Later that year, a Chinese ship became the focus of an investigation into the apparent sabotage of data cables under the Baltic Sea, linking Finland and Sweden to Estonia. The incident happened just a few months after Finland joined NATO, and with an application from Sweden nearing completion. Russia threatened 'counter-measures' in response, with Beijing supporting Moscow's criticism of NATO expansion. Concerns over vulnerable undersea infrastructure led to northern European countries setting up a joint expedition force in December 2023, Britain contributing seven Royal Navy ships and a maritime patrol aircraft.

Concerns were intensified by a lack of communications between the US and Chinese militaries of the type that existed in the last Cold War with the Soviet Union to prevent incidents spinning out of control. At a security conference in Singapore in June 2023, China's recently appointed defence minister, Li Shangfu, re-buffed efforts by his US counterpart to establish military-to-military dialogue aimed at putting what the Americans called 'guardrails' around the relationship. Li quoted approvingly from a Chinese song saying, 'When friends visit us, we welcome them with fine wine. When jackals or wolves come, we will face them with shotguns.' Li vanished two months after the conference, apparently purged amid corruption rumours. His abrupt departure followed the disappearance of top generals of the elite PLA Rocket Force, which oversees land-based missiles, including China's nuclear arsenal. China's foreign minister also vanished amid suggestions of sexual impropriety or possibly espionage. For a while, America's desire for a security dialogue appeared to flounder on account of their being nobody to talk to in the opaque court of President Xi Jinping.

The first edition of this book speculated about the future of Taiwan in the light of Russia's aggression against Ukraine and whether Moscow's bungled assault and Western sanctions might give Beijing pause for thought and make the island safer from invasion in the short term. The answer is a tentative yes, though ahead of Taiwan's January 2024 presidential election, the PLA intensified its 'grey zone' coercion of the island, ranging from cyber-attacks and military intimidation (practising for a blockade) to large scale disinformation campaigns. The Chinese Communist Party is studying and learning from Russia's military missteps while looking at ways of hardening its economy and financial system against possible sanctions. At the same time, it will certainly be taking account of divisions and weakening resolve in Western capitals over support for Kyiv as it calibrates its pressure on Taiwan. Xi has also tightened his embrace of Russia's leader Vladmir Putin, effectively underwriting his aggression with stepped-up trade and diplomatic cover, while falling short (often just short) of overt military aid. Leaked documents exposed a formal agreement to share and amplify each other's disinformation and propaganda. The two countries also continued to carry out joint military exercises, and in March 2023 they were joined by Iran for naval exercises in the Gulf of Oman. New geopolitics were fast turning into a competition between autocracies and democracies – with China first among equals in the autocratic camp.

China's deteriorating economy became another factor in the debate about Taiwan. The island's president speculated that China was too overwhelmed with domestic problems to attempt an invasion any time soon, though it could equally be argued that stepping-up aggression against Taiwan might be increasingly tempting for the CCP as a means of distraction from mounting economic problems. The term 'Peak China', introduced in the first edition of this book to describe a country where growth is stalling and which may be facing the sort of decline it has long wished on the West, is gaining ever greater currency. The CCP seems incapable of implementing the more market-friendly policies that might reboot the economy for the simple reason that these would threaten its own power – and the consolidation of power around Xi and the extension of the Party into every aspect of life in China are central to Xi's increasingly authoritarian rule.

There is a sense of economic paralysis and drift in Beijing. Zombified property companies are kept on life support and soaring levels of youth unemployment have seemingly severed the unwritten pact whereby young people were encouraged to grasp the economic opportunities of rapid growth in exchange for political acquiescence. A conference to mark the tenth anniversary of the $1 trillion Belt and Road Initiative (BRI), a global infrastructure scheme that has become a catch-all for just about everything the CCP does internationally, was a subdued affair. Mounting bad debts among the recipients of Chinese loans, and the CCP acting like an international loan shark in its reluctance to join international efforts to provide relief or accept write-downs on the billions it has lent, spoiled the celebrations for many. Not surprisingly, there is an increasing global wariness towards Beijing, even among the bigger recipients of aid. China's soft power has always been limited; its chief attraction has been its economy and the hunger of others for a share of the spoils. As the economy splutters, so China loses its power to seduce and to coerce – and also to finance its breakneck pace of military expansion and modernisation.

In the West, the term 'de-risking' has replaced 'decoupling' as countries move to lessen their dependence on an increasingly hostile Beijing. 'De-risking' is more nuanced but adds up to much the same thing. The United States has intensified its efforts to cut China off from advanced technologies with military applications, particularly the fastest microprocessors and the machines to make them. Washington continues to add to its lists of Chinese companies deemed a risk to security or complicit in human rights abuses. The challenge in 'de-risking' is particularly acute in 'green' technologies, from solar panels to electric vehicles and batteries, where strategic thinking and heavy subsidies have given China a firm grip on every stage of these critical supply chains. It is only beginning to dawn on Western capitals that creating dependencies is a geopolitical strategy of the CCP, and that in the case of renewables, wresting control from Beijing may well mean delaying targets for net-zero emissions.

The benign international environment that abetted China's rapid rise is over, though Western policy towards China still lacks coherence – no more so than in the UK, where a summer 2023 report by Parliament's Intelligence and Security Committee said that China was engaged in a 'whole of state' assault on the UK and that the Government's approach was 'completely inadequate'. 'China's size, ambition and capability have enabled it to successfully penetrate every sector of the UK's economy,' it stated.

The government argued that the findings were out of date and that it is now armed with a powerful new set of security tools that include stricter rules governing public procurement, foreign interference and inward investment. However, these are still largely untested and they leave much to the discretion of ministers and officials. The return to government of David Cameron as UK Foreign Secretary in November 2023 was hardly an encouraging sign; as Prime Minister, he had fired the starting gun for the no-holds-barred race for Chinese money that resulted in the CCP becoming deeply embedded in the most sensitive corners of the British economy. During his time out of office, Cameron pursued business projects linked to China. These included an ultimately failed attempt to set up a $1 billion UK–China investment fund, in which his role might have been 'in some part engineered by the Chinese state' to give credibility to Chinese investment, according to Parliament's Intelligence and Security Committee. He also praised China's BRI and promoted a major Chinese investment project in Sri Lanka made under its banner. His return was welcomed by Beijing, with China's foreign minister urging London to 'establish a correct understanding of China'.

Western intelligence agencies remain deeply concerned that the level of CCP interference and penetration of Western democracies is not sufficiently appreciated. In a rare joint statement, the intelligence chiefs of the US, UK, Canada, Australia and New Zealand (the Five Eyes alliance) came together in October 2023 to warn about Beijing's continuing and prolific intellectual property theft, hacking and spying – and the potential for artificial intelligence (AI) to turbo-charge this. 'China has long targeted businesses with a web of techniques all at once: cyber intrusions, human intelligence operations, seemingly innocuous corporate investments and transactions,' said FBI Director Christopher Wray. 'Every strand of that web had become more brazen, and more dangerous.' The scale of the CCP's disinformation operations was underlined a month later when Meta, which owns Facebook, said it had taken down more than 4,700 fake and misleading accounts based in China which were being used to spread polarising content about US politics and US–China relations. An invitation to China to attend an AI Safety Summit at Bletchley Park, Britain's wartime code-breaking centre, in November 2023, was widely condemned. The summit was designed to consider the risks of AI, and critics pointed out that one of the biggest risks was these powerful new tools ending up in the hands of the CCP.

In early December 2023 it was revealed that Sellafield, Britain's most hazardous nuclear site, had been hacked by groups linked to China and Russia. The breaches in the systems at the site where nuclear waste is stored involved the installation of sleeper malware, which can be later activated to spy or to sabotage systems. The hack, which was denied by Sellafield, was reportedly first detected as far back as 2015. Incredibly that was also the year when the Cameron government formally invited Beijing to become a partner in the UK's nuclear industry as an investor and also to build its own power station.

Since I wrote *The Fire of the Dragon*, the many fronts and multiple tools of China's new Cold War described in the book have continued to expand, while tensions have intensified. At the same time, Western delusions about Xi Jinping's China are falling away – though not nearly as fast as they should. In Britain, ministers continue to shy away from labelling China as a threat and argue for separating security and human rights concerns from the need to engage with Beijing economically. China makes no such distinction and continues to use trade, investment and market access as means of coercion. While it is a truism to say that Chinese cooperation is required on issues such as climate change and global disease prevention, Beijing shows little interest in either. It's approach, where it has one at all, is self-interested and transactional. There are those who argue that Xi Jinping (like Vladimir Putin) was initially misread by the West, which only woke up when the threat became too obvious to ignore. If that is the case, it was a wilful misreading. As we see in the pages that follow, the nature of the man and his rule should have been obvious to those who cared to look.

London, January 2024

## Introduction:

# *China's New Cold War*

'We will never allow anyone to bully, oppress or subjugate China. Anyone who dares to try to do that will have their heads bashed bloody against the Great Wall of Steel forged by over 1.4 billion Chinese people.'

*Xi Jinping, in a Tiananmen Square speech marking the 100th anniversary of the Communist Party, 1 July 2021*

There was no snow-swept Glienicke Bridge, Berlin's famous 'bridge of spies', over which so many prisoner exchanges took place during the last Cold War. No slow, tense walk to freedom so beloved by Hollywood film-makers. But the choreography was familiar enough, and their two aircraft could well have passed in the night. Hers was a specially chartered Air China jet from Vancouver to the southern Chinese city of Shenzhen, where she was welcomed back with flowers and a cheering flag-waving crowd. The two Canadians were flown home from China in a Royal Canadian Air Force Challenger aircraft and greeted in Calgary by Prime Minster Justin Trudeau. 'You've shown incredible strength, resilience, and perseverance,' he told them.[1] It was 25 September 2021, the first prisoner swap of China's new Cold War, and from the Communist Party's perspective a triumph of hostage diplomacy.

Meng Wanzhou was the chief financial officer of Huawei, the Chinese technology giant, which is closely linked to the Communist Party. She is also the eldest daughter of the company's founder and chief executive, Ren Zhengfei, a former army officer and a Party member. Meng, dubbed the 'princess of Huawei', was arrested at the request of US prosecutors while changing aircraft in Vancouver in December 2018. The US sought her extradition, accusing her of fraud relating to Huawei's dealings with Iran, which is under American sanctions. Ten days after her arrest, Chinese security agents snatched the two Canadians, who were working in China, and accused them of spying. Michael Kovrig, a former diplomat, was employed by the International Crisis Group, a think tank, while Michael Spavor was a business consultant.[2]

Meng's lengthy extradition hearings were slow, but hardly uncomfortable for her. It was a judicial process, heard in open court and freely reported upon. She had top legal representation, was given bail and allowed to live in her C$13 million Vancouver mansion. She could receive visitors, including her children and husband, who were given special permission to enter Canada during the Covid-19 pandemic, and she could go out during the day. In China, the 'Two Michaels', as they became known, were held in grim concrete cells initially without access to families or lawyers. They were granted a single consular visit per month. For their first six months they were kept in solitary confinement in an interrogation centre run by the Ministry of State Security.[3] After one and a half years, they were formally charged with espionage by a closed court, though no evidence was presented. Spavor was found guilty and sentenced to eleven years in prison; Kovrig was waiting to be sentenced at the time of his release.

In September 2021, Meng reached a deal with US prosecutors. Charges against her were conditionally dropped, but were retained against Huawei, which the US regards as an arm of the Chinese state. These charges included fraud, sanctions busting and economic espionage. The deal paved the way for Meng's release from house arrest, and for the near simultaneous freeing of the 'Two Michaels' from their grim cells. Washington insisted there was no direct link, and was keen to discourage the Cold War comparisons, but the parallels were unmistakable.

A month after the 'Two Michaels' were freed, General Mark Milley, chairman of the US Joint Chiefs of Staff, used a Cold War metaphor to describe a Chinese weapon test, which appeared to be more advanced than comparable American systems and stunned US officials. He said it was 'very close' to being a 'Sputnik moment' for the US – a reference to the shock of the Soviet Union's first successful launch of a space satellite in 1957.[4] The People's Liberation Army (PLA) reportedly tested a nuclear-capable hypersonic weapon designed to evade America's nuclear defences.[5] The test involved the launch of a rocket into space, which circled the globe before releasing into orbit a highly manoeuvrable hypersonic glider. The nuclear-capable glider – which has been likened to a weaponised space shuttle – had the ability to surf along the earth's atmosphere before powering down to its target at up to five times the speed of sound (hence the hypersonic).[6] Hypersonic weapons are far more difficult to detect and destroy than traditional ballistic missiles, and several states, including the US, Russia, the UK and Japan are working on the technology. The Chinese test was a 'very significant technological event,' General Milley said. 'It has all our attention.'[7] It also played to a wider fear that the US might be losing its technological edge. Separately, researchers spotted that China was building hundreds of missile silos in the western provinces of Gansu and Xinjiang. A Pentagon assessment said that China planned to quadruple its nuclear weapons stockpile by 2030 in what appeared to be a move away from its previous policy of minimum deterrence.[8]

At the time, the US was reassessing how it could best defend the democratic self-governing island of Taiwan in the event of a Chinese invasion or blockade. The island was coming under increasing pressure, including the almost daily despatch by Beijing of waves of fighter jets and bombers designed to intimidate the island and test its defences. There were comparisons to West Berlin, a city that was emblematic of the long stand-off with the Soviet Union during the last Cold War. It was argued that the very existence of lively, democratic Taiwan was seen by the Chinese Communist Party as an existential threat in much the same way that the walled-off German city once rankled with Moscow, and that Taiwan was equally deserving of support.[9] To many in Washington, China's nuclear moves contained a thinly disguised message – that America was deluding itself if it thought a conflict over the island could be contained to the immediate area and not endanger the American homeland.

The intimidation of Taiwan was only the most egregious example of China's growing international aggression, yet Western political leaders struggled to redefine their relationship with Beijing and articulate coherent policies to deal with it. Addressing the United Nations General Assembly in September 2021, President Joe Biden said, 'We'll stand up for our allies and our friends and oppose attempts by stronger countries to dominate weaker ones, whether through changes to territory by force, economic coercion, technological exploitation, or disinformation.' Then he added: 'But we're not seeking – I'll say it again – we are not seeking a new Cold War or a world divided into rigid blocs.'[10] That same caution was on display in Britain's House of Commons, when Prime Minister Boris Johnson faced criticism that his China policy was incoherent. 'Those who call for a new Cold War on China or for us to sequester our economy entirely from China . . . are, I think, mistaken,' Johnson said.[11] He repeated that sentiment during a summit of the NATO military alliance. 'I don't think anybody around the table today wants to descend into a new Cold War with China,' he said.[12] The British government preferred to describe China as a 'systemic competitor'. The EU opted for 'systemic rival', while NATO said China presents Western democracies with a 'systemic challenge'. The Biden administration used the term 'strategic competition' to describe an all-encompassing rivalry which was becoming the defining foreign-policy challenge of the era.

The caution reflected a belief among many Western leaders that they could compartmentalise their Beijing relationship – confronting China on security and human rights issues, while at the same time enjoying constructive trade and investment ties and cooperating on issues of mutual interest, such as climate change and health. As this book will explain, this view misunderstands the nature of Xi Jinping's China. Western leaders may also have feared that Cold War analogies could become self-fulfilling.

Chinese Communist Party leader Xi Jinping had no such reticence in identifying Western democracies – and the US in particular – as enemies, using language worthy of the most unreconstructed of Cold War warriors. 'We will never allow anyone to bully, oppress or subjugate China. Anyone who dares to try to do that will have their heads bashed bloody against the Great Wall of Steel forged by over 1.4 billion Chinese people,' he warned during an hour-long address in Tiananmen Square in July 2021 to mark the Party's centenary.[13] He said China would not allow 'sanctimonious preaching' over human rights, pledged to continue to build up and modernise his military and reiterated his 'unshakable commitment' to take Taiwan.[14] Military jets swept over the square, forming the number 100, and a hand-picked crowd sang 'Without the Communist Party there would be no new China'.

For Xi, the anniversary celebrations were a high point of a year of nationalist triumphalism, during which he and his 'wolf warrior' diplomats appeared to ditch the language of diplomacy in favour of threats and abuse at any perceived offence. 'The East is rising while the West is declining' became a common refrain of Party propaganda. It encapsuled the Party's view that the West – and again America in particular – is in terminal decay and decline and that China's time has come. Xi was portrayed as a transformative figure, restoring the country's position as a global power, facing off against a hostile West. The Chinese people were urged to 'follow the Party forever' – though a more appropriate slogan might have been 'follow Xi forever', as he prepared to consolidate his grip in a manner not seen since Mao Zodong. His cult of personality was stoked by a 12,000 word homage published by state media, which described him as 'a man of determination and action, a man of profound thoughts and feelings, a man who inherited a legacy but dares to innovate and a man who has forward-looking vision and is committed to working tirelessly'.[15] A communique praised Xi's 'decisive significance in advancing toward the great rejuvenation of the Chinese nation'. A Party congress in late 2022 will effectively allow him to remain in power for life.

In November 2021, Xi held his first summit with US President Joe Biden, a full ten months after Biden's inauguration. The meeting was by video link and lasted three and a half hours. It took place at a time when relations were at their worst for four decades, clouded by distrust. Expectations were low, though they did recognise the need for what they called 'guardrails' to ensure that their intense competition did 'not veer into conflict'.[16] Biden told Xi that the US 'strongly opposes unilateral efforts to change the status quo or undermine peace and stability across the Taiwan Strait'. Xi warned Biden not to 'play with fire', and that China was prepared to take 'decisive measures' if the island moves towards formal independence.[17] Biden is thought to have met Xi at least eight times during the decade before he became president. He was once a strong advocate of engagement – a policy broadly defined as welcoming and embracing China's rise and avoiding too much criticism in the belief that both China and the world would become better places as a result. This was the prevailing orthodoxy since the normalisation of relations in 1979, but by the time Biden became president it had been largely discredited. Not only did Biden maintain Donald Trump-era tariffs and sanctions, but he also even extended them. The need to lessen American dependence on Chinese products and supply chains, and to protect US technology, is now one of the few areas of bipartisan agreement in Washington. The question for policy makers there is no longer *whether* decoupling the US economy from that of China is a good idea, particularly in advanced technology, but *how* best to manage the process.

At the time of the summit, Xi had not left China for nearly two years. That was ostensibly because of Covid-19, but it seemed symptomatic of something larger – a growing self-isolation. China was turning in on itself in a way that seemed to amplify the Communist Party's arrogance and insecurities. In Xi's world view, every setback, every criticism, is part of a conspiracy to contain China's rightful rise – an outlook that blinds Beijing to the impact of its own imperial behaviour and the extent to which this is generating global concern.

Xi's cult of victimhood and deep animosity towards Western democracies are shared by Russian president Vladmir Putin and have driven their ever-closer relationship. In early February 2022, on the opening day of the Winter Olympics in Beijing, they met in person in the Chinese capital to cement what has been dubbed an 'axis of autocracy'. They said there were 'no limits' to their partnership and pledged to work together to build a new international order. Putin supported Xi's stance on Taiwan and in return Xi echoed Putin's criticism of NATO enlargement and his demand for 'security guarantees' from the West.[18] Three weeks later, Putin sent his tanks into Ukraine. Xi then parroted Putin's justifications for the aggression and avoided criticising the man he has described as his 'best friend'. The principles of 'sovereignty' and 'non-interference' have long been staples of Communist Party propaganda. Putin flagrantly violated both, but Xi could not bring himself even to describe Russia's aggression as an invasion, his barbarity as a war.

George Orwell's Big Brother is frequently invoked in describing the dystopian surveillance state that the Communist Party is building in China – though in reality Orwell could never have imagined the repressive new technologies that Xi Jinping is harnessing to underpin his rule. Less well known is that Orwell also coined the phrase 'Cold War'. He did so in an essay, 'You and the Atom Bomb', published in *Tribune* magazine in October 1945, four years before the publication of *Nineteen Eighty-Four*. The essay reflected on 'a state which was at once unconquerable and in a permanent state of "Cold War" with its neighbours'. He envisaged the destructive power of the atom bomb putting an end to large scale 'hot' wars, and instead resulting in a perpetual 'peace that is no peace' as two or three superstates fought in multiple other ways while avoiding an unthinkable head-on conflict.[19]

As this book will explain, Xi Jinping's China has become a master of those multiple other ways to influence and coerce. Western leaders say they do not want a new Cold War, but it is a little too late for that. The Chinese Communist Party is already waging a form of cold war and until now it has been very effective because Western democracies have been largely absent from the battlefield. Far from trying to contain China, as Beijing frequently claims, the West has facilitated its rise, and is only now – belatedly – waking up to the reality of Xi Jinping's China and the threat it represents to liberal democracies.

Popular culture often provides useful pointers about the real world. The old Cold War kept Hollywood busy, yet major studios today are extremely reticent about casting the Chinese Communist Party as a villain. Hollywood's priority has been to gain access to the lucrative China market, and to that end they stripped movies of anything that might upset Party censors. The Chinese movie industry has no such reticence when it comes to casting the West as villains. The top two grossing movies of recent years were *Wolf Warrior 2*, a Rambo-style action film, and *The Battle at Lake Changjin*, a Korean War epic, both of which depict Americans as almost comic-book enemies. While Hollywood pursues profit from China and kowtows to the Party, China's propaganda machine is going into battle with a chilling sense of purpose – the new Cold War is in full swing in China's biggest home-grown movies, and in the broader language and imagery of Party propagandists.

This book is the story of China's new Cold War. It is different from the last one – China is richer and more deeply embedded in the global economy than was the Soviet Union. That makes the rivalry not only more complex, broader and deeper, but potentially more dangerous. China's integration into the world economy has given it multiple new tools of coercion and influence that were never available to the Soviet Union, and which it has not hesitated to use as it bids to become the dominant global power. China is also engaged in one of the largest military build-ups ever seen during peacetime, yet there are none of the protocols and little of the depth of mutual knowledge about capabilities and intensions that existed and provided a level of stability during the last Cold War. There is no nuclear hotline, and Beijing has consistently rejected conversations about arms control.

It is China's behaviour that is driving a belated response from Western democracies, and a broader wariness towards Beijing across the world. China's new Cold War has technological, economic and strategic dimensions – and it is being played out globally, from the South China Sea to the deserts of Afghanistan, the Arctic, the Himalayas and in cyberspace. While it does not have the sharp ideological divide of the last Cold War, it is still about fundamental values – look no further than the 1.5 million Uyghurs held in 're-education camps' in Xinjiang or the crushing of liberties in Hong Kong to understand that.

The book is divided into three broad parts. The first seven chapters following this introduction examine the many fronts and flashpoints of China's new Cold War, and the multiple tools the Party is deploying. Chapter 1 begins in the Taiwan Strait, the narrow stretch of water that separates China from Taiwan, where the danger of conflict is higher than at any time in decades. The Strait has seen conflict before – in both 1955 and 1958, the United States considered the use of nuclear weapons against China should it try and invade Taiwan. Once again the area is tense, with China carrying out military drills on an almost daily basis. The People's Liberation Army is far more formidable than in the past, one of the key purposes of its modernisation being to take Taiwan and deter American intervention. In Chapter 2, we broaden the focus to the South China Sea, 90 per cent of which China claims as its territory – a territorial grab the size of which the world has rarely seen before. Beijing justifies this with vague 'historic rights'. Its claims have been ruled illegal under international law, a ruling China ignores. It has built and militarised artificial islands and intimidates other claimants. The United States and its Western allies conduct an increasing number of tense 'freedom of navigation' patrols through the area.

Chapter 3 moves to Southeast Asia, where China has vigorously asserted its influence, largely by economic means, and where it has at times treated nations as the vassal states of old, demanded fealty in exchange for trade, investment and access to China's market. The nations of the area seek to balance their sovereignty with their desire for the economic benefits. Beijing has sunk billions of dollars into the region, much of it into railways, pipelines, ports and other infrastructure that serve Beijing's strategic interests. The region has become a front line in the rivalry with the United States and its allies. In Chapter 4, we focus on the 'roof of the world', and China's tense stand-off with India along their disputed border. A 2020 clash of almost medieval barbarity left twenty Indian soldiers dead and up to 38 from the PLA, when China sought to grab territory high in the Himalayas. The clash put an abrupt end to what had been burgeoning economic relations between the two Asian giants. Beijing has also become increasingly aggressive with other border disputes, notably in Bhutan. Chapter 5 examines the new frontiers of China's Cold War – from the struggle in the frozen Arctic for control of key minerals that are crucial for technologies of the future, to Beijing's efforts to exert its technological influence globally through what it calls a 'digital silk road'. Chapter 6 looks at China's use of the dark cyber world – how it uses cyberspace to push its interests through disinformation, spying and sabotage. In so doing, its tactics are increasingly converging with those of Russia. Chapter 7 examines the warming relationship between Moscow and Beijing. The two are growing so close militarily that rattled Western analysts speculated about whether they were coordinating activities against Ukraine and Taiwan. Historic animosities run deep, and their relationship in many ways is a marriage of convenience – but no less dangerous for it.

The second broad section, covering Chapters 8 to 11 focuses more closely on Taiwan, where the Chinese Communist Party's intimidation is at its most egregious, and where the dangers to global peace are most stark. In a similar way that Xinjiang can be seen as a laboratory for high-tech means of repression, so Taiwan can be regarded as a proving ground for China's 'grey zone' warfare. It is also where the potential costs to outsiders are highest – morally, strategically and economically. Chapter 8 looks more closely at the 'grey zone' warfare China is already waging against the island. This includes military intimidation, economic and information warfare, and cyberattacks. China is seeking to deny Taiwan international space and intimidate those who deal with the island. Beijing even sought to deny Taiwan access to Covid-19 vaccines. This chapter also looks at how a military conflict might unfold. Chapter 9 examines the history of Taiwan, and China's spurious claims over it. It examines the origin and unsustainability of the 'One China Policy', a fudge that has kept the peace for five decades, and of America's policy of 'strategic ambiguity' over the defence of the island. Chapter 10 seeks to explain why Taiwan matters. It looks at the island's evolution into possibly the world's most successful new democracy, and how in terms of political development China and Taiwan have moved rapidly in opposite directions. It examines how China's repression in Hong Kong has destroyed any dwindling support for unification on the island and how Taiwan's democracy might well be Taiwan's most important form of defence. Chapter 11 looks at Taiwan's remarkable economic success. It also examines its significance as a vital cog in the global economy, particularly for advanced technology, where it dominates the production of high-end microprocessors. Disruption would be extremely costly for the world economy.

The final section of the book examines the increasing tit-for-tat and geopolitical manoeuvrings as Western democracies push back. They examine and assess the strategies being used and developed to counter Beijing – as well as the ambiguities of Western policy. They also ask whether Beijing has now reached the peak of its powers, with cracks beginning to emerge in its global strategy, largely of its own making. In Chapter 12 we examine the role of Japan, constitutionally barred from having an army, but in practice building one of the most powerful forces in Asia. It is increasingly outspoken about Chinese aggression, including Beijing's claims over Japanese-controlled islands, and the security of Taiwan. It is becoming a key, but understated, player. Chapter 13 looks at the evolving but still confused policy of Britain towards China, as London seeks to find a new post-Brexit role in the world. It has identified Beijing as a significant security threat – a 'systemic competitor' – but believes it can pursue deeper trade and investment ties, even though Beijing has not hesitated to use these for coercion elsewhere.

Chapter 14 looks at the experiences of Australia and Lithuania. Both were targeted by Beijing with threats and economic sanctions – Australia after calling for an independent inquiry into the origins of Covid-19, and Lithuania for allowing Taiwan to open a diplomatic office in Vilnius under its own name. Both stood firm in the face of this bullying. The chapter asks whether they can provide a model for standing up to Beijing. Chapter 15 seeks to draw conclusions about how this rivalry might develop and the most effective ways of countering Beijing, while also avoiding a 'hot war'. It also poses the question as to whether we may now be witnessing 'Peak China' as the country faces economic headwinds at home and a world increasingly prepared to push back. There is considerable evidence to support this, but Peak China may also be a more dangerous China. There then follows an epilogue, written from Taipei as Taiwan gradually eased Covid-19 restrictions, and more fully assessing the impact of the Ukraine war.

Names often provide a challenge for authors of books about China and Taiwan, some of them going to extraordinary lengths to avoid calling Taiwan a country. The official name of China is the People's Republic of China (PRC), while the official name of Taiwan is the Republic of China (ROC), a legacy of when the defeated nationalists retreated to the island after losing the Chinese civil war to the communists in 1949. They set up their ROC government in exile on Taiwan, dreaming of retaking the mainland. The name 'Republic of China' is no longer so widely used, and most of those who live on the island self-identify as Taiwanese and refer to their country as Taiwan. This is not an academic textbook, and I have no wish to avoid offending China – I shall therefore use the name Taiwan, refer to the PRC simply as China, and call Taiwan a country. As this book will demonstrate, Taiwan has all the attributes of a country, and a very successful one at that. The fact it is not recognised as such and is denied its formal right to self-determination is down to Beijing's bullying.

The Chinese Communist Party has been described as a master of 'salami slicing', the practice of slowly accumulating advantages, whether this be in grabbing territory or other strategic gains. Each advance is calculated to remain below (often just below) a bar that might provoke a reaction. In isolation, each slice creates anger but is not sufficient to trigger sanctions. However, over time they add up to a substantial change in the strategic picture, whether that be in the South China Sea, the Himalayas, trade practices or cyberspace. As this book will demonstrate, not only have Western democracies set the bar far too high, but an emboldened China is carving bigger slices, doing so with greater frequency and confidence, and with a growing appetite for risk. As Richard Moore, the head of Britain's Secret Intelligence Service (MI6) said in a rare interview in November 2021, 'The days of Deng Xiaoping's "hide your strength, bide your time" are long over,' and he warned, 'Adapting to a world affected by the rise of China is the single greatest priority for MI6.'[20]

The Chinese Communist Party frequently accuses its critics of having a 'Cold War Mentality'. The label is used for those who criticise its repression at home, and against those who have the audacity to criticise, or seek to stand up to, its bullying and territorial claims worldwide. By this definition, a Cold War mentality is precisely what is needed by Western democracies and like-minded allies as they push back against Xi Jinping's China.

# CHAPTER 1

# *The Taiwan Strait: The Most Dangerous Place on Earth*

'China's gone from bide our time, to this is our time. There are fewer and fewer inhibitions'

*Rear Admiral Jim Ellis, commander of the USS Independence battle group during the 1996 Taiwan Strait crisis*

The beach on the Taiwanese-controlled island of Little Kinmen is lined with rusting, barnacle-covered spikes, designed to thwart an invasion. They point towards the Chinese coast, which at low tide is less than two miles away. The towering glass-walled high-rises of sprawling Xiamen, one of China's most prosperous cities, loom through the haze.

Little Kinmen is the nickname for Liehyu, the baby sister of the main island of Kinmen, and the closest Taiwanese-controlled islands to China. Taiwan itself is 140 miles east, across the Taiwan Strait. Little Kinmen once endured what military historians regard as one of the largest and most intense artillery bombardments in military history. In 1958 Chinese forces blockaded the islands, and for forty-four days, beginning on 23 August of that year, they rained down an estimated half a million shells in an effort to 'liberate' the place.

The US, fearing the assault was a step towards an attack on Taiwan itself, responded with an enormous show of force, and Secretary of State John Foster Dulles threatened 'massive retaliation'. American warships escorted Taiwanese supply vessels across the Taiwan Strait, while the US Air Force helped Taiwan gain control of the skies above it. Plans were drawn up to use nuclear weapons, initially against strategic targets such as Chinese military airfields, but also against cities including Shanghai and Guangzhou. The Soviet leader, Nikita Khrushchev, warned that an American attack on China would be viewed as an attack on the USSR.[1]

A classified US study of the 1958 confrontation disclosed by Daniel Ellsberg, who also leaked the classified history of the Vietnam War known as the 'Pentagon Papers', suggests that American military leaders doubted that conventional weapons would deter China's leader, Mao Zedong, if the crisis escalated. Ellsberg quotes Christian Herder, who succeeded Dulles as secretary of state, as saying: 'The Cuban Missile Crisis is often described as the first serious nuclear crisis, those of us who lived through the Quemoy [Kinmen] crisis definitely regarded that as the first serious nuclear crisis.'[2] Thankfully, the bombardment of Kinmen ended with a whimper rather than a bang – when Chinese forces ran short of ammunition. The two sides then settled into a bizarre routine under which they bombarded each other with shells containing propaganda leaflets on alternate days of the week. This informal arrangement lasted for twenty years.

For Kinmen, the 1958 confrontation was the second of that decade. In 1955, the Taiwanese repulsed another invasion attempt, during which two American military advisers were killed. Then too the use of nuclear weapons against China was considered, but American President Dwight Eisenhower pushed back against his generals. Back then Kinmen resembled one giant military bunker. It covered only seventy square miles, but was of huge military and strategic importance. It's granite rocks hid a subterranean world of military fortifications – tunnels, forts and caves that would not be out of place in a James Bond movie. Up to 100,000 Taiwanese soldiers were stationed there, and travel in and out was highly restricted – restrictions that remained in place until 1994.

Today the old scars and fortifications are tourist attractions. It takes little more than half an hour to drive across the main island, but Kinmen has one of the highest densities of military museums to be found anywhere in the world. There is even an 823 Artillery Bombardment Victory Monument roundabout (the 823 referring to the date in 1958 when the bombardment began), which takes the form of a giant upright shell. A landmine museum has one of the most comprehensive – and scary – collections of these devices. When the two sides were not firing shells they were blasting propaganda at each other, and the Beishan Broadcasting Wall still stands on the larger island, a tall box-like concrete tower facing the Chinese coast and packed with dozens of powerful speakers. For nearly three decades it broadcast music and anti-communist propaganda, 'sonic warfare' as it was dubbed. Now it has become an art installation, a stage on which musicians experiment with sound. So many shells were fired that to this day Chinese shell cases and shrapnel sustain a local cottage industry, a string of workshops melting them down to make kitchen knives and other ornaments. The Bishop of Taiwan even has a project to transform shell cases into crosses.

Since direct links with China were established in 2008, Beijing has preferred to bombard tiny Kinmen with tourists, who have flocked to this bizarre little Taiwanese outpost. Before they were halted in 2020 by the Covid-19 pandemic, some forty-four ferries were making the half-hour crossing between Kinmen and Xiamen every day. The tourists wandered the narrow streets of Kinmen town, poked around the old fortifications, peered back at China through powerful binoculars and took selfies against the smoggy backdrop. It is hard to know what they made of the place, but one of the key tenets of China's 'patriotic education' and propaganda is that Taiwan is part of China, a breakaway province, and in this telling Kinmen is part of Fujian province – just like Xiamen – and by hook or by crook the renegade will soon be returned to the motherland.

For their part, the people of Kinmen happily pocket the tourist dollars, while keeping their Taiwanese flags proudly flying. Some 140,000 people now live on the islands, a figure that has increased by around 4 per cent a year over the decade to 2020. The main island now boasts its own university, which contains a plaque with a quote from the poet Luo Fu, who served as a naval officer in Kinmen. 'The sound of opening a bottle of liquor is better than the sound of pulling a trigger', it reads – a reference to another thriving Kinmen industry, producing fiery sorghum wine.

The islanders have welcomed (and benefited from) China's appeals to their hearts and to their wallets – the 'win-win' promises of joint prosperity, so beloved of Communist Party propagandists. Drinking water is now pumped from China and there has been talk of connecting the islands to China's electricity grid, building a bridge to Xiamen and turning Kinmen into a special economic zone. But at the same time, Kinmen has embraced Taiwanese democracy and sovereignty – its de-facto independence. The islanders have preferred to treat Beijing's frequent and noisy threats of war should Taiwan formally declare independence as so much background noise. In this sense their little islands are a microcosm of the Taiwanese fudge – embodying all the contradictions, the smoke and the mirrors that have characterised relations between the two sides for decades.

It is a fudge that has avoided the open hostilities of the 1950s – but it is becoming increasingly difficult to sustain. 'Kinmen should become a bridge of peace between Taiwan and Mainland China,' Chou Yang-sun, a professor of Chinese affairs at the university, told a visiting journalist in late 2020.[3] Though Wang Jui-sheng, a first year student, was more troubled about the intentions of their giant neighbour: 'China is angry at Taiwan and acting all the more brutish.' He said the people on Kinmen were increasingly unsettled. 'I'm worried about the chance of military conflicts between the two sides, possibly even in the near future.'[4] Wang is part of a new generation of Taiwanese, children of what has become one of the world's most prosperous and successful democracies. He was perhaps being more realistic than the professor. Even the ferries that bring the tourists from Xiamen embody the contradictions that underlie the relationship. They are a source of prosperity, but at the same time civilian vessels form a key part of Beijing's invasion planning. At shipyards all along China's east coast, ferries are being retrofitted, strengthening them for carrying military equipment and troops; new ferries must be built to military specifications.[5]

It would be premature and dangerous to regard the fortifications that honeycomb these islands as merely relics of a bygone era. The Taiwanese military still has a heavy presence on Kinmen – though the parts of the subterranean honeycomb they use are firmly off limits to tourists. Few doubt that Kinmen would again be one of China's first targets in the event of war, since it forms a natural barrier to Xiamen harbour, and would need to be subdued if China was to ensure safe passage for its Taiwan-bound invasion fleet. Seizing these smaller islands may also be part of China's 'anaconda strategy', whereby instead of a full assault on the main island of Taiwan, China progressively squeezes its prey until it surrenders. As we shall see later in this book, many other elements of this strategy are already in place. What is for certain, is that as the drums of war from China's leader, Xi Jinping, grow increasingly louder, few people can hear them more clearly and menacingly than the people of Kinmen, who have borne the brunt of Beijing's violence in the past.

On the other side of the narrow stretch of water from Kinmen, China's People's Liberation Army has engaged in a massive military build-up and modernisation, which have two principal aims that could not be achieved in the past – to invade Taiwan and at the same time deter intervention from the United States. Under Xi Jinping, the PLA has carried out increasingly aggressive drills designed to demonstrate its ability to do both.

Xiamen itself is home to the PLA's 73rd Group Army, believed to be China's main Taiwan invasion force. Early in 2021, it was reported that the PLA had deployed to the area a new and powerful long-range ballistic missile system, the PLC-191.[6] These are mounted on forty-five-tonne trucks, and each unit is able to fire multiple missiles with a range of more than 200 miles, giving them the capability to hit targets not just on Kinmen, but all down Taiwan's west coast. The system joins a dizzying array of new and modernised weapons deployed by the Chinese military. A series of pyrotechnic-laden documentaries broadcast by state television to celebrate the fifth anniversary of the PLA's Rocket Force, showed ten types of missile designed for use against the island.[7] Estimates vary, but China is thought to have between 1,000 and 2,000 missiles trained on Taiwan and its outlying islands.

In addition, the PLA has developed intermediate-range ballistic missiles dubbed 'aircraft-carrier killers' by state media. These were first test-fired into the South China Sea from a base in Zhejiang province in August 2020 during military drills.[8] The DF-21D and its bigger brother, the DF-26B, are anti-ship missiles with ranges between 1,200 and 3,000 miles, and developed with the principal purpose of countering US aircraft carrier groups. During exercises three days after Joe Biden's inauguration as US president, Chinese fighters reportedly simulated an attack on a US aircraft carrier in the region.[9] It was later reported that the PLA had built mock-ups of an American aircraft carrier and other warships at a military training facility in the remote desert in western Xinjiang province. The 'aircraft carrier' appeared to be on tracks designed to simulate the ship's movement.[10]

China has stepped up its aerial harassment of Taiwan with waves of heavy nuclear-capable bombers and sophisticated fighter jets bearing down on the island in numbers and with a frequency not seen before. In 2020 alone, China conducted 380 incursions into Taiwan's air defence identification zone (ADIZ), a buffer zone of international airspace where foreign planes face questioning by controllers and potential interception, according to the Taiwanese government.[11] In 2021, the figure more than doubled to 969 incursions, according to a database compiled by Agence France-Presse.[12] Over four days straddling China's October 1st National Day holiday weekend, 149 aircraft entered Taiwan's ADIZ, including a record 56 on the Monday alone.[13] The US State Department labelled China's actions 'provocative' and 'destabilising'.[14] As the year progressed, Taipei was forced to scramble its forces on an almost daily basis at the approach of these aerial armadas.[15] Chinese warplanes regularly crossed the Taiwan Strait 'median line', an informal border that previously had been largely respected by both sides. Satellite images appeared to show China expanding and upgrading three military airbases on its coast opposite Taiwan. The images showed newly built aircraft hangars, potential munitions bunkers, extended runways, tarmac aprons and a possible missile defence system.[16]

The aerial incursions were coordinated increasingly with large-scale drills involving navy and ground forces in which thousands of troops simulate an invasion of Taiwan. In April 2021, the PLA conducted simultaneous naval exercises to the east and west of Taiwan. The Chinese aircraft carrier, *Liaoning*, was given pride of place, while fifteen warplanes tested the island's air defences.[17] Chinese state television showed amphibious fighting vehicles rolling onto beaches and shelling targets marked on the distant mountainside.[18] Waves of attack helicopters skimmed across the sea as part of another 'assault exercise'.[19] In a series of increasingly belligerent statements, Xi Jinping publicly called on the PLA to prepare to fight 'at any moment'. While inspecting marines in Chaozhou City, he said they must 'put all [their] minds and energy on preparing for war'.[20] During a meeting of China's rubber-stamp parliament, the National People's Congress, he told PLA commanders to 'step up preparations for armed combat', citing 'security threats from Taiwan independence forces'.[21]

In evidence to a US senate armed services committee hearing in March 2021, Admiral Philip Davidson, then Washington's top military officer in the Indo-Pacific, said he feared China would invade Taiwan within the next six years. 'I cannot for the life of me understand some of the capabilities that they're putting in the field, unless . . . it is an aggressive posture,' Davidson told the senators.[22] His successor, Admiral John Aquilino, avoided a timescale, but warned, 'My opinion is that this problem is much closer to us than most think and we have to take this on.' He said that taking control of Taiwan was now Xi Jinping's 'number one priority' and was cautious about America's ability to deter him. 'The Chinese Communist party has generated some capabilities in the region that are designed to keep us out,' he said, reiterating that 'The most dangerous concern is that of a military force against Taiwan.'[23] Another senior US official said, 'There's concern he [Xi] sees capstone progress on Taiwan as important to his legitimacy and legacy. It seems that he is prepared to take risks.'[24]

The incoming Biden administration declared its commitment to Taiwan was 'rock-solid'.[25] The newly elected president attended back-to-back meetings of the leaders of the G7 group of developed economies and NATO, the Western military alliance, both of which issued warnings about China's global behaviour. Beijing responded by flying another wave of military aircraft into Taiwan's air defence buffer zone.[26] The G7 communique stressed the 'importance of peace and stability across the Taiwan Strait' – the first time such a statement had ever referred directly to Taiwan. The NATO statement was unusually strong, warning that China poses a 'systemic challenge' to the rules-based international order. Beijing called the NATO statement 'slander of China's peaceful development'.[27] The sense of growing alarm in the first part of 2021 was captured by the cover image of the *Economist* newspaper, which showed Taiwan at the centre of a radar screen sandwiched between little bleeps representing American and Chinese forces. It labelled the island 'The most dangerous place on earth'.[28]

The year 1996 was a watershed year for Taiwan, China and the US – and for the complex relations around the Taiwan Strait. It was the year Taiwan held its first fully democratic presidential election, an event that would set the island on course to become what is widely regarded today as the world's most successful new democracy. China fired missiles close to the island and carried out military exercises in an effort to influence the election. In response, the US put on a massive display of military power, sending two aircraft carrier battle groups to the area. Beijing's intimidation did influence the election, but not in the way it hoped – it solidified support behind the candidate the Communist Party loathed, but the experience was a key factor in China's decision to rapidly expand and modernise its military.

The winner of the 1996 election was Lee Teng-hui, who is widely regarded today as the father of modern Taiwanese democracy. He also sought to nurture a separate non-Chinese identity for the island – efforts that turned him into a hate figure for Beijing. When he died in 2020, aged ninety-seven, President Tsai Ing-wen declared, 'President

Lee's contribution to Taiwan's democratic journey was irreplaceable and his death is a great loss for the country.'[29] Later in life Lee became a strong advocate of independence, though he had long argued that there was no need for Taiwan to antagonise Beijing by formally declaring independence, since it already was a sovereign state – a commonly held view on the island.

Surprisingly, Lee was a member of the Kuomintang (KMT), or Nationalist Party – the party of Chiang Kai-shek. Chiang established the Republic of China on Taiwan in 1949 after retreating from China with his defeated army at the end of the Chinese civil war against Mao Zedong's communists. Chiang tolerated little opposition; his rule over Taiwan was at times brutal and corrupt, as I shall examine more fully later in this book. He surrounded himself with hardline mainlanders who dreamed of reconquering China. When he died in 1975 power passed to his son and former head of the secret police, Chiang Chin-kou, who eased some of the harder edges of his father's rule and formally lifted martial law in 1987. When this Chiang died a year later he was succeeded by Lee, who set about trying to further soften the party's iron rule, and to give a stronger political voice to those who had lived in Taiwan before 1949.

Although the KMT was dominated by mainlanders, Lee himself was a native of Taiwan, born in a farming community near Taipei in 1923, which was around halfway through Japan's half century of colonial rule over the island. Until 1996, the president of Taiwan had been chosen by members of the tightly controlled national assembly. Lee changed the rules and the elections of that year were the first under which the president was directly elected by the people. That unnerved China, as did Lee's Taiwanese pedigree, Beijing being suspicious of anything it saw as flirting with a separate non-Chinese identity. China's anger was further exacerbated when the year before the election the US allowed Lee to visit Cornell University, where he had studied, which in Beijing's eyes gave recognition to its 'renegade' province.

I spent several weeks in Taiwan at that time, covering the election and the growing tensions across the Strait. Lee, tall and charismatic, seemed to revel in needling Beijing. In one interview he declared that relations between Taiwan and China had the character of relations between two separate states. This was heresy, not only in the eyes of Beijing, but even in his own party, where many still looked forward to eventual union between the sides, though not under communist rule. At a Taipei rally I attended, Lee cut an imposing figure; he looked like he was enjoying himself, a smile fixed permanently on his face. 'They're the ones who are scared, right? And all they can do is try and frighten the Taiwan people, using military exercises to try and undermine confidence,' he said.

Lee did cancel a planned visit to Matsu, another string of Taiwanese-controlled islands, around 130 miles to the northeast of Kinmen. The islands are named after the goddess of the sea, believed to protect fishermen and sailors. They are ten miles from the Chinese coast, where the nearest Chinese city is Fuzhou. Lee's office cited security reasons for the cancellation, perhaps feeling a rally there was just a little too provocative. I went anyway, driving into the main town of Nangan to the sound of countless explosions – firecrackers, thankfully. A festival was underway in honour of Zao Jun, the Taoist Kitchen God. There were around 20,000 soldiers stationed on Matsu at the time, and it too resembled a fortress. But instead of the drums of war, I found at one base the heavy beat of percussion for a traditional lion dance, preparations for the forthcoming Chinese New Year. The Communist Party might be huffing and puffing a few miles away, but here they were not going to allow Beijing's tantrums to get in the way of a good celebration or their giving thanks to the god who keeps a protective eye over their food. The most common response to questions about China's threats began with a shrug – 'We're used to it'. It wasn't so much bravado as weary acceptance, the background noise that went with the territory. It was something they'd learned to live with.

I also visited Kinmen, where travel restrictions had only recently been lifted. The flight from Taipei took a little over an hour, but felt far longer as the small aircraft was buffeted by the area's notoriously strong winds, the Taiwan Strait acting as a kind of wind tunnel. Back then, Kinmen still resembled a military garrison, Taiwanese forces heavily dug in, warily monitoring the Chinese coast. They still heavily outnumbered the civilian population, among whom memories were still raw of curfews, blackouts and hours spent in the underground shelters required by every village. Along the coast, many villages were deserted, houses still bearing the scars of the shelling.

In 1996, direct travel to China was still not allowed, and to visit relatives, some living just across that narrow stretch of water, meant travelling to the main island of Taiwan and then down to Hong Kong to enter from there. Unofficially, smuggling was rife, and small boats would head out to sea every night under the cover of darkness to meet and trade with enterprising counterparts from Xiamen and the villages around it. The level of smuggling, and the military's willingness to tolerate it, depended on the level of tension, and as the election approached the smugglers were staying at home. Yet even these front-line islands were gripped by election fever; roads were lined with Taiwanese flags and countless election posters.

As the 23 March election day approached, China deployed 150,000 troops to Fujian province, bordering the Taiwan Strait, and carried out a series of military exercises. The PLA fired M-9 nuclear-capable ballistic missiles into Taiwanese territorial waters, splashing down in shipping lanes close to the island's two main seaports, Keelung in the north and Kaohsiung in the south. One missile passed almost directly over Taipei, the Taiwanese capital, before landing some twenty miles off the coast. US military analysts warned that China appeared to be 'bracketing' the island in preparation for a direct attack. US Defense Secretary William J. Perry warned Beijing of 'grave consequences' should a missile strike Taiwan. He diverted an aircraft carrier battle group, centred on the USS *Nimitz*, to the area, where it joined the USS *Independence* battle group, already on location, carrying out exercises 200 miles off the northeast of Taiwan.[30]

The pilots who fly C-2A Greyhounds will tell you that although they are not the best-looking aircraft, these stubby twin-engine workhorses are the unsung heroes of a battle group – their lifeline, ferrying essential supplies out to the carrier. It also takes a certain class of pilot to land a Greyhound on a moving ship almost inch perfect to catch the restraining cord, which pulls the aircraft to an abrupt halt, and will later launch it from the deck like a giant slingshot. A few days before the 1996 presidential election in Taiwan, I flew on a Greyhound from the American base in Okinawa, Japan, to spend a weekend on USS *Independence*, and can testify that landing and taking-off from a carrier deck beats most fairground rides I've ever been on.

I was still recovering from the landing when I met Rear Admiral Jim Ellis, the commander of the battle group. While my cameraman carried out some last-minute checks on our equipment, I tried a little small talk. 'Nice boat,' I said. He fixed me with a wry smile and pointed out to sea, where a small vessel was bobbing in the distance. 'Sir,' he said, 'that's a boat. This is a ship.' And it was quite a ship – more than

1,000 feet long, with four acres of flight deck and more than 5,000 crew. It could carry more than seventy aircraft, and day and night F-14 and F-18 fighter jets screamed back and forth from the deck, up to thirteen of them in the air at any one time. They practised air intercepts and bombing runs. 'Our purpose in being here is to demonstrate the commitment of the United States to peace and stability in the region,' Ellis told me.

There were seven support vessels in the battle group, five warships and two submarines. The USS *Independence* was then thirty-seven years old, the oldest and most experienced ship in the navy's active fleet. It had participated in almost every major US navy operation during that time, including during the Vietnam War, the invasion of Grenada and Operation Desert Shield, when it enforced a no-fly zone in the Persian Gulf in the build-up to the first Gulf War. At the time of the Taiwan deployment it was based out of Yokosuka, a Japanese port city that sits in the shadow of Mount Fuji, about thirty miles southwest of Tokyo, from where its main focus of operations had been the Korean peninsula.

Together with the *Nimitz* battle group, this was the largest gathering of US naval power in the area since the 1958 Kinmen island crisis. It was designed to deter, and it succeeded in keeping China at bay. Although Beijing huffed and puffed it could not disrupt the election, and as we shall see later, Taiwanese democracy has gone from strength to strength. But China did learn, and when soon afterwards the PLA embarked on a massive expansion and modernisation, it was determined that never again would the US navy have such free rein in those waters. In military jargon, China embarked on a strategy of A2/AD – anti-access/area denial, designed to keep the US navy away from its shores by threatening unacceptable losses should it attempt another 1996-type intervention.

More than twenty-five years after he commanded the USS *Independence* battle group, and oversaw its drills off the Taiwan coast, Rear Admiral Jim Ellis recognises that things have changed dramatically. 'They [China] swore that it would never happen again, and they've now fairly successfully been able to craft a strategy that would make it much more challenging and much more difficult,' he told me by Zoom from his home in California. 'I couldn't go where I went and do what I did with impunity now. It's a different environment. I was concerned about the Chinese submarines and the potential vulnerabilities and that type of thing, but they didn't have the DF-21s, the carrier-killer missiles, the robust capabilities that they've now built.' What hasn't changed is Beijing's sense of acute paranoia. 'I laughed when I learned through intelligence sources after the fact that in 1996 China thought I was selected, that my carrier battle group was chosen to go to Taiwan, because of the name of my flagship, the USS *Independence*. They thought that was the reason. And I thought to myself, if only we were that clever.'

Ellis went on to head US naval forces in Europe, and led US and NATO forces in combat and humanitarian operations during the 1999 Kosovo crises. His final assignment before ending his military career in 2004 was as Commander of the US Strategic Command, which oversees America's strategic nuclear arsenal. He is, in other words, a man of considerable experience. He now heads the national security task force at the Hoover Institution at Stanford University, which has brought him full circle – back to Taiwan. 'China's gone from bide our time, to this *is* our time,' he told me. 'There are fewer and fewer inhibitions.' No other subject is commanding as much attention among US policy makers and military strategists as Taiwan. In the face of growing Chinese aggression, there is a recognition that the ambiguity that has characterised policy for decades, the fudges, the smoke and mirrors surrounding the island's status and America's willingness to defend it, are no longer tenable. It is built on a fiction that is no longer sustainable. 'It has become *the* issue, quite frankly,' Ellis said.

The Taiwan fudge is built on the decades-old 'One China Policy', to which all sides supposedly subscribe. It is less a policy and more an agreement to disagree. Over the years it has become an evolving exercise in verbal contortion and obfuscation. At its heart is the notion that there is only one China, of which Taiwan is a part. When it was first agreed between Beijing and Washington in 1972 it did not seem an unreasonable fudge, since at that time both sides of the Taiwan Strait claimed to be the rightful ruler of all of China. But it side-stepped the question of what 'One China' means in practice, avoiding any detailed discussion of when or how any unification should come about. Many now question *if* that goal is any longer desirable or feasible at all, given that so many of the original assumptions no longer stand – if indeed they ever did. As I shall examine later in this book, the two sides have grown apart, and a majority in democratic Taiwan no longer identify with China and want nothing to do politically with the increasingly dystopian state that Xi Jinping is building.

The 'One China Policy' is a creature of a different era. Its first appearance was in the Shanghai Communique, issued during the groundbreaking 1972 visit to China by Richard Nixon. It was designed to placate Beijing while preserving as far as possible Washington's relationship with Taiwan, with whom the US had a formal alliance at the time. That alliance had been in place since the 1949 retreat by Chiang Kai-shek's defeated and bedraggled Nationalist army and its establishment on Taiwan of the Republic of China's government in exile. During that period Taiwan was viewed by the US through the prism of the Cold War struggle against communism – plucky Chiang as the leader of 'Free China' on Taiwan enjoyed strong American diplomatic and military backing as the rightful ruler of all China.

The narrative shifted with the geopolitical tide, and seven years after Nixon and his secretary of state, Henry Kissinger, broke the ice with Beijing, the Carter administration normalised relations, switching diplomatic recognition from Taipei to Beijing. The switch was motivated at least in part by another Cold War calculation that saw China as a useful counterweight to the Soviet Union, the two communist giants having fallen out. US military personnel were duly withdrawn from Taiwan, although the US continued to supply sufficient weapons for the island's defence, while at the same time being vague about what it would do in the event of an invasion – a policy that became known as 'strategic ambiguity'.[31]

A later iteration of the 'One China Policy' stressed the need to strive for a 'peaceful resolution' of the Taiwan question, which implied that unity would only come about in an amicable way and by mutual agreement. When China embarked on its policy of reform and opening under paramount leader Deng Xiaoping this did not seem an unreasonable goal to many policy makers in Washington, and even in Taipei. They assumed that at some point in the future the two political and economic systems might converge – that more openness and prosperity in China would lead to greater liberalism and democracy and thereby make some sort of unity more palatable to Taiwan. As Rear Admiral Jim Ellis now sees it:

> To some degree, we kind of gave up our formal commitment to Taiwan's defence in the seventies because we assumed that

> China was going to become a caring parent at some point and embrace the child again. In a sense the context in which those promises were made was predicting a future that has not arrived and now appears will not arrive vis-à-vis China, and so does that change the basic assumptions and tenets of that agreement? I don't know.

Over the years, the 'One China Policy' has treated Taiwan as part of a larger narrative, a bit-part player on a wider geopolitical canvas, rather than an important player with agency to be examined and respected in its own right. The Taiwan–China spat is all-too-frequently portrayed as a family quarrel, the unfinished business of the Chinese civil war, rather than treating Taiwan as a country with a long and distinctive history and culture – and a well-deserved right of self-determination.[32] It is remarkable how many contemporary commentators accept Beijing's narrative at face value, particularly the Communist Party's talk of 'reuniting' the island, when history shows Taiwan's relationship with China to be far more complex and Beijing's sovereignty claims debatable to say the least.

As I shall examine in more detail later, two developments in particular have rendered the 'One China Policy' largely obsolete: the flourishing of democracy on Taiwan and the adoption by Xi Jinping of an increasingly chauvinistic nationalism in China, which sees the 'recovery' of Taiwan as a defining principle. The two sides of the Taiwan Strait are moving rapidly in opposite directions. Democracy and diversity have become part of a growing and distinct Taiwanese identity, underpinned by a successful tech-driven economy. The island is possibly the most liberal place in Asia and standards of living among the highest in the world. China under Xi Jinping, has grown richer too, but it has become a dark and dangerous place for anybody who expresses criticism of the Party; Xi has turned himself into the most powerful leader since Mao Zedong, intolerant not only of dissent but of any separate cultural or ethnic identities within China, as evidenced by his repression of the Uyghurs in Xinjiang. Technology is important to Xi too, but as a tool to underpin his rule, as he has built a surveillance state the likes of which the world has not seen before.

Because Taiwan is now a flourishing democracy, its 23 million people need to be persuaded of the benefits of unity, yet Xi has shown himself to be a deeply unattractive partner. By his actions, he has made it far less likely that unity will be the democratic will of the Taiwanese people any time soon. The island is a threat to Xi because it represents an alternative future, the embodiment of a rival set of values and an alternative model of what China could become. For this reason it has attracted parallels to West Berlin during the last Cold War, with calls for its defence to be taken as seriously as that of the once-walled German city.[33] If China were to lunge at Taiwan, it would constitute much more than a territorial grab. It would be a direct challenge to others who hold those values – first and foremost the United States.

As a pragmatist, Deng Xiaoping saw Taiwan as an issue that could be dealt with by future generations, preferring to concentrate on economic development. His successors, Jiang Zemin and then Hu Jintao upped the rhetoric on Taiwan, but never had the military strength to do much about it. Xi Jinping now has the means and the ideology. His 'Chinese Dream' is a dream of national rejuvenation, underpinned by historic grievance and ethnic superiority. The restoration of the great Han Chinese nation has no room for the sort of complex identities that characterise modern Taiwan, or any competing notions of sovereignty or governance. The 'recovery' of Taiwan is central to Xi's world view, and in this sense Xi has become a prisoner of his own rhetoric.

Over the years, China's policy on Taiwan has combined coercion and persuasion – the carrot and the stick, as epitomised by the Kinmen islands. Threats have been interspersed with efforts to enhance economic, cultural and social ties. China has appealed to Taiwanese hearts and wallets, while warning of the dire consequences should Taiwan formally reject its embrace. Neither has worked, and Xi has now shifted firmly towards coercion. Beijing has sought to isolate Taiwan internationally, and has grown louder and more aggressive in its intimidation of the island, as well as those countries, companies and even high profile celebrities who deviate from its narrative about the island being part of China. At the same time as flexing its military muscles and heightening its rhetoric, the Communist Party has embarked on a campaign of 'grey zone' warfare against Taiwan. This takes on many forms, including economic coercion, cyberattacks, influence operations and disinformation. A toolkit increasingly familiar to those dealing with China globally as Beijing seeks to further its interests worldwide – no more so than in its own backyard, the South China Sea.

## Chapter 2

# The South China Sea: The Biggest Territorial Grab Since the Second World War

'China, my friend, how politely can I put it?
Let me see . . . O . . . GET THE FUCK OUT.'

*Teddy Locsin Jr, secretary of foreign affairs of the Philippines, May 2021*

It was perhaps one of the most undiplomatic diplomatic missives of all time. In May 2021, Teddy Locsin Jr, the Philippines' secretary of foreign affairs, launched a Twitter tirade against Beijing over the presence of more than 250 Chinese 'fishing boats' around a reef inside his country's territorial waters in the South China Sea. 'China, my friend, how politely can I put it? Let me see . . . O . . . GET THE FUCK OUT.' He went on to liken Beijing to an 'ugly oaf'.[1]

His boss, President Rodrigo Duterte, himself no slouch when it comes to foul language, told Locsin to calm down, but it was easy to understand his anger and frustration. 'All the diplomatic protests that the secretary of foreign affairs filed have been ignored as if nothing was filed at all. The continued incursions and bullying finally got his goat,' tweeted Panfilo Lacson, a member of the Philippines senate.[2] It was all the more galling because Duterte had tried hard to cosy up to China, turning his back on his traditional American allies. So desperate was he not to offend Beijing, that he had even sought to undermine his own government's victory at an international tribunal in 2016, which invalidated China's extensive claims in the area.

The Chinese boats were discovered at Whitsun Reef, a boomerang-shaped feature in the Spratly Islands, around 175 miles from the Philippine island of Palawan, and well within the country's 200-mile exclusive economic zone (EEZ). They stayed there for several weeks. Satellite photographs showed them tied together in neat rows, large Chinese flags fluttering on their bows. Beijing claimed they were merely fishing vessels taking shelter from bad weather. But it was unprecedented in scale and duration, and analysts familiar with Beijing's tactics identified them as part of a 'grey zone' maritime militia, which China has used increasingly to spearhead its territorial claims.[3]

Whitsun Reef hardly seems like prime real estate. It is eight miles long and only appears above water at low tide. It is also more than 650 miles from China (nearly four times its distance from the Philippines), but to China it was another feature ticked off in its efforts to take control of the South China Sea, 90 per cent of which it claims as its own territory. That's an area of more than 1.25 million square miles, more than thirteen times the size of the United Kingdom. Territorial expansion by imperial powers is usually associated with land-based armies on the march, but China's assertion of sovereignty over such a vast area still represents a territorial grab on a scale not seen since the Second World War.[4]

In 2013, the Philippines challenged China's territorial claims under the United Nations Convention on the Law of the Sea (UNCLOS), which both countries had ratified. It was regarded as a landmark case, and followed China's grabbing of a rock called Scarborough Shoal, which lies within the Philippines' EEZ in another part of the South China Sea. Beijing responded to the legal challenge by imposing an economic boycott against bananas and pineapples from the Philippines, both important exports. Thousands of tons were impounded and destroyed in Chinese ports.[5]

Amid the rising tension, I visited the headquarters of the Philippine army's Western Command in Puerto Princesa on Palawan Island, the closest point to the disputed Spratly Islands. My aim was to hitch a lift on a resupply vessel to the rusting hulk of the *Sierra Madre*, a Second World War tank-landing ship that had been deliberately grounded on Second Thomas Shoal to mark Manila's claim to that reef. It was home to a lonely contingent of Philippine marines, and the only way to get supplies to them was by wooden fishing boats or other small vessels that by night ran the gauntlet of the far better equipped Chinese coastguard. The 100-mile crossing was precarious at the best of times, and to our disappointment the navy decided it was too risky and provocative to take along a camera crew at such a tense moment.

Instead, they invited us to witness the storming of a secluded bay, further down the coast. It was part of annual war games with US forces, an exercise known as *Balikatan* – which means shoulder-to-shoulder. We watched as a joint force, crouching in their inflatables, guns at the ready, swept into the bay. Then, under cover of a thick fog created by smoke grenades, they launched an ear-piercing attack on a 'terrorist compound'. Against a background of lingering pops and bangs, a spokesman for the US marines said it was all routine stuff, though his feisty Philippine counterpart was rather more forthcoming. 'China, they claim it all,' said Neil Estrella, gesturing towards the South China Sea. He was an exuberant man with mirrored sunglasses, which kept slipping down his nose. 'They'll be claiming America next,' he added with a disdainful laugh. The US and Philippines have a mutual defence treaty, but even as they exercised together in Palawan there was growing bitterness in Manila that the US had not been at their shoulder at Scarborough Shoal, which had turned into an embarrassing retreat in the face of Chinese might.

When the Permanent Court of Arbitration in the Hague ruled three years later, in June 2016, it was overwhelmingly in favour of Manila. Its unanimous 500-page verdict was a blistering rebuke of Beijing's 'historic claim' to the South China Sea, which was determined to be unlawful under the UNCLOS convention. The tribunal said China had violated the Philippines' sovereign rights in its exclusive economic zone by interfering with Philippine fishing and petroleum exploration.[6] Beijing quickly made clear it had no intention of being bound by international law, angrily rejecting the ruling. The *Global Times*, a Chinese Communist Party newspaper, described the ruling as 'radical and shameless', saying it 'brazenly violated China's territorial sovereignty and maritime rights'.[7]

Chinese money was rumoured to be behind Duterte's successful presidential bid, and he took office just days before the ruling. When it was announced, he was sombre and low key. It was almost as if he had lost the case. He seemed fearful of China's response, having received warnings from Beijing of possible 'confrontation' if he insisted the ruling be enforced.[8] Duterte was also rapidly falling out with America. In early October 2016, after President Barack Obama criticised his brutal war against drugs, in which thousands of suspects were gunned down in extra-judicial killings, Duterte said the US president could 'go to hell'.[9] A few days after that declaration Duterte made his first visit to

Beijing, where he announced what he called his 'separation' from the US, at one point telling a crowd in the Chinese capital, 'I will not go to America any more. We will just be insulted there. So, time to say goodbye my friend.'[10]

In practice military links between the Philippines and the US continued, albeit at a lower level, but there was little political trust. Duterte clearly believed that a more conciliatory approach to China would pay dividends, and that's the way it looked initially, China responding with promises of billions of dollars for infrastructure. Duterte described the tribunal ruling as 'just a piece of paper' to be thrown in the trash, and called China a friend and benefactor.[11] Perhaps he calculated that there was no way the UNCLOS ruling could be enforced, and that the Philippines' armed forces are in any case no match for those of China. His supporters continued to point at the unreliability of the US in the Scarborough Shoal stand-off.[12] He threatened repeatedly to completely tear up the Visiting Forces Agreement (VFA) with the US, the cornerstone of their mutual defence treaty.

In late 2021, as Duterte approached the end of his six-year term in office, little of the promised investment from Beijing had materialised, and instead of gratitude, he got contempt. The Chinese boats began swarming around Whitsun Reef, ignoring the Philippines' impotent anger. Duterte had built his presidency around insulting America and kowtowing to China. Five years after the law on the sea ruling, that policy had come to nought. He had provided an object lesson in how not to handle China. His government turned gingerly back to the Americans, while a disdainful Beijing pressed on with its increasingly aggressive efforts to turn the area into a Chinese lake.

Chinese maps depict its vast South China Sea territorial claim as lying within a U-shaped line stretching hundreds of miles to the south and east of Hainan island, the country's most southerly province. It is a broken line, presumably because it is a sea border rather than a land border, and for this reason it is often referred to as the 'nine-dash line'. Every map produced or sold in China must show the line (with a tenth dash in the East China Sea to embrace Taiwan), and designate the area inside as Chinese territory. It appears in all Chinese school textbooks and passports, where it can be seen hugging the coast of the Philippines, Malaysia, Brunei and Vietnam, all of which have claims that compete with China and frequently overlap each other – as does

Taiwan. It is the most contested piece of water in the world, but there is no claim on the scale or with the audacity as that of Beijing. The nine-dash line has also been likened to a cow's tongue, which is perhaps the most apt description because it suggests something slippery, organic and yet powerful – a device that can be deployed in numerous different ways, and for Beijing that means stoking nationalism at home while furthering Beijing's strategic and economic interests.

The line first appeared on an official Chinese map in 1947, two years before the Communist Party seized power (although some scholars date its origin back to the early 1930s). Back then it had eleven dashes and encompassed 90 per cent of the South China Sea and hundreds of bits of rock, reefs, shoals and sandbars – most of them uninhabited or uninhabitable, many only visible at low tide, and frequently referred to simply as 'features'. Mao Zedong scrapped two of the lines in 1952 when, in a display of socialist solidarity, he handed over the Gulf of Tonkin to Vietnam. The map was then filed away for fifty-seven years. Little was heard of it until 2009, when the nine dashes reappeared on a map Beijing submitted to the UN – ironically during a dispute with Vietnam, with whom relations had become a good deal less fraternal.

It is only since 2010 that Beijing has turned up the volume of its claims and become increasingly aggressive in enforcing them. That has coincided with the rise to power of Xi Jinping and the Communist Party adopting a far more nationalistic tone. The claim to the sea is based on 'historic rights', Beijing asserting that its control of the area goes back centuries and that the two main island chains – the Spratlys in the southeast and Paracels in the northwest – were an integral part of the Chinese empire. There is little evidence to support that assertion, which is rubbished by most experts outside China and was dismissed by the UNCLOS tribunal as incompatible with international law.

The claim is deliberately ambiguous. China has never precisely spelled out what the nine-dash line means in detail – whether it is just claiming islands within it or blanket sovereignty over the entire marine space, including all the water, all the resources and all the features that lie within the area of the cow's tongue. But it is increasingly behaving as if it does own the lot, and aggressively patrolling the island chains with a beefed-up coastguard that would put many small navies to shame. In September 2021, Beijing introduced a new law requiring all foreign vessels to give notice before entering 'Chinese territorial waters'. As with many Chinese laws, it lacked specifics. It also appeared to breach the law of the sea, and was immediately dismissed by the US, with a top commander saying that attempts to enforce it could lead to 'instability and potential conflict'.[13]

The Spratly Islands, named after a British whaling captain who recorded them in 1843, have been the particular focus of contention. They comprise more than 100 features – mostly coral reefs and shoals sitting astride strategically important fisheries and shipping lanes, and possibly above reserves of oil and natural gas. In 2013, China began large-scale land reclamations in seven locations. The island-building was dubbed the 'great wall of sand' by Admiral Harry Harris, the Commander of the US Pacific Fleet.[14] In September of that year, President Barack Obama challenged Xi Jinping on the island-building during a summit in Washington. Xi reiterated that China had sovereignty over the area 'since ancient times', but pledged not to militarise his new islands. 'Relevant construction activities that China is undertaking in the Nansha [Spratly] islands do not target or impact any country and China does not intend to pursue militarisation,' he said.[15]

It was a lie. A little over a year later the estimated area of artificial land was estimated at thirteen square kilometres (five square miles).[16] China was transforming the reefs and atolls into island fortresses, building military airstrips and naval bases, while deploying anti-aircraft and anti-missile systems.[17] The Philippine-based *Inquirer* newspaper obtained aerial photographs that showed 'Lighthouses, radomes, communication facilities, hangars and multistorey buildings' had been built. It also noted the presence of underground tunnels, missile shelters, radars and high-frequency antennae.[18]

China pressed on with its construction and its broad assertions of sovereignty, combined with threats and harassment towards those who questioned it. A July 2019 defence white paper reiterated that the area was an 'inalienable' part of Chinese territory and that China 'exercises its national sovereignty to build infrastructure and deploy necessary defensive capabilities on the islands and reefs in the South China Sea'.[19] Beijing designated the area a 'core interest', a label it uses for issues regarded as beyond debate. Or as Yuan Yubai, commander of the People's Liberation Army Navy's northern fleet, has put it, 'The South China Sea, as the name indicates, is a sea area that belongs to China . . . from the Han dynasty a long time ago where the Chinese people have been working and producing from the sea.'[20]

While Beijing's claim to the South China Sea is a key part of Xi's nationalist agenda, it is also motivated by strategic considerations, and underpinned by a deep sense of insecurity. China is enclosed on three sides by land borders, and counts fourteen countries as neighbours. Looking out to the east, beyond its only sea border, it is confronted by an island barrier extending from Russia's Kamchatka Peninsula in the north to Borneo in the south. Part of that barrier is formed by Japan, South Korea and the Philippines, all US allies, as well as by Taiwan. The South China Sea is a strategic and economic chokepoint. China remains heavily dependent on Middle Eastern oil, and some 80 per cent of those supplies cross the South China Sea after passing through the Malacca Strait from the Indian Ocean. Around 40 per cent of China's total trade takes the same route.[21] It is the sort of challenging geography that feeds Communist Party paranoia about being 'contained'.

China undoubtedly has strategic interests in the South China Sea, but so does the rest of the world. It is one of the most important global trade routes, with goods valued at $3.37 trillion transiting the area annually.[22] Estimates of the volume of world trade carried through the South China Sea range from 20 per cent to 33 per cent.[23] Almost a third of global crude oil and over half of global liquefied natural gas (LNG) passes through the area each year. As an energy supply route it is critically important to the economies of Japan, South Korea and Taiwan. More than half the world's fishing vessels are in the South China Sea, and millions depend on the sea for food and livelihoods – though fish stocks are dwindling because of overfishing, which rivals blame on aggressive expansion of China's huge fleet.

There has been considerable speculation about the riches that might lie beneath the seabed, but surveys for oil and gas have been limited and have become another source of tension with China. Beijing has impeded exploration efforts by other states and pressured Western oil companies not to cooperate with them. Estimates of the value of oil and gas reserves vary widely. China has produced a figure of up to $60 trillion dollars, ten times the value estimated by the US, which reckons most reserves lie at the margins of the South China Sea rather than beneath disputed reefs and islands.[24] The US has accused China of using coercion to block development in the area and preventing neighbouring states from accessing $2.5 trillion of energy reserves.[25]

For China it was a sort of Holy Grail – a 600-year-old book of navigational instructions that provided 'undeniable proof' of China's sovereignty over disputed islands. The handwritten book supposedly belonged to Su Chengfen, a retired fisherman, and in the run up to the UNCLOS tribunal ruling in 2016, his weathered face was all over Chinese state media, explaining how his book had been handed down from generation to generation, guiding him and his distant relatives to far-flung rocks and reefs across the South China Sea. 'It is ironclad proof . . . We can deduce China's historic fishing and sailing rights in the South China Sea, as well as ownership,' screamed the *China Daily*, quoting Gao Zhiguo, the director of the China Institute for Marine Development Strategy.[26]

Except the book didn't exist. When a BBC television team tracked down a rather baffled Mr Su to his house in the fishing port of Tanmen, on the east coast of Hainan Island, they found him busy building a model boat in his yard close to the beach. 'It mainly taught us how to go somewhere and come back, how to go to the Paracels and the Spratlys, and how to come back to Hainan Island,' he said of the book. But when asked to show it, he said he'd thrown it away. 'It was flipped through too many times. The salty seawater on the hands had corroded it . . . In the end it was no longer readable so I threw it away.'[27] If the book was ironclad proof of anything it was the extraordinary lengths that Beijing is willing to go to manipulate the truth in order to press its narrative on the South China Sea. Hainan, a tropical island which juts off the south coast of China, is home to many of China's often surreal propaganda efforts, mobilising myth and emotion to justify its behaviour.

Hainan hosts the National Institute for South China Sea Studies (NISCSS), and a vast new China Museum of the South China Sea, which is located in Tanmen. The museum has a shiny double sloping roof that is supposed to represent waves, or perhaps a ship, depending on which way you look at it. 'She sometimes squats on the earth, and sometimes floats in the air, accompanied by the coconut wind and sea melody, silently, like a god,' gushed one architectural website.[28] If that sounds other-worldly, then that is appropriate, since both the museum and institute peddle an alternative reality, based on mythology rather than history. Their overwhelming purpose is to bolster China's claims that the sea has belonged to China since ancient times. Their efforts run in tandem with those of the well-funded National Conservation Center for Underwater Cultural Heritage. They have weaponised archaeology, whereby every relic, from shipwrecks down to the smallest fragment of cup, plate or saucer hauled from the depths, becomes a propaganda prop, used to demonstrate China's 'unalienable' rights to the South China Sea.

If there is a man who has come to symbolise China's mythology of the sea it is Zheng He, a eunuch general who undertook a series of epic voyages to the South China Sea and Indian Ocean during the Ming Dynasty in the early fifteenth century. He has been enlisted as a symbol not only of China's territorial rights, but also its 'peaceful rise'. Propaganda depicts him as a bold explorer who extended China's influence and controlled the seas, but who sought no more than 'friendship and cooperation'.[29] At a conference in 2017 to promote Chinese investment, Xi Jinping said: 'These pioneers won their place in history not as conquerors with warships, guns or swords. Rather they are remembered as friendly emissaries.'[30] There is no doubting the scale of He's endeavours. Each of his seven voyages consisted of between 50 and 250 giant ships, with more than 20,000 heavily armed men – easily the most advanced navy of that time. But more neutral historians describe his voyages as exercises in 'gunboat diplomacy', designed to shock and awe – controlling trade routes and unleashing plunder and slaughter on those unwilling to bow to the authority of the Chinese empire.

What is perhaps most intriguing about that period is how suddenly it was all abandoned. Just as China's naval power appeared to reach a peak, Ming rulers turned inwards. They banned all seafaring activities, closed their shipyards and shrank their navy to a small coastal force. Indeed, apart from that brief period of Ming hyperactivity, as represented by He, successive Chinese empires paid very little attention to maritime exploration – they largely cut themselves off from the sea. It is no surprise that the modern law of the sea is very cautious about vague claims of 'historic rights' – especially around the South China Sea, where patterns of power and influence if they existed at all were fluid and shifting. There is little evidence that anybody exercised sovereignty in any meaningful or sustained way. There was little concept or need of it. The overriding imperative was trade – towards which imperial China has had a distinctly skittish attitude over the centuries.

Fishermen like Su Chengfen are often depicted in Chinese propaganda as hardy and skilled operators, living off their wits, employing knowledge and instincts (and ancient books) handed down from one seafaring generation to the next to navigate the distant seas. In reality there is little that is traditional about many of the hulking fishing boats that line the shore in Tanmen. These are modern 500-ton steel-hulled vessels equipped with state-of-the-art satellite navigation and communications equipment. Their crews, who receive basic military training, are members of Tanmen's maritime militia, which Xi Jinping has designated a 'model unit'. It even has its own museum at its office in the port's local government compound.[31] The Tanmen militia played a key role in the 2012 stand-off at Scarborough Shoal, when its boats harassed and obstructed those of the Philippines. The following year, Xi Jinping visited the port and praised their efforts and visited their museum. 'Build big boats, charge forth on the deep sea, and catch big fish,' Xi urged – an ambiguous instruction that triggered a frenzy of construction and modernisation. The government has heavily subsidised boatbuilding, with subsidies conditional on militia membership. The militia now comprises hundreds of boats, and there are militia units at several ports on Hainan Island, as well as in Sansha, a municipality in the Paracel Islands charged with administering all China's claims in the South China Sea.

It was boats from the maritime militia that in 2021 occupied Whitsun Reef, and triggered the expletive-laden tweet from the Philippines' secretary of foreign affairs. They have been described as 'little blue men', likened to the armed 'little green men' without insignia whom Russia sent to occupy Crimea in 2014.[32] Others have described them as reservists. Their principal role appears to be to maintain a presence, to fly the flag, particularly in the distant Spratly Islands, and to collect intelligence.[33] Though they can be more aggressive if required, using their heavy hulls to ram the comparatively flimsy wooden hulls of rival fishing fleets.

Hainan might be at the heart of Chinese myth-making over the South China Sea, but it is also the base for the coercive assets used to enforce Beijing's territorial claims with increasing aggression. The maritime militia have been described as 'blue hulls', the first tier in China's three-tier system of enforcement. The others being the 'white hulls' of the coastguard and the 'grey hulls' of the navy.[34] The Chinese Coast Guard (CCG) has expanded rapidly with the express purpose of enforcing China's territorial claims. By 2020, the CCG had an estimated 260 ships capable of operating offshore and more than 1,000 confined to coastal waters. The largest increase has been in large ocean-going patrol ships of more than 2,500 tons, from just three in 2005 to an estimated sixty in 2020. Their equipment includes helicopters, interceptor boats, deck guns and high-capacity water cannon.[35] The CCG is the world's largest coastguard, with more ships than the coastguards of all regional neighbours combined, and includes the world's two largest maritime law enforcement vessels.[36]

Since a 2018 reorganisation the CCG has taken on a far more assertive role. It has escorted Chinese research vessels conducting seismic surveys in Vietnam's exclusive economic zone, and impeded Malaysian oil exploration.[37] In April 2020, a 3,500-ton coastguard ship rammed and sank a wooden-hulled Vietnamese fishing boat in waters claimed by Hanoi.[38] In early 2021 China introduced a new 'Coast Guard Law' granting its vessels the authority to manage, control and open fire on foreign ships violating its 'jurisdictional waters'.[39] The law gave the CCG the right to forcibly board non-compliant foreign vessels engaged in 'illegal' activity in Chinese-claimed waters. Like many Chinese laws, it is ambiguously worded but empowers the CCG to employ 'all means necessary, including the use of force' to stop foreigners found infringing Chinese 'sovereignty'. China's rattled neighbours pointed out that since China's territorial claims have been invalidated by an international tribunal then the Coast Guard Law itself was in violation of international law. Beijing was unmoved.

Hainan is also home to some of China's most advanced naval assets. They are concentrated at two adjacent bays – Yalong Bay and Yulin Bay – on the southern tip of the island, just to the east of the city of Sanya, a popular tourist destination. In April 2021, on the seventy-second anniversary of the founding of the People's Liberation Army Navy (PLAN), Xi Jinping visited the Yalong Bay base and commissioned three new warships – a helicopter carrier, capable of carrying dozens of helicopters, as well as jump-jets, tanks, and up to 1,200 troops, a guided-missile destroyer, and a nuclear-powered submarine, believed to be capable of carrying a dozen intercontinental ballistic missiles.[40] State television showed hundreds of white-clad sailors standing to attention along the decks of the ships and on the harbourside, bursting into synchronised applause as an impassive Xi stood on a platform in front of them. The Communist Party leader was clad in a khaki open-necked shirt, and presented flags and naming certificates to the captains and political commissars of the three warships. The *Global Times* said the combination of the helicopter carrier and destroyer will be 'very powerful in island seizing'. It quoted Song Zhongping, described as a military affairs expert, saying, 'These vessels will play important roles in solving questions in places like the island of Taiwan and the South China Sea.'[41]

Yalong Bay contains Asia's largest nuclear submarine base; Yulin Bay has a mix of facilities, hosting a fleet of destroyers and conventional submarines, but is reportedly expanding to handle nuclear submarines and aircraft carriers. It is regarded as the hub for deployments to the South China Sea.[42] It had been assumed that stationing vessels permanently at the artificial islands that Beijing has built in the Spratlys is a challenge because of the rough seas around them and their sheer distance from China. But there has been speculation that Beijing is looking to base submarines at Fiery Cross, which has the most advanced facilities, including a runway long enough to take any aircraft, from fighter jets to heavy transport planes and bombers. The waters around the reef quickly plunge to depths of more than 2,000 metres, which would seem to make it ideal as an outpost for a submarine fleet, tightening potential control over the sea lanes.

Of all the South China Sea claimants, Vietnam is best equipped to stand up to China, but it is cautious about how it does so. Hanoi is still haunted by a 1988 clash, which left sixty-four of its soldiers dead, a video of which is still available online. The video, shot from a Chinese ship, is grainy, the explosions muffled. It is accompanied by a frantic Chinese commentary and stirring martial music – all of which contribute to making the spectacle even more harrowing to watch. The Vietnamese soldiers are standing on a submerged rock, up to their knees in water. One of them is carrying a large flag, fluttering from a pole above him. Then comes a steady burst of heavy machine-gun fire from the Chinese ships and the water seems to explode all around the soldiers, erupting in spouts that dwarf their flag. Within a few seconds, the soldiers can no longer be seen – ending what can best be described as a turkey shoot.[43] This was the day China seized Johnson South Reef in the Spratly Islands, and secured the first of its holdings in the Spratlys. Fourteen years earlier China expelled South Vietnamese forces from the Paracel Islands to the north, which are now completely under the control of Beijing. Neither date is officially commemorated in Vietnam, but popular anger runs deep, and occasionally spills over. In May 2014, China's deployment of an oil rig into an area near the Paracel Islands claimed by Hanoi triggered a tense stand-off at sea and deadly anti-Chinese riots and arson in Vietnam. The rioters targeted Chinese-owned factories and businesses and left at least two people dead. Beijing evacuated 3,000 of its nationals.

Visitors to Hanoi do not have to look far for memorials or museums dedicated to what Vietnam calls the 'American War', the nineteen-year conflict that ended with the fall of Saigon in April 1975 and victory for Ho Chi Minh's guerrilla army. But relations with Washington have warmed in recent years – largely as a result of a common concern about Beijing. Vietnamese historians will tell you that the American War was a skirmish compared with the millennia-long struggle with China, which first forcibly incorporated Vietnam into the Han empire in 111 BC. Much of modern Vietnamese nationalism defines itself in opposition to China. As recently as February 1979, China invaded Vietnam with 200,000 soldiers with the aim of teaching Hanoi a 'lesson' for its overthrow a month earlier of the Khmer Rouge regime in neighbouring Cambodia, which Beijing supported. Up to 50,000 soldiers died in a month of bitter fighting close to the border before China declared 'victory' and withdrew. The People's Liberation Army had proven no match to the ferocious defence of the battle-hardened Vietnamese forces. This remains the last full war that China has fought to date.[44]

Vietnam has an estimated forty-nine outposts spread across twenty-seven features in the Spratly Islands. Most are submerged reefs or banks, though around ten are islets of varying sizes.[45] It has been busy beefing up fortifications, and on one of the islets has reclaimed land to build an airstrip, hangars and a protected harbour. It is not hard to see why maritime borders are so important to Hanoi. Some one-third of the country's population live along the coast and half the country's GDP comes from marine activities.[46] It has more than 2,000 miles of coastline, and claims an exclusive economic zone stretching 200 miles over its continental shelf into the South China Sea.

Quantifying who occupies what feature in the South China Sea can be a challenging exercise, since it depends on what you mean by a feature and how you define occupation, and both can be muddied by those making the claims. An 'occupation' can range from a pillbox or other simple structure (or the Philippines' beached ship) erected as a sign of sovereignty on an otherwise uninhabitable submerged reef, all the way to China's large artificial islands. China now controls all the Paracel Islands (which it calls the Xisha Islands), which number around 130 features. They are the closest to China, but are also claimed by Vietnam and Taiwan. The largest, Woody Island, has been turned into a major military garrison with airport, hangars and a civilian population of about 1,400. China occupies seven features in the Spratly

Islands which, as we have seen, have undergone vast land reclamation and include major military installations. The Philippines occupies nine or ten features in the Spratlys and Malaysia occupies five. Taiwan occupies a single Spratly island, Itu Aba, the largest natural land feature in the area, which it has also been fortifying.[47] Furthermore, it occupies Pratas Island, in the northern part of the South China Sea, between Taiwan and Hong Kong. It is a lonely outpost, but well situated to give Taiwan early warning of any attack that China might mount against it from the south and for anti-submarine warfare missions.

To complicate things further, neighbouring states have expunged the name 'China' from their description of the sea. Vietnam calls the area the East Sea, the Philippines calls it the West Philippines Sea, while Indonesia prefers the North Natuna Sea. Jakarta does not claim any of the disputed islands, but China's cow's tongue overlaps with parts of Indonesia's internationally recognised economic zone, and there have been tense stand-offs around Indonesia's Natuna Islands.

For its part, Malaysia has pursued a less confrontational approach with Beijing, but its patience has been severely tested as China has repeatedly harassed Malaysian energy exploration vessels operating in Malaysia's territorial waters. Chinese coastguard and navy ships intruded eighty-nine times between 2016 to 2019, according to Malaysian government figures.[48] A particular flashpoint has been the Kasawari gas field, just forty-four miles off the coast of Sarawak (East Malaysia), which is 1,200 miles from China. In June 2021, Malaysia scrambled fighter jets after sixteen Chinese military planes approached Sarawak and failed to respond to radio challenges. Kuala Lumpur lodged a diplomatic protest over what it called a 'breach of airspace and sovereignty.[49] The aerial intimidation appeared to be coordinated with harassment by the Chinese coastguard of Malaysian pipe-laying vessels.[50] Malaysia, in common with other South China Sea claimants, has resisted pressure from Beijing to enter into joint energy developments, and analysts saw China's military harassment as a warning to Kuala Lumpur not to proceed on its own.[51]

Beijing believes it has more than enough military clout to prevail over any local rivals, and that its growing maritime dominance will intimidate them into silent acquiescence, both individually and through their largely toothless regional grouping, the Association of Southeast Asian Nations (ASEAN). China also has enormous economic clout in the neighbourhood – and it has shown itself to be more than willing to use trade, investment or access to its market as weapons of influence, to reward and to punish. ASEAN and China have tried for twenty-five years to agree a regional code of conduct in the South China Sea, and they are still trying, but China is unwilling to put its name to anything that might constrain its behaviour.

'Nowhere is the rules-based maritime order under greater threat than in the South China Sea,' said US Secretary of State Antony Blinken on the fifth anniversary of the UNCLOS ruling. He accused China of seeking to 'coerce and intimidate Southeast Asian coastal states, threatening freedom of navigation in this critical global throughway'.[52] Most of the nations around the South China Sea have quietly welcomed greater American engagement after the divisive Trump presidency, though remain wary of publicly taking sides in the growing US–China stand-off. Both the US and China have escalated and intensified military operations in the South China Sea in what has been described as a 'feedback loop' in which Beijing is pushing its claims with ever-growing assertiveness and Washington is responding by stepping up what it terms 'Freedom of Navigation Operations'.[53] The US also increased reconnaissance flights, and in August 2021 alone, there were six naval task groups on operational deployment in the region – two from the US, and one each from Australia, Japan, India and the UK, according to the US Naval Institute.[54]

Beijing's single-minded pursuit of its strategic interests in the South China Sea has left little room for diplomatic (or legal) niceties, or for engagement on anything other than Beijing's terms. The Communist Party cloaks its claims in historical myth and nationalist emotion. It is also grounded in a view of the world that increasingly harks back to a period of history when the region was a patchwork of supplicants, paying tribute to the Chinese emperor – an attitude that is at its most explicit in Beijing's push into Southeast Asia.

## Chapter 3

# *Southeast Asia: Paying Tribute to the Emperor*

'China is a big country and other countries are small countries, and that's just a fact.'

*Yang Jiechi, director of China's Central Foreign Affairs Commission, July 2010*

Hundreds of ancient temples were spread across the vast plain, their towers and red-brown brickwork seemed to come alive in the late afternoon sunshine. 'China,' my guide sniffed. 'The great Kingdom of Bagan was destroyed by China.' We were standing on an elevated tier of one of the larger temples, looking out at the remains of one of Southeast Asia's greatest empires. Between the eleventh and thirteenth centuries the Bagan (or Pagan) Dynasty unified most of what is now modern Myanmar. The empire was a prolific temple builder, around 2,000 of which still remain in various states of disrepair, but the empire was shattered by the invading armies of Kublai Khan. The last king of Bagan, Narathihapate, fled at their approach, and in classrooms across today's Myanmar he is known as Tayok-pyay-min, the cowardly 'king who ran away from the Chinese'. Despite this, poems and songs in the country still celebrate resistance against China down the ages.

Not long before my visit, an earthquake shook the temples, causing severe damage. There'd been offers of help with repairs and restoration from across the world – including from China. But the way my guide saw it, Chinese archaeologists were about as welcome as Kublai Khan. 'There's restoration and there's restoration. The Chinese, they want to create Disney, not restore history,' he complained. I was sympathetic. I'd seen how the Chinese Communist Party had demolished much of old Lhasa in Tibet, only to build a tacky replica in its place. 'They won't be allowed to do that here,' I assured him. 'They do as they like,' he replied.

Early the following morning I took a boat up the Irrawaddy to Mandalay. The river is treacherous at the best of times, and during the monsoon season it becomes bloated and dangerously unpredictable. My boat spluttered and strained against the current before the captain decided the best course was to hug the shore, where the water was calmer. He said he needed to be especially wary of the shifting sandbanks and wrecks – lots of wrecks, he said with a smile. It was September 2017, and I was researching a book – my second novel, *Zero Days*, a cyber thriller, with lots of hacking and other digital skulduggery. My main character comes to Myanmar to investigate the case of an archaeologist blackmailed into handing over priceless artefacts by cyber crooks who hack into and take control of his pacemaker. I was looking forward to Mandalay, which was Myanmar's last royal capital, and in my mind a thriving centre of Buddhist culture and religion. I thought it would make a good backdrop for scenes from the novel, and I imagined my protagonist wandering among the old wooden houses and temples.

It took more than thirteen hours to cover 100 miles of river, and it was dusk by the time we moored at a scrappy jetty on the outskirts of the city. From there I shared the backseat of a decrepit Nissan taxi with a single voracious mosquito, a tiny escapologist which ducked and weaved to avoid my flailing arms and clapping hands. It began to rain heavily, and the traffic crawled along flooded roads which in parts resembled mini versions of the Irrawaddy. I looked out at the smudgy outlines of sprawling construction sites and ugly buildings that resembled stacks of egg-boxes hung with neon signs. I spotted a glass-fronted hotel called the New Dragon, another called the Great Wall, a hotpot restaurant with a Mandarin-language menu, advertisements for Chinese fashion brands and smartphones. Was I back in China? The taxi driver seemed to sense my surprise, and he took up where my Bagan guide had left off. 'The Chinese are master here,' he said in broken English. 'Everything is China.'

Mandalay is 165 miles southwest of the border with China's Yunnan province and has become a major crossroads for transport, trade and all manner of smuggling. By one estimate almost two-thirds of the local economy is in Chinese hands and up to half the city's 1.2 million population is Chinese.[1] While a Chinese community has long existed in Mandalay, most have come more recently, though local businesspeople say the precise figure is hard to determine because many obtain Myanmar citizenship by bribing immigration officials. The city is still thought to be home to more than half of Myanmar's monks, but the old monastic centre is now lined with shops packed with jostling Chinese traders looking to get their hands on the jade and other gemstones that Myanmar is renowned for. Stores in the city's markets are packed with Chinese-made clothes, consumer goods and cosmetics. China has extended its influence on local media, and the city administration signed a deal with the Chinese telecoms giant Huawei to supply surveillance cameras and other equipment as part of what is described as a 'safe city' project.[2]

China is by far Myanmar's most important trading partner, investor and benefactor, but it is in Mandalay, the country's second city, that China's influence is at its most stark. There is certainly a new prosperity, but it is not hard to find the resentment at what is seen as the aggression and cultural insensitivity of the new arrivals. Local comedians have labelled the country the 'Chinese Republic of the Union of Myanmar', and the city 'Mandalay, Yunnan'. While 'The Death of Mandalay', a song by popular local singer Lin Lin, laments that 'The city where I was born is no longer there. Who are these people in the city?' As the historian Thant Myint-U writes, 'Fear is too strong a word. But an anxiety about China is deeply ingrained in Burmese thinking.'[3]

On 1 February 2021, the Myanmar military seized power, annulling a general election in which the National League for Democracy (NLD) of Aung San Suu Kyi won a resounding majority. For almost a decade the men in uniform had just about tolerated civilian rule, all the time retaining considerable power for themselves. Now they wanted it all back, returning Myanmar to the dark days of brutal military dictatorship that had blighted the country between 1962 until 2011. There was strong international condemnation – but not from Beijing, which stalled a UN Security Council resolution condemning the coup, at one point describing the military takeover as a 'major cabinet reshuffle'.[4] There were reports that Myanmar's military chief had shared bogus claims of electoral fraud used to justify the coup with China's foreign minister, Wang Yi, during a visit by Wang just three weeks before the takeover. This fed suspicions that Beijing was involved in the takeover, or at the very least had been forewarned.[5]

When the coup triggered widespread protest, the army responded with characteristic brutality, turning their guns on the protesters, killing hundreds, while jailing thousands more. The anger on the streets was aimed at the men in uniform, but also at China. Protesters besieged the Chinese embassy in Yangon, Myanmar's main commercial hub, carrying placards reading 'Shame on you China', 'Myanmar's military dictatorship is made in China' and 'China get out of Myanmar'.[6] There were arson attacks on Chinese-owned garment factories in an industrial zone of the city – the Communist Party's *Global Times* claimed thirty-two had been vandalised, sustaining $37 million of damage.[7] Passions were further inflamed by allegations that China had helped bolster internet controls for the military and had supplied drones to monitor the protests.[8] In Mandalay, protesters shouted 'Chinese business, Out! Out!' and ominously for Beijing they threatened action against critical Chinese-owned gas and oil pipelines. 'China's gas pipeline will be burned,' they chanted. Social media carried many more threats.[9] Soon after, three guards were slashed to death at the Mandalay pipeline substation by unidentified machete-wielding assailants.[10] The city is a key staging post for the twin pipelines which stretch almost 500 miles across Myanmar from the Indian Ocean to the border with China. The gas pipeline opened in 2013, and carries supplies from Myanmar's offshore fields; the oil pipeline entered service in 2017 and sits alongside it, bringing Middle Eastern crude from a Chinese-built port on Myanmar's coast. Beijing urged the military regime to tighten security measures, insisting that 'any damage to the pipelines would cause huge losses for both countries'.

The pipeline is one of the most prominent projects under China's Belt and Road Initiative (BRI), which also include multi-billion dollar investments in energy, mining, railways, roads, industrial parks, a new city next to Yangon and a deep-water port. These are often labelled as components of the 'China–Myanmar Economic Corridor'. As of March 2020, the Myanmar government reported more than $21 billion of approved Chinese investment.[11] The BRI is often described as an international infrastructure project, though it lacks any real coherence. It is better understood as a tool for Beijing's broader economic and geopolitical goals, an umbrella term under which all manner of projects are grouped. In the case of Myanmar, the overriding purpose is to give China access to the ocean – 'the long march to the sea', as it has been dubbed. As we saw in Chapter 2, geography has not been kind to China, and much of its policy in Myanmar – and Southeast Asia in general – is designed to lessen its economic dependence on the South China Sea and Malacca Strait trade route. Myanmar has been described by Chinese analysts as 'China's California', a proxy for the western coast that it lacks.[12]

Myanmar is also an important source of raw materials for Beijing, and one of China's largest investments is the Letpaduang copper mine, which occupies a fortified compound near the central Myanmar town of Monywa. A February 2017 Amnesty International report said the project was 'plagued by human rights abuses', citing land confiscations, environmental damage and harassment of activists and villagers opposed to the mine.[13] When Myanmar was under civilian rule, the mine did come under scrutiny, but it has powerful backers – it is a joint venture between China's Wanbao Mining and a conglomerate owned by the Myanmar military. Wanbao is a subsidiary of Norinco, a Chinese state-owned arms manufacturer, which supplies weapons and other equipment to Myanmar's army. Soon after the 2021 coup, the miners went on strike, and it was reported that the mine had suspended production 'because of the recent turmoil'.[14]

Chinese gangs are also heavily implicated in more illicit trade, again working hand-in-hand with the Myanmar military or the ethnic armies who control the country's borderlands, from where they smuggle timber, wildlife, gems and drugs. A March 2019 Human Rights Watch report accused the Myanmar and Chinese authorities of looking the other way and allowing the trafficking of ethnic Kachin women and girls as 'brides' to families in China. The balance of the sexes in China is skewed heavily towards men, a legacy of the country's now abandoned one-child policy under which a preference for boys meant that girls were frequently aborted.[15]

China's projects came under scrutiny when Myanmar began its tentative liberalisation and opening to the West in 2011. A proposed $3.6 billion Myitsone Dam in northern Kachin state, which borders China, was suspended. The project planned to dam the Irrawaddy River, flood an area the size of Singapore and export 90 per cent of the power generated to China. Other projects, including a deep-water port at Kyaukphyu on the Bay of Bengal, were renegotiated to cut costs and give a bigger stake to Myanmar. The Letpaduang copper mine was suspended, but then allowed to continue. Although these projects were negotiated by the previous military government, it was widely assumed that the decision by the military to allow a return to guided civilian rule was motivated at least in part by a desire to lessen dependence on Beijing, which had become too claustrophobic, even for the generals. At first it seemed to work, and a visit by US Secretary of State Hillary Clinton in late November 2011 was followed a year later by that of President Barack Obama. The president addressed a packed hall at the University of Yangon. 'I stand here with confidence that something is happening in this country that cannot be reversed,' he said. 'The will of the people can lift up this nation and set a great example for the world. And you will have in the United States of America a partner on that long journey.' I was in the audience that day, and thought Obama looked tired, that his delivery was unusually flat. But there was no denying that the first ever visit to Myanmar by a US president was an historic moment. A huge mural spray-painted on a wall in downtown Yangon, showing the smiling American leader and the words 'Welcome OBAMA' seemed to capture the popular mood. He posed with opposition leader Aung San Suu Kyi at the lakeside villa where she spent years under house arrest. Western countries began the process of removing sanctions that had been in place for two decades.

During the years of military rule, when the West shunned and sanctioned the generals, Beijing had protected them – supplying arms, diplomatic support against charges of human rights abuses, as well as investment and trade. Yangon had few alternatives. Now Beijing watched in dismay as Suu Kyi's NLD won the November 2015 general election, the first free election in twenty-five years. The military still barred her from the presidency because her children are British nationals, but the position of 'State Councillor' was created, which made her de facto head of a quasi-civilian government. Beijing's influence appeared to be waning – until the persecution and the mass exodus of the Rohingya Muslim minority, which began in August 2017, changed the equation again. Suu Kyi, the Nobel Peace Prize Laureate and democracy icon remained silent in the face of army atrocities and Buddhist nationalist abuse and violence. She faced withering criticism from her erstwhile supporters in Western democracies, which reimposed targeted sanctions. As in the past, China stepped forward to defend what the West found unpalatable. Beijing restored its influence, shielding Suu Kyi's regime and the military in the UN, watering down a Security Council statement drafted by the UK and obstructing UN attempts to investigate the violence. Beijing promoted itself as a mediator between

Myanmar and Bangladesh, to which hundreds of thousands of Rohingya fled.[16]

China also stepped up its role as a 'broker' in Suu Kyi's efforts to strike a lasting peace deal with the country's patchwork of ethnic groups, many of which have been fighting the central authorities for decades. Beijing cultivated strong links with many of these ethnic armies, particularly in the borderlands between the two countries, and has not hesitated to use this leverage to its advantage. When China's Foreign Minister Wang Yi visited Myanmar in January 2021, he urged the government to speed up construction work on the 'China–Myanmar Economic Corridor', the label for all those expensive infrastructure projects Yangon had been hesitating over. He also said China would continue to support the peace talks with the ethnic minority armies. The two issues were not explicitly linked, at least not in public – they did not need to be.[17]

Beijing maintains a particularly close relationship with the 30,000-strong United Wa State Army (UWSA), the largest rebel force, which is armed by China and has been accused of employing child soldiers. It runs a slice of territory the size of Belgium, which sits in northeast Shan state on the border with China's Yunnan province and beyond the authority of the government in Yangon. Panghsang, the capital of this self-styled Wa State, is so dependent on China that it is almost indistinguishable from it. The city sits astride a river border crossing, and unlike most cities in Myanmar it has well-made concrete roads and an air of prosperity. A string of casinos and brothels cater largely to visitors from China, and it is connected to the Chinese internet and mobile phone system. China's currency is widely used and Mandarin spoken, while the Wa elite send their children to Chinese schools and are treated in Chinese hospitals.[18] The Wa State sits at the heart of the notorious 'Golden Triangle', and much of its wealth was built on heroin production, of which it was the world's biggest producer. It claims to have kicked the opium habit, but it has branched out into methamphetamine drugs, for which it remains one of the largest production hubs.

Relations between the Wa and the Chinese Communist Party go back a long way. The USWA emerged from the break-up of the Communist Party of Burma, which led an insurgency in the early days of independent Burma (as Myanmar was then called). It was strongly backed by Mao Zedong, who at that time was busy spreading revolution across Southeast Asia. Rather like the Wa, China ditched ideology for the pursuit of narrow and calculating self-interest. Mao's obsession with revolution was abandoned by Deng Xiaoping, who ushered in the more pragmatic era. Today, China sees the Wa as an instrument of coercion, a relationship that gives Beijing considerable leverage with the government in Myanmar. As we shall see later, it has also been deployed to stoke uprisings in India.

Mao's China was by far the biggest supporter of Pol Pot's genocidal Khmer Rouge regime, which killed an estimated 2 million Cambodians between 1975 and 1979. The Cambodian genocide killed around a quarter of the population. Per capita that is truly horrifying, though the absolute number is dwarfed by the total number of Chinese murdered by Mao or who died as a result of his disastrous policies, where credible estimates range from 40 to 70 million. Much of this has been written out of official Chinese history, as has Mao's support for the Khmer Rouge. It does not fit with official propaganda about China's 'non-interference' and 'peaceful rise', and its presentation of itself as a victim and not an aggressor in international politics.

In 1979, a young Hun Sen, Cambodia's foreign minister in the government that followed the ousting of the Khmer Rouge, condemned 'the barbarous regime of the Pol Pot clique, instrument of Beijing's expansionist policy'. Hun Sen was a soldier in the Khmer Rouge, but defected and then fought alongside Vietnamese forces to defeat Pol Pot. A decade later, as prime minister, he wrote that 'China is the root of all that is evil in Cambodia'.[19]

The country is still littered with memorials to those who died in the killing fields – from stupas containing piles of skulls and bones to more simple village shrines. The execution grounds have been carefully documented and almost 20,000 mass burial pits have been identified across the country. Yet China's complicity is being erased from the official history in Cambodia too – and Hun Sen, still prime minister, is now the man doing the whitewashing. In 2018, a slick and endlessly rebroadcast government film about the defeat of Pol Pot, *Marching Toward National Salvation*, set the tone – it did not mention China a single time. Beijing is now Hun Sen's main patron, and for China, the man who fought against the Khmer Rouge is now their most reliable asset in Southeast Asia, blocking criticism at regional bodies such as ASEAN and strongly backing China's position on the South China Sea and beyond.

In his early years as prime minister, Hun Sen was heavily reliant on Western aid, which acted as a restraint on his authoritarian inclinations. But Chinese money and political support emboldened him, and in 2017 he cast off any lingering pretences of democracy. He dissolved the main opposition party and arrested its leader Kem Sokha for treason, claiming he had colluded with foreign powers, including the United States, to topple the government. Hun Sen gave himself the title of 'glorious supreme prime minister and powerful commander', and when the English language *Cambodia Daily* condemned his 'descent into outright dictatorship' it was promptly shut down. The West echoed the newspaper's criticism, but Beijing saw things differently, praising Hun Sen for his 'effort to uphold national security and stability'.[20] The prime minister suspended annual joint military exercises with the United States – and for the first time participated in exercises with China.[21] By 2018, more than half of all foreign investment in Cambodia was coming from China, mostly under the umbrella of its Belt and Road Initiative, and ranged from roads and airports to power plants – even entire towns. Half the country's rapidly rising foreign debt, amounting to more than a quarter of GDP, was owed to Beijing.

Nowhere better illustrates the rapid expansion of Chinese influence than the once sleepy coastal town of Sihanoukville, which sits on a peninsula on the Gulf of Thailand. It has been transformed by a China-funded construction frenzy, which has sprouted new hotels, apartment blocks, restaurants, bars, resorts and gambling dens, all emblazoned with Mandarin-language neon signage. Land prices increased tenfold between 2014 and 2019. Before Covid-19 hit travel, nine out of every ten visitors were from China, and the shops were stacked with Chinese goods. Crime and violence also soared as Sihanoukville became a base for Chinese organised crime – a hub for online gambling and other online scams, human trafficking and drugs, all seemingly under the protection of corrupt local police.[22]

In a fast-expanding special economic zone just outside Sihanoukville, 90 per cent of the more than 100 companies are Chinese, and the zone is protected by private Chinese security guards. Beijing is financing a new four-lane $2 billion motorway – the nation's first – linking the town with the capital Phnom Penh, and described as 'another testament to the unbreakable ironclad friendship between Cambodia and China'.[23] Sihanoukville is not without its own reminders of the Khmer Rouge genocide, with two burial pits identified on the southeastern outskirts of town, each of which contained the remains of 1,000 bodies.[24] In early 2022, Google Earth revealed the giant scars from construction bearing down on the closer of the two – and it seems only a matter of time before this grim reminder of China-backed barbarity is encased by China-financed concrete.

Across the bay to the north of Sihanoukville the new Dara Sakor International airport has been carved out of the jungle by an opaque Chinese company called Union Development Group (UDG). This Tianjin-based firm has been granted a ninety-nine-year lease to some 20 per cent of Cambodia's coast, where it pledged to build what amounts to a new metropolis. Company publicity boasts of investment worth $3.8 billion in tourist resorts, luxury golf courses, casinos, marinas, up-market homes, container ports and industrial parks, but at the time of writing all it has to show for itself is a single resort complex attracting very few visitors – and of course the jungle airstrip. It seems to defy economic logic – but it does make a lot of strategic sense to China's military planners. The airport's two-mile-long runway is the longest in Cambodia, far longer than required for commercial aircraft, or the wildest of optimistic forecasts about tourism, but more than suitable for China's long-range fighter jets, surveillance aircraft, military transport planes and bombers. In September 2020, the US blacklisted UDG, saying it was building on land forcibly seized from local people, and Mike Pompeo, US secretary of state in the Trump administration cited 'credible reports' that Dara Sakor could be used to host Chinese military assets.[25]

Nor is Dara Sakar the only military foothold Beijing is establishing in the area. On a peninsula the other side of Sihanoukville, sits the Ream Naval Base, which includes a number of facilities originally built by the US and is home to a fleet of around a dozen Cambodian Navy patrol boats. Cambodia reportedly signed a secret deal with Beijing granting the People's Liberation Army exclusive rights to part of the installation. Under the deal, the PLA would be able to post military personnel, store weapons and berth warships, according to a draft of the agreement.[26] The deal allows China to build two new piers and dredge the port to facilitate larger vessels, turning it into Beijing's first naval base in Southeast Asia. Basing air force and naval assets in Cambodia – or using the facilities for logistics or as staging posts – would help China enforce its territorial claims in the South China Sea while complicating US efforts to come to the assistance of Taiwan in the event of conflict over the island.

The scene was Hanoi in July 2010, the event a regional security meeting of the sort that rarely generates great passion, at least not in public. That isn't regarded as the ASEAN way, preferring disputes to be handled in a low-key fashion behind closed doors – if at all. This time it was tense. US Secretary of State Hillary Clinton and top Chinese diplomat Yang Jiechi attended, and they eyed each other warily. When Clinton raised the issue of a binding code of conduct for the South China Sea, Yang lashed back, telling her in effect to mind her own business. Then, addressing leaders from Southeast Asia, Yang said: 'China is a big country and other countries are small countries, and that's just a fact.'[27] The audience was shocked – and not just by the arrogance. For many it harked back to a Chinese imperial mindset, a China-centric view of the world that treated the region as inferior to *Zhonggou*, the Middle Kingdom – and one that demanded lesser states know their place.

It is a mindset that has its roots in the ancient Chinese cultural concept of *Tian xia* (literally 'all under heaven'), with China (and the emperor) at the centre of a universal order, surrounded by lesser tributary states and barbarians.[28] Imperial China's old default position was to deal with foreigners on the emperor's terms or not at all. By this reading, ideology plays no part – states are judged, rewarded and cajoled according to their willingness to accept China's primacy. 'Revanchism is an intrinsic part of the story of China's "Great Rejuvenation",' according to Bilahari Kausikan, Singapore's former top diplomat. Few Asian diplomats have spent more time in the company of Chinese envoys, and he says their sense of cultural superiority and demand for almost Pavlovian deference leaves little room for the give-and-take of Western diplomacy. 'China does not merely want consideration of its interests. China expects deference to its interests to be internalised by ASEAN members as a mode of thought,' he says.[29] This is seen by Beijing as a natural state of affairs, particularly in China's backyard. Restoration of something resembling the ancient order is regarded by today's Communist leaders not only as the natural scheme of things, but almost as destiny, intrinsic to the 'great rejuvenation' of the Chinese nation.

Rather like China's 'historic' claim to the South China Sea, Beijing's ancient relationship with Southeast Asia is also mythologised by its

Communist Party leaders. Much of the Southeast Asia of old did pay tribute to the Chinese empire, a ritual that dates back more than two millennia. Tributary missions, with envoys bearing gifts and messages for the emperor and receiving others in return, varied in frequency and size, but there is much debate about their actual meaning. They were certainly ritualised, but for the Southeast Asian kings (who rarely went in person) they did not have the same connotation as they did for China. They were seen more as a way of humouring the emperor – practical gestures necessary for ensuring mutually beneficial trade.[30] Southeast Asian kingdoms never saw themselves as part of the Chinese order alone, foreign relations were more complex and shifting. There were competing centres of power. The vast temple complexes of the region, from Myanmar's Bagan to Cambodia's Angkor Wat and Indonesia's Borobudur, are evidence of the profound Indian influence across the region, for instance.

Like their forebears, the modern states of Southeast Asia have sought to strike a difficult balance between seeking to accommodate (and profit from) a rising and at times overbearing China, and protecting their sovereignty. 'Only the irredeemably corrupt or the terminally naïve take seriously Beijing's rhetoric about a community of common destiny,' says Bilahari Kausikan, drawing on thirty-seven years of experience in Singapore's diplomatic service.[31] That still adds up to a lot of countries susceptible to China's blandishments, and to them might be added the deeply repressive who have been shunned by Western democracies or multilateral lenders. A key component of Communist Party rhetoric is 'non-interference', which in practice means finding common cause with the most corrupt and unsavoury of regimes. They are the ones most likely to bend to China's will because of a lack of alternatives. We have seen this in the case of Myanmar and Cambodia, but this is also evident in Thailand. The Thais have historically been masters of balancing and hedging multiple foreign relationships, but more recently the kingdom became one of the West's most dependable allies. That changed after Western democracies criticised a 2014 military coup. China stepped in with economic and diplomatic support, and as a result was able to extend its influence with Bangkok. A year after the coup, the Thai military government showed its gratitude by deporting to China a group of 100 Muslim Uyghurs who had fled to Bangkok, where they were seeking asylum. The UN High Commissioner for Refugees called the deportation a 'flagrant violation of international law'. That same year, a Hong Kong bookseller, a high profile critic of Beijing, was abducted from his Thai holiday home, seemingly with the complicity of the Thai authorities.

Ironically, it is the Southeast Asian countries most accommodating to China who have been on the receiving end of one of Beijing's most flagrant power plays. China controls the source of major Asian rivers including the Mekong, Salween and Brahmaputra, and has embarked on an enormous programme of dam building without consideration of the impact on countries downstream. China has eleven mega-dams on the northern reaches of the Mekong River alone, giving Beijing enormous power over the economies and ecosystems of those countries who share the river and the millions who depend on it for their livelihoods. The Mekong is a lifeline for Thailand, Myanmar, Cambodia and Laos, as well as Vietnam, but Beijing has rejected any discussions of dam construction or management with the downstream countries. China regards the Mekong as a sovereign resource and not one that should be shared.[32] China could quite literally turn off the tap, and in 2019, was blamed for doing just that and triggering a severe drought in the lower Mekong basin, even after record rain and snowfall in the upper reaches. As a result, crops failed and the fish catch fell to some of the lowest levels in years. 'China is impounding much more water than it ever has before and is causing erratic and devastating changes in water levels downstream,' according to an investigation by the Stimson Center, a Washington DC-based think tank.[33] As a consequence, the dry season water flows of the Mekong has been likened to 'an erratic stock chart with random peaks and nadir'.[34]

There are echoes here of the Philippines and its failure to get any meaningful return or respect for its courting of China in the South China Sea. Mekong-dependent Cambodia, Laos, Myanmar and Thailand have been the Southeast Asian countries most willing to do Beijing's bidding, but on an issue fundamental to their national wellbeing, their muted complaints have been shrugged off. None have been rewarded with any meaningful say over such a key resource.

With China's growing influence in the region has come a wave of Chinese migration, described as the 'the shock troops of China's growing economic presence', extending China's power and reach.[35] Many came to work on projects under the Belt and Road Initiative, others in search of economic opportunities of various shades of legality. As we have seen, in places such as Mandalay and Sihanoukville, they now outnumber the local people, often generating resentment. There are estimated to be hundreds of thousands now working out of Manila, the capital of the Philippines, where Chinese online gambling operations now outnumber the city's thriving international call centres. In Laos, along the Mekong River where the country borders Myanmar and Thailand, China is building the 'Golden Triangle Special Economic Zone', which has been characterised as 'a Chinese city of gambling, smuggling and sleaze'.[36] The town's currency is the Chinese yuan, a local security force was recruited in China, and the signage is in the simplified Chinese characters. China is also now the region's biggest source of tourists. It is hard to put a precise figure on the number of migrants, since so many are working informally, but it certainly numbers in the millions.

The newer migrants are not to be confused with Southeast Asia's more long-standing ethnic Chinese communities, which are thought to number more than 30 million. They have long played a prominent role in trade and business, building large family-run enterprises along the Pacific Rim – and characterised as the 'Lords of the Rim'.[37] In some countries, such as Thailand, they are well integrated; in others, such as Indonesia and Malaysia, less so, and have long faced discrimination and sometimes outright violence. When China began to open up, the overseas Chinese were the first to sense the new opportunities and were among the biggest early investors. Yet historically China's attitude towards them has been ambiguous at best. As recently as 1998, when anti-Chinese riots erupted in Jakarta, Beijing's response was relatively muted, regarding it as a purely Indonesian domestic affair.

In contrast, Xi Jinping has adopted a more expansive view of what it means to be Chinese, and the obligations this carries to the motherland (which is indistinguishable in his thinking from the Communist Party). He has blurred the distinction between foreigners of Chinese descent who were born and long-settled overseas and are citizens of other countries, who are referred to as *huaren*, and the more recent migrants, or *huaqiao*, who may be overseas temporarily for work or education. He has lumped them all together calling them *haiwai qiaobao*, which roughly translates as 'overseas sojourner-siblings', whose task should be to 'promote the revival of the Chinese nation'. The job of reaching out to this extended Chinese family has been handed to the Party's United Front Work Department, an organisation whose brief it is to spread Party influence both openly and through clandestine means.[38] In this way, Xi emphasises ancestry and ethnicity over citizenship – it is a racial understanding of what it means to be Chinese, under which however deep the roots of an ethnically Chinese person in another country may be, no matter what passport they are carrying and no matter how long ago their ancestors left home, they are still seen as having obligations to China, as embodied by the Party. It is a chilling extension of the Party's reach, and is a particular challenge to those countries in Southeast Asia with a history of racial tensions and distrust towards their ethnically Chinese citizens. Xi is putting overseas Chinese communities in a particularly difficult and dangerous bind, stoking suspicion about their loyalties in their adopted countries.

Nowhere in the world is China's influence being felt as strongly as in Southeast Asia. China wants to dominate in its own backyard, and it is emerging as a key theatre in the battle for influence with the United States. The ten countries that comprise the Association of Southeast Asian Nations are collectively no minnow. Brunei, Cambodia, Indonesia, Laos, Malaysia, Myanmar, Philippines, Singapore, Thailand and Vietnam are home to almost 700 million people and have thriving economies with a GDP of almost $3 trillion. China is the region's largest trading partner, while Chinese investment in the region increased thirtyfold in the decade to 2021, with commitments of around $42 billion. Much of this is in infrastructure – massive cross-border road, rail and pipeline projects under the umbrella of the BRI.

As we have seen, talk of the old tributary relationship between Southeast Asia and China too often overlooks the complexities of foreign relations, it also ignores the enormous historic influence of India. Contemporary India has taken a back seat as China has extended its influence. It has had a difficult relationship with China over the years, but the two had appeared to be drawing closer economically – until a barbaric clash on the roof of the world, which seemed to defy logic or common sense, but gave a fresh insight into the mindset of Xi Jinping.

## Chapter 4

# *Brawling on the Roof of the World*

'You are over-confidently provoking the PLA and Chinese people – this is like doing a handstand on the edge of a cliff!'

*Global Times, September 2020*

The Galwan Valley is one of the most desolate and inhospitable places on earth. Situated high in the Himalayas, it is where the Indian territory of Ladakh meets Tibet and it marks the disputed border between India and China. On the night of 15 June 2020 it was the scene of a ferocious hand-to-hand battle of almost medieval barbarity, with soldiers wielding rocks, sticks, fence posts, and even clubs wrapped with barbed wire or embedded with nails. The moonlit clash, which triggered the worst crisis in decades between the nuclear-armed neighbours, took place along a narrow ridge, at an altitude of 14,000 feet. By the time it was over twenty Indian soldiers were dead and scores injured – struck down by blows from the improvised weapons or sent tumbling down the steep ravine and into the freezing river waters below.[1] They were the first combat deaths between the two sides since 1975, when four Indian soldiers were killed in a remote pass in another area of the border. China later admitted to losing four soldiers 'defending and guarding the country's borders', according to the *Global Times*. The paper quoted a PLA soldier from a nearby garrison saying, 'I would rather sacrifice my life than lose one inch of my country's territory.'[2] Other reports suggest that as many as thirty-eight Chinese soldiers may have died.[3]

The fighting took place without firearms because a 1996 agreement bars the use of live ammunition in the immediate area. Tanks, machine guns and artillery are kept to the rear. A report later emerged in Beijing claiming that Chinese forces had cleared two strategic hilltops of Indian soldiers by firing a microwave weapon, which focused high-frequency electromagnetic pulses or beams to cause irritation and pain. The weapon 'turned the mountain tops into a microwave oven', according to Jin Canrong, a professor of international relations at Beijing-based Renmin University. He claimed in a lecture that the weapon had been fired from below and within fifteen minutes those occupying the hilltops all began to vomit. 'They couldn't stand up, so they fled. This was how we retook the ground. We didn't publicise it because we solved the problem beautifully. They [India] didn't publicise it, either, because they lost so miserably.'[4] There has been no independent confirmation of the claim.

Tensions had been building for weeks along the remote and poorly demarcated border, which is referred to as the Line of Actual Control (LAC). Satellite images showed China steadily building its forces and establishing positions in areas which had traditionally been patrolled by both sides in the summer, when the harsh climate allowed. Indian press accounts suggested the fighting took place when an Indian patrol tried to dislodge Chinese soldiers from one of these buffer zones. Indian defence analysts had warned a month before the fighting that the PLA was moving to take control of the entire valley, which overlooks a strategically important road India had recently upgraded. By one estimate, China annexed up to twenty-three square miles of territory.[5]

Beijing blamed India for the clash and then claimed the area had always been Chinese territory. 'China always owns sovereignty over the Galwan Valley region,' asserted Zhao Lijian, the Chinese Foreign Ministry spokesman, warning that if India wanted to avoid conflict, it should restrain its forces.[6] India's external affairs minister, Subrahmanyam Jaishankar, retorted that China's assertion 'reflected an intent to change the facts on the ground in violation of all our agreement'.[7] It was an attempted land grab right out of Beijing's South China Sea playbook.

In an address to the nation, Prime Minister Narendra Modi said, 'India wants peace. But on provocation, India will give a befitting reply.'[8] He rushed tens of thousands of additional troops and heavy equipment to the border region. He moved to restrict Chinese economic activity in India, banning dozens of apps, including the popular TikTok short video app, and generally tightening oversight of Chinese companies. Imports of Chinese-made mobile phones and other goods were delayed at Indian ports. Curbs were placed on Chinese companies bidding for government contracts, requiring them to receive 'political and security clearance' from the Foreign and Home Ministries. Talk turned to loosening dependence on India's giant neighbour.[9] 'This is a turning point – a very serious junction in the relationship,' said Nirupama Rao, India's former foreign secretary and its former ambassador to the US and China. 'With what happened in Galwan – and so much blood being shed – it can't be business as usual.'[10]

To many China-watchers, the timing of Beijing's actions made no sense. Yes, the border dispute had been simmering for decades, and yes, China was the 'all-weather friend' of rival Pakistan, but trade and investment ties between Delhi and Beijing were growing and deepening. India was not a member of China's Belt and Road Initiative, but China's tech companies in particular were big investors in India, having pumped billions into Indian start-ups. Alibaba, Tencent and Huawei led the charge, excited by India's young and increasingly tech-savvy population, which they saw as a vast and relatively untapped market. India was also a fast-growing market for Chinese consumer goods, which were flowing in record amounts. At the time of the Galwan Valley clash, China enjoyed a big trade surplus.

Political ties were also growing closer. Nine months before the clash, Prime Minister Modi met Xi Jinping for a two-day summit in the southern Indian temple town of Malappuram, posing for photos designed to convey their warming relations, and sitting down for a sumptuous meal of local delicacies that included 'mutton Ularthiyathu' and 'lobster Malabar'.[11] A year before that Modi had travelled to Wuhan, where he took a boat ride with Xi and strolled with him amid the plum blossoms.[12] There was a consensus in Delhi in favour of deepening their relationship.

After all, this was supposed to be the 'Asian century', and India and China together could be its drivers. More optimistic economic analysts had begun to refer to the pair collectively as 'Chindia', to reflect the enormous potential of a partnership encompassing a third of humanity. Within a few years they would together account for more than half of global output, so the story went. It was surely a win-win situation, to borrow a favourite phrase of Xi Jinping – if only they could set aside their historic differences. That was always a big 'if', but the timing of China's incursions still seemed bizarre. Not only did the clash damage the prospects for Chinese companies in India and shatter bilateral political relations, but it pushed Delhi closer to the US and to regional powers Australia and Japan. It also came at a time when Beijing had its hands full elsewhere – locked in an increasingly bitter trade dispute with the Trump administration, intensifying repression in Xinjiang and Hong Kong, and stoking tensions in the Taiwan Strait and South China Sea. Why pick another fight?

Indian analysts suggested China had deliberately made its land grab while Delhi (and the rest of the world) was preoccupied with the fight against Covid-19. Beijing, then emerging from its own initial outbreak, had been mobilising troops for some time close to the LAC, while India had delayed its regular summer exercises because of the outbreak. Others speculated that Xi was keen to stir nationalist sentiment at home to distract attention from his early Covid-19 stumbles and cover up. There might have been an element of both, but the Galwan Valley in June 2020 clearly presented an opportunity for Xi to push for strategic advantage over an old rival, which he did with little concern for the geopolitical fallout or the economic cost. A more generous interpretation is that Xi miscalculated, and did not fully appreciate the depth of Indian anger and the strength of its response. There was some cautious optimism when the two sides began a series of military-to-military talks to try and diffuse the tensions. But they proceeded haltingly in an atmosphere of hostility and distrust. Then the lights went out in Mumbai.

On 13 October 2020, four months after the Galwan Valley clash, India's financial capital and a city of 20 million people was plunged into darkness. Trains stopped running, traffic ground to a halt, the stock exchange was suspended and businesses shut down. Mumbai was one of the hardest hit cities in the world by Covid-19 at the time, and hospitals treating thousands of patients were forced to switch to back-up generators to keep ventilators running. India is no stranger to blackouts, but this was one of the worst in decades in Mumbai. The state of Maharashtra's energy minister, Nitin Rout, hinted at sabotage, and the state government, which owns the transmission network, ordered an investigation. A month later, its cyber department suggested that a malware attack could have been responsible.[13] Yashasvi Yadav, the department's inspector general revealed that over a five-day period just after the Galwan Valley clash, a large-scale phishing attack had targeted Indian banking, information services and infrastructure. 'At least 40,300 cyberattacks were attempted,' he said. 'Most of them can be traced to the Chengdu area of China.' The implication was that malware had been pre-positioned within the computers of power-generating companies, and later triggered to bring down the Mumbai grid, but he offered few additional details.[14]

Recorded Future, an American cybersecurity company, collected further disturbing evidence of malicious code placed inside India's power systems. In a report published in February 2021, the company said ten Indian power sector organisations, including four out of five 'Regional Load Despatch Centres', which are responsible for managing the power grid through balancing supply and demand across the country, had been targeted in what it described as a 'concerted campaign against India's critical infrastructure'.[15] By closely examining the tactics, techniques and procedures of the hackers, Recorded Future concluded that the malware had come from a Chinese state-sponsored group called RedEcho. It did not believe the purpose was espionage, since there were limited opportunities to steal information, and the available data was of little value. Instead it suggested that the malware had been pre-positioned inside the computer systems to be triggered later for future operations – possibly for sabotage. The investigators could not firmly link their discovery to the Mumbai outage, but a few days after their report was published, the cyber department of the state government of Maharashtra submitted its findings on what it called the 'attack on the state's power grid'. The results closely correlated with those of the American company. 'So, from the findings of the cybercrime department and electricity department experts, it seems that the October 12 blackout could have been due to it [sabotage],' said Home Minister Anil Deshmukh.[16] Deshmukh was cautious, never singling out China. 'There were attempts to log in to our servers from a foreign land,' he said. 'We will investigate further'. India likes to boast of its own significant cyber capabilities, and it could be that the minister's caution reflects embarrassment that his own systems were so easily compromised.

Recorded Future also uncovered evidence that a suspected Chinese state-sponsored group had hacked an Indian media conglomerate that publishes the respected *Times of India*, a police department and an agency responsible for India's national identification database. This time the purpose seemed to be to steal information, rather that sabotage, with the Unique Identification Authority of India being a potentially rich target. It could be used by hackers to identify 'high-value targets, such as government officials, enabling social engineering attacks or enriching other data sources'.[17]

For its part, Beijing issued a boilerplate denial of the hacking. 'It is highly irresponsible to accuse a particular party when there is no sufficient evidence around,' said Wang Wenbin, a spokesman for China's Ministry of Foreign Affairs. 'China is firmly opposed to such irresponsible and ill-intentioned practice.'[18] However, as tensions continued at the border, Beijing appeared to be telling Delhi, 'back off, or the lights could go off across the country'.[19]

The state of Assam in India's northeast is perhaps best known to outsiders for its tea. The hills north of the town of Tezpur on the banks of the mighty Brahmaputra River are blanketed with vast tea gardens. Workers, almost all of them women in bright saris, move amid the thick bushes plucking the bright green leaves and placing them in baskets on their backs. It is a remarkably tranquil scene, yet the area serves as a bitter reminder of past Chinese aggression. In a brief border war in 1962, China captured much of the area to the north of Tezpur, and in the years that followed the region was buffeted by a China-backed insurgency. In recent years, the violence has been more sporadic, but five days after the power went out in Mumbai, Beijing threatened to reignite the rebellion.

'These armed separatist factions in Northeast India have now been weak under the strong crackdown by the Indian military, but they have not been completely wiped out,' noted the *Global Times*, which is strongly nationalist and often deployed by the Party as an attack dog.[20] 'Because of a lack of external support, they find it difficult to develop and grow. But if there is support, it would empower them to launch insurgencies,' it noted darkly. The paper took issue with an interview Indian media had run with Taiwan's foreign minister, Joseph Wu, and advertisements carried in several outlets for Taiwan's 10 October national day before issuing a stark threat: 'If India's nationalists move forward by fanning the Taiwan flame, what awaits them will be insurgence and chaos in its northeast.' Beijing does not usually object to such low-level or private contacts with Taiwan, and the warning – like the power outage – was taken as a broader threat linked to the continuing tension at the border.

There are those in Tezpur who still remember the 1962 border war and the *hahakar*, or pandemonium, as Indian forces retreated, leading to a mass evacuation of the town. Tezpur was the nearest sizeable settlement to the fighting, and the tea gardens were abandoned as townspeople and workers fled south across the Brahmaputra River.[21] In the event the PLA never made it that far south, Mao Zedong ordering an abrupt retreat after a month of fighting.

Tezpur is the hometown of award-winning Indian film-maker Hiren Bora, who was twelve year's old at the time and recalls how his grandfather told his family to collect all their belongings and flee, while the patriarch himself stayed behind to defend the town. In 2019, Bora made a film about the incident, *Seema – The Untold Story*, a tribute to Tezpur. 'The Chinese Aggression of 1962 was a huge event in Northeast India's history, but it's hardly been portrayed in popular culture – neither in books nor films, the way Indo-Pak conflicts have been,' he said.[22] Perhaps that is because there is no glory in the sort of ignominious defeat India suffered, but it is seared into the national consciousness when Indians look towards their northern neighbour.

Assam and the six smaller surrounding states of the northeast are often referred to as the 'seven sisters' and comprise Arunachal Pradesh, Assam, Manipur, Meghalaya, Mizoram, Nagaland and Tripura. They form an odd-looking appendage to the main part of India, to which the area is attached by a narrow corridor known as the 'chicken's neck'. Myanmar lies to the east, Bangladesh to the southwest, Nepal to the west, Bhutan to the northwest – and of course China looms large to the north. China claims Arunachal Pradesh as its own, calling it South Tibet

After the 1962 war, Mao supported a patchwork of insurgent groups in the area, which were mostly ethnic or tribal-based, though many paid lip-service to a vague notion of 'Maoism'. Two groups, the United Liberation Front of Assam (ULFA) and the National Democratic Front of Boroland (NDFB), have remained active. China long ago gave up its overt military support for the groups, but the extent to which links to Chinese security services remain is the subject of considerable debate in India. Paresh Baruah, the head of the ULFA, lives in a border town in the Chinese province of Yunnan, where he has been interviewed by Indian media, and weapons – often crude, but effective – come from gun factories and arms bazaars in Wa-controlled areas of Myanmar, where these groups are also given refuge. As we have seen, the United Wa State Army (UWSA) has especially close links with China. Other ethnic insurgent groups of the region have also based themselves in Myanmar and China's Yunnan.[23] China has used the groups as a means of putting pressure on India to control the activities of Tibet's exiled spiritual leader, the Dalai Lama, and the Tibetan government in exile, which is based in the Indian hill town of Dharamshala.[24] If China were to act on its threat and open a sort of proxy front as the two sides face off in and around the Galwan Valley, it would represent a grave escalation of the crisis, but be entirely in keeping with Beijing's use of these groups.

India shares a 2,520-mile border with China, which runs through rivers, glaciers and deserts of snow in the west to mountains blanketed in thick forests in the east. It is punctuated by numerous territorial disputes, though there are two principal areas of contention – one in the east and one in the west. In the west, India claims Aksai Chin, a high-altitude desert administered by China and lying beyond the Galwan Valley, which saw the 2020 clashes; in the east China claims the Indian state of Arunachal Pradesh, which lies in the Himalayan foothills beyond Assam. In establishing the border, British cartographers typically chose mountain peaks for their lines, which were regarded as more defensible. The literature on the legitimacy of these lines, the intentions behind them, and whether they reflected ethnic realities or the actual boundaries of areas under British administration (or whether they were formally administered at all) is voluminous. India has generally accepted the boundaries inherited from the British; China has dismissed them as colonial legacies, preferring a far more expansive interpretation of its territory based on the (often mythical) boundaries of imperial China.

The picture is further complicated because the boundary in the east, known as the McMahon Line after British diplomat Henry McMahon, was agreed in 1914 between British India and Tibet, which had declared itself independent after the 1911 collapse of the Qing Dynasty. The line followed the highest ridges of the Himalayas. In the west, Aksai Chin, which translates as 'desert of white stones', was largely uninhabited. Reaching heights of more than 15,000 feet, its main importance was as an ancient trade route, traversed in the summer by caravans of yaks from Tibet and Xinjiang. An early British line placed the area inside India, its extremities defined by the Kunlun Mountains in the north; a later map placed the border along the Karakoram mountains, locating Aksai Chin in China. The British preference varied over time, depending on its strategic interests, but by 1914 (when the McMahon line was being agreed), Britain settled on the earlier map, which was adopted in 1947 by newly independent India. Although China would later selectively use the maps to its advantage, it has no historic claims over the area.

Thus, the border areas were a dispute waiting to happen – though India's first prime minister, Jawaharlal Nehru, didn't necessarily see it that way. 'He saw China as a friend and as a natural partner in leading post-colonial Asia. And even after the communist take-over of China, his vision of close Sino-India cooperation remained strong,' writes Thant Myint-U, the Burmese historian and writer.[25] India initially had a buffer in the form of independent Tibet, but that was short-lived. In October 1950, the People's Liberation Army led a military assault on Tibet, and the following year Tibetan leaders signed a treaty giving Beijing control over Tibet's external affairs and accepting military occupation. Tibet's borders were now China's borders. There was a nod towards political autonomy, but it was short lived, and by 1956 Tibet was in open rebellion. Three years later, following a failed uprising in Lhasa, the Dalai Lama fled to India, where he established his government in exile in Dharamsala, further complicating India's relations with Beijing.

The 1962 border war took place while the world was transfixed by the Cuban missile crisis. It was fought in both the east and west, with India defeated on both fronts before China abruptly withdrew to the original line in the east, but kept the Aksai Chin in the west. Much has been written about the cause and conduct of the conflict. It has been argued that Mao's primary intention was to teach Nehru a lesson and weaken his position in the emerging non-aligned movement.[26] He succeeded in both – Nehru was broken by the conflict, and within two years he was dead. The conflict also usefully drew attention away from Mao's internal problems – his disastrous Great Leap Forward to modernise China had triggered widespread famine at the time and millions were dying. It also emphasised the vastly different world views of the lawyerly Nehru and the revolutionary Mao, Nehru earnestly believing in the universal applicability of laws and agreements, while Mao never paid much attention to either – a mindset equally applicable to Xi Jinping today.[27]

To the northwest of Assam, sandwiched between India and China, sits the tiny Himalayan Kingdom of Bhutan – *Druk Yul*, the Land of the

Thunder Dragon. This remote and mountainous Buddhist nation of just 800,000 people was almost completely cut off for centuries, only tentatively opening to the outside world in the 1970s. There were no roads or currency until the 1960s, and television only arrived here in 1999; it remains fiercely protective of its ancient traditions – but has still not been able to escape the predatory attention of Xi Jinping's China.

In 2011, the year before Xi assumed power in Beijing, I visited Bhutan to report on a royal wedding – the marriage of thirty-one-year-old King Jigme Khesar Namgyel Wangchuck – the 'Prince Charming of the Himalayas', as he was often called – to Jetsun Pema, a basketball-loving student and daughter of an airline pilot. The traditional Buddhist ceremony took place in an ancient fortress at 8.20 a.m. on 1 October – an auspicious time and date selected by a royal astrologer – and was followed by three days of celebrations. Tens of thousands of people, dressed in traditional robes, travelled to the capital Thimphu to try and catch sight of the royal couple and to witness elaborate displays of song, dance and archery – the national sport. No heads of state were invited, since the king wanted it to be a 'wedding of the people'. It was during that visit that I learned about Gross National Happiness (GNH), a concept coined by Bhutan as an index of wellbeing that takes account of a range of cultural and environmental factors, as well as the economy. I also learned that Bhutan has no formal diplomatic relations with China, and I did wonder if there was a link between the two – that the absence of China's scowling 'wolf warrior' diplomats might have boosted the index. Unfortunately, the years following the wedding have seen Beijing nibbling at the edges of Bhutan in a way guaranteed to wipe the smile off the happiest of faces.

Relations between Bhutan and India have been traditionally very close, based on culture, mutual interests – and a suspicion towards China. Bhutan is not a formal protectorate of India, but Delhi still regards itself as a protector of the tiny kingdom, and in 2017 sent troops into an area called Doklam, a plateau which Bhutan regards as its territory, but across which China had started to build a road. For India, the Chinese road-building had a wider strategic significance, since the area is close to the 'chicken's neck' – the narrow and strategic Siliguri Corridor, which as we have seen is a lifeline linking India's remote northeast to the rest of the country. Indian troops intervened to stop the construction and then stationed themselves in the disputed area to ensure that it did not recommence, triggering a tense stand-off with Beijing. The confrontation lasted for two months, with both sides building up forces in the area. On this occasion it was resolved peacefully, with India withdrawing its troops and the road construction ending – but it did not end Beijing's designs on Bhutan's territory.[28]

In May 2021, an investigation by Robert Barnett, a writer and researcher on modern Tibetan history and politics at the University of London's School of Oriental and African Studies (SOAS), revealed that China had gone beyond nibbling at the edges of Bhutan and had bitten off an entire chunk of territory that for centuries had been regarded as a sacred part of the Himalayan kingdom.[29] Using satellite imagery, Chinese media reports and other open-source maps and documentation, he showed that China had built three villages, sixty-six miles of new roads, a communications base, a small hydroelectric power station and at least five military or police outposts in the far north of Bhutan. 'This involves a strategy that is more provocative than anything China has done on its land borders in the past. The settlement of an entire area within another country goes far beyond the forward patrolling and occasional road-building that led to war with India in 1962, military clashes in 1967 and 1987, and the deaths of 24 Chinese and Indian soldiers in 2020,' he wrote in *Foreign Policy* magazine. The land grab breached a 1998 treaty Beijing signed with Bhutan in which it undertook 'not to resort to unilateral action to alter the status quo of the border'.

One of the areas in Bhutan grabbed by China is Beyul Khenpajong, which has an average altitude of 12,000 feet and is of huge religious significance to Bhutan. Beyul means 'hidden valley', and the term has been used in traditional Bhutanese literature and myth since the fifteenth century to describe sacred mountain areas ringed by high ridges. According to legend, these could only be discovered by those with special spiritual powers. Even Chinese maps until at least the 1980s showed the areas annexed by Beijing as part of Bhutan. Satellite images and media photographs now show a large new administration building in the newly built village of Gyalaphug with a hammer and sickle and a signboard in Chinese reading, 'The Party and Serve-the-Masses Center', according to Barnett. A giant painting of China's national flag covers the wall of one building, while a large red banner proclaims loyalty to the new power in the mountains: 'Resolutely uphold the core position of General Secretary Xi Jinping! Resolutely uphold the authority of and centralized and unified leadership by the Party Central Committee!' it reads.

China was also reportedly building another village, Pangda, inside Bhutanese territory close to the Doklam Plateau, where the 2017 stand-off with India took place. Beijing also made a sudden claim over the 740-square-mile Sakteng Wildlife Sanctuary in the east of Bhutan. The government in Thimphu had approached the US-based Global Environmental Facility for aid on projects in the park, but the Chinese representatives objected, saying the area was in dispute, which it had never been before.[30] It was an absurd claim, but widely seen as an attempt to drag tiny Bhutan into China's dispute with India, possibly by forcing Thimphu to hand over land on the Doklam Plateau in order to get back the occupied areas in the north – a trade that would never be accepted by India, which sees the security of Bhutan as deeply entwined with its own.

A year after the June 2020 Galwan Valley clash, China convened a virtual regional meeting. Nepal, Pakistan, Bangladesh, Sri Lanka and Afghanistan were all there – but not India. The meeting was ostensibly to discuss Covid-19 and poverty reduction, but it also sent a powerful message to Delhi about the strong and growing clout Beijing now wields in what India has long regarded as its own backyard.[31] China has lavished particular attention on Nepal in an effort to wrest it away from India, which has long treated the Himalayan nation as a sort of Hindu little brother and a vital part of its sphere of influence. Beijing offered billions of dollars for factories, power plants and highways, while Nepal's tourist industry is increasingly geared towards Chinese visitors and mountain climbers. Beijing is also exerting a growing influence on Kathmandu's often chaotic politics, and Nepal has responded to Chinese blandishments and pressure with a crackdown on the activities of the country's 20,000-strong Tibetan refugee community. Beijing has sought to discourage Nepal from accepting any more Tibetans fleeing from China. It has deployed aid with political precision; when an earthquake struck in 2015, China immediately sent search-and-rescue teams and medical supplies. Kathmandu dutifully refused Taiwan's offer of rescue teams, and warned India's army rescue groups to keep away from Chinese airspace, even though the area in most need lay in the border areas between China and Nepal.[32] When Nepal was hit with a surge in coronavirus cases in spring 2021, Beijing ostentatiously offered a million doses of vaccines. At the time, Delhi – often dubbed the 'pharmacy to the world', because of the size of that industry in India – had stopped exports in order to deal with its own coronavirus crisis.

The danger from Nepal's growing dependence on China became clear in February 2022, when a Nepalese government report leaked to the BBC accused China of encroaching into Nepal along their shared border. Beijing denied the accusation and the Nepalese government publicly played down the report – seemingly out of fear of upsetting its Chinese benefactor.[33]

China has close and long-standing relations with Pakistan – Beijing supplied Pakistan with critical technology and know-how for its nuclear weapons programme. Islamabad is also the biggest recipient of funds under the Belt and Road Initiative (BRI) – $62 billion has been earmarked. China does not have any formal alliances, but Pakistan (together with Russia) is just about as close as it gets. The Chinese Communist Party describes the relationship as an 'all-weather strategic partnership of cooperation'. Pakistan is a major buyer of Chinese weapons, including battle tanks and combat drones, and the relationship between the two militaries is getting closer. In May 2021, they conducted joint exercises in Tibet, close to the disputed border with India, one of a growing series of drills that have alarmed military strategists in Delhi.[34] A key component of the BRI is Gwadar port on the Arabian Sea in Pakistan's Baluchistan province. India fears that the port, fenced off to protect against Baloch separatists, will become a base for the Chinese navy. China has already taken control of Hambantota port in Sri Lanka in lieu of unpaid debts, and is building another at Kyaukphyu in Myanmar. Jittery Indian strategists call this network of potential military bases around the Indian Ocean, China's 'String of Pearls'.

In early 2022, the Himalayan border was still simmering. Several rounds of talks produced few tangible results. There are ongoing skirmishes, the two sides trading accusations of incursions across the ill-defined line separating them. Pledges of de-escalation were overshadowed by a relentless build-up of weapons and soldiers on both sides, with an estimated 200,000 troops deployed. China reportedly stationed long-range bombers close to the Himalayas.[35] One Indian military officer said the military build-up was 'like never before' and included bringing in more heavy artillery and moving squadrons of fighter jets to within easy reach.[36] The Communist Party's *Global Times* thundered: 'We must warn India seriously: You have crossed the line! Your frontline troops have crossed the line! Your nationalist public opinion has crossed the line! Your policy toward China has crossed the line! You are over-confidently provoking the PLA and Chinese people – this is like doing a handstand on the edge of a cliff!'[37] Beijing claimed the Indian military had trained more than 10,000 exiled Tibetans to pose as local herdsmen in an effort to infiltrate China's borders.[38] In this febrile atmosphere a network of informal border protocols that had largely kept the peace before the June 2020 clash has been abandoned. 'The whole architecture for maintaining peace and tranquillity has collapsed and is lying in ruins,' said Gautam Bambawale, India's former ambassador to Beijing.[39] He called the border tensions a 'recipe for disaster'.

Some of the additional Indian forces were deployed from the Pakistan border, hitherto considered by India to be its most serious threat. 'The crisis over the last year has brought home the reality to India's decision makers that China presents the biggest strategic challenge in the future, and it has led to shifting the attention away from Pakistan,' said Sushant Singh, a senior fellow at the Center for Policy Research and visiting lecturer at Yale University. Delhi began to rethink its strategic ties. It sought to bolster its relationship with the United States, as well as regional powers Australia and Japan.

One result has been India's renewed interest in the long dormant Quadrilateral Security Dialogue (the Quad) comprising the US, Australia, Japan and India. In September 2021, two Indian warships joined a Quad exercise off the coast of Guam, a US territory in the western Pacific Ocean. Indian warships also joined the UK's HMS *Queen Elizabeth* aircraft carrier and its battle group for drills in the Bay of Bengal, and took part in bilateral exercises in the South China Sea with the navies of Vietnam, the Philippines, Indonesia, Singapore and Australia.[40] To add a little niggle to his strategic moves, India's Prime Minister Narendra Modi, let it be known in July 2021 that he had telephoned China's nemesis the Dalai Lama and personally wished him a happy eighty-sixth birthday, disregarding any potential anger from Beijing.[41]

A poll of young Indians by the Observer Research Foundation found that for 77 per cent of respondents, China was the most distrusted country (the same proportion found the US the most trusted).[42] A posting on Weibo, China's Twitter-like social media platform, triggered particular outrage. It showed two photographs, side by side, one of the launch of a Chinese space shuttle, the other a mass cremation in India, then reeling from Covid-19. The caption read, 'China lighting a fire versus India lighting a fire'. The tone was triumphant, mocking India's coronavirus catastrophe. It did not however come from some twisted nationalist blogger – but instead from the official account of the Communist Party's powerful Central Political and Legal Affairs Commission.[43] Furthermore, during the torch relay that kicked off the 2022 Winter Olympics in Beijing, the Communist Party chose as a runner Qi Fabao, a PLA officer wounded during the Galwan clash. It seemed almost calculated to provoke, and within a day, Delhi duly announced a diplomatic boycott of the games.

It has often been claimed that economic integration acts as an important deterrent to conflict and an incentive for following agreed rules – that at a global level this will make China a responsible partner, while strong bilateral economic ties will blunt political or strategic differences. The brawl on the roof of the world, and subsequent collapse of India–China relations, belie this claim. Beijing's actions were diplomatically and economically counterproductive, but that held little sway with Xi Jinping. It demonstrates not only that Xi is prepared to take risks, but that in his paranoid world view, everything is subordinate to China's widening definition of its strategic and security interests. It is an important lesson for the world as Beijing expands into new frontiers.

## CHAPTER 5

# *From the Frozen Arctic to the Digital World: The Frontiers of China's New Cold War*

'We have no intension of interfering in other countries' internal affairs . . . What we hope to create is a big family of harmonious coexistence'

*Xi Jinping, May 2017*

Narsaq has long been popular with rock pickers – the amateur geologists who come during the summer months to scour Kuannersuit, a cloud-rimmed mountain that sits behind the small Greenland town. They collect the strikingly colourful stones that can be found lying around in abundance. The town sits on the shore of a deep fjord on the southern tip of the world's largest island, a sleepy collection of green, red, yellow and ochre wooden houses. In the winter, when the snow and ice close in, it is best reached by dog sled, though the traffic of helicopters, landing on the local football pitch has been rising steadily year round as Narsaq has taken on a new role – as a geopolitical flashpoint between China and the West.

Kuannersuit contains one of the world's biggest untapped deposits of rare earths, seventeen obscure minerals that occur jointly in nature and have magnetic and conductive properties that give them multiple and vital applications in our digital lives. They are crucial to modern electronics, used in small amounts in just about everything from microchips, screens, medical devices, rechargeable batteries and magnets to missile guidance systems, fighter jets and other state-of-the-art weaponry. They enable the tech that drives clean energy – including wind turbines and electric vehicles. 'In just a period of decades, rare earth elements have seeped deeply into the fabric of modern technology and industry and have proven exceptionally challenging to duplicate or replace,' according to an industry report.[1] Demand is set to soar as concerns rise over climate change and countries push to reduce the use of fossil fuels.

China controls the market, and has been increasingly willing to use that leverage. It currently mines as much as 80 per cent of the world's rare earths and does around 90 per cent of the processing, which is expensive and messy. In 2010, China limited exports of rare earths to Japan after a collision involving a Chinese fishing boat and a Japanese coastguard patrol vessel off disputed islands in the East China Sea.[2] In 2019, Beijing threatened to use the minerals as part of the unfolding trade war with the United States.[3] In early 2021, Beijing looked at adding rare earths to a list of materials that could be restricted in order to 'help safeguard national security'. Officials reportedly consulted industry executives about how such a ban would impact the US defence industry, especially the F-35 fighter jet programme.[4]

Luckily rare earths are not so rare; they are called rare because of their atomic properties. That China has cornered the market is a result of an aggressive industrial policy, heavily subsidising and protecting the Chinese companies involved, while being willing to tolerate environmental damage from the toxic process of extracting the minerals. Significant known deposits exist in China, Brazil, Australia, Vietnam, India, the US – and of course in Greenland, which by one estimate could hold a quarter of the world's reserves.[5]

Greenland Minerals, an Australian company, was given an exploration licence for the Kuannersuit project in 2007, attracted by the promise of the rare earths, but also a vast deposit of uranium in the same area. Exploring is different to developing, and the process of getting the necessary permits to begin serious digging of a vast open-pit mine that would scoop out a chunk of the mountain, was slow and contentious. It faced fierce opposition from environmentalists. The town of Narsaq was split. The fishing industry that once sustained it was dying, and the population fell by almost a fifth in the decade to 2019, by which time Narsaq was home to just under 1,400 people. The conflicting issues facing the town were explored in a moving 2016 documentary *Kuannersuit; Kvanefjeld*.[6] In a series of interviews set against a stunning backdrop of mountains and fjords littered with icebergs, it explored the town's hopes and fears – some residents seeing Kuannersuit as a saviour that would create hundreds of jobs and kick-start the town, others talking in apocalyptic terms about the destruction of the environment and an indigenous culture tied to the land. For some it had become a subject no longer raised in public, because of the fierce and divisive passions it provoked between neighbours – even within families in this closely knit community. It also divided national politics, with supporters arguing that the riches from the mine would give Greenland a road to independence; at present the vast, ice-covered island is an autonomous Danish territory.

Then into this contentious mix waded Beijing. In late 2016, Greenland Minerals announced that it was entering into a strategic partnership with a Chinese mining company called Shenghe Resources, which bought 12.5 per cent of its shares to become the largest shareholder. The two companies also agreed that Shenghe could in the future buy a controlling stake of up to 60 per cent of the Australian company. There was an outcry when this was revealed in a disclosure the Chinese company made to the Shanghai Stock Exchange. Greenland Minerals sought to 'clarify' the statement, at first denying the option existed, and then insisting it was non-binding, and merely an agreement to enter into negotiations to sell Shenghe a majority stake once all licences for the mine had been obtained.[7] But to students of China's global ambitions, the Greenland acquisition carried an unmistakable message: that Beijing was intent on holding on to its near monopoly over one of the world's most strategically important raw materials.

In 2019, Shenghe entered into a partnership with state-owned China National Nuclear Corporation (CNNC), under which their joint venture would import from Greenland those rare earths that when processed produce uranium and thorium, radioactive substances which can be used as nuclear fuel.[8] CNNC is a nuclear power producer with deep roots in China's nuclear weapons programme. On its website, the company describes itself as 'a leading element of national strategic nuclear forces and nuclear energy development. It undertakes missions to ensure national security and facilitate domestic economic development.'[9] In 2020, the US included CNNC in a list of companies linked to the Chinese military, and Donald Trump later issued an executive order barring Americans from investing in any companies on that list, arguing that such investments posed a risk to national security.[10]

Taken in isolation this would have been worrying enough, but Beijing's ambitions went far wider. Greenland, whose population of just under 60,000 is about twice that of Arctic polar bears, was firmly in the strategic cross-hairs of a resource-hungry China (population 1.4

billion) determined to extend its influence into the Arctic. In 2017, China offered to bankroll and build three airports in Greenland, including in the capital Nuuk, home to around a third of the population. Its short runway could at the time receive only small propeller planes. To Greenland this offered the promise of bigger jet aircraft and of opening the country to more international tourism. A Chinese government-owned company also offered to buy an abandoned naval base, and a Chinese state owned university announced it would build a polar research antenna on the island.[11] In 2018, in its first policy paper on the Arctic, China declared itself a 'near-Arctic state' with an interest in developing shipping in the region, carrying out scientific research and exploiting the region's oil, gas, minerals, fisheries and other natural resources – opportunities likely to open up as global warming takes its toll on the polar ice cap.[12] The People's Liberation Army Navy was increasingly active in the Arctic region, including the deployment of warships to within forty-six miles of Alaska's Aleutian Islands in the Bering Sea.[13]

Little wonder that these ambitions set off alarm bells in Washington and Copenhagen. There was concern that Greenland would struggle to pay back loans for the airports estimated at $555 million, resulting in China taking control of runways with potential military applications just a few hours flight from the US east coast. They piled pressure on Greenland, which eventually accepted an alternative package of cheap loans for the airport backed by Denmark, with the US offering support with airport infrastructure. There was to be no Chinese involvement. Denmark blocked the purchase of the naval base, and the Greenland government denied it had given approval for the research antenna.[14]

During the Second World War, the US had thirteen army bases and four naval bases on Greenland; now the US Air Force's Thule base, its northernmost facility, is all that remains, housing part of a ballistic missile early warning system. Established under a long-standing treaty between Denmark and the US, the base shot to fame (or perhaps infamy) in 1968 at the height of the Cold War when a B-52 bomber laden with four nuclear bombs crashed into the sea ice around seven miles west of the base. It was trying to make an emergency landing following a cabin fire caused by a crew member stuffing cushions in front of a heating vent.[15] The bombs didn't explode, but they did rupture, resulting in radioactive contamination of the area. The incident severely strained relations between the US and Denmark, and is one reason why the anti-nuclear sentiment (and environmentalism more broadly) is so strong in Greenland.

In 2019, President Donald Trump expressed interest in buying Greenland, an offer that was roundly condemned by the Greenland and Danish governments – the Danish prime minister calling any discussion of a sale 'absurd'.[16] To most observers it seemed like a rather hare-brained proposal – though it was not without a certain logic. A year later, the US opened a consulate in Nuuk and went on a charm offensive, offering trade and security cooperation, and a beefed-up aid package. It agreed to let Greenland take over the maintenance of the Thule base, a move that should help the local economy.[17] It signed its own memorandum to cooperate on rare earth mining and to promote investment in the sector.[18] By 2021, the European Union was also waking up to its dangerous dependence on China, and Greenland was enticed to join the EU's European Raw Materials Alliance. This was an effort by the block to diversify supplies of strategic raw materials, with the promise of investment and seed money for mines and processing plants.[19] Surveying the broader security environment, NATO Secretary-General Jens Stoltenberg said, 'The melting of the ice in the Arctic could lead to the heating up of geopolitical tensions between different powers in the world.'[20] He cited Russian activities and the growing China presence and said the impact of global warming on the Arctic was 'changing the security landscape'.

That still left Greenland Minerals and its Chinese partner in charge of the giant Kuannersuit mine, but in April 2021 the project was grounded on the rocks of Greenland politics. In a snap general election that month, Inuit Ataqatigiit (IA), a left-leaning pro-environment party, finished first with 37 per cent of the vote and set about forming a coalition government. IA had long been a fierce opponent of the mine, and in November 2021, Greenland's parliament passed legislation banning uranium mining and stopping the Kuannersuit project.[21] Shares in Greenland Minerals fell sharply, though the company suggested it would look for ways to revive the project.[22] A few weeks later, the government stripped another Chinese company, General Nice, of its licence to an iron ore deposit near the capital Nuuk, because it failed to make guarantee payments. The government demanded the company return all geological data and clean up the area.[23]

The Greenland story is one of neglect by Western democracies, in spite of the area's abundance of critical raw materials. The US, EU and

Denmark realised belatedly that they were being outplayed by Beijing in this isolated but strategically vital corner of the Arctic. It is just one example of the way the West has allowed itself to become a spectator as China has gained control of supply chains critical to the technologies of the future.

Re-chargeable lithium-ion batteries are vital for 'clean energy'. They power electric vehicles, as well as most portable consumer electronics such as mobile phones and laptops. The market is expanding rapidly, and it too is dominated by China. By one estimate, Chinese companies in 2019 accounted for 80 per cent of the world's output of raw materials for advanced batteries, controlling the processing of most minerals critical to their manufacture – including rare earths, lithium, graphite, manganese, nickel and cobalt. More than 100 of the 136 lithium-ion battery plants planned by 2029 are based in China.[24] China has been buying up lithium mines worldwide and processes almost 60 per cent of the world's supply. It produces two-thirds of the world's graphite, though has only a quarter of the world's reserves. It mines only 6 per cent of the world's manganese, but refines 93 per cent. Nickel is spread quite evenly around the world, but China still controls two-thirds of the chemical processing.[25] China has only 1 per cent of the world's cobalt reserves, but dominates its mining and refining. More than two-thirds of the world's cobalt production comes from the Democratic Republic of the Congo in Africa. In 2020, fifteen of the nineteen cobalt-producing mines in Congo were owned or financed by Chinese companies.[26]

The Chinese companies, whether state-owned or nominally private, enjoy a seemingly unlimited line of credit from Beijing as part of a methodical strategy to dominate the clean energy economy. By one estimate, state-backed institutions have provided $12 billion in loans and other financing to cobalt miners in Congo.[27] Mining deals have frequently been part of broader contracts under which China pledged to provide roads, bridges, power stations and other infrastructure. More recently, there have been signs of unease in Congo at the rapid embrace of China. In December 2021, the Chinese embassy urged its citizens to leave three provinces in the eastern part of the country after unrest targeted Chinese workers. At the same time, the Congolese government was reportedly reviewing contracts, and Chinese companies were facing accusations of failing to fulfil promises, lax safety standards and corruption.

The availability and reliability of supplies of critical minerals – and control of those supply chains – will be crucial in the years ahead, as by most estimates the world is likely to face a severe shortage as it transitions away from fossil fuels. The International Energy Agency predicts supplies of rare earths and battery-grade nickel will be tight, but warns that in a scenario consistent with climate change goals, 'expected supply from existing mines and projects under construction is estimated to meet only half of projected lithium and cobalt requirements and 80% of copper needs by 2030'.[28]

In November 2021, the world received a worrying glimpse of what the future might hold when it faced a potentially crippling shortage of magnesium, over which China also has a near monopoly. The motor industry warned of an imminent shutdown, as magnesium is a raw material for the production of the aluminium alloys used for gearboxes, steering columns, fuel tank covers and seat frames. There is no substitute for magnesium in the production of aluminium sheets. Stockpiles began to run low after a power shortage shut Chinese factories that supply 85 per cent of the world's magnesium. European officials held urgent consultations with China's leaders, fearing that China would direct its dwindling output to its own industry, cutting off exports completely.[29] The price of magnesium surged by 75 per cent in a month to a record high of more than $9,000 a tonne. Europe was particularly vulnerable as it had shut all its own magnesium production, unable to compete with cheap imports from China. The Europeans had accused China of large-scale dumping, selling at below cost to force out rivals, and over two decades Chinese producers created their near monopoly. It is a familiar accusation of predatory trade practices, and it had left the world almost entirely dependent on Beijing for a key commodity.

The worst fears did not come to pass; the car industry muddled through, but it was a sobering experience for them and for Western leaders. It also animated the conversation around the tables at the annual dinner of the London Metals Exchange (LME) held that same month in the Great Room of the Grosvenor House Hotel. The previous year it was cancelled because of Covid-19 and they were glad to be back, champagne in hand, almost 1,000 guests in tuxedos and elegant dresses. The 144-year-old exchange is the world's oldest and biggest trading venue for industrial metals, and they toasted the reopening of 'the ring', one of the last bastions of the almost theatrical practice of open-cry trading, which had been closed for eighteen months because of the coronavirus. Yet the atmosphere was less raucous than usual and there was much talk of erratic markets and metal shortages. They might also have reflected on their own strange position, another sort of bastion – just about the only part of the metals supply chain that is not dominated by China. Chinese brokers have sought a foothold in the exchange, but their progress has been limited by red tape, cultural clashes and a lack of a clear strategy.[30] While Chinese bulldozers have powered their way to mining and refining prominence, their traders have so far been held at bay by the whimsical ways of the LME.

When China declared that it was a 'near-Arctic state' its stated ambition was to tap the area's resources and open new shipping lanes made possible by global warming, forming what it called a 'Polar Silk Road'.[31] In doing so, it was placing its Arctic aims under the umbrella of its Belt and Road Initiative (BRI). We have already met the BRI in several guises. It encompasses multiple 'silk roads' of land, maritime and digital variety. Marco Polo would probably have been rather puzzled by Beijing's increasingly expansive use of the term, but the BRI has grown into an amorphous catch-all for the Communist Party's global ambitions, its efforts to remake the world order and its aggressive use of economic power.

The BRI is a curious beast. It was peddled as a multi-trillion dollar programme of infrastructure investment that would supposedly replicate the ancient trade routes linking East and West by sea and land. In the process the world would be blessed with Chinese-built roads, railways, ports, airports, power stations, telecoms and, of course, mines. Xi Jinping described it as 'a project of the century, which will benefit people across the world', and 'a big family of harmonious coexistence.'[32] China claims more than 138 countries have signed up. Putting a precise figure on spending is hard, since programmes are opaque and memorandums of understanding and funding pledges do not always translate into spending. It is now China's principal foreign policy initiative, and has become a rather incoherent catchphrase for just about all aspects of what Beijing does abroad, covering all manner of projects and with no real geographic boundaries. Bruno Maçães, a former Europe Minister in the Portuguese government, who has written extensively on the BRI, has described it as 'a giant project of international political engineering'.[33]

The BRI is massively overhyped and under-principled – unencumbered by any troublesome notions of transparency and good governance, and lacking the environmental, labour or human rights protections that typically accompany lending from multilateral institutions or the West. It has enabled China to export industrial overcapacity and capital, while shaping the world in its own image and according to its own interests. In many ways it is a classic neo-colonial enterprise, and one that harks back to the ancient China-centric view of the world we have already encountered in Southeast Asia. Projects typically involve the import of Chinese labour, and are saddling the recipients with large and possibly unpayable debts.

The infrastructure element of the BRI has attracted a great deal of attention. These are the projects the Communist Party likes to advertise, as if the BRI is one big charitable organisation, an enormous benevolence fund. Others have pointed to the strategic advantages China is leveraging from its construction, particularly of ports – and especially after Sri Lanka was forced to hand over its new $1.3 billion Hambantota port to a Chinese company after failing to make repayments.[34] In Africa, Djibouti's crippling external debt is the highest of any low-income country as a proportion of GDP, much of it owed to China, and Beijing has leveraged this dependency by establishing an additional strategic foothold in the country: Djibouti is now the site of China's only overseas military base.[35] From Cambodia to Myanmar to the United Arab Emirates, it has invested in dozens of port facilities that have the potential for military use.

Of all Xi Jinping's 'silk roads', it is the digital version that is perhaps most intriguing, and where China's grip is at its most insidious. It increasingly underpins the other elements of the BRI and illustrates the extent and nature of Communist Party ambition. Take Africa, long-neglected by Western powers and dubbed 'China's second continent'.[36] Beijing is now Africa's biggest investor, trade partner and aid donor. This has created such a dependency that not even the revelation that Chinese cyber spies plundered the files of the African Union (AU) raised much of a complaint.[37] The AU, which represents fifty-five African states, could not afford to upset its benefactor, which installed a backdoor into computer systems in the new AU headquarters in Addis Ababa, which was built and gifted by Beijing – one of numerous parliaments and other public buildings China has donated across the continent. The Chinese telecoms giants Huawei and ZTE have between them built most of Africa's telecoms infrastructure (hence the 'digital silk road'). Huawei claims to have built 70 per cent of Africa's 4G telecoms networks.[38] Beyond the network nuts and bolts, it also supplies smartphones, computers and a range of surveillance kit. Its products are considered cheap and robust, and sales have been assisted by the seemingly unlimited credit line from the Chinese government that has benefited the mining companies.

One of Huawei's flagship products is what it calls 'safe city solutions,' a suite of advanced surveillance tools developed and honed in China, and which offer 'omnipresent sensing' and 'real time warning and surveillance deployment' that will 'promote the digital transformation of the public safety industry', according to a company brochure.[39] These are popular with autocrats worldwide – 71 per cent of 'safe city' agreements are in countries rated by Freedom House as 'not free' or 'partly free', and include Angola, Egypt, Ethiopia, Kazakhstan, Russia, Saudi Arabia, Thailand, the United Arab Emirates and Uzbekistan.[40]

The 'digital silk road' can best be seen as an ecosystem of technologies, ranging from 5G telecoms networks, cloud computing and other data storage, to GPS satellite positioning systems and other internet infrastructure. In essence, the Chinese Communist Party is peddling techno-authoritarianism, modelled on the surveillance state it has built at home – and which is at its most egregious in the repression of the Uyghurs and other Muslim minorities in Xinjiang. They will also give China potential control over enormous pools of data – another source of power and influence.

Other components of the 'digital silk road' under development include a centralised digital currency, the digital yuan. In many ways this is the ultimate surveillance tool, giving real time information on every transaction an individual makes – how much, where, how often, for what. There is nowhere left to hide. Internationally it is seen as a way of challenging the dominance of the US dollar.[41] Among client states created by the BRI, use of the digital yuan may become a condition of doing business with China. It was heavily promoted ahead of the 2022 Beijing Winter Olympics, during which the government hoped its digital yuan would be used by visitors and athletes. 'If wrongly implemented, it gives a hostile state the ability to surveil transactions,' warned Sir Jeffrey Fleming, the director of GCHQ, Britain's signals intelligence agency in a rare interview. 'It gives them the ability... to be able to exercise control over what is conducted on those digital currencies.'[42]

At the same time, China is putting enormous energy into shaping the vital international technical standards that define the interoperability and security of emerging technologies. Standards are the technical rules of the highway, and an enormous source of power and influence. Some 200-odd global organisations and bodies are involved in standards-setting, and China has been very active in these forums. For instance, between 2016 and 2019, all twenty submissions to the International Telecommunications Union (ITU) on facial recognition technology came from China, most relating to how footage and audio recordings are stored and analysed.[43] International standards are voluntary, but they are usually adopted by developing countries in Asia, Africa and the Middle East, key markets for China. Beijing stands to gain a big technological and commercial edge if its standards are adopted, though the impact goes well beyond that. Technology is rarely neutral – the same tech can be deployed in many ways and serve multiple purposes. Standards embody political, economic and wider moral and ethical values. For instance, human rights groups have complained that the process by which the facial recognition standards are adopted by the ITU allows little opportunity to challenge the rules or to adopt safeguards on the grounds of privacy or freedom of expression.

While the BRI is an instrument for China to push its economic, technological and strategic interests, it is also creating a network of dependencies. This is not a 'bloc' of ideological and military allies that the Soviet Union controlled during the last Cold War, but it is creating compliant states who can be dragooned into providing political support for China, stifling criticism in international forums or parroting Beijing's narrative on issues such as Taiwan, Hong Kong and Tibet.

The Communist Party's well-documented campaign of mass detention of up to 1.5 million Uyghur and other Muslim minorities, forced labour, forced sterilisation and cultural destruction, all underpinned by stifling surveillance, has been characterised in the West as genocide and crimes against humanity.[44] But not by Imran Khan. 'Frankly, I don't know much about that,' said the prime minister of Pakistan at a time the repression was being widely reported.[45] He ducked and dived, saying Pakistan respected China as it was. 'How come this is such a big issue in the Western World?' he asked, before getting to the crux of the matter. China had been 'one of the greatest friends to us in difficult times', he insisted, and any tricky conversations happened 'behind closed doors'.[46] Pakistan is the biggest recipient of BRI projects, worth more than $62 billion, and including the strategically important seaport at Gwadar, on the Arabian Sea, which will be linked to China via a planned 2,000-mile network of road and rail links.[47] China refers to Pakistan as an 'ironclad friend' – an appropriate label because the country has been shackled and muzzled by its dependence on China. While Khan is quick to condemn perceived 'Islamophobia' elsewhere in the world, he is unable to bring himself to condemn the biggest and most egregious assault on the Muslim faith of our times.

Most Muslim-majority countries, including Malaysia and Indonesia, have largely avoided the subject out of fear of retribution. In October 2021, forty-five countries signed a statement supporting China's policies in Xinjiang, which they described as a province in which 'People of all ethnic groups enjoy their happy lives in a peaceful and stable environment.'[48] Among the signatories were the usual crop of anti-Western autocrats, including Cuba, Russia, Belarus and Iran, joined by a rollcall of countries that have received substantial Chinese largesse – among them, Angola, Cambodia, Egypt, Iraq, Mozambique, Myanmar, Nepal, Pakistan, Sri Lanka, Syria, Tanzania, Uganda and Zimbabwe. The Middle East, where Beijing has worked hard to extend influence, was also well-represented, the UAE, Bahrain and Saudi Arabia all endorsing the statement, which went on to say, 'We note with appreciation that China has undertaken a series of measures in response to threats of terrorism and extremism in accordance with the law to safeguard the human rights of all ethnic groups in Xinjiang.' Beijing had reason to be well-pleased with its investments. Ukraine supported a Canadian-led call for independent observers to be allowed into Xinjiang, but removed its name after China threatened to block a planned shipment of at least 500,000 doses of Chinese Covid-19 vaccines to Kyiv if it did not do so, according to diplomats.[49]

China also targeted companies which had expressed concern about the use of forced labour in Xinjiang's cotton fields and factories. Prominent Western clothing brands faced an orchestrated campaign of nationalist boycotts and threats, stirred up by Chinese social media. H&M was one of the hardest hit, all but disappearing from the Chinese internet, its products removed from major Chinese e-commerce platforms. The company then posted a statement on its Weibo account saying it 'respects Chinese consumers' and that it 'does not represent any political position'.[50] Burberry, Adidas, Nike, Uniqlo and Lacoste were also targeted. In the West, many companies had built notions of human rights and environmentalism into their brand image, and were now discovering how uncomfortably that sits with sourcing and business in China. US chip-maker Intel apologised following a backlash over a letter to suppliers urging them not to source products from Xinjiang.[51] It later amended the letter to delete references to the province.[52]

The German car manufacturer VW tied itself in knots over Xinjiang in a manner worthy of Imran Khan. It has a factory in Urumqi, the capital of the province, and when pressed repeatedly about human rights at the 2019 Shanghai Motor Show, chairman Herbert Diess said he was 'not aware' of the existence of detention camps.[53] In a later interview, the head of the company's China operations, Stephen Wallenstein, did not deny the existence of the camps, but said 'I can assure you, we do not have forced labour.' Though, when pressed further, he said that he could not be absolutely certain.[54] China is VW's biggest market, but critics have argued that it has a special ethical responsibility because it was founded by the Nazi Party in 1937 and used forced labour – including concentration-camp prisoners – in its factories during the Second World War.[55]

The Communist Party upped the pressure on companies by introducing what it called an 'anti-sanctions law', which gives the authorities the explicit right to take punitive action against companies or individuals who obey foreign sanctions against China. In other words, any company complying with Western sanctions relating to the repression in Xinjiang and Hong Kong, or against blacklisted Chinese tech companies, could see their China-based executives arrested or deported and their assets seized.[56] Banks in particular are likely to be in the cross-hairs. They have been explicitly warned by the US authorities that they will be closely scrutinised for any dealings with sanctioned entities or individuals, while China created a Beijing Financial Court to hear lawsuits against banks or other financial firms deemed to have damaged the 'legitimate interests' of Chinese domestic investors.[57] It remains to be seen how this plays out in practice, and of course, the Party does not really need the backing of the law to carry out coercion. It is above and beyond the law, but it does nevertheless drastically raise the stakes.

Companies are being pushed even more to the heart of geopolitical tensions and being told, in effect, to pick sides. China wants to control what they say as well as what they do. Under Xi Jinping, the Party has become more punitive and vindictive towards individuals, companies and countries that stray, often inadvertently, into an expanding list of no-go areas, where they are required to support China's position as a price for market access and investment. The Party has sought to enlist foreign companies in lobbying efforts on its behalf. In November 2021, it was reported that the Chinese embassy in Washington had pressed executives, companies and business groups to fight against China-related bills in the US Congress. These included the US Innovation and Competition Act, legislation aimed at boosting US competition with China and funding much-needed semiconductor production. Chinese officials warned companies they would risk losing market share or revenue in China if the legislation was passed. 'We sincerely hope you . . . will play a positive role in urging members of Congress to abandon the zero-sum mindset and ideological prejudice, stop touting negative China-related bills, delete negative provisions, so as to create favourable conditions for bilateral economic and trade cooperation before it is too late,' said one letter.[58]

Amazon was enlisted by the Party's propaganda department to help boost Xi Jinping's cult of personality. In December 2021, it was reported that the American e-commerce giant had scrubbed bad customer reviews and ratings of Xi Jinping's books from its China website. The company agreed to a Chinese government demand that only five-star ratings of Xi's turgid speeches be allowed. In response to criticism, Amazon said it 'complies with all applicable laws and regulations, wherever we operate, and China is no exception'.[59] That has become a boilerplate response from companies accused of complicity with Communist Party repression.

The Communist Party also sought to enlist the support of British companies at a time of growing scrutiny in the UK of Chinese investment and human rights abuses. Premier Li Keqiang held what was described as a virtual dialogue with thirty companies, including AstraZeneca, Clifford Chance, BP, Jaguar Land Rover, PWC, Rio Tinto, Standard Chartered and HSBC, during which he said, 'China also hopes Britain will provide a fair, just and non-discriminatory business environment for Chinese companies to invest in the country,' according to the *Xinhua* news agency.[60] There was no explicit threat to their business interests in China – there didn't need to be. Many companies need little encouragement to see things from the Communist Party's perspective – a condition that has been described as a version of Stockholm Syndrome, whereby a hostage comes to develop feelings of trust, sympathy and affection for their captor.[61]

The use of economic instruments to achieve political ends has been described as geoeconomics, and China is the world leader. This can include the coercive use of market access, trade and investment, in all of which Beijing has a well-established track record. This is why we should be so concerned about the supply chains for technologies critical for the future, where we began this chapter. Geoeconomics has been China's preferred mode of combat, and has been remarkably successful, largely because the Chinese Communist Party controls so many geoeconomic tools and so much wealth. The US is a richer country, but the government does not have so much direct control over how those riches are deployed. Washington has not been shy about using economic sanctions, and has leveraged its control over the international dollar-based financial system, but in the West geopolitical tools are more dispersed and its influence more constrained, with many trade and investment decisions in private hands.

Geoeconomics can also be indirect, such as when China's economic influence threatened to undermine the credibility of the World Bank and International Monetary Fund, the world's leading multilateral financial institutions. In October 2021, an independent investigation found that while she was chief executive of the World Bank, Kristalina Georgieva, had pressured staff to improve China's position in the bank's annual investment rankings.[62] This happened at a time when the bank was seeking more money from China, its third-largest shareholder. The bank's *Doing Business* report ranks countries according to their business climate, and China was set to fall several places before her alleged intervention. By the time the report was published, Georgieva had left the bank, and was managing director of the IMF. Critics demanded she resign in order to protect the integrity of both institutions and their data, in which companies and organisations have traditionally placed great trust. Georgieva remained in her place, saying she fundamentally disagrees with the report's conclusions and denies ever asking for data to be changed.

The era of classic Western colonial expansion produced the axiom that 'trade follows the flag' – whereby territorial control was deemed necessary in order to develop the trade that would support home industries. China has turned this on its head. The flag is following trade, dependencies are created through economics, and Beijing increasingly looks for ways to protect its growing global interests and assets. One aspect of this is the growth of Chinese 'private' security, another is the search for overseas bases. In April 2022 Beijing reached a security agreement with the Solomon Islands allowing Chinese military personnel, police and occasional 'ship visits', ostensibly to 'protect the safety of Chinese personnel and major projects' in the Pacific island nation.[63] Australia, New Zealand and the US all cried foul, but it is unlikely to be the last such agreement as China seeks to challenge American military dominance in the Pacific and beyond.

Geoeconomics has been described as one element of 'war by other means', the use of a suite of coercive tools that falls short of full-on military conflict.[64] Cyberweapons are also part of that toolbox. China has long excelled at cyber espionage, but has been broadening its repertoire. It is embracing online disinformation with relish, teaming up with cyber criminals where needed, and branching into sabotage, as it expands its capabilities into the darkest corners of cyberspace.

# Chapter 6

# *Disinformation, Spying and Sabotage: The Cyber Panda Bears Its Claws*

> 'How China evolves in the next decade will probably be the single biggest driver of the UK's future cyber security.'
>
> *UK's National Cyber Security Centre, Annual Report 2021*

The Swiss biologist was angry. He claimed on his Facebook and Twitter accounts that he'd uncovered attempts by the United States to subvert the World Health Organization investigation into the origin of Covid-19. There had been 'enormous pressure and even intimidation from the US side as well as certain media outlets,' wrote Wilson Edwards in July 2021. 'The WHO sources told me the US is so obsessed with attacking China on the origin-tracking issue that it is reluctant to open its eyes to the data and the findings.'[1] Edwards's post was enthusiastically spread by China's state media and on the social media accounts of its diplomats. A headline in the Communist Party's *People's Daily* accused the US of 'leveraging WHO into political tool', while the *China Daily* demanded: 'Put science first on virus.' The Party's propaganda machine eagerly presented the words of this esteemed biologist as further evidence of American perfidy.

Edwards would have had good reason to be pleased by the impact of his post – if he had existed. The following month, a puzzled Swiss embassy in Beijing tweeted: 'Looking for Wilson Edwards, alleged 🇨🇭 biologist, cited in press and social media in China over the last several days. If you exist, we would like to meet you! But it is more likely that this is a fake news, and we call on Chinese press and netizens to take down the posts.'[2]

The embassy said there was no record of any Swiss citizen with the name Wilson Edwards, and there were no articles in the field of biology cited under his name. The Facebook and Twitter accounts he used were created on the same day that he published the Covid-19 posts, which were identical on both platforms. His Facebook profile was illustrated by a picture of an Oxford University library and listed three friends. There were no other posts. As well as being spread by Chinese state media, the posts were shared and amplified by hundreds of fake Facebook and Twitter accounts.[3]

Wilson Edwards's moment of fame was brief. His social media accounts were deleted soon after the Swiss embassy exposed him, and the state media articles praising his wisdom and foresight began disappearing from the internet. His was a fictitious profile, almost certainly a creation of China's propaganda machine, which at that time was in overdrive churning out conspiracy theories about the origin of the coronavirus, aiming to draw attention away from China's own culpability. Most experts agree that the place to start looking for clues is where the virus first emerged in December 2019 – the Chinese city of Wuhan. The most credible theories are a natural spillover from an animal (most likely a bat) to a human via some intermediary, or a leak from a local research laboratory that was studying bat viruses. Epidemiologists believe that understanding the origins of Covid-19 is important in the fight against future pandemics, but attempts by the WHO and others to get at the truth have faced obstruction from China, which has denied access to data, facilities and people. The invention of Wilson Edwards was one part of a concerted effort by the Communist Party to use Western social media to muddy the waters.

Disinformation, a key element of what intelligence agencies used to call 'active measures', has a long and at times colourful history, particularly during the last Cold War – 'a vast test lab of disinformation and professional, organised lying', as that period has been described by Thomas Rid, a professor at Johns Hopkins University, who has written a history of disinformation.[4] The aim back then was to sow division, doubt and distrust, spotting and exploiting the cracks in order to weaken the target – aims that essentially remain the same today. What has changed is the means. The internet has become a great enabler of peddlers of alternative reality. As Rid describes it, 'The internet didn't just make active measures cheaper, quicker and more reactive, and less risky; it also, to put it simply, made active measures more active and less measured.'[5]

Russia inherited from the old Soviet Union a strong pedigree in active measures, which it deployed with gusto during the 2016 US presidential election, won by Donald Trump. These measures included troll factories which created fake American social media accounts and spewed racially and politically divisive content and fake news articles. Russian hackers also targeted key individuals and institutions associated with Hillary Clinton's presidential campaign, stealing and then leaking embarrassing internal emails.[6]

China was slower to the disinformation game, but has been quick to catch up. As recently as 2018, Beijing had almost no diplomatic presence on Western social media – which is banned from operating inside China itself. Over the next two years, its presence grew rapidly, and by the time the coronavirus hit, around 200 Chinese diplomats were growling and trolling their way around Twitter and Facebook. They had become the foot soldiers for China's aggressive 'wolf warrior' diplomacy, named after a series of Rambo-style nationalistic movies of that name. Western social media became their platform of choice, from which to broadcast their threats and vitriol to an international audience.[7] They are now the vanguard of China's increasingly aggressive efforts to shape the international narrative on a growing range of subjects. They work in concert with state media, which has rapidly extended its international presence online and offline. Between 2009 and 2021, *Xinhua*, the state news agency doubled the number of its foreign bureaus to 200, China Radio International more than tripled its hours of programming in sixty-five languages, and China Global Television Network (CGTN) established itself as a new brand overseas, with twenty-four channels in five languages.[8]

Diplomats and state media work in concert with a shifting array of bogus accounts. Early in the Covid-19 pandemic, Beijing used tens of thousands of fake and hijacked Twitter accounts to portray itself as a leader and benefactor in public health. At the same time it rubbished the faltering efforts of Western democracies and spread baseless theories about the origins of the virus. The EU accused China of running 'a global disinformation campaign to deflect blame for the outbreak of the pandemic', and sending out a 'huge wave' of false facts. Brussels cited one case in which the Chinese embassy in Paris claimed French care workers had abandoned their jobs leaving residents to die, and asserted falsely that French lawmakers had used a racist slur against the head of the World Health Organization, Tedros Adhanom Ghebreyesus.[9]

The Alliance for Securing Democracy, a Washington-based advocacy group, calculated that between April and May 2020, accounts connected to the Chinese government pumped out 90,000 tweets as part of China's Covid-19 disinformation blitz, with the messaging becoming increasingly aggressive and conspiratorial.[10] In June 2020, Twitter shut down 170,000 accounts linked to China, which it said were engaged in 'a range of coordinated and manipulated activities'.[11] YouTube deleted almost 2,500 channels in the second quarter of 2020 alone, 'as part of our ongoing investigation into coordinated influence operations linked to China'.[12] CGTN was banned from advertising on Twitter over concerns it was spreading disinformation about the pro-democracy protests in Hong Kong.

The Party's disinformation machine was initially at its most assertive on Covid-19, but soon turned to Hong Kong and Xinjiang, as China faced global criticism for its repression in both. Posts heaped vitriol on think tanks, politicians, media and researchers who highlighted human rights abuses. The *Economist* newspaper described this as China's 'new scold war'.[13] At the same time, posts amplified fringe media, obscure 'experts' and conspiracy theorists in support of China's alternative reality. At times the messaging was clunky, even surreal – as when Party-linked organisations used Facebook for a series of sponsored video posts showing happy, thriving Uyghurs in Xinjiang – dancing, singing and generally fulfilling every kitschy ethnic stereotype, pausing only to praise the benevolence of the Communist Party. Staff at Facebook reportedly raised concerns on internal message boards and in other internal discussions that the firm was complicit in this state propaganda, but to no apparent effect.[14]

A report by the Australian Strategic Policy Institute found that the frequency of tweets about Xinjiang from Chinese state media and diplomatic Twitter accounts reached an all time high in 2020 – an average of almost 500 tweets per month, almost double the year before. 'The CCP [Chinese Communist Party] is using tactics including leveraging US social media platforms to criticise and smear Uyghur victims, journalists and researchers who work on this topic, as well as their organisations,' the institute reported, saying it expected these efforts to escalate.[15] Though diplomats at the Chinese embassy in Washington got a little over-enthusiastic, and the embassy's Twitter account was suspended after tweeting that Uyghur women had been 'emancipated' from extremism and were no longer 'baby-making machines'.[16] The tweet followed accusations that China was using forced sterilisation, forced abortion and coercive family planning against minority Muslims. Twitter said the tweet violated its policies against 'dehumanising people'.

Wilson Edwards, the fictional biologist and scourge of the Americans over Covid-19, was quite easily rumbled. Of more use to Beijing are real Westerners, however fringe or obscure, who nevertheless depict China in a positive light. State media has made increasing use of gullible foreign video bloggers, usually teachers or business people resident in China. Their videos, uploaded to YouTube, typically combine footage of travel or everyday life with attacks on foreign media 'lies' about human rights, while loudly defending China.[17] In March 2021, the Foreign Ministry discovered a Canadian YouTuber called Daniel Dumbrill, who had uploaded a twelve-minute video presentation in which he accused the US of using Xinjiang as a pretext to contain China, warning against 'brainlessly swallowing and regurgitating' Western propaganda.[18] Dumbrill was based in Shenzhen, where he ran a craft beer bar. That might not seem the most credible base for an aspiring geopolitical pundit, but the Foreign Ministry played his conspiracy-laden video before its weekly press conference. And, although YouTube is blocked in China and only accessible using a VPN anti-censorship tool, the presentation was widely shared by Chinese state media. They depicted Dumbrill as an international expert. It was also spread via Chinese social media.

It is a key tenet of Communist Party propaganda that Western democracies, and the United States in particular, are decaying and in terminal decline. During summer 2020, that became the foundation of a broader and more aggressive disinformation campaign, as Beijing began to stoke some of the most difficult and divisive issues in America. Protests over policing and race provided the opportunity, and Chinese diplomats embraced the Black Lives Matter movement with relish. They used it as a means to attack the US government for hypocrisy and double standards on human rights. When US state department spokesperson Morgan Ortagus tweeted that freedom-loving people around the world must hold the Communist Party to account for its repression in Hong Kong, Chinese government spokesperson Hua Chunying replied, 'I can't breathe,' the last words of George Floyd, who was murdered by a police officer during his arrest.[19]

During the 2020 US presidential election campaign and its messy aftermath, Beijing largely avoided showing a preference for either Donald Trump or Joe Biden. Instead, a government that would never dream of allowing free elections in its own country mocked America's democratic process, with Party-controlled media highlighting chaos, disfunction and the threat of violence, all amplified by social media.[20] When a mob stormed the US Capitol building, the Communist Party Youth League described it as a 'beautiful sight' on its Twitter-like Weibo platform, while the Chinese Foreign Ministry drew parallels with the 2019 break-in and seizure by Hong Kong protesters of the city's Legislative Council complex.[21]

In early 2021, the United States saw a rise in violent crime against Asian-Americans, which many commentators blamed on the anti-Chinese rhetoric of President Donald Trump and other Republican politicians. In March of that year, a man went on a shooting rampage at three massage parlours in the city of Atlanta. He killed eight people, six of them women of Asian descent, sparking fear and anger in the Asian-American community.[22] Two weeks later, a sixty-five-year-old Asian-American woman was brutally attacked in Manhattan, an assailant knocking her to the ground, kicking and punching her as she walked to church near Times Square. The assailant shouted anti-Asian slurs and told her, 'You don't belong here'.[23]

The New York attack was captured by a surveillance camera and the footage quickly went viral, attracting widespread condemnation and outrage. It also made for a productive afternoon for Zhao Lijian. From his Beijing office, the Chinese government spokesman re-tweeted twenty posts and shared the video twelve times on his official Twitter account. 'We can't help but wonder, who will be the next victim? When will it all end?' he told his 1 million followers. The American posts he re-tweeted were not necessarily the angriest, but they were full of despair at the state of the country. 'What the hell is wrong with people?', 'This is incredibly difficult to watch', 'Oh my God, what is happening to this country?' 'This is a state of emergency', were among them.

Zhao's words were amplified by state media, who used Facebook, Twitter and YouTube accounts to stoke a narrative of American racism and hatred. One Twitter post from the *Global Times* showed the Statue of Liberty, gun in hand, towering over a tiny cardboard cut-out figure marked 'Asian' and with a target on its chest.[24] Another cartoon, shared by China Global Television Network (CGTN), the international arm of

China's state broadcaster, depicted an American Covid-19 vaccination centre and a young Asian asking the doctor, 'By the way, is there also a vaccine for racism?'[25] Hate crime was framed as being a consequence of the US government's more assertive stance against Beijing. 'Experts say [hate crime] results from US politicians' smearing of China as culprit of Covid-19. Worsening bilateral ties play part in discrimination surge,' the *Global Times* tweeted.

Beijing made liberal use of what has been dubbed 'whataboutism', using spurious comparisons in order to deflect attention away from Chinese repression.[26] This was employed after evidence was published of the use of forced labour in Xinjiang's cotton fields. In response, spokesman Zhao Lijian tweeted, 'It is a historical fact that the #UnitedStates forced black slaves to collect cotton. Who on earth engaged in forced labor?' Later he tweeted: 'Shocking conspiracy of the US & West: destabilise #Xinjiang & contain China's development. The cotton smears are just part of the bigger plot' – assertions that were dutifully amplified by Party-controlled media.[27] As more Western politicians began to characterise China's behaviour in Xinjiang as 'genocide', the *Global Times* claimed America was in the grip of 'racist terror'. It asserted without evidence that in San Francisco people were joining a 'slap an Asian' challenge, encouraged by social media to slap anyone of Asian appearance they encountered on public transport.[28]

On paper at least, China's state-controlled news outlets and its tweeting diplomats appear to have some of the highest ranked accounts on Twitter and Facebook. By the end of 2021, CGTN had 13.4 million Twitter followers and 117 million followers on Facebook, the *Global Times* had 1.8 million on Twitter and 65 million on Facebook, and *China Daily* had 4.2 million on Twitter and 105 million on Facebook. *Xinhua*, a state news agency has 12.3 million on Twitter and 92 million on Facebook. Obscure diplomats have quickly built followings to rival Hollywood celebrities. Can there really be a market for such stultifying propaganda? China has learned very quickly one of the basic rules of social media – that engagement is driven more by confrontational, provocative and conspiratorial content, than by dry facts and diplomacy. It has also embraced many other dark social media arts.[29] The figures are almost certainly false, inflated by automated programs (bots) that generate fake followers and fake likes. The idea is to give the pages more credibility and reach, and thereby pull in legitimate users. Bogus or highjacked accounts are also used as 'amplifiers' in order to push postings and get them trending.[30]

Liu Xiaoming, China's ambassador to the UK between 2010 and 2021, joined Twitter in 2019, quickly acquiring a following of 119,000. Between June 2020 and February 2021 his posts were re-tweeted more than 45,000 times, but almost half of these were from fake accounts, many impersonating British citizens, according to an investigation by the Associated Press and Oxford Internet Institute.[31] 'This fiction of popularity can boost the status of China's messengers, creating a mirage of broad support. It can also distort platform algorithms, which are designed to boost the distribution of popular posts, potentially exposing more genuine users to Chinese government propaganda,' the AP reported.

Wikipedia, one of the most visited sites on the internet, has become another battleground. The online encyclopaedia, which is managed and updated by volunteers, is blocked in China, where it can only be accessed with a VPN anti-censorship tool. But that has not stopped the Communist Party from trying to influence its content in a manner that threatened 'the very foundations of Wikipedia', according to the Wikipedia Foundation, the US non-profit that owns the site. In September 2021, the foundation said it had been infiltrated by a group that attempted to control the content and promote the 'aims of China'. 'This case is unprecedented in scope', said foundation vice-president Maggie Dennis, who claimed there had been 'credible threats' to other volunteers. The foundation banned seven users from China and removed administrative privileges from a further twelve. The foundations said it had set up a disinformation team.[32]

The irony is that China's ability to disseminate propaganda and disinformation to a Western audience is being enabled largely by American social media platforms – platforms that are blocked in China, where the mere act of trying to access them can lead to interrogation and jail. As we have seen, Twitter, Facebook and YouTube do crack down on Chinese disinformation when it becomes impossible to ignore, but their actions are inconsistent and patchy. Twitter and Facebook now label Chinese accounts as 'state-affiliated', or belonging to 'key government officials', but the AP/Oxford investigation said the labelling was inconsistent, the criteria not clear and disclosure weak in languages other than English.

***

China also has its own social media with a growing international presence, and over which it exercises more direct control. The most important of these is the WeChat app, or Weixin in China, which is owned by the tech giant Tencent. Within China, where it is known as the 'app for everything' because of its range of services, it is an important component of the surveillance state, a weapon of social control, censorship and disinformation. Its international version is aimed mainly at Chinese speakers, for whom it has become a vital way of keeping in touch with friends, family and developments in China. It has also been used as a tool by Chinese security officials to intimidate exiled Uyghurs, Tibetans and other dissidents, often with threats relayed via relatives at home.[33]

The broader danger is that by pumping nationalist propaganda into Chinese-speaking communities, shaping what they read and see, it is creating bubbles and magnifying divisions.[34] As we have seen, in Xi Jinping's world view, the overriding loyalty of ethnic Chinese people wherever they live and however long they have been away from the motherland, should be to the Party. In the US, after the spate of anti-Asian violence, China was quick to present itself as the champion of these communities. Older established migrant communities and political exiles have little time for Communist propaganda, but newer arrivals, particularly those who have travelled overseas more recently for economic or educational opportunities, may be more receptive to WeChat enabled propaganda and nationalist blandishments.

Then there is TikTok. The short-video-sharing app is China's first truly global internet success story, which quickly acquired 100 million active users in the US and 3.7 million in the UK. It is owned by the Chinese company ByteDance, and is popular among sixteen to twenty-four-year-olds. It has been criticised for its zealous collection of personal data and the security of that data.[35] In 2021, it agreed to pay $92 million to settle a class-action lawsuit alleging it illegally tracked users and shared biometric data from photos and videos, without their consent. The data, which included face scans, was allegedly shared with third parties, some in China. The company denies any wrongdoing.[36]

At the heart of the TikTok app is an opaque algorithm that determines what a user sees. That is not unusual, but whereas on Twitter and Facebook users are mostly served content from accounts they subscribe to, on TikTok the videos can come from anywhere, the app taking account of a range of inputs.[37] These include the type of videos you look at, the duration, your likes, comments and sharing, as well as user data, such as age, gender and location. While the company does employ engineers abroad, control is firmly in the hands of secretive China-based teams, who have been experimenting with advanced inputs including facial and voice recognition, and sentiment analysis. The precise recipe of the algorithm is not known, but is so sensitive that in August 2020, when it looked as if the Trump administration might force ByteDance to sell its American app, Beijing added content-recommendation technology to its export control list.[38] In China the company deploys this tech to censor content and promote Communist Party propaganda. It claims (as does WeChat) that it does not censor its international app, but all Chinese companies by law must cooperate with the Communist Party on 'national security', a very elastic concept. While the overseas algorithm might not be massaged as blatantly as in China, there is ample room for more subtle manipulation.

This all comes at a time when the Communist Party has succeeded in bringing much of the world's Chinese-language media under its control. This was clear at a 2019 conference in China, which brought together more than 400 representatives of this media from sixty countries, including America, Australia, Britain and Canada. A senior Party official told them it was their 'duty and mission' to 'retransmit' news from China's state-controlled press at 'important times'.[39] There are reckoned to be more than 1,000 Chinese-language media outlets outside China. Before the Tiananmen Square massacre, the largest were owned by people from Hong Kong or Taiwan and strongly anti-communist, but the Party has tamed them through direct or indirect subsidies and the provision of content.

China remains the global leader in the use of cyber espionage for commercial and economic gain, and has hacked the computers of Western companies on an industrial scale. The targets closely align with the advanced technologies that the Party has identified as those in which it wants to lead the world, such as artificial intelligence and green energy. The US's Office of the National Counterintelligence Executive described Chinese actors as the 'world's most active and persistent perpetrators of economic espionage'.[40] While General Keith Alexander, then head of US Cyber Command and the National Security Agency, famously described America's loss of intellectual property and other industrial information through cyber espionage as 'the greatest transfer of wealth in history'.[41]

The Obama administration tried to make a distinction between legitimate espionage for military or political purposes, and stealing to gain a commercial edge. At a summit in September 2015, Barack Obama struck a deal with Xi Jinping supposedly outlawing hacking for economic gain.[42] A month later China agreed a similar cyber non-aggression pact with Britain. The deal didn't last, since the Communist Party never recognised Obama's distinction between different types of hacking. To the Party they are one and the same thing; Chinese companies, whether state-owned or nominally private, are instruments of state power and Party policy. And the hacking was too effective. The deal, however, enabled Beijing to blunt a growing threat of sanctions, and gave breathing space to reorganise, retool and refocus its cyber forces. Then they came roaring back with a greater degree of ambition. Obama was stung by Xi's duplicity. He was an advocate of engagement with China, and his frustration at Beijing's persistent breaking of agreements is evident in his memoir, *A Promised Land*. He writes that China's rise has been facilitated by systematically 'evading, bending, or breaking just about every agreed-about rule of international commerce'.[43]

In July 2021, the United States joined Britain, the EU, Australia and other allies in accusing China of working with criminal groups to breach Microsoft email systems, which affected tens of thousands of companies and public sector organisations worldwide. The coordinated condemnation was unprecedented. US Secretary of State Antony Blinken said China's Ministry of State Security 'has fostered an ecosystem of criminal contract hackers who carry out both state-sponsored activities and cybercrime for their own financial gain'.[44] President Joe Biden told reporters: 'My understanding is that the Chinese government, not unlike the Russian government, is not doing this themselves, but are protecting those who are doing it, and maybe even accommodating them being able to do it.'[45] China has typically exercised more direct control over its hacking groups, which cyber researchers have given the moniker 'panda', dividing them into sub-species of not-so-cuddly bear according to their techniques, tools and targets. Most are closely affiliated with the PLA or Ministry of State Security. 'Electric Panda', 'Stone Panda' and 'Putter Panda', are three of the more active. While Beijing does use front organisations – it nurtured a network of 'patriotic hackers', deployed against targets perceived to have offended China – they have been closely supervised. The Microsoft hack was the first time Western allies had explicitly linked Beijing to criminal contractors, and made a direct comparison with the tactics of Moscow, which has long used cybercrime gangs to give its hacking a veneer of deniability.

The March 2021 attacks, which exploited a vulnerability in Microsoft Exchange server software, began as a sweeping state-sponsored cyber espionage operation, harvesting emails, contacts and other information. But it quickly escalated into a hacking free-for-all, as cybercriminals piled in after the spies. Many were criminal ransomware gangs, who typically insert code that encrypts data and 'freezes' systems, effectively holding the networks hostage until large sums of money are paid, usually in cryptocurrency, for the key to decrypt the system. The hack was characterised as 'untargeted, reckless and extremely dangerous'.[46]

The Chinese Communist Party has long cooperated with computer experts in Chinese universities on cybertheft operations, and now appears keen to nurture a new generation of hackers. In 2017, China banned Chinese security researchers from taking part in international hacking contests, only to start its own annual competition, the Tianfu Cup, a few months later. In October 2021, prize money amounting to $1.5 million was offered for those who could find bugs in popular browsers, as well as the Microsoft Exchange server and the new iPhone 13 Pro.[47] 'Bug-bounty' contests are not unusual, but what is most striking about China's version is its strong links to the country's security and defence establishment, which receives early access to high-value bugs discovered through the competition. A zero-day exploit (a hitherto unknown bug) for the iPhone, discovered during the 2018 contest, was used for two months after the contest to spy on Uyghur dissident targets overseas before Apple released a security update.[48]

China's cyber tradecraft can be somewhat lacking. Beijing's cyber spies often leave a forensic trail, eagerly picked up by security researchers and rival intelligence agencies, but the evidence does underline the sheer scale and ambition of the Communist Party's activities against both business and government targets. Stung perhaps by the Microsoft Exchange hack, the Microsoft Digital Crimes Unit reported in December 2021 that it had seized websites belonging to a Chinese hacking group that had been used to gather intelligence on government agencies, think tanks and human rights groups in the US, UK and twenty-seven other countries. Microsoft said the attacks were 'highly sophisticated and used a variety of techniques but nearly always had one goal: to insert hard-to-detect malware that facilitates intrusion, surveillance and data theft'.[49] A separate report from the cybersecurity firm Recorded Future revealed that throughout 2021, suspected Chinese hackers had been targeting rival claimants in the South China Sea and Southeast Asian countries strategically important to its Belt and Road Initiative. The targets included navies, the offices of prime ministers, and Ministries of Defence and Foreign Affairs.[50] While in Florida in October 2021, the FBI raided the Florida office of PAX Technology, a Chinese provider of point-of-sale devices used by millions of businesses and retailers globally. The devices were suspected both of spreading malware and for being used as 'command and control' tools for staging attacks and collecting information, according to security researchers.[51]

In a May 2021 speech at a conference of the Chinese Academy of Sciences, Xi Jinping declared, 'Technological innovation has become the main battleground of the global playing field, and competition for tech dominance will grow unprecedentedly fierce.'[52] That's certainly the way it feels to FBI director Christopher Wray, who said in February 2022 that Beijing's hacking operations and its theft of American ideas and innovation had reached a new level – 'more brazen, more damaging than ever before'. He said the bureau had 2,000 investigations focused on China. 'There's just no country that presents a broader threat to our ideas, innovation, and economic security than China,' he warned. The bureau was opening new cases to counter Chinese intelligence operations every twelve hours or so.[53]

In its 2021 annual report, Britain's National Cyber Security Centre, which is part of GCHQ, said cyber 'incidents' in Britain were running at a record level, and that Covid-19 vaccine research had become a prime target for hackers. It said that in the twelve months to November 2021, 20 per cent of 777 incidents were vaccine-related, including attacks on research, distribution and supply chains. It did not name the suspected perpetrators, but did warn: 'China remained a highly sophisticated actor in cyberspace with increasing ambition to project its influence beyond its borders and a proven interest in the UK's commercial secrets. How China evolves in the next decade will probably be the single biggest driver the UK's future cyber security.'[54]

While it cannot quite be described as a division of labour, the use of cyberweapons by Russia and China has in the past been very different. Russia was the vandal seeking through disinformation and hack-and-leak operations to undermine Western democracy. At the same time it engaged in cyber sabotage. It was blamed for a series of crippling attacks in Ukraine between 2015 and 2017 that hit the power grid, the Kyiv metro, businesses and government. It was earlier accused of attacking computer systems in Georgia and Estonia, during times of tension with both. In May 2021 a Russia-based gang with close links to the intelligence services was blamed for an attack that shut down the Colonial Pipeline, one of America's largest fuel pipelines.[55] China in the past has preferred to work within Western systems, hacking and trawling through computers for know-how that will help China's rise. Cyber espionage can best be understood as one branch of a vast system for acquiring technology. This system also includes more conventional espionage, as well as the common practice of forcing companies to hand over technical know-how as a price for doing business in China. Other tech is acquired from carefully targeted university and other research tie-ups.

China's malign activities in cyberspace are beginning to look more like those of Russia, in their embrace of disinformation, but also in its apparent use of sabotage. The attack on the Mumbai power grid described in Chapter 4 is something right out of the Russian playbook. One crucial difference is that China appears to care still about its international image in a way that Russia has long given up on. Beijing is quick to feign outrage when accused of hacking – 'The US has repeatedly made groundless attacks and malicious smears against China on cybersecurity,' Liu Pengyu, spokesman for the Chinese embassy in Washington, said after the Microsoft accusations.[56] The merger of cyber tactics is disquieting, but it's only one way that Russia and China are growing closer, much to the growing alarm of Western democracies.

## Chapter 7

# *The Awkward Dance of the Panda and the Bear*

'Friendship between the two States has no limits, there are no "forbidden" areas of cooperation'

*Joint statement after a Xi-Jinping–Vladimir Putin summit, 4 February 2022*

Hours before the lavish opening ceremony of the 2022 Winter Olympics in Beijing, which was boycotted by Western leaders in protest at human rights violations, Xi Jinping and Vladimir Putin put on their own chilling performance for the world. During a summit meeting the Chinese and Russian leaders declared there were 'no limits' to their partnership and pledged to intensify their collaboration against the West and to build a new international order. 'Friendship between the two States has no limits, there are no "forbidden" areas of cooperation,' they said in a joint statement.[1] It was Xi's first in-person meeting with a foreign leader in nearly two years, and it came at a time when Russia had massed more than 100,000 troops along its border with Ukraine. While not specifically mentioning Ukraine, Xi endorsed Putin's aims, calling for an end to NATO enlargement and supporting Russian demands for security guarantees from the West. In return, Putin endorsed China's stance on Taiwan.

Their relationship had been growing closer for some time. At a virtual summit the previous December, Xi addressed Putin as 'old friend', while Putin called the Chinese leader 'esteemed friend'.[2] The two shared a deep paranoia and hostility to the West. 'At present, certain international forces under the guise of democracy and human rights are interfering in the internal affairs of China and Russia,' Xi told Putin at their December summit. 'China and Russia should increase their joint efforts to more effectively safeguard the security interests of both parties.'[3] The Russian leader said that 'close collaboration on the global stage' had become a 'tangible factor of stability in international relations.'[4]

The two men also shared a profound sense of historic grievance, and imperial dreams of re-building their former empires. Putin fantasised about re-establishing the *Russkiy Mir*, the mythical Russian World, which he would later use to justify his invasion of Ukraine. For Xi it was the Chinese Dream of national rejuvenation. Both are almost messianic visions of restoring national greatness. They saw the world in terms of big power politics and spheres of influence, with no room for self-determination and the rights of pesky democracies like Ukraine or Taiwan to make their own security and political choices. At the time of the Olympic summit, the nightmare for strategists in Washington was that Putin's military build-up around Ukraine was being coordinated with that of Xi in and around the Taiwan Strait, where military intimidation of Taiwan had reached new levels of intensity. Western analysts anxiously toggled between spy satellites covering the two regions.

China does not have formal alliances in the Western sense. It does not fit with Beijing's sense of its own centrality, which is incompatible with an alliance system that might require obligations, commitments and a degree of equity. But it does have a hierarchy of partnerships, of which Russia sits at the top – the relationship officially designated as a 'comprehensive strategic partnership of coordination for the new era'. Their relationship in primarily defined in terms of opposition to Western democracies – and to the US in particular. In an annual worldwide threat assessment, the US Director of National Intelligence has described China and Russia as more aligned than at any point since the mid 1950s.[5]

Their joint military drills have become more frequent and more complex. They are able to learn from each other's tactics and procedures, helped by the fact that Russia is a big supplier to China of advanced weapons, including fighter jets and missile systems. Russia also had a less tangible, but highly valuable asset to pass on – the combat experience that the PLA lacks, Russian troops having fought in wars from Georgia and Chechnya to Ukraine and Syria.[6] The drills appeared to be going beyond symbolic shows of camaraderie, aimed increasingly at coordinating command and control and enhancing battlefield interoperability.[7] In August 2021, some 13,000 troops and hundreds of aircraft, drones, artillery pieces, antiaircraft batteries and armoured vehicles took part in a drill in northwest China.[8] Two months later, Chinese and Russian warships, including destroyers, frigates, a refuelling vessel and missile-tracking ship, sailed through the 12-mile wide Strait of Tsugaru separating Japan's northern island of Hokkaido from its main island of Honshu. It was part of a four-day joint exercise that was greeted with particular alarm in Washington and Tokyo.[9]

China and Russia complement each other economically. Resource-hungry China devours Russian energy, commodity and agricultural exports, while manufactured goods and investment flow the other way. Between 2016 and 2020, 77 per cent of China's total arms imports were from Russia.[10] Although China has fast developed its own substantial arms industry, Moscow has played an important role in Beijing's military modernisation, increasing substantially the technological sophistication of its exports. In return, Moscow has imported know-how in an area where China excels – the 'Great Firewall' system of internet filtering and control.[11] As we have already seen, the nature of Russian and Chinese malign cyber activities has been converging.

To many Western strategists, the Olympic summit, and China's support for Russia's invasion of Ukraine 20 days later was a defining moment – the creation of a new 'axis of autocracy', with far reaching implications. However, those with a keen sense of history were not so sure. The Xi–Putin partnership seemed opportunist, a marriage of convenience. There seemed too much baggage for it to be sustainable. Historic suspicions and animosities run deep, and Beijing is encroaching further into areas of traditional Russian influence. Certainly, Xi Jinping and Vladimir Putin share a dangerous imperial nostalgia, a nostalgia underpinned by wilfully distorting history. However, those bad histories can clash – no more so than in the areas where their empires once faced off, in Central Asia, Mongolia and the Russian Far East.

In July 2021, China's Foreign Minister Wang Yi, became the first high-profile guest in Damascus after Bashar al-Assad's 're-election' as president of Syria.[12] Assad, 'the butcher of Damascus', claimed to have won 95 per cent of the vote in a poll described by Britain and the EU as 'neither free nor fair'. Wang offered Assad membership of China's Belt and Road Initiative (BRI) to speed up the reconstruction of a country whose economy was in ruins. For Assad, the promise of billions of dollars in Chinese investment seemed like a perfect accompaniment to the Russian and Iranian guns and muscle that kept him in power during a ten-year civil war that claimed half a million lives. To outsiders it seemed further proof that no regime was too odious to become a partner of the Chinese Communist Party, but it also raised intriguing questions about China's relationship with Russia. Was Moscow really willing to see its influence seep away to Beijing?

Two weeks after this visit to Damascus, Wang shifted his focus to Afghanistan. He met with senior leaders of the Taliban in the northern Chinese city of Tianjin. Among those present was the group's co-founder, Mullah Abdul Ghani Baradar, who headed its political committee. Wang said he expected the Taliban to play an important role in Afghanistan's 'peace, reconciliation and reconstruction process'.[13] At the time, the Taliban was advancing rapidly across the country as the US withdrew. China has invested heavily in other parts of Central Asia and Beijing sensed opportunity as well as danger in the Taliban's advance. When the Taliban seized power in Kabul, two and a half weeks after the Tianjin meeting, the Communist Party greeted America's chaotic retreat with a mixture of glee and trepidation. Its well-oiled propaganda machine revelled in the fall of Kabul and the humiliation of the US, but at the same time Beijing fretted over the threat of instability on its doorstep spilling over into Xinjiang province, which shares a short border with Afghanistan.[14]

Beijing reached for its cheque book, offering in effect, to buy the Taliban. It held out the promise of massive investment in the country as part of its BRI, in exchange for the Taliban curbing the activities of the Afghanistan-based East Turkistan Islamic Movement, which China blames for violence in Xinjiang (East Turkistan is the Uyghurs' preferred name for Xinjiang).[15] Most independent observers believe the movement's membership and influence is exaggerated by Beijing, which uses a very wide definition of terrorism to justify its repression.

The bigger prize for Beijing was access to a stock of mineral deposits in Afghanistan worth an estimated $1 trillion, including the world's biggest deposit of lithium, an essential component of the rechargeable batteries that will supposedly power our green future. An initial priority was the development of the world's second largest copper mine, nineteen miles southeast of Kabul, for which China already has a contract, but the project was stalled as a result of security concerns. Chinese officials hinted that Afghanistan could become an extension of its China–Pakistan Economic Corridor, to which Beijing has pledged an estimated $62 billion for roads, railways, ports and other infrastructure

– the biggest recipient of BRI funds. For Beijing, Pakistan was a perfect role model – Beijing's largesse has gagged Prime Minister Imran Khan, who has dutifully parroted the propaganda lines of his benefactor, denying knowledge of the repression in Xinjiang.

Yet clamping down on Uyghur activities was a big ask of the Taliban, an Islamist group, even assuming a degree of pragmatism in the face of mass starvation and economic collapse. The Taliban itself was split, and facing armed opposition from more radical groups. The danger for China was underlined in early October 2021 when a bomber from the Islamic State-Khorasan (ISIS-K) group, killed nearly fifty people at a mosque in Kunduz. The group said that the bomber was Uyghur and that the attack was a punishment on the Taliban for their close cooperation with China.[16] Chinese assets in Pakistan were also targeted, and in July 2021 nine Chinese engineers working on a dam project were killed in a bus explosion in Pakistan's Kohistan province. In an effort to appease China, Pakistan initially described it as a mechanical failure, only later admitting that traces of explosive had been found.[17]

Beijing complemented its cheque-book diplomacy with fresh security moves. It hastily arranged a joint 'anti-terrorism exercise' with Tajikistan, which shares an 835-mile border with Afghanistan. Chinese and Tajik forces took to the hills outside the capital Dushanbe, while in a letter to his Tajik counterpart China's Minster of Public Security Zhao Kezhi said, 'The current international situation is changing and the regional counterterrorism situation is not optimistic.'[18] China reportedly established a military outpost in eastern Tajikistan, close to the narrow frontier between Afghanistan and China's Xinjiang province.[19] It also provided finance to bolster a special forces unit of Tajikistan's police on the Afghan frontier.[20] It is not clear how far any of this was coordinated with Russia, which has its largest foreign military base in Tajikistan, close to the Afghan border. Tajikistan also sought reassurance from the Collective Security Treaty Organisation (CSTO), a Russia-led bloc that groups former Soviet states. Russian Foreign Minister Sergey Lavrov said Russia would 'do everything to prevent any aggressive moves against our allies'.[21] For good measure, the foreign ministers of Tajikistan and Uzbekistan were invited to Washington for talks with US Secretary of State Antony Blinken.

Little wonder that many commentators reached for the analogy of the 'Great Game' to describe what was developing in and around Afghanistan. The nineteenth-century rivalry between Britain and

Russia, during which the two empires struggled for influence and control in Central Asia, has become a thing of myth and legend – likened to a 'vast chessboard' on which took place 'a shadowy struggle for political ascendency'.[22] It's a tempting analogy, but not a particularly accurate one – the contemporary rise of China is defined by sharper elbows, the canvas far broader. Afghanistan has also been described as the 'graveyard of empires', a sobriquet for the failure of foreign intervention. Thirty-two years before the American withdrawal, it was the Soviet Union making for the exits after a disastrous decade-long occupation. The British empire tried and failed on three occasions. Dreams of stabilising the country go back a long way – will China become the next power with imperial ambitions to be sucked in? Certainly Beijing has invested a lot of money in Central Asia. In Beijing's eyes it is the original Silk Road, the revival of which was the idea on which its BRI was founded. However, it is a region long regarded by Russia as its own backyard.

In the language of the Junggar people who dominated the area in the seventeenth and eighteenth centuries, Khorgos means 'place of much camel dung'. It sits on the Kazakhstan–China border, or more accurately *they* sit on the border. The Chinese version of Khorgos is a gaudy new city of skyscrapers, wide boulevards and plenty of hustle, while across the frontier the Kazakh version is more modest, little more than a village, though with big aspirations. In recent years, Khorgos had also become an umbrella name for a vast trading hub straddling the border. The image of yellow cranes against a backdrop of desert and distant snow-capped mountains has been used in Chinese Communist Party propaganda as a pin-up for its Belt and Road Initiative – promoted as a key transit point on its new Silk Road linking Asia with Europe.

Khorgos Gateway, to give its precise name, has been touted as one of the world's largest dry ports – a particularly apt description since it is the furthest place on earth from an ocean. It is where cargo is sorted and then moved between trains for onward travel – necessary because of different railway gauges on each side of the border.[23] For the moment, the remote outpost is not quite the global hub it aspires to be since most of the goods are from China and go to countries of the former Soviet Union. It also requires massive subsidies to make it viable – up to 40 per cent of shipping costs by one estimate are paid by Beijing.[24] The dry dock is complemented by a special economic zone which straddles the border. Before the Covid-19 pandemic put a dampener on trade, the International Center for Business Cooperation (ICBC), a visa-free and duty-free mall, was packed with Kazakh traders snapping up Chinese consumer goods. Khorgos is also an important junction for a pipeline bringing natural gas to China from Turkmenistan, another former Soviet state, which accounts for 70 per cent of China's total natural gas imports.[25]

On the Kazakh side of the frontier, a planned new border city (also called Khorgos) has barely got off the drawing board, and for the moment the nearest Kazakh settlement is Zharkent, eighteen miles away. Zharkent has a population of around 43,000, including Kazakhs, Russians, Dungan (Chinese Muslims or Hui) and Uyghurs, for whom it is an important cultural centre. Its make-up is testament to the complex history of the area.[26] It was once part of the Qing empire, a garrison town, which was razed to the ground during a Muslim rebellion.[27] It was eventually incorporated into the Russian empire under the 1881 Treaty of Saint Petersburg – one of the many 'unequal' treaties supposedly imposed on China during what the Communist Party refers to as the 'century of humiliation'. Between 1942 and 1991, before the Soviet Union disintegrated and Kazakhstan gained its independence, the town was called Panfilov after Ivan Panfilov, a Soviet Second World War hero. Uyghurs left neighbouring Xinjiang province in China in large numbers during the late 1950s and early 1960s to escape the repression and hardship of Maoist China, and there are now reckoned to be around 300,000 Uyghurs living in Kazakhstan. There are also some 1.5 million ethnic Kazakhs living in Xinjiang, the largest ethnic group after the Uyghurs and Han Chinese, further complicating life for Kazakhstan's rulers, as they seek to do business with China.

It was in these border regions of Kazakhstan that the first reports emerged of a new kind of repression – of a surveillance state the likes of which had not been seen before, an algorithmically-driven police state. In 2018, word began to seep out of the mass incarceration in Xinjiang of Uyghurs and other Muslim minorities, including ethnic Kazakhs, in a vast network of 're-education camps'. China demanded Kazakhstan quash the reports and deport back to China those who carried them across the border. In July of that year, in Zharkent's dreary Soviet-era courthouse, the trial took place of Sayragul Sauytbay, a Chinese citizen and an ethnic Kazakh, accused of crossing the border illegally. The forty-one-year-old kindergarten teacher had worked in one of the camps, and her emotional testimony provided the first public evidence of what China was then strenuously denying. It was 'very, very scary. Just one glimpse would frighten you,' she said. 'People didn't dare speak, even a word out loud. Everyone was silent. Endlessly mute.'[28] Kazakhstan was in a bind. Beijing was applying intense pressure to hand her back, but the government could not ignore growing Kazakh nationalist anger at the reports. The court found her guilty of illegal border crossing but refused to deport her. The government also refused her request for asylum, silencing her until she and her family were taken in by Sweden. The Sauytbay case set a pattern. Ethnic Kazakhs who fled to Kazakhstan from Xinjiang were typically given short or suspended prison sentences, but not deported.[29] However, the authorities did crack down on activists seeking to draw attention to the repression next door, and refused to even acknowledge the existence of the camps.

In a few short years, China has edged out Russia as Kazakhstan's biggest trading partner.[30] Beijing sees its relationship with Kazakhstan as the most important in Central Asia. It was in the Kazakh capital Astana (since renamed Nur-Sultan) that Xi Jinping launched the BRI in 2013, signing deals worth $30 billion, mostly in oil, gas and other natural resources and related infrastructure.[31] Yet the shared trade and development rhetoric of the BRI has always been the glossy veneer for a project that is essentially about security and geopolitics. This is at its most stark in Kazakhstan, which Beijing has sought to enlist in its fight against 'extremism' in Xinjiang – an umbrella term the Communist Party uses for all opposition to its rule.

A common Turkic heritage with the Uyghur people as well as personal ties across the border have put the Kazakh government in a difficult spot, especially as Chinese repression has become so stark. Before the Covid-19 pandemic, there were protests across the country against Chinese proposals to move old and polluting factories to Kazakhstan, and land reforms that would allow China to acquire large swathes of Kazakh farmland, as well as Chinese migration and the repression in Xinjiang.[32] When the coronavirus first struck in the Chinese city of Wuhan, the Kazakh authorities cut transport links with China, suspended the issuance of visas to Chinese citizens and halted work on the Kazakh side at Khorgos – measures that were welcomed with an enthusiasm that seemed to go beyond fear of the virus.[33] Nationalist sentiment was further enraged in 2020 when Chinese media ran stories asserting that Kazakhstan was historically a vassal state of China during the Qing Dynasty and that Kazakhs longed to return to the motherland. The Kazakh Foreign Ministry lodged a protest with the Chinese ambassador.[34]

Such comments also create unease in Moscow, which knows it cannot compete with China's spending power in Kazakhstan, but has strong cultural, linguistic and security links. Some 3.5 million – around 20 per cent – of Kazakhstan's population are ethnic Russian, mostly in the north of the country. The Soviet Union tested its nuclear weapons in Kazakhstan, carrying out 456 tests at Semipalatinsk, a site the size of Wales, with little regard for the environment or human health.[35] The vast Baikonur Cosmodrome in southern Kazakhstan remains the home of the Russian space programme, on a lease that runs until 2050.[36] Kazakhstan is embedded in Moscow's economic and security architecture – including the Eurasian Economic Union, and the CSTO, the military alliance. By the end of 2021, President Putin had visited Kazakhstan twenty-eight times, more than any other country.

When protests erupted across the country in January 2022, during which government buildings were stormed or set on fire, Kazakhstan turned to the CSTO to help suppress them. Russian 'peacekeeping troops' eagerly answered the call. Dozens of protesters were killed, as well as police and security forces. The unrest was sparked by rising fuel prices, but intensified by long-standing political and economic frustrations. Much of the anger was aimed at Nursultan Nazarbayev, a Kazakh Communist Party leader in Soviet days who then became president of independent Kazakhstan. His autocratic rule lasted until 2019, when he resigned, but he and his cronies retained considerable power. The country has some of the world's largest oil fields and 40 per cent of global uranium production, but little of the riches have trickled down. A 2019 report by the consultancy KPMG estimated that just 162 people owned half of the country's wealth.[37] While Nazarbayev and his family and cronies enriched themselves, the average salary in 2021 was the equivalent of £420 a month.[38]

In spite of the rampant corruption, most observers acknowledge that Kazakhstan was adept at balancing the powers competing for its natural wealth. However, the response to the 2022 protests marked a shift closer to Russia, which has never had much respect for the sovereignty of former Soviet republics. Putin has described the break-up of the Soviet empire as 'the greatest geopolitical catastrophe of the century', and said that he would reverse it if he had a chance to alter modern Russian history.[39] Moscow's intervention seemed initially to take Beijing by surprise, though it soon endorsed Moscow's actions.

After the Sino-Soviet split in the late 1950s, the fortified frontier between the Soviet Union and the People's Republic of China became a tense and hostile place. It was closed for the best part of three decades – the front line of a shadow cold war, as the two communist giants vied for leadership of the world revolutionary movement. A border clash in the Russian Far East in March 1969 left hundreds dead and brought the two sides to the brink of full-scale war. The border with the then Kazakh Soviet Socialist Republic also saw numerous skirmishes. The most serious took place later in 1969 when a Soviet patrol ambushed and killed thirty-eight Chinese soldiers near Lake Zhalanashkol, some 160 miles northeast of Khorgos. At the time, the Soviet Union made thinly veiled nuclear threats against its neighbour.[40] The Soviet and Chinese sides of Central Asia became isolated from each other. Mao Zedong regarded the Soviet Union as a bully who spoke the language of socialism and fraternalism but behaved like an imperialist. A similar accusation could well be levelled today against Xi Jinping's China.

The frontiers of Kazakhstan, together with Kyrgyzstan, Tajikistan, Uzbekistan and Turkmenistan, were all established by the Soviet Union during the 1920s and '30s, following the Bolshevik Revolution. Kazakhstan, Kyrgyzstan and Tajikistan inherited the old external frontier of the Tsarist Russian empire and these are the Central Asian nations that now border China. Uzbekistan and Turkmenistan are further to the east. Each Soviet Socialist Republic was established by Stalin on broad ethnic lines, while at the same time ensuring there were large minorities of other groups in each administrative unit. The idea was to create dominant ethnic groups in each republic, but not too dominant – sufficient to play them off against one another and at the same time avoid the emergence of any pan-Islamic or pan-Turkic movements. The Soviet Communist Party nurtured local elites in each republic (those not purged by Stalin) through whom it ruled. Though real power lay in Moscow, the republics were allowed considerable leeway, just as long as they maintained stability and fulfilled their economic quota, mostly supplying raw materials ranging from oil to minerals and cotton.

Across the border, Chinese colonial rule in Xinjiang was more openly chauvinistic than that of Russia in its part of Central Asia. Although there were periods of relative liberalism, Beijing's rule has been characterised by the imposition of Han Chinese practices and culture through mass migration and the repression of a Uyghur culture and religion deemed inferior and threatening – a policy that has culminated in today's gulag of 're-education' camps. Many Uyghurs originally saw the Soviet Union as a source of revolutionary inspiration, and a short-lived East Turkistan Republic established in 1944 was initially backed by the Soviets. When Mao's communists seized power in China in 1949, they moved to crush the ETR, and by the end of the following year the People's Liberation Army had captured most of the area of the fledging republic.

When the Soviet Union collapsed in 1991, many of its constituent republics enthusiastically seized their new independence. In Central Asia feelings were more mixed. Independence was in many ways unwanted and unexpected.[41] For the most part the old Soviet elite became the authoritarian rulers of new sovereign states within the borders of the former Soviet republics. Little changed apart from the signs on the doors and the flags. The old guard retained their grip, as they have mostly done ever since, rigging elections and enriching themselves along the way. At the time of independence it was widely assumed that Turkey and Iran would be the big beneficiaries in Central Asia – Turkey because of strong linguistic and cultural links, Iran because of a revival of long-repressed religious fervour. Turkey was the first country to establish diplomatic relations with the new Central Asian states, and Ankara assumed they would be happily guided by their Turkic big brother. However, neither Iran nor Turkey gained much traction. In 2001, Central Asia became part of the military and logistical network for the United States-led war in Afghanistan. The former Soviet states were happy to leverage the language of the 'war on terror' for their own repressive purposes, signing security cooperation agreements to provide Washington with logistical support and overfly rights. For a while the US had military bases in Uzbekistan and Kyrgyzstan.

Tajikistan remains the poorest and most dysfunctional of the old Soviet Central Asian republics. Together with Kyrgyzstan, it has been named among the eight countries of the world at highest risk of debt distress because of BRI projects.[42] In 2020, Tajikistan's public debt amounted to $3.7 billion, or 44.9 per cent of GDP, with China by far the biggest and fastest growing creditor.[43] The debt to Beijing has continued to increase in spite of a 2011 deal in which China wrote off an undisclosed sum in exchange for almost 500 square miles of disputed territory in the Pamir mountains, which straddle the border.[44] The opaque deal raised alarms across the region, as did a spate of more recent articles in the Chinese media that appeared to extend China's territorial claim to the entire mountain range and beyond.[45]

China sought to expand its influence through an organisation called the Shanghai Cooperation Organisation (SCO), founded in 2001 and grouping Central Asian states with Russia and China. Its original aims were to strengthen cooperation and mutual trust, but it evolved to focus on China's three broadly drawn demons of 'terrorism, separatism and extremism'.[46] In 2017, Russia brought in India and Pakistan, a move that was widely seen as an effort to dilute the organisation and reduce Chinese influence.[47] Moscow has sought to strengthen relations with India more broadly, in spite of the tense border clashes between Delhi and Beijing that we examined earlier. In December 2021, Russia and India revealed plans to step up defence cooperation in Central Asia, including the joint manufacture of defence equipment in the region and joint military and counterterrorism drills.[48]

It has been said that China and Russia have a tacit agreement in Central Asia, that Russia dominates the security side, while China covers the economics, and in this way they complement each other.[49] That is far too simple a distinction for what is a complex and mutually suspicious relationship. As we have seen many times in this book, the BRI itself is a geopolitical tool with aims that go far beyond trade and investment – and while China certainly has the deepest pockets in the region, it also has the deepest insecurities.

While Communist Party repression in Xinjiang and Tibet has generated attention and alarm internationally, the Party's activities in the Chinese territory of Inner Mongolia are less well documented. However, the pattern is familiar – a policy of ethnic harmonisation that is seeking to impose Han Chinese culture and erode Mongolian tradition and language. It is troubling in its own right, but also has broader implications for the relationship between China and Russia.

Beijing has encouraged Han migration to the extent that only one in six of the province's 24 million population are now Mongolian. In September 2020, the government sharply curtailed use of the Mongolian language in public schools, provoking widespread protests and school boycotts.[50] Religious freedom had already been greatly restricted – many Mongolians follow a Tibetan form of Buddhism that recognises the Dalai Lama as the ultimate authority. Bainu, a Mongolian social media platform in China, was closed down to prevent parents from organising, but many were able to send videos to friends and relatives across their northern border into the independent nation of Mongolia, where there was widespread outrage at the treatment of their brethren.[51] The highly indebted Mongolian government was more cautious. It was keen not to upset China, which buys around 90 per cent of its exports, and knows a thing or two about Chinese coercion – after a 2016 visit to Mongolia by the Dalai Lama, China imposed trade restrictions, forcing Ulaanbaatar to promise that it would never happen again.[52] It seems like a familiar story, but as Mongolians in Ulaanbaatar are fond of telling visitors, they are the decendents of Genghis Khan and know a thing or two about big power politics.

'Our location is strategic because Mongolia sits on the backbone of China, while punching the underbelly of Russia,' said Tsakhiagiin Elbegdorj, president of Mongolia from 2009 to 2017, during which he met Xi Jinping thirty times.[53] He has since become one of China's harshest critics. He wrote to Xi via the Chinese embassy in Ulaanbaatar after the language crackdown, accusing the Chinese leader of presiding over a 'growing atrocity that seeks to dissolve and eliminate Mongolians as an independent ethnicity through their language'. The letter was returned with a warning not to meddle in China's internal affairs.[54]

The Mongolian state is built around the memory of Genghis Khan, who conquered more than half the known world in the thirteenth century. The main airport, university and hotels – even vodka, beer, energy drinks and cigarettes – are named after him. There are countless monuments and statues – an hour's drive from the capital sits a 131-foot-tall statue of the warrior on horseback, wrapped in 250 tons of stainless steel.[55] Genghis Khan (which means 'universal ruler') has a rather more bloodthirsty reputation among most historians, but after centuries of dominance by China and Russia, Mongolia seized upon him as a symbol of national identity. His grandson Kublai Khan conquered China and founded the Yuan Dynasty. Mongolia was later absorbed by the Chinese Qing Dynasty, and declared independence after the Qing collapsed in 1911. However, it quickly fell under the influence of the Soviet Union, becoming a Soviet satellite state, regarded by Stalin as a useful buffer between him and China.

Early in 1990, amid a wave of anti-communist uprisings and with the Soviet Union on the verge of disintegration, Mongolia experienced its own peaceful democratic revolution, which ushered in a messy multi-party democracy. After a shaky start, the new democracy rode the back of soaring commodity prices in the early 2000s. Foreign miners rushed in to exploit abundant supplies of coal, copper and gold, and briefly Mongolia was the world's fastest growing economy. The new wealth allowed it to manage the precarious balance between Russia and China, while reaching out to Japan and the US. For a while it seemed to work. Ulaanbaatar became a wild frontier city – until boom became bust. Commodity prices retreated, and in 2017 Mongolia was forced to go cap in hand to the International Monetary Fund.[56] The economy was held up as a classic example of the 'resource curse' – in which countries blessed with natural resources squander their advantage through a variety of reasons, from over-dependence to mismanagement and corruption.

Mongolia is a country of dunes and grasslands, six times the size of the United Kingdom, but with a population of just 3.3 million – the world's most sparsely populated sovereign nation. Almost a third are still nomadic or semi-nomadic. Economic stresses were further compounded by border closures because of Covid-19, which severely hit trade with China.[57] However, to Mongolia's giant neighbours economic stress equals strategic opportunity. Both pushed for investment concessions – underpinned by their broader imperial nostalgia. Chinese nationalists consider the very existence of Mongolia as an affront, believing the imperial Qing Dynasty borders are their rightful frontier. Russia is pressing ahead with a proposed new gas pipeline that will transit Mongolia; Russia provides 92 per cent of Mongolia's energy, but the pipeline is primarily a shortcut to get gas to China.[58] It is also seen as an instrument to rebuild influence in Mongolia, where Russian is still widely spoken, and which still uses the Cyrillic alphabet

Russians celebrating the 160th anniversary of the founding of their far eastern port city of Vladivostok were surprised to learn that its real name is Haishenwai and that it is rightfully part of China. The claims were spread on social media by Chinese diplomats and journalists in July 2020 and seemed guaranteed to strike a raw nerve in Russia's Far East, where popular suspicion and fear about China are at their most raw.[59] The geography and demographics of the area provide some of the explanation: Russia, vast, resource-rich and underpopulated facing a China that is resource hungry and crowded. The border is 2,615 miles long, and more than 1,000 miles of it follows the Amur river.

For all the warming of ties between the two neighbours, the border remains heavily fortified. Although trade across the frontier, legal and illegal, has grown rapidly, there is on the Russian side widespread anti-Chinese sentiment – a neurosis that at some point Beijing will transform its economic dominance into political control, and the Russian Far East, where the population is continuing to shrink, will simply be subsumed by a voracious China.[60]

As we have seen, this is where the most violent border clash took place in 1969, which raised fears of all-out war. The border along the Amur River was established by the 1858 Treaty of Aigun between the Russian Empire and Qing Dynasty, under which China ceded 230,000 square miles north of the river to Russia. A later treaty ceded a huge swathe of land further east around modern-day Vladivostok on the Sea of Japan. In theory, at least, the dispute has been settled, the border finalised, but these treaties are still regarded in China as 'unequal'. In the nationalist mindset, they rank alongside the ceding of Hong Kong as a cause of grievance, another legacy of the Party's much-vaunted 'century of humiliation'.[61] Chinese school textbooks still show the area, as well as large swathes of central Asia, as being part of historic Chinese lands. In the Chinese nationalist narrative Russia is one of the villains who inflicted 'humiliation' on China.

With so many areas of real and potential contention, it is not surprising that their new found warmth has been greeted with some scepticism. Tod Wolters, NATO's Supreme Allied Commander Europe, described it as a 'partnership of convenience', but no less dangerous for it. He said it demanded heightened vigilance, since it could be 'to the detriment of Europe and corresponding and surrounding nations.'[62] Others see it as a tactical alignment based on nothing more than mutual pragmatism, played up in public, but plagued by private mistrust and rivalry.[63] Russia continues to have warm relations with and sell advanced weapons to Vietnam as well as India, both of whom have seen tension with Beijing. On purely economic grounds, China is the senior partner – China's economy is roughly nine times larger than that of Russia. Moscow would appear to need Beijing more than Beijing needs Moscow, and after the invasion of Ukraine Russia was clearly hoping Beijing would help cushion it from the effects of Western sanctions.

In the wake of Russia's aggression and amid accusations of atrocities against civilians, a chorus of Western leaders urged Xi Jinping to use his influence to restrain Putin, and to live up to his much-vaunted claim to believe in the sanctity of 'sovereignty and 'non-interference'. Instead, Xi continued to echo Russia's justifications, and the Chinese Communist Party leader could not bring himself to call it an invasion. Chinese state media echoed Russian claims to be 'denazifying' Ukraine, and likened the rise of supposed Ukrainian 'Naziism' to the Hong Kong protests – with both presented as examples of 'foreign forces interfering with domestic affairs'. Chinese commentators echoed bogus Russian claims that video of murdered Ukrainian civilians was staged. A foreign ministry spokesman promoted Russian conspiracy theories about American military 'biolabs' in Ukraine bristling with 'dangerous pathogens'.[64]

There has been much speculation about whether China was tipped off in advance of the invasion – that is certainly the view of US intelligence, which claims Chinese officials asked Russia to hold off until the Olympics had ended.[65] Beijing denied that, but it seems inconceivable that Xi did not have at a least broad knowledge of what was planned. Perhaps Putin convinced him it would be over quickly. Instead the invasion was bungled and Putin flaunted his barbarity to the world in a manner that could not be easily glossed over. What can be said for certain is that Xi was closely watching both the conflict and the reaction from the West as he calibrated his plans for Taiwan, to which we now turn.

# CHAPTER 8

# *Target Taiwan: The Chinese Anaconda Tightens Its Grip*

'The historical task of the complete reunification of the motherland must be fulfilled, and will definitely be fulfilled.'

*Xi Jinping, October 2021*

Taiwan is an independent country. That seems like a self-evident statement; after all, the island has all the trappings of a sovereign state – its own flag, army, constitution, borders, president and legal system. It has a distinct identity and culture and a strong sense of national pride in its achievements. That Taiwan is not recognized internationally is because for more than seven decades it has been treated as a pawn in a larger geopolitical game – but mostly it is because of bullying by China.

Those five words – Taiwan is an independent country – can lead to severe retribution against the individual, company or country speaking or even implying them. Ask John Cena, the professional wrestler and star of *F9,* the latest instalment of the *Fast and Furious* movie franchise. Not many things intimidate Cena, at least not in his movie persona. *Fast and Furious* movies might be the ultimate in strutting macho melodramas, but Cena was reduced to a quivering wreck in the face of Communist Party anger when he accidentally called Taiwan a country. In a May 2021 interview with the Taiwanese broadcaster TVBS, he said 'Taiwan is the first country that can watch' the new movie. Trigger Chinese outrage and a quick retreat. 'I made a mistake,' he said in a rapidly released apology video. 'I'm very sorry for my mistakes. Sorry. Sorry. I'm really sorry. You have to understand that I love and respect China and Chinese people.'[1] China is a huge market for *Fast and Furious*, and Cena has a big personal following there, neither of which he wanted to jeopardise.

Cena joined a long list of celebrities and companies who have issued grovelling apologies or 'corrections' after stepping into a political minefield that under Xi Jinping has become especially difficult to navigate as he has sought to deny Taiwan any political space, while aggressively asserting China's claims over the island. In a trailer for *Top Gun: Maverick*, the 2022 sequel to the 1986 classic *Top Gun*, eagle-eyed viewers noticed that Tom Cruise's iconic leather jacket had been altered with the removal of a Taiwanese flag that had been among several on the back of the original.[2] The new movie was financed in part by Tencent, a Chinese technology company.

In 2018, China ordered 44 international airlines, including British Airways, Lufthansa and United Airlines, to remove from their websites any reference to Taiwan that would suggest it was an independent country, a move Donald Trump dismissed at the time as 'Orwellian nonsense'. The airlines meekly obeyed, fearful that Beijing would otherwise take punitive action against their China businesses. The BA and Lufthansa websites changed their references to 'Taiwan, China', while American carriers, the last to comply, dropped the Taiwan reference and just listed the airports.[3] That same year, the Chinese authorities briefly shut down the Marriott website, claiming the hotel chain had 'seriously violated national laws and hurt the feelings of the Chinese people' by listing Tibet, Taiwan, Hong Kong and Macau as separate countries in a customer survey. In a statement the company said, 'Marriott International respects the sovereignty and territorial integrity of China. We don't support separatist groups that subvert the sovereignty and territorial integrity of China. We sincerely apologise for any actions that may have suggested otherwise.'[4]

The Communist Party has a particular obsession with maps, scrutinising each and every one, in and out of the country, to see that they adhere to the Party's version of what constitutes its territory. In 2019, customs officers seized and destroyed 30,000 maps that were due for export from Qingdao port in Shandong province because they did not show Taiwan as part of China.[5] Foreign publishers are avoiding putting any type of map – even historic maps – in books for China, since the censorship process is now so tortuous.[6] And it does not stop at the Chinese border: as Qingdao was enforcing Beijing's geography, Chinese students in London were being mobilised by their embassy to demand changes to a London School of Economics art installation, an upside down globe that showed Taiwan in a different colour to China.[7] The

LSE added a disclaimer in the form of a plaque beneath the artwork reading, 'The designated borders, colours and place names do not imply endorsement by the LSE concerning the legal status of any territory or borders.' An asterisk was added beside Taiwan.

During the opening ceremony of the Olympic Games in Tokyo in summer 2021, the American broadcaster NBC displayed a map on the screen as each team entered the stadium, showing their location in the world. When the China map popped up, there was no Taiwan, and Beijing exploded in indignation, the Chinese Consulate in New York claiming the map was incomplete and 'hurt the dignity and emotions of the Chinese people'.[8] Taiwan has been barred from competing under its own name at the Olympics since 1970, when the International Olympic Committee formally recognised Beijing. Since 1981, Taiwan has competed as 'Chinese Taipei' – a name that appears on no maps. Its team is not allowed to display the Taiwanese flag.

In Paris in 2018, Beijing pressured the French government to prevent the Taiwanese team at the Gay Games in that city from competing under its own name. As a result, the organisers changed the team's designation from 'Taiwan' to 'Taipei', but the team was still able to wave the Taiwanese flag and hold a banner reading 'Taiwan' at the opening ceremony. That was enough for the organisers to insist Taiwan compete as 'Chinese Taipei' or 'Taiwan region' and keep the flag under wraps at the next Gay Games, scheduled for 2022 in Hong Kong. As a result, the Taiwan team pulled out.[9]

Taiwanese film-makers were surprised to find that they too represented 'Chinese Taipei' when they participated in the 2021 Venice International Film Festival. Films made by Tsai Ming Liang, an acclaimed Taipei-based film-maker, were submitted under the name 'Taiwan', as they had been in the past, but organisers changed the name in the event listings. The festival made no public statement about the change, and provided no explanation to the Taiwanese. It seemed a festival that has long trumpeted its willingness to stand up for artistic freedom was not willing to stand up to pressure from China.[10]

Not even the most innocuous of nongovernmental organisations has been spared. At the United Nations, Chinese diplomats have obsessively scrutinised applications by NGOs for UN consultative status, blocking those that do not use the 'correct terminology' for Taiwan. Consultative status is important since it allows NGOs to participate in UN proceedings. China has been the most active country in stalling groups that include a South Korean NGO that maintains long-distance walking trails, the Women's Entrepreneurial Day Organization and the World Yoga Community, which were required to modify their websites to the satisfaction of Beijing.[11]

Individually, many of Beijing's actions can seem petty – examples of Communist Party petulance and small-mindedness. But they demonstrate just how far the Party will go to deny Taiwan any international breathing space. Cumulatively they are designed to force the island to take to the global stage only on China's terms – if at all. But there are times when the impact is far more immediate and damaging – as when Taiwan was hit with a serious flare-up of Covid-19 in April 2021. Beijing's spite became a matter of life and death as it sought to limit Taipei's access to vaccines. Until then, Taiwan had weathered the pandemic well, but its vaccination programme had barely got off the ground. President Tsai Ing-wen said a deal with Germany's BioNTech for the purchase of 5 million shots had been close to completion but was torpedoed by Beijing. 'Because of China's intervention, up to now there's no way we can complete it,' she said.[12] The island's health minister, Chen Shih-chung, said they were close to issuing a press release announcing the contract, when BioNTech asked that the word 'country' be removed from the joint announcement. 'BioNTech suddenly sent a letter, saying they strongly recommend us to change the word "our country" in the Chinese version of the press release,' he said.[13] A week later BioNTech told Taiwan the completion of the deal was on hold due to a 'revaluation of global vaccine supply and adjustment times'. The company, which co-developed its vaccine in partnership with Pfizer, declined to comment on Taiwan's accusations.

China denied applying pressure to BioNTech. It offered to supply the vaccine through Fosun, a Shanghai-based pharmaceutical company, which claimed it had the exclusive licence to distribute BioNTech's vaccine throughout 'Greater China', including what it described as the 'Taiwan Region'. Beijing also offered to donate its own Chinese-developed shots for free. Taiwan turned them down. It accused China of 'faking kindness' and inhumanely blocking vaccines at a time of great need on the island. Taipei has a long-standing policy against buying Chinese-made vaccines, and would never go along with a deal that labels the island as a province of China.[14] BioNTech's commercial ties with Fosun go far deeper than just distribution. In the early days of the pandemic, the Shanghai company bought exclusive Chinese rights to develop and commercialise Covid-19 vaccine products developed using BioNTech's mRNA technology. It agreed to buy a stake in the German firm worth $50 million, and to pay up to $85 million in licencing fees, which may go some way to explain BioNTech's reluctance to cross China – a depressingly familiar story.[15]

Japan and the US stepped forward to donate vaccines to Taiwan, the Japanese government sending an initial 1.2 million doses of AstraZeneca's Covid-19 shot, while America shipped 2.5 million doses of Moderna's vaccine.[16] The American Institute in Taiwan, the de facto US embassy, said the donation reflected the US commitment to Taiwan 'as a trusted friend and an important security partner'.[17] The Grand Hotel Taipei and the Taipei 101 skyscraper, the city's most iconic buildings, were lit up with giant messages of thanks to the US.[18] Eventually, in July 2021, an arm's-length deal was struck with BioNTech under which two of Taiwan's tech giants, Hon Hai Precision Industry (better known as Foxconn) and the chip giant Taiwan Semiconductor Manufacturing Co., stepped in as intermediaries. They agreed to buy millions of jabs, worth $350 million from the German company, and then donate them to the government's Centres for Disease Control for local vaccination.[19]

At the time, China was engaged in aggressive 'vaccine diplomacy' worldwide, and by August 2021 had supplied more than half a billion doses of its home-grown vaccines to more than 100 countries. But there were serious doubts about the effectiveness of the Chinese vaccines, particularly against new variants of Covid-19, and global health experts criticised the Chinese government and its vaccine manufacturers – state-run Sinopharm and privately owned Sinovac – for a lack of transparency about their clinical trials and efficacy data.[20] China's principal aim was to portray itself as a generous benefactor, particularly to poorer countries, and to highlight the apparent stinginess of the West, but more coercive goals were never far from the surface. Paraguay, which at the height of the pandemic recorded the world's highest ratio of deaths to population, was reportedly approached by a broker offering Chinese vaccines in return for cutting diplomatic ties with Taiwan. At the time, Paraguay was one of only fifteen countries with which Taiwan had official ties.[21]

The battle against the coronavirus also bore witness to another facet of China's campaign against Taiwan – Beijing's effort to block Taipei's membership of international organisations. As Beijing has sought to expand its own influence over global governance – Chinese nationals now head four of the United Nations' fifteen specialist agencies – so it has worked to eliminate that of Taipei. In theory at least, the UN is supposed to be a force for global good, promoting international cooperation. In practice, some voices have always been louder than others, and as China has played a more active role, so it has sought to use the UN to advance its own narrow interests and ambitions.[22]

The World Health Organization, currently headed by the China-friendly former Ethiopian Foreign Minister Dr Tedros Adhanom Ghebreyesus, is a particular case in point. In the run-up to the Covid-19 pandemic, the world should have had much to learn from Taiwan's first-class health system, in particular its experience with infectious diseases. Since the SARS outbreak, which originated in China in 2002, Taiwan has built one of the world's most advanced systems of health surveillance, designed to try and identify the emergence of new diseases. It made advance preparations for the next outbreak, including building isolation wards and virus research laboratories. Between 2009 and 2016, Taiwan was able to share its knowledge and experience, participating as an observer in the World Health Assembly (WHA), a body that controls the WHO, and consists of all member states. Then in 2017 Beijing slammed the door shut, using its influence to corral enough countries to block Taiwan completely.

In December 2019, Taiwan identified worrying internal hospital reports emerging in Wuhan that indicated a possible new and threatening virus. The health authorities in Taipei then alerted the WHO, raising concerns in an email about a number of 'atypical pneumonia cases' in the Chinese city that had been 'isolated for treatment', suggesting there was a fear the virus could pass between humans.[23] Taiwan's vice-president Chen Chien-jen, an epidemiologist by training, said the warnings were ignored. The WHO rejected the criticism, claiming Taiwan merely requested information and did not issue a warning.[24]

During the first sixteen months of the pandemic, the response in Taiwan was one of the world's swiftest and most effective. It won global praise, and it seemed there was much that Taipei could share, yet still China's bullying denied it a seat at the world's top table for health. Beijing ignored calls from the G7, a grouping of Western industrial democracies, for Taiwan to attend the WHA, and when New Zealand publicly supported a role for Taipei, it was warned by Beijing to 'immediately stop making wrong statements on Taiwan, to avoid damaging our bilateral relationship'.[25]

The seizure of power by the Taliban in Afghanistan in August 2021 and the messy departure of the US provided plenty of fuel to China's narrative of the arrogant superpower in decline. 'The fall of Kabul marks the collapse of the international image and credibility of the US', crowed Xinhua, the state news agency.[26] Beijing quickly leveraged the events in Afghanistan to pile psychological pressure on Taiwan, warning that Washington was an unreliable ally. 'Afghanistan today, Taiwan tomorrow,' ran a headline in the Communist Party tabloid the *Global Times* before continuing, 'US will abandon Taiwan in a crisis given its tarnished credibility.'[27] While an editorial in the same newspaper warned Taiwan to have a 'sober head' because 'once a war breaks out in the [Taiwan] Straits, the island's defense will collapse in hours and the US military won't come to help'.[28] It carried a cartoon of an American bald eagle ushering the Taiwanese president towards a hole in the ground, and suggested her officials would flee as quickly as their Afghan counterparts.

One commentator in Taipei accused Beijing of 'cheap psychological warfare', but social media on the island was soon buzzing with speculation about whether the US would indeed come to the island's defence. President Tsai Ing-wen herself took to Facebook. 'Recent changes in the situation in Afghanistan have led to much discussion in Taiwan,' she wrote. 'I want to tell everyone that Taiwan's only option is to make ourselves stronger, more united and more resolute in our determination to protect ourselves.'[29] The US withdrawal from Afghanistan coincided with yet more Chinese exercises off Taiwan's south coast. The drills were no doubt planned well before the events in Kabul, but the coincidence of the two raised tensions across the Strait.

The mixture of psychological pressure and military intimidation against Taiwan has reached new peaks under Xi Jinping, and are at the heart of an intense strategy of what has been described as 'grey zone' warfare against the island – a term that covers all manner of tools and techniques of harassment and intimidation that fall short (often only just short) of actual shooting warfare. We have already explored many of these in other contexts, but it is across the Taiwan Strait that they are at their most egregious. Rather in the manner that Xinjiang has served as a sort of laboratory for surveillance and other repressive technology, so Taiwan has become a testing ground for the coercive toolbox of China's new Cold War.

Disinformation is often described by Taiwan as 'cognitive warfare'. Officials in Taipei accused Beijing of using it to spread fake news about the Covid-19 outbreak on the island, including reports that President Tsai Ing-wen had been infected and it was being covered up, and that tens of thousands of Taiwanese people were flocking to China to get vaccinated. China-originated reports also sought to undermine faith in Taiwan's own vaccine programme with false claims that elderly people were dying from the jab – reports blamed for a fall-off in uptake. Other reports claimed Taipei was giving away shots to maintain the loyalty of its diplomatic allies instead of providing them to its people.[30] Most were traced to Chinese state media or China-based trolls or content farms. They were typically amplified by an army of bots using the messaging app Line, which is popular in Taiwan, or other online discussion boards. Taiwan's own feisty media also played an inadvertent role in magnifying disinformation when it picked up reports online without rigorous checks. In response Taiwan has become a pioneer in techniques to counter disinformation.

Throughout 2021, China continued to send menacing forays of aircraft towards and around Taiwan on an almost daily basis. Pressure has also come from the sea; Taiwan's Defence Ministry said that in the first ten months of 2020 it conducted more than 1,200 missions to intercept Chinese military vessels, an increase of a third over the previous year. China can gain useful intelligence from the nature and speed at which Taiwan's air force and navy react, though experts say the broader aim is to wear down and exhaust the island's defence forces and erode their will to fight. The tactics are 'super effective', according to Admiral Lee Hsi-ming, a former head of Taiwan's military. In an interview with the Reuters news agency, he said: 'You say it's your garden, but it turns out that it is your neighbour who's hanging out in the garden all the time. With that action, they are making a statement that it's their garden – and that garden is one step away from your house.'[31]

One of China's latest weapons in its 'grey zone' armoury is the sand dredger. Hundreds of these hulking monsters were deployed off Taiwan's Matsu Islands, the Taiwanese-controlled islands that sit just off the coast of China, and which we visited in Chapter 1. Scores have been expelled by the Matsu coastguard, only to come creeping back, their loud rumblings echoing day and night across the islands.

Fishermen complain that the dredging is killing their industry, and in 2020 dredgers cut an undersea communications cable six times, disrupting internet and telecoms connectivity. 'These huge titans are intruding into Taiwan's waters and wearing down our coastguards,' said Lii Wen, a Matsu opposition politician, while Su Tzu-yun, an analyst at the Institute for National Defense and Security Research, a think tank backed by Taiwan's Defence Ministry, described the invasion of the sand dredgers as 'psychological warfare'.[32]

China has also stepped up cyberattacks. In July 2021, Taiwanese officials claimed they was facing 30 million cyberattacks every month – an astonishing 700 attacks every minute. They said about half of these originated from China, and that Taiwan has become one of the top targets of cyberattacks anywhere in the world.[33] Most were probes or scans, searching for weaknesses in computer systems – often characterised by cyber security experts as reconnaissance missions. Officials insisted their defences were largely holding, and they were successfully defending against the overwhelming majority. But there were still several hundred breaches, with targets including Government agencies and officials, educational institutions and tech companies. The aims of the hackers ranged from espionage to vandalism and sabotage, and Taipei warned its people to be on the alert for 'omnipresent infiltration'.[34]

Economic ties between Taiwan and China, which have grown closer in recent years, have been leveraged increasingly as a means of coercion. As we shall examine in more detail later, Taiwanese companies have invested heavily in China and shifted production lines there. This has no doubt helped the island's economy, but also created dependencies and vulnerabilities, which Beijing has not hesitated to exploit. Even tourists have been used as a tool against Taipei. After constraints on travel were relaxed in 2011, the number of tourists from China grew rapidly to the point where by 2016 they constituted the biggest single group of visitors. Then when President Tsai Ing-wen took office that year, beating China's preferred candidate, China showed its disapproval by drastically curbing travel, dealing a serious blow to the island's tourism industry.[35]

At the same time as honing his 'grey zone' toolkit, Xi Jinping is overseeing one of the largest military build-ups and modernisations ever seen during peacetime – much of it designed to invade Taiwan and deter America from intervening. Every year since 2000, America's Department of Defense has been required by law to submit to Congress a report on military and security developments involving China. To mark its twentieth year, the 2020 report was something of a retrospective. It recalled how the very first report had described the People's Liberation Army as a sizeable but largely archaic force that lacked the capabilities, organisation and readiness for modern warfare, and was focused largely on waging a large-scale land warfare along China's borders. It went on:

> The PLA's ground, air, and naval forces were sizable but mostly obsolete. Its conventional missiles were generally of short range and modest accuracy. The PLA's emergent cyber capabilities were rudimentary; its use of information technology was well behind the curve; and its nominal space capabilities were based on outdated technologies for the day. Further, China's defense industry struggled to produce high-quality systems. Even if the PRC could produce or acquire modern weapons, the PLA lacked the joint organizations and training needed to field them effectively.[36]

No longer. 'The PRC [People's Republic of China] has marshalled the resources, technology, and political will over the past two decades to strengthen and modernize the PLA in nearly every respect,' the DoD reported, and it warned: 'China is already ahead of the United States in certain areas.' It described how China now had the largest navy in the world, with 350 ships and submarines at the time the report was written, compared with a US naval force of 293. China was also ahead in land-based conventional ballistic and cruise missiles and in integrated air defence systems, and had restructured its forces to be better suited to joint operations. The report noted that an invasion of Taiwan would still be one of the most complicated and difficult military operations, but that the PLA continues to build the ability to do so, while at the same time, 'The PLA is developing capabilities to provide options for the PRC to dissuade, deter, or, if ordered, defeat third-party intervention during a large-scale, theater campaign such as a Taiwan contingency.' For members of Congress, it made for sobering reading.

The warning was echoed by Sir Stuart Peach, NATO's most senior military officer. 'It is quite shocking how quickly China has built ships, how much China has modernised its air force, how much it has invested in cyber and other forms of information management, not least facial recognition,' he said in a June 2021 interview, shortly before he stepped down.[37] Peach, who headed NATO's military committee for three years, then posed the question, 'What do you do if you're a leader in China with a modernised powerful large force? You deploy it, you move it around.' The interview came just a few days after NATO warned for the first time that Beijing posed 'systemic challenges' to the rules-based international order.

Back in 2000, when America's Defence Department was making its first report to Congress, the PLA simply did not have the capability to invade Taiwan. It could huff and puff about 'separatist forces' on the island, but the threats had a *pro forma* feel about them. They brought to mind the Daleks in the BBC series *Dr Who*, who screamed 'exterminate, exterminate' so frequently it became background noise. At that time, Taiwan's US-supplied armed forces were considered to be technically superior, better trained and more than able to repulse any attack. By law the US is required to supply Taiwan with arms sufficient for its defence. The 1979 Taiwan Relations Act states that 'The United States will make available to Taiwan such defense articles and defense services in such quantity as may be necessary to enable Taiwan to maintain a sufficient self-defense capability.' In practice, US presidents have interpreted this in different ways over the years, but arms sales have included advanced fighter jets, air defense missiles, naval frigates and anti-ship missiles, attack helicopters, anti-tank weapons, tanks, and other weapons and equipment.[38]

The Taiwan Relations Act is one of the cornerstones of what has become known as 'strategic ambiguity'. It does not explicitly state that the US will come to the defence of Taiwan should China attack, but it does commit America to 'consider any effort to determine the future of Taiwan by other than peaceful means, including by boycotts or embargoes, a threat to the peace and security of the Western Pacific area and of grave concern to the United States'. This was largely academic at a time when China's rise appeared to be benign and its military prowess limited. Neither is now the case, and as the military balance across the Taiwan Strait has moved sharply in China's favour, few strategists see much hope of the island holding out for long without US help. 'China's multi-decade military modernization effort has eroded or negated many of the military advantages that Taiwan has historically enjoyed in the context of a cross-Strait conflict,' as the Department of Defense puts it.[39] In terms of raw numbers, Taiwan is now significantly out-gunned, as the DoD lays out in stark detail:

## Taiwan Strait Military Balance, Ground Forces 2020

| | CHINA | | TAIWAN |
|---|---|---|---|
| | Total | East and Southern Theatres | Total |
| Total Ground Force Personnel | 1,030,000 | 412,000 | 88,000* |
| Group Armies | 13 | 5 | 3 |
| Combined Arms Brigades | 78 | 30 (5 amphibious) | N/A |
| Mechanised Infantry Brigades | N/A | N/A | 3 |
| Motorised Infantry Brigades | N/A | N/A | 6 |
| Armour Brigades | N/A | N/A | 4 |
| Air Assault/Army Aviation Brigades | 15 | 5 | 2 |
| Artillery Brigades | 15 | 5 | 3 |
| Airborne Brigades | 7 | 7 | 0 |
| Marine Brigades | 8 | 4 | 3 |
| Tanks | 6,300 | | 800 |
| Artillery Pieces | 6,300 | | 1,100 |

*Only includes active-duty personnel

Source: US Department of Defense

## Taiwan Strait Military Balance, Air Forces 2020

| | CHINA | | TAIWAN |
|---|---|---|---|
| | Total | Eastern and Southern Theatre | Total |
| Fighters | 1,500 (2,700*) | 600 (750*) | 400 (500*) |
| Bombers/Attack | 450 | 250 | 0 |
| Transport | 400 | 20 | 30 |
| Special Mission Aircraft | 150 | 100 | 30 |

*Totals in parenthesis include fighter trainers

Source: US Department of Defense

**Taiwan Strait Military Balance, Naval Forces 2020**

| | CHINA | | TAIWAN |
|---|---|---|---|
| | Total | Eastern and Southern Theatre | Total |
| Aircraft Carriers | 2 | 1 | 0 |
| Cruisers | 1 | 0 | 0 |
| Destroyers | 32 | 23 | 4 |
| Frigates | 49 | 37 | 22 |
| Corvettes | 49 | 39 | 0 |
| Landing Ships, Tank/Amphibious Transport Dock | 37 | 35 | 14 |
| Medium Landing Ships | 21 | 16 | 0 |
| Diesel Attack Submarines | 46 | 32 | 2 |
| Nuclear Attack Submarines | 6 | 2 | 0 |
| Ballistic Missile Submarines | 4 | 4 | 0 |
| Coastal Patrol (Missile) | 86 | 68 | 44 |
| Coastal Guard Ships | 255 | N/A | 23 |

Source: US Department of Defense

A 2019 study for the International Institute for Strategic Studies estimates that China is targeting 1,200 short-range ballistic missiles, 400 land-attack cruise missiles and an unknown number of medium-range ballistic missiles at the island. It predicts that the ability of the US to successfully intervene on behalf of Taiwan in any conflict will have gone by 2030, such is the pace of China's modernisation:

> Taiwan could once arguably have held its own in a fight with its much larger neighbour, but the cross-strait military balance is now decisively in China's favour. Meanwhile, although the US would still almost certainly prevail in a conflict with China over Taiwan today – albeit with significantly greater cost and risk than was previously the case . . . its ability to do so is rapidly eroding, and will probably be gone within a decade.[40]

China's official defence budget for 2021 was 1.36 trillion yuan (just under $210 billion, based on the exchange rate at that time), a 6.8 per cent increase over the previous year – and a figure that has almost doubled over a decade. China is the second largest military spender in the world after the US, but the figure is difficult to dissect because it is short on detail and excludes a number of major items, including research and development and paramilitaries. Most outside analysts believe the true figure is considerably higher – the Stockholm International Peace Research Institute database gives a figure of just over $252 billion for 2020, almost 40 per cent higher than the official figure given for that year ($183.5 billion).[41] SIPRI's China estimate is still less than a third of US expenditure, but dwarfs Taiwan's planned 2022 defence budget of $16.89 billion.[42]

How precisely would China use its formidable arsenal against Taiwan in order to achieve 'national unification', as the Communist Party likes to describe the subjugation of the island? Drawing on PLA writings and its own analysis, the US Department of Defense identifies four military options which could be used individually or in combination:[43]

- **Air and maritime blockade.** China would aim to prevent any maritime or sea traffic reaching Taiwan, cutting it off from vital supplies and severing it from the rest of the world in a bid to force the island's capitulation. In some scenarios this would be accompanied by targeted missile strikes and the possible seizure of Taiwan's offshore islands. This would be accompanied by large-scale cyberattacks against critical infrastructure and information warfare aimed at isolating the Taiwanese people.
- **Limited force or coercive options.** This would involve the targeted use of force against Taiwan's military, political and economic targets, aimed at undermining confidence of Taiwan's population in its leaders. It could be accompanied by the use of special forces against infrastructure or leadership targets.
- **Air and missile campaign.** China would use missiles and other air strikes against defence targets, including air bases, ports and communications facilities in order to degrade Taiwan's defences. It would likely be accompanied by an attempt to take out Taiwan's leaders. The aim would be to break the island's will to fight. Some analysts have also suggested this phase might be accompanied by

missile and air strikes on US assets deployed nearby – possibly including bases in Japan and Guam.[44]

- **Invasion of Taiwan.** Most analysts regard this as the final part of any campaign against the island. Judging by what we have seen of China's preparations, this would likely comprise a joint operation by air, sea and electronic assets, aiming to break through degraded shore defences and establish a beachhead on the island. Of all the options open to China, most experts agree this is the hardest to pull off.

Estimates vary, but it is assumed that if it came to an invasion, anything between 300,000 and 2 million combat troops, along with thousands of tanks, artillery pieces, rocket launchers and armoured personnel carriers would need to cross the Taiwan Strait. It would be an operation of unprecedented size and complexity, and the preparations would be impossible to hide. Ian Easton, a Taipei-based analyst who has studied PLA writings on Taiwan, likens it to a deadly relay race in which every team member must perform at their best and dropping the baton at any time could be fatal.[45] It is all very well having all the shiny new kit, but China's ability to join it all up is untested. This is what military types often refer to as C4ISR – the sophisticated command, control, communications, computers, intelligence, surveillance, and reconnaissance networks required to get the most out of (and defend) the deadliest of conventional weapons.[46]

China has not fought a war on any scale since its 1979 invasion of Vietnam, a very different type of conflict, which did not end well for Beijing. It should not be forgotten that the PLA is the armed wing of the Communist Party. It is a political military, answering to the CCP and is not a professional military in the Western sense. Modern warfare requires an enormous amount of flexible and innovative thinking, the ability to adapt to a changing battlefield and to adopt new doctrines as needed. China has worked hard to modernise thinking and practices in what used to be a sclerotic, bloated and corrupt machine (much like the Party), but again it is untested.

Perhaps Taiwan's most important allies are the island's geography and the climate of the Taiwan Strait. The coastal terrain of the main island is described by Ian Easton as a 'defender's dream', with only fourteen beaches regarded as suitable for an amphibious landing. Most of the east coast is made up of cliffs, while beaches on the west coast are lined with densely populated towns, mud flats, paddies or other coastal ponds. 'From the perspective of Chinese military experts, there are simply no good places to land on Taiwan with a large enough force to quickly steamroll into Taipei,' Easton writes.[47] Then there are the treacherous waters and winds of the Taiwan Strait, known as *heishuigou* or the 'Black Ditch' in local dialect, which means there are only two realistic windows for an invasion every year – late March to the end of April, or late September to the end of October.

In planning its defence, Taiwan has leveraged these natural advantages. The island's geography has been extensively studied by military strategists, and Taiwan's elaborate defences against attack from the sea include forests of steel spikes, layers of sea mines to protect the approaches to vulnerable beaches and what has been dubbed 'seawalls of fire' – an underwater system of pipelines that would release gas and oil ahead of advancing invasion forces, which would be ignited by gunfire.[48] Assuming they got ashore, combat operations could be equally as daunting, and if China eventually prevailed against Taiwan's army, the PLA would then have to subdue a hostile population – though tough internal repression is one area in which Beijing does have plenty of experience. Lazy comparisons are often made to the D-Day landings during the Second World War, which took place along a relatively flat fifty-mile stretch of seafront in rural Normandy. Not only would an operation against Taiwan be much more difficult in practical terms, but the analogy is extremely spurious. The D-Day landings were an act of liberation from the Nazis, an invasion of Taiwan would be an attempt to impose tyranny on a democracy.

Speaking in October 2021, against the background of increased military intimidation of the island, Xi Jinping said, 'The historical task of the complete reunification of the motherland must be fulfilled, and will definitely be fulfilled.'[49] Over the years, China has combined the carrot and the stick in its efforts to bring that about, but under Xi there has been a sharp shift towards the latter. Beijing has always avoided putting a timescale on its ambitions, but it has long been assumed that 2049, the 100th anniversary of the communist's seizure of power in China was the target for seizing Taiwan. However, time is not on Xi's side. With each year that passes, Beijing is losing more hearts and minds on Taiwan. Perhaps that is why Xi Jinping has shown far greater urgency, and the threatening rhetoric has reached new levels. The Daleks seem a good deal more menacing. 'National unification' is a central part of

Xi Jinping's nationalist agenda – his 'Chinese Dream' of the national rejuvenation. He is armed with an 'anti-secession law' that states that 'non-peaceful means' would be deployed in the event 'that possibilities for a peaceful reunification should be completely exhausted'. He appears to be dangerously boxing himself in over Taiwan. Yet while his military is now immensely more powerful than in the past, Taiwan would still be no push over – with or without American intervention.

China's military planners no doubt hope that resistance fades away quickly, and the steady application of pressure, the anaconda strategy, pays dividends – that Taiwan loses the will and ability to fight well before the invasion forces wade ashore. One of the aspects of the US withdrawal from Afghanistan that Chinese state propaganda played up (alongside US reliability as an ally) was how quickly the old regime abandoned the country, drawing comparisons with what might happen in Taiwan. For all Xi's chest-thumping, an attempted invasion would be a big gamble that could quickly spin out of control. The stakes are huge, and not just for Taiwan and the strategic balance in the region – it is hard to see how Xi (and perhaps even the Communist Party itself) could survive a humiliating defeat over the island, whose 'recovery' they have made such a centrepiece of their identity.

Under US pressure, Taiwan's defence strategy is changing and becoming smarter. Strategists know they cannot match China gun for gun and are increasingly looking at how they can make better use of the island's natural advantages. Instead of investing in costly high-profile pieces of kit, they are increasingly looking at such weapons as smart mines, drones, highly mobile missile launchers, coastal cruise missile defences, and small, fast and resilient ships. It is a more asymmetrical type of warfare that has been dubbed the 'porcupine strategy', aiming to raise the cost of any attempted invasion and make the island more indigestible. 'The PLA's weakness is in the phase of sea transit,' according to a report from Taiwan's Defence Ministry. 'The [Taiwanese] Armed Forces must take full advantage of the natural barrier of the Taiwan Strait and fight in a resilient manner.'[50] The Taiwanese military increasingly assumes a blockade of airports and ports, cutting off air and sea lines of communications, would be Beijing's initial strategy, though Taiwan's defence minister warned that China will be able to launch a full-scale invasion by 2025. Chui Kuo-cheng told the *China Times* in October 2021 that the current tensions were the worst in forty years.[51]

In November 2021, China announced that it would hold those supporting 'Taiwan independence' criminally liable for life. Those deemed 'stubbornly pro-independence' would be barred from China and from dealing with Chinese entities, and as long as they lived be subject to Communist Party 'justice' for the 'crime' of supporting self-determination. It marked another ratcheting up of the rhetoric. Yet, for all Beijing's noise, its intimidation of the island, its growling at anybody who as much as implies Taiwan has a separate identity or hinting that it has a right to determine its own future, there is one overriding factor that is too frequently overlooked – the People's Republic of China's claim over the island is legally and historically extremely flimsy.

## CHAPTER 9

# *The Myth of 'One China': Why Taiwan is an Independent Country*

'We don't want to be bothered with unification, don't want to be ruled by others and we're proud to tell anyone we are Taiwanese.'

Lee Teng-hui, former president of Taiwan, speaking at an election rally in January 2012

The tranquil shrine is surrounded by trees and seems strangely out of place in the centre of Tainan, a bustling coastal city in the southwestern corner of Taiwan. A horizontal plaque above the entrance reads, 'Unrivalled among the ancients', and in its main hall is a sculpture of a seated man in traditional robes, with a small beard and an impassive almost solemn look on his face. This is Zheng Chenggong, better known as Koxinga. The shrine in Tainan is the best known of more than a hundred temples across Taiwan dedicated to him, and the sculpture is one of many images and statues in his memory. Yet like so much else in Taiwanese history, Koxinga is a deeply contested figure.

He was born on Hirado Island in Japan in 1624, the son of a Japanese mother and a Chinese father, who is variously described as a merchant or a pirate. At the time, the distinction was blurry, but Koxinga's father was a powerful man, heading a sprawling maritime trading empire that stretched from his home province of Fujian in China to Japan. Koxinga stayed with his mother in Japan until he was seven years old, then joined his father in China, moving into the family mansion in Quanzhou, which sits just up the coast from Xiamen, looking out onto the Taiwan Strait. By then his father was a military leader of the Ming Dynasty, the embattled empire appointing him 'Admiral of the Coastal Seas'. By most accounts Koxinga was a diligent student, studying classics and successfully sitting imperial exams, and becoming a military commander aged twenty-two. By then the Ming were coming under pressure from the northern Manchus, who in 1644 captured Beijing and established the Qing Dynasty.

The remnants of the Ming retreated south, first to Nanjing and then to the southeast coast. Koxinga's mother, who had belatedly joined her husband and son in China, killed herself, and his father defected to the Qing. But Koxinga continued the fight, and among the many heroics attributed to him was the sinking of the Manchu fleet off the Kinmen islands in 1656. By then he was leader of the resistance, but it was crumbling fast and soon confined to Kinmen and an enclave around Xiamen. Koxinga knew his days were numbered. He needed a new base from which to rebuild, so he assembled a force of 25,000 soldiers and 400 war junks and sailed for Taiwan, then a fledgling Dutch colony. In 1662, after a nine-month siege of the main Dutch fortification at Fort Zealandia, just outside modern-day Tainan, the Dutch were expelled, and Koxinga established the Kingdom of Tungning on the island. From Taiwan, he plotted his return to China to resume battle against the Qing, but died, probably of malaria, aged thirty-seven, a year after his victory over the Dutch. He was succeeded by his eldest son, who ruled the kingdom until 1681. The Manchus took advantage of the messy succession struggle and in 1683 an invasion fleet put an end to the short-lived kingdom.[1]

That all leaves plenty of room for myth-making, at which Beijing excels. China has built its own statue of Koxinga, a fifty-feet high granite monstrosity that looks out over Xiamen harbour. In Beijing's narrative, you'll be lucky to find anything about his Japanese heritage – travel guides claim this 'son' of Xiamen and 'famous hero' was born in China.[2] He is used by the Communist Party to bolster an increasingly strident cultural nationalism, celebrated primarily for despatching foreign colonialists and supposedly making Taiwan an inalienable part of China. As another Xiamen city guide puts it, Koxinga was 'the great nationalist who recovered Taiwan from Dutch imperialists, restoring it to its proper place in Chinese territorial domain'.[3] The 'great admiral' has been enlisted into Beijing's campaign to 'recover' Taiwan; an annual lantern festival in Koxinga's 'hometown' of Quanzhou ends with local people shooting firecrackers at hanging castles made of paper and bamboo. The fiery ritual is supposedly inspired by artillery training Koxinga's army undertook while preparing to invade Taiwan. With the area around Xiamen bristling with missiles aimed at the island, the message is hardly subtle. The Party has also used him to stress 'brotherhood' and 'common ancestry' between the two sides of the Taiwan Strait, while for China's current leaders he also represents a broader vision of China's imperial ambitions.[4]

Taiwan doesn't see it that way. Koxinga is regarded as the original ancestor, the man who created the free nation-state of Taiwan, and who represents the beginning of separate Taiwanese identity. Many biographies also credit Koxinga with bringing a degree of order and administrative efficiency to Taiwan. The Dutch before him only ever controlled the western plains of the island, with much of the coast remaining a haven for pirates, smugglers and outlaws of every ilk. The heartlands were the home of headhunting tribes – even Koxinga was cautious about venturing too far into the interior. Many in Taiwan view Koxinga not as a man who established Chinese rule, but as a great sage who 'heroically led persecuted, fearful and dissident Chinese to a new land of hope and promise away from the chaos of the mainland'.[5] As Koxinga consolidated his position on Taiwan, the Manchus ordered all people living within ten miles of the Chinese coast to move inland in an effort to cut Koxinga off from supplies and support. Millions were forced to abandon fertile land and fishing grounds, and many followed Koxinga to Taiwan rather than endure the resulting poverty.[6]

The image of the island as a place of refuge from mainland tyranny and hardship still endures. Wu'er Kaixi, a leader of the 1989 Tiananmen Square protests who we will meet later in this book, is now a prominent political commentator on the island. Wang Dan, another veteran of Tiananmen Square, lived and taught in Taiwan before moving to the United States. More recently, many participants of the pro-democracy movement in Hong Kong sought refuge in Taiwan – not all of them successfully. In August 2020, the Chinese coastguard intercepted twelve activists who fled from Hong Kong by speedboat in a bid to reach Taiwan and claim political asylum.[7] They were kept for months without charge and without access to their families or independent lawyers before being jailed after a closed trial in the Chinese city of Shenzhen.[8] Their plight attracted enormous attention and sympathy in Taiwan. As we shall see later, Communist Party repression in Hong Kong has had a profound impact on attitudes on the island.

Yet another view of Koxinga can be found among Taiwan's indigenous people, the ancestors of the headhunters of folklore, to whom he is just another colonialist – like the Dutch before him, and the Qing,

Japanese and the nationalists of Chiang Kai-shek who came later. Those who lived in the remote, rugged and inhospitable eastern areas of the island, had a fearsome reputation for hostility to outsiders, and consequently were largely left to their own devices. It was not until Japan occupied Taiwan that any serious attempt was made to forcibly assimilate them. The Japanese colonialists also had their uses for Koxinga, stressing his mixed heritage in propaganda to prove a deep connection between the Taiwanese and Japanese people, while Japanese nationalists attributed his martial spirit to his Japanese blood.[9] Perhaps the only firm conclusion to be drawn from these multiple interpretations of Koxinga's legacy is that Taiwan has a very complex history. It has all contributed to the multiple identities of modern Taiwan. It is certainly not the monochromic version of the past that the Chinese Communist Party would wish to impose to justify its dubious claims.

Too many contemporary Western analyses of Taiwan give the impression that the island's history began in 1949, when Chiang Kai-shek retreated to the island with his defeated Nationalist army. The dispute with China too often is presented as a family quarrel, an unresolved issue from the civil war. Or else Taiwan is treated as a bit player, a pawn in a wider geopolitical game, its future and its interests to be haggled and traded over, rather than the enormously successful democratic state and economic and technological powerhouse it has become – fully deserving of respect and support in its own right. Taiwan is all too frequently described as a 'question', an 'issue' or a 'problem', rather than something with its own intrinsic values. Not only does this play into China's narrative, but it dehumanises the Taiwanese people, and denies the island's achievements, its complexities, and its rich and separate history.

Beijing's assertion of sovereignty over the island has a dubious basis in law and history. Needless to say, Taiwan's history goes back well before 1949. In the colourful words of Taiwan-based author John Grant Ross, 'Until the early twentieth century, Taiwan was one of the wildest places in Asia. Its coastline was known as a mariners' graveyard, the mountainous interior was the domain of headhunting tribes, while the lowlands were a frontier area where banditry, feuding, and revolts were a way of life.'[10] Taiwan's indigenous people trace their roots on the island back thousands of years. Their ancestors are thought to have migrated from Oceania and Southeast Asia. Today they comprise around

2.5 per cent of Taiwan's population, with sixteen recognised tribes living across the country, and they have become an important part of modern Taiwan's identity. Until the Second World War, the island was more commonly referred to as Formosa – or Ilha Formosa. This means 'beautiful island' and is thought to have originated in the early part of the sixteenth century with passing Portuguese traders. Between 1626 and 1638, the Spanish established trading bases on the island, including in Keelung on the northern tip, from where they attempted to expand ties with Japan. Their efforts however were short-lived and a combination of poor trade, typhoons, malaria and hostile indigenous tribes, drove them away. The Dutch had better staying power. The Dutch East India Company (VOC) established its base in 1624 close to what is now the city of Tainan. The Dutch began to open the island to the outside world, created an administrative structure, and brought in Chinese settlers to work the land. They traded in sugar, rice, silk and satin, porcelain, pepper, nutmeg and cinnamon, and kept the indigenous tribes at bay with a combination of co-option and brutality. It seems to have been lucrative for them, and they would no doubt have stayed longer if not for the arrival of Koxinga.

As we have seen, Koxinga's initial aim was not so much the conquest of Taiwan, but to use it as a military base for loyalists who wanted to restore Ming rule in China. The short-lived kingdom he created was defeated in 1683 by Qing military commander Admiral Shi Lang. More recently, when China acquired its first aircraft carrier, bought second-hand from Ukraine, there were reports that it would be named after Shi. But Beijing changed its mind, eventually commissioning the refitted vessel in 2012 as *Liaoning*. It's not clear why, but it does indicate the challenges faced by those manipulating history. Naming the ship Shi Lang would have sent a message of intent to Taiwan, but could perhaps have complicated the propaganda that depicted Koxinga, whose descendants Shi defeated, as a great Chinese patriot and anti-colonial warrior.[11]

The Qing ruled Taiwan for 212 years, but only partially and with no great enthusiasm. The aim had been to defeat the last remnants of Ming resistance to the Manchus, rather than to occupy the island. 'Taiwan is nothing but an isolated island on the sea far away from China, it has long since been a hideout of pirates, escaped convicts, deserters and ruffians, therefore, there is nothing to gain from retaining it,' stated one report to the Qing emperor, which also advocated shipping Han

Chinese migrants 'back to their homes in China.'[12] The emperor also had his doubts, stating in 1683, 'Taiwan is outside our empire and of no great consequence.'[13] He even offered to have the Dutch buy it back, but reluctantly chose to retain his new possession. The Qing were in a state of almost constant warfare with the indigenous people – by one estimate there were more than 100 recorded rebellions, some requiring the deployment of thousands of troops from the mainland. This has been characterised by Taiwanese historians as 'Every three years an uprising, every five years a rebellion', with the Manchu treated as a foreign colonial regime.[14] At the time of Koxinga's death, the number of Chinese settlers roughly equalled the indigenous population, but as more settlers arrived they increasingly encroached on traditional aboriginal land, and the number of conflicts soared.

Yu Yonghe, a writer who travelled across the island shortly after it fell into Qing hands, divided the indigenous people into two categories: plains savages, who had to some degree been assimilated, and whom he described as 'cooked', and the mountain tribes whom he called 'wild' or 'raw savages'. He wrote a memoir in 1697 entitled *Small Sea Travel Diaries*, which provides a colourful flavour of the fear the indigenous tribes instilled in the Qing occupiers:

> The wild savages live in holes in the ground and they drink blood and eat hair . . . The plains savages fear them and do not dare enter their territory. The wild savages are especially fierce and strong; they often come out to burn houses and kill people. Then they return to their lairs so there is no way to get near them. When they kill, they take the head, and when they return they cook it. They strip the skull and sprinkle it with red powder, setting it before their door.[15]

In 1729, the Qing administration tried to seal off the 'wild savages', prohibiting Chinese settlers from venturing into the mountain areas. A 'boundary line' known as the 'red line' because of the colour of the markings was established running down the western side of Taiwan's central mountains. It was a recognition that the rugged eastern part of the island was ungovernable. Qing officials disavowed responsibility for anything that happened beyond the red line, and the area remained beyond the control of the Qing administration for the rest of its rule over the island.[16]

The Qing Dynasty's patchy rule over Taiwan ended in 1895, with China's defeat in the First Sino-Japanese War. Under the Treaty of Shimonoseki, Beijing ceded Taiwan to Japan 'in perpetuity'. It would take decades for Japan to bring the aboriginals in the mountains under control – the first time that had been done. There was resistance and plenty of brutality, but for the most part Japan's colonial rule over the island and its integration into the Japanese empire is remembered in modern Taiwan as relatively benign, at least compared with elsewhere in Asia – especially in China. As John Grant Ross writes:

> Japanese colonialism in Taiwan is not a story of blacks and whites. It was a mixture of militarism, harsh rule, and economic exploitation, counterbalanced with progressive, honest, and efficient government. In many ways, Japanese rule was superior to the Chinese governance that came before and after it, and old people still speak of the Japanese occupation (1895–1945) as a time of law and order, a time when there was no need to lock your door. Colonization on the beautiful isle was the least harsh of Japan's overseas adventures and today the legacy is as much goodwill as animosity. The president, for example, works in the Japanese-built Presidential Office Building.[17]

Lee Teng-hui, Taiwan's first democratically elected president, studied in Japan and spoke better Japanese than Mandarin. Fifty years of Japanese occupation had many lasting impacts, influencing the physical layout and management of cities, customs and even cuisine, as the island took on a more hybrid identity, which is still very evident today.[18] The island became more economically advanced than China, its residents enjoying a higher standard of living.[19]

It is not clear how important strategic considerations were in Japan's decision to annex the island in 1895 as a prize of war. It may well be that it merely saw Taiwan as a logical extension of the island chain of which Japan is part, but as Tokyo's imperial ambitions grew it quickly came to appreciate the island's wider significance. It became a base for expansion into Southeast Asia, and during the Second World War it was an important staging post and supply base for Japanese forces. And as with the early pirates who based themselves in Taiwan, Japan quickly appreciated the island's ideal location from which to harass shipping along the Chinese coast and in the sea lanes between Japan and Southeast Asia.[20] As the Second World War progressed, Taiwan's strategic importance was well appreciated by the US military. A restricted document published in 1944 by the Office of the Chief of Naval Operations said, 'The movement of Japanese troops and supplies throughout the southern theatres of action depends upon the efficiency of the airfields and ports of Taiwan,' before going on to say, 'The island of Taiwan (Formosa) dominates the China coast and all coastwise shipping between Japan and southeastern Asia. Japanese officials refer to it as "the nation's great plane carrier in the South".'[21] As we shall see later, this notion of the island as an 'unsinkable aircraft carrier' and its wider strategic significance are now playing into contemporary discussions of Taiwan's strategic significance – not least in Japan.

Tokyo's rule over Taiwan ended with Japan's defeat in 1945, at which point the victorious allies handed the island to the Republic of China, which was then ruled by Chiang Kai-shek's nationalists. Yet China showed no real interest in regaining Taiwan until the early 1940s. Chiang was far more interested in regaining Manchuria and also getting his hands on Korea and the Ryukyus Islands (which include Okinawa) than he was on Taiwan.[22] Neither was there unanimity in American ranks about the wisdom of handing over the island to Chiang. George Kerr, an American diplomat based in Taiwan at the time, drafted a memorandum for the US War Department in which he advocated independence or else a temporary Allied trusteeship until such a time as the Taiwanese could hold a plebiscite to decide their own future.

Kerr went on to write what remains one of the most influential books ever written in English about Taiwan.[23] The title, *Formosa Betrayed*, sums up his own feelings about American policy and Washington's decision to hand the island to Chiang. 'We were treating five million Formosans as chattel property, to be transferred from one sovereignty to another without reference to their wishes,' he writes.[24] He likens it to the decision to allow Russia to occupy Prague and Berlin, and characterises Taiwan as 'an island, settled long ago by Chinese who had left China proper to get away from it and with a centuries-long tradition of separation and pioneer independence'.[25] The book bristles with anger. Kerr regarded Chiang Kai-shek as an unreconstructed thug, and his book chronicles the incompetence, corruption and brutality of the Generalissimo's rag-tag nationalists as they took control of the island.

Initially, Chiang's forces appear to have been welcomed in Taiwan, or at least given the benefit of the doubt. 'Although there was a degree of apprehension in Taiwan about the new regime, the ROC troops and administration were initially welcomed. However, the KMT regime's misrule ensured that this goodwill was quickly lost,' writes Dafydd Fell, a Taiwan scholar at London's School of Oriental and African Studies (SOAS).[26] Low quality and brutal officials were sent to Taiwan and locals were largely excluded from government. 'For most Taiwanese, it was clear that one cruel but efficient colonial regime had been replaced by a cruel, corrupt and inefficient one.'

Economic mismanagement and corruption soon triggered an island-wide rebellion. It was sparked by what became known as the '2-28 incident', which is widely regarded as the single most important event in modern Taiwanese history. On 28 February 1947, anger boiled over after agents from the Monopoly Commission assaulted a cigarette seller, who they accused of peddling contraband. An angry crowd gathered, one of whom was shot dead. Two of the agents were caught and beaten to death, and rioting quickly spread to cities across the island. Martial law was declared, and with it an orgy of indiscriminate violence by Chiang Kai-shek's forces.

George Kerr, who was by then a vice-consul in the US consulate in Taipei, witnessed some of the violence. He was at home with friends when Nationalist army trucks came rolling slowly down the road in front of his house. 'From them a hail of machine-gun fire was directed at random into the darkness, ripping through windows and walls and ricocheting in the black alleyways,' he writes. During a lull in the fighting he took refuge in the compound of a local hospital, from where he watched the horrifying events unfold from the upper window of one of the buildings.

> From an upper window we watched Nationalist soldiers in action in the alleys across the way. We saw Formosans bayoneted in the street without provocation. A man was robbed before our eyes – and then cut down and run through. Another ran into the street in pursuit of soldiers dragging a girl away from his house and we saw him, too, cut down.
>
> This sickening spectacle was only the smallest sample of the slaughter then taking place throughout the city, only what could be seen from one window on the upper floor of one rather isolated house. The city was full of troops.[27]

Estimates of the number killed in the aftermath of 2-28 vary between 18,000 and 28,000. It was hard to say for sure, because the events of 1947 remained a taboo topic in Taiwan for forty years – talking about it in public could get you jailed, and school textbooks made no mention of it. It was only after martial law was lifted in 1987 and Taiwan began to move towards democracy that the island began to confront its uglier past. In 1995 President Lee Teng-hui made an official apology, and two years later, on the fiftieth anniversary of 2-28, the date was made a national holiday.

In the immediate post-war years, George Kerr was not the only American official wary of Chiang Kai-shek. Many were uneasy about handing Taiwan to China and supportive of allowing the island to determine its own future.[28] The official position was that the Republic of China was occupying the island on behalf of the victorious allies until such a time as its status could be determined, and there were discussions in Washington about taking the future of the island to the United Nations. But such talk was soon overshadowed by Chiang's imminent defeat at the hands of Mao in the Chinese civil war, and the rapidly unfolding Cold War against the Soviet Union and communism more generally. By the time the Nationalist army retreated to Taiwan in 1949 and Chiang established his government-in-exile there, dreaming Koxinga-like of retaking the mainland, calculations were changing fast. The following year, North Korean forces attacked South Korea across the 38th parallel, and in October 1950, Mao entered the war, sending a quarter of a million Chinese 'volunteers' across the Yalu River in support of the Communist North – a figure that was to rise to more than three million as the fighting ground on.

Taiwan was suddenly on the front line and crucial to American interests and prestige in the region.[29] President Harry Truman sent the American 7th Fleet to patrol the Taiwan Strait, fearful that an unpredictable Mao might follow his Korean invasion with an attack on Taiwan. 'In these circumstances the occupation of Formosa by Communist forces would be a direct threat to the security of the Pacific area and to the United States,' Truman said.[30] Over the years, Truman had blown hot and cold on the future of Taiwan, but as he despatched the fleet he suggested it was still to be resolved. 'The determination of the future status of Formosa must await the restoration of security in the Pacific, a peace settlement with Japan, or consideration by the United Nations,' he said.[31] The despatch of the fleet was also designed to deter Chiang from any precipitate moves against the mainland. But through the lens of the intensifying Cold War, Chiang was soon transformed in American eyes into the plucky leader of 'Free China', whose corruption and repression of the Taiwanese people and other political opponents was largely overlooked. He enjoyed strong American diplomatic, economic and military support, and dressed up much of his brutality in the language of the fight against communism. Martial law in Taiwan lasted for thirty-eight years, from 1949 to 1987, and the repression of this period became known as the 'White Terror'. Official records state that military courts tried 140,000 people and between 3,000 and 8,000 were executed, although many believe the true figures are far higher.[32]

As we have seen, it was another Cold War calculation that motivated to a large extent the Kissinger–Nixon opening to China, the normalisation of relations and the switching of diplomatic recognition from Taipei to Beijing. By 1972, when Nixon set this in motion with his visit to Beijing, China and the Soviet Union had fallen out and China was seen as a useful counterweight to Moscow. Taiwan was collateral damage. The 'One China Policy' and 'strategic ambiguity' fudges were born of this era, efforts to paper over the cracks and open to wide interpretation – the smoke and mirrors that have become increasingly unsustainable as the years have passed.

To this day, the precise legal status of Taiwan remains unresolved. Supporters of China's claim over Taiwan point to several wartime documents that appear to commit the allies to 'restore' the island to the Republic of China. But there is doubt over their legal status. The most prominent of these documents, the Cairo Declaration of 1943, has been described as neither a treaty nor a binding document. It was not signed, and was merely issued as a press release setting out the policy intent of the wartime allies.[33] George Kerr, the US diplomat who was seeking to shape policy on Taiwan at the time, saw Cairo as a sop to Chiang, quickly forgotten by the allies, but with dangerous long-term implications: 'Before the Chiangs had reached home Roosevelt and Churchill had changed their minds about some of the secret commitments made on the Generalissimo's demand . . . Roosevelt, Churchill and Chiang had "divided up the bearskin before the bear was dead".'[34] Other foreign policy analysts point out that the Cairo Declaration, together with others from Yalta and Potsdam, were always subject to any final peace settlement.[35] That settlement didn't arrive until 1951, when Japan formally relinquished sovereignty over Taiwan as part of the

Peace Treaty of San Francisco, signed in that city. However, the treaty did not determine the legal status of the island, and some scholars have pointed out that with no subsequent international treaties, Taiwan's sovereignty remains undetermined under international law.[36] This all makes for a complex picture, but underscores the frailty of China's claims over Taiwan. What can be said for certain is that there are two entities that have never ruled over Taiwan: the People's Republic of China, which came into being in 1949, and its ruling Communist Party.

At the end of the Second World War, when Taiwan was handed to the Republic of China, the population of the island was around 6 million. Most had migrated from southeastern China over the previous three centuries. These are usually referred to as the native Taiwanese and can be subdivided into two broad groups: the Hoklo, whose ancestors came from southern Fujian province, and the Hakka, who trace their roots to southeast Guangdong province. Taiwan's earliest inhabitants, the aboriginal people, made up around 2–3 per cent of the population, depending on how they are defined. After the defeat of the Nationalists by Mao in 1949, between 1.5 and 2 million mainlanders followed Chiang Kai-shek to the island, coming from all over China. 'The Formosans resented every new arrival. Too much had taken place in the past and the future seemed too uncertain,' writes Kerr.[37]

Over the centuries there has been considerable intermarriage – according to one study around 85 per cent of Taiwan's Hoklo and Hakka people have some aboriginal ancestry.[38] Taiwan's population now stands at around 23.5 million people, and it has become a trend in the last decade or so for Taiwanese to search for any indigenous roots, as a way of expressing their separate identity.[39] The biggest divide remains between the aboriginals and native Taiwanese on the one hand, and the 'mainlanders' who arrived in 1949 and their descendants on the other. Though more blurred than before, this divide continues to run through Taiwanese politics and society.

The mainlanders imposed the Mandarin language on Taiwan and this remains the official language of government and the law, though Hokkien (also known as Taiwanese) is widely spoken and is the common language of everyday life. As we shall see, the Taiwanese people have increasingly celebrated their indigenous culture, and sought to discover their roots. However, the island's contemporary political leaders, even the strongest advocates of independence, have been cautious about publicly renouncing the 'One China Policy', not wanting to provoke Beijing. Perhaps the most outspoken was Lee Teng-hui, Taiwan's first directly elected president. After he left office, he said, 'We don't want to be bothered with unification, don't want to be ruled by others and we're proud to tell anyone we are Taiwanese.'[40] He wrote, 'It is an unquestionable fact that Taiwan does not belong to China' – sentiments well rooted in history, but which earned him the title 'scum of the nation' from China's state media.[41]

There was a time when the United Nations and newly emerging independent states were animated by the principle of self-determination, especially when it related to colonialism and its legacies. In Taiwan's case, that principle has been subordinated to the politics of raw power. Even states that emerged themselves from brutal colonialism are cowed into a numb compliance with China's demands – too afraid to even utter the name 'Taiwan'. During the often fraught negotiations between China and Britain leading up to the 1997 handover of Hong Kong, Beijing made it clear to the last governor, Chris Patten, that as far as it was concerned the future of Hong Kong had nothing to do with the Hong Kong people. Xi Jinping has adopted much the same approach to Taiwan. Yet Taiwan is a thriving democracy – far more so than Hong Kong ever was. No settlement can be imposed on the Taiwanese people. Indeed, its most effective defence might well be democracy itself.

# Chapter 10

# *Why Taiwan Matters*

'In a digital democracy, transparency is about making the state transparent to the public. Under digital authoritarianism, the word 'transparency' means making citizens transparent to the state.'

*Audrey Tang, Taiwan's digital minister, describing Taiwan's Open Government National Action Plan, July 2021*

It is an unusual cartoon, not what you'd expect of a political leader, which is probably why it spread so quickly online. It shows Taiwan's premier Su Tseng-chang wiggling his backside and gesturing towards a caption that reads, 'We only have one butt, don't hoard, don't trust rumours.' It was released in the early stages of the Covid-19 pandemic, in response to online rumours that toilet paper supplies were running low because it was being diverted to manufacture facemasks. A concise graphic explained that Taiwan's toilet paper is made from pulp sourced from South America, while masks are made locally from non-woven fabric.[1] 'Because of that, the panic buying died down. It's piggybacking on an earlier meme, *wǒmen yǒu yí gè dì qiú* – we only have one earth. It's a very popular environmental protection slogan,' says Audrey Tang, Taiwan's digital minister. The premier's wriggling backside rapidly spread online. 'And the panic just went down – I think over a weekend.'

At other times during the pandemic the government used a cartoon dog, a Shiba Inu called Zongchai, to put across important public health messages. Zongchai roughly translates as 'chief executive' and it appeared on Facebook updates and posters, at one point explaining social distancing in terms of keeping three dog-lengths apart. A pigeon in a facemask provided information about travel restrictions. When reports emerged that some schoolboys were being bullied for wearing pink facemasks, male health officials started wearing them at press briefings. To counter rumours of facemask shortages, Tang's team created an app that updated facemask inventories at local pharmacies every thirty seconds.

Tang is the architect of these tactics, which she calls 'humour over rumour'. I met her in Taipei in May 2022 in the grand Japanese colonial-era building that houses the executive branch of Taiwan's government. The atmosphere of the building was stuffy and sober, but Tang's corner office had the informal air of a scrappy tech start-up, with young staffers buried in their computers and walls festooned with Post-it notes. Attention spans are short online, and she told me 'humour over rumour' requires speed and brevity. Two hours is the deadline. 'When we detect a viral conspiracy, the counter measures need to be rolled out within a couple of hours,' she says, with 200 words or fewer containing the facts of an issue. 'The idea very simply put is to make the clarifications even more viral than the conspiracy theories, and we do that by piggybacking on the popular internet memes, piggybacking on self-deprecating humour and things like that.' In this way, she hopes to take back control of the narrative. She works closely with comedians who she has described as 'cherished colleagues'. She talks about her work in a mix of tech-speak and language from the pandemic, saying she is creating 'nerd immunity', inoculating people from disinformation, and tackling an 'infodemic' of false information, which can be more dangerous than any virus.

Initially, Taiwan was one of the most successful countries in the world in combating the coronavirus. During the first fifteen months of the pandemic, the island had just ten deaths and 1,000 documented cases.[2] It had a clear plan and swiftly closed its borders, there was a culture of mask-wearing and an efficient tech-driven system of track, trace and isolation was quickly set up. Public messaging was clear and engaging, and where intrusive tracking was deployed it was done in an open and transparent way and with tight oversight, designed to maintain popular consent – all a sharp contrast to the tactics deployed across the Taiwan Strait, where China's fight against Covid was characterised by claustrophobic surveillance, grim threats and warnings, and a casual brutality towards those defying the Party's hungry algorithms. There could not have been a starker demonstration of two very different systems in action.

The 'infodemic' of disinformation that Tang and her colleagues had to tackle included claims that Covid was completely out of control and the government did not know how to protect its people.[3] After April

2021, when Taiwan faced a spike in cases, the disinformation shifted towards vaccines. The aim was to undermine public confidence in the government's programme and the willingness of allies to help, and to force the island to accept Chinese vaccines. When Japan donated vaccines to Taiwan, online posts falsely claimed the shots had killed scores of elderly. The *Global Times*, a Communist Party tabloid, demanded that Taiwan suspend the vaccine 'for the sake of public health'.[4] There were reports that the Taiwanese economy was suffering badly, citing as evidence a wave of company shutdowns. Tang and her team countered that one with a Facebook post of a cartoon of Chinese zombies on the march through a moonlit graveyard, alongside a caption explaining how the Economics Ministry had closed a number of front companies – the zombies – in a campaign against money laundering.[5]

According to research by the V-Dem Institute, based at the University of Gothenburg in Sweden, Taiwan (along with Latvia) is the liberal democracy most exposed to false information spread by foreign governments.[6] It has been described as 'an open field for a bad actor.'[7] This is in part because it is such an open and vibrant place with a very high rate of internet penetration, but also because Taiwan uses a version of Mandarin Chinese which is similar to the bad actor across the Strait. It is the front line of the Communist Party's international influence operations, which have intensified as Beijing has stepped up its 'grey zone' warfare against the island.[8]

While the coronavirus presented a particular challenge, disinformation was intense in the run-up to the January 2020 presidential election, when Beijing sought to damage Tsai Ing-wen of the more independence inclined Democratic Progressive Party (DPP). She was bidding for a second term in office against Han Kuo-yu of the Kuomintang (KMT), the modern incarnation of Chiang Kai-shek's nationalists, who advocated a more accommodating policy to China. The two parties are usually referred to by their party colours: green for the DPP, and blue for the KMT. Since Taiwan embraced democracy, both have become fairly broad churches, with differing shades of opinion. In office they have for the most part been pragmatic and cautious in their China policy, defending Taiwanese interests while seeking to avoid overly antagonising Beijing. China has been unable (or unwilling) to grasp the complexities of Taiwanese society and its competitive politics. It routinely turns up the volume of threats when the DPP is in government (or fighting for office). This can best be seen as Beijing burnishing its nationalist credentials for a home audience, since in Taiwan it frequently achieves the opposite of what Beijing wants, galvanising support behind those being attacked.

During the campaign for the 2020 presidential election, there were false reports questioning whether Tsai Ing-wen's doctoral dissertation was authentic (the London School of Economics confirmed that it was), of protesters besieging her office and of electoral fraud. Other reports sought to undermine her broader democratic credentials. A fake government notice was circulated saying her government was deporting protesters who fled Hong Kong. Another false report asserted that Joshua Wong, a Hong Kong democracy activist widely admired in Taiwan, had attacked an old man. As with the US presidential election, the goal was to undermine confidence in the democratic system – the legitimacy of the DPP in particular.

In addition to Tang's 'humour against rumour' campaign, the government strengthened laws against spreading harmful rumours, and pressured social media companies, including Facebook, Google and the messaging service Line to more effectively police their platforms. There has been a proliferation of fact-checking platforms aimed at de-bunking disinformation soon after it appears. One of the best known is Cofacts, a chatbot set up by G0V.tw, an online community of technologists and hackers. People are able to send a suspicious article to the chatbot, which will run it against a comprehensive database of flagged content which has been checked by humans, before informing the user about the veracity of the content – all in the space of a few seconds.[9] An organisation called DoubleThink Lab is using machine learning algorithms to try and trace disinformation to its source in Chinese content farms, the online portals that generate fake stories. It also monitors around a million accounts on the Chinese social media sites Weibo and WeChat, and keeps tabs on thousands of Chinese news sites. Puma Shen, the chairperson of DoubleThink Lab, says that an open society like Taiwan cannot eliminate disinformation without compromising its own values. Instead, transparency is the key. 'Punishment is not the right way, but revealing, telling people that it is made in China is the way to go,' he says. That sentiment is echoed by Audrey Tang. 'We can't fight it, the infodemic, through takedowns. I mean there are jurisdictions that use takedowns, the same as they use lockdowns,' she said. 'But we're a liberal democracy. So instead of takedowns we work though public notice, humour over rumour to make sure people understand.'

Much of China's disinformation and propaganda is aimed at

influencing young people, seen as more impressionable and disaffected from politics. As we shall see later, neither of these assumptions hold true, but authorities have stepped up warnings about using Chinese-made apps. Public agencies are already barred from using them, Taiwan's intelligence agencies fearing they could be used to harvest personal information. Officials have cautioned against the use of a popular face-swapping app called Quyan, on which users upload a photograph and then edit their face onto celebrities. Officials fear that when combined with other personal data requested on sign-up, users are leaving themselves wide open to identity theft, or else the information could be used by Chinese intelligence services to create files on individuals.[10]

Young Taiwanese found their own ways to hit back with humour. A Mandarin-language ballad by Taiwan-based rapper Namewee satirising nationalistic Chinese internet users was for a while the most popular YouTube video in Taiwan and Hong Kong. The song, 'Fragile', targeted 'little pink' internet users, a disparaging term for China's patriotic keyboard warriors. 'You're a bad listener, but you can't stop talking and retaliating. I wonder how I have offended you. You assume the world is your enemy,' Namewee rapped. The song also surged briefly in streaming services in China itself, but censors soon swung into action and it was quickly taken down.[11]

In spite of the barrage of disinformation from China, Tsai Ing-wen was the winner of the January 2020 presidential election, earning a second term in office. She achieved a record number of votes, suggesting voters are not only becoming more immune to disinformation, but that it might have been counterproductive, especially at a time when Beijing was stepping up intimidation in multiple other ways. That's certainly how Foreign Minister Joseph Wu saw it. 'Disinformation this year doesn't seem to have the same effectiveness,' he said after the election, comparing it to local elections three years earlier.

To Audrey Tang it is an ongoing battle. Her broader mission is to use technology to improve the way the government interacts with its people – to make tech a servant of democracy. She is an immensely gifted individual, teaching herself to code at eight, and is often referred to as a child prodigy. She was reading classical literature in a variety of languages and solving simultaneous equations by the time she was in first grade, according to her parents.[12] She started her own company at sixteen, and worked for a while in Silicon Valley. In March 2014, she joined Taiwan's student-led Sunflower Movement, which seized control of the national legislature in Taipei. They were protesting against a proposed China free-trade deal negotiated by the then KMT government that many feared would allow Beijing too much influence over key parts of the Taiwanese economy.[13] The sunflower was adopted as a symbol of hope (sunflowers turn towards the sun), and the movement grew into one of the largest protests in Taiwan's history, spreading to the streets around parliament as well as other cities. It succeeded in having the trade deal put on hold, effectively halting the process of greater integration with the economy with China. A notable feature of the movement was its use of the internet and social media to mobilise and organise – with Audrey Tang in charge of communications.

Tang describes herself as a 'conservative anarchist'. 'Basically it's a way to say live and let live with existing institutions, repurposing them if you will, instead of disrupting them or taking them down,' she tells me. She was invited to join the new DPP government in 2016 as a minister without portfolio with responsibility for digital affairs. Then aged thirty-five, she was the youngest-ever minister. She was also the first transgender and non-binary official in the cabinet – 'I'm the first *openly* transgender non-binary minister,' she corrects me. She recalls having to fill in a form when she became a government employee which required her to state her gender – she ticked neither box. When asked what pronoun she prefers, she answers, 'Whatever.' That's her official Twitter designation. 'In my Twitter bio, where people say "he slash him" or "she slash her" or "they slash them", I wrote star slash star. Which is a very geeky way to say whatever.' In computer coding, */* means and/all. She says colleagues respect her openness. 'I'm non-binary on pretty much anything, not just gender,' she says, rejecting rigidly defined political positions. She is also a believer in what she calls 'radical transparency', whereby transparency should be the root or default position in just about everything. To this end she releases a transcript of every conversation and interview she makes in her official capacity. On joining the government she said she did not want access to any classified information which she could not release.

In her mission to make government more transparent, Tang has sought to tap the skills of tech activists in the civic hacker movement, from where she came – the term 'hackers' used here in the traditional, positive sense of problem solvers, rather than its more malign form. Taiwan has a vibrant tech culture, and one early result is a platform called Pol.is, which shares views on policy issues. The aim is to trigger informed debate, gauge the degree of public support on issues and search for a consensus where possible. It has been described as 'a tool for turning crowds into coherence'.[14] A related project is vTaiwan, which has been likened to a crowdsourcing platform, except that rather than being tapped for money, participants are contributing opinions and ideas. It came into its own during spirited debate over online alcohol sales and the future of Uber on the island.[15] Another online platform overseen by Tang hosts and debates online petitions. The petitions are not legally binding, but if one attracts more than 5,000 signatures, participating government agencies must within two months give a point-by-point response and explain why a proposal has been rejected or accepted. Every year since 2018, a presidential hackathon has offered prizes for innovations tackling issues ranging from telemedicine in outlying islands to practical tools for achieving net-zero greenhouse gas emissions.

Tang rejects the top-down approach to government, and sees these initiatives as a way of modernising governance and nurturing public trust. It is early days, and there is debate about the true impact of these projects on public policy, but Tang is keen to draw a clear line between what Taiwan is trying to achieve and the use of technology by the Chinese Communist Party. 'In a digital democracy, transparency is about making the state transparent to the public. Under digital authoritarianism, the word "transparency" means making citizens transparent to the state' is the way she summed it up when launching a new Open Government National Action Plan.[16] She returns to geekery to describe her wider objective. 'So democracy to us is not something static, it's like a semi-conductor or any computer code, it's something that people can contribute to, can improve and share the innovation with the world . . . what we're doing is improving the democratic system so that it has higher bandwidth, lower latency and connects to more.'

Tang has also turned to Taiwan's hacking community for help to fend off Chinese cyber-attacks, now running at unprecedented levels. 'White hat' hackers as they are known (as supposed to the malign 'black hats') are encouraged to stress test government systems and infrastructure, looking for vulnerabilities and letting the government know about them. 'So before we roll out new cyber security services and so on I often personally say let's just have half a year and have the white hats test this infrastructure before they are officially rolled out.'

As China's disinformation campaigns have become more aggressive and increasingly global, Audrey Tang's advice is being sought by other liberal democracies looking for the best strategies to counter Beijing. In November 2021, a delegation of EU lawmakers met the digital minister in Taipei and peppered her with questions about Taiwan's experience. The group was sent by the European Parliament's special committee on foreign interference and disinformation and was the latest in a series of top-level interactions between Brussels and Taiwan.[17]

'What she's doing is amazing,' said Wu'er Kaixi, shaking his head slightly as he pours out his admiration for Audrey Tang. 'She comes from the digital world, she knows that well, she was a coder, and now she is using all these technologies to bridge government and people.' It was September 2021, and I was speaking to Wu'er Kaixi by video link to New York, where the former Tiananmen Square student leader was staying, part of his first trip from his home in Taiwan since before the Covid-19 pandemic. The conversation had quickly turned to the island's transgender digital minister. 'She makes the whole world look at Taiwan and say, "so cool",' he told me. 'She is one of the smartest people I have ever met.' Most important in his view is that Tang, by using tech to improve democracy, is further distancing Taiwan from Xi Jinping's grim surveillance state, which is marching headlong in the other direction – towards a digitally powered totalitarianism. The political gulf between the two sides of the Taiwan Strait has never been wider. 'Beijing is saying democracy is not working, you have to adopt our authoritarian approach,' he says. 'But Taiwan is reforming democracy. The task was laid down to Audrey, asking her to use modern technology to bridge people and government and then she's coming up with all kinds of solutions.'

Wu'er Kaixi was a student at Beijing Normal University in Beijing at the time of the 1989 Tiananmen Square protests. He emerged as one of the key leaders, shooting to prominence as the hunger striker who interrupted and rebuked Chinese Premier Li Peng on national television – two weeks before Li sent in the tanks. He was smuggled out of China through Hong Kong after the massacre, and for a while he was number two on Beijing's most wanted list. He travelled first to France and later studied at Harvard University before settling into exile in Taiwan, where he is now a leading political commentator.

I met him many times over my years reporting from Asia, often on Tiananmen Square anniversaries, interviewing him about his determination to keep the memory alive. He became a fierce advocate for Taiwanese democracy, witnessing it take root on the island in a way he had once dreamed about in China. Pre-Covid, he used to travel a lot, and when he spoke to me from America he was making up for lost time. He had visited Germany, France and Turkey before landing in New York, where he caught up with fellow exiles and supporters from the Tiananmen days, and was preparing to travel to Washington DC to meet policy makers. He said he was amazed how quickly perceptions of China had changed, the world finally waking up to the threatening reality of Xi Jinping's rule. With that has come a far greater curiosity about Taiwan and the dangers it is facing. 'It's amazing. People are talking about Taiwan much more frequently than before,' he said. 'Our success in fighting off Covid, but also our determination to defend our democracy, when everybody else has been caving in to China.' He said the most common sentiment encountered on his travels was how wrong the world has been about a China that has become, 'so big, so dangerous, so threatening'. He was telling everyone who'd listen about the need to push back against Beijing and reduce dependence – and he's been saying that Taiwan matters, and it merits support. 'Taiwan deserves to be seen as a player in its own right, rather than a pawn in a bigger game,' he said.

Two days before our conversation Wu'er Kaixi was appointed general secretary of Taiwan's Parliamentary Human Rights Commission. Some of the warmest congratulations came from exiled Uyghur groups at a time of appalling abuses in their homeland of Xinjiang (or East Turkistan, as Uyghurs call it). They know Wu'er Kaixi as Uerkesh Davlet, his Uyghur name, since he is of Uyghur heritage. This, together with his role in Tiananmen Square, gives him a unique status in the eyes of many human rights activists – and also in the eyes of Beijing, which has persistently blocked his efforts to visit his parents, who he has not seen since 1989. They have been denied passports to meet him overseas.

Wu'er Kaixi cut his teeth as a student leader, which is one reason why he has been so encouraged by the growth of civic activism in Taiwan – especially the greater involvement of young people in political and social issues. 'Civil society is much more vivid these days, day by day,' he said. The Sunflower Movement's occupation of parliament, which gained widespread public support, was the most visible sign of this new activism. However, it was only part of a much broader youth-led protest movement that swept the island and encompassed issues ranging from the environment, labour rights and media reform, to forced evictions and aboriginal land rights. Wu'er Kaixi gave a speech to the young protesters when they had control of parliament. 'The young generation taking up their responsibilities and acting upon it, that is precisely the hope of this democracy,' he told them.

Young people were at the forefront of a movement that successfully fought for marriage equality. The island has a large and thriving LGBTQ+ community, and they were rewarded in May 2017 when the Supreme Court ruled that the Civil Code's definition of marriage was unconstitutional. The court gave Taiwan's parliament two years to amend laws to legalise same-sex marriage. There was fierce opposition from evangelical and other conservative groups, but the law was finally changed in 2019, making Taiwan the first place in Asia to do so. The island's annual Pride celebration is the largest on the continent, and Taipei is widely regarded as the most LGBTQ+ friendly city in the region.[18] The high-profile LGBTQ+ community is very influential in Taiwan's creative scene, enjoying a freedom denied in China. Beijing's attitude to the movement could not be more different, marked by bigotry and intolerance. The Communist Party has targeted sexual and gender minorities, launching a campaign against 'effeminate' entertainers, and closing dozens of social media accounts associated with the LGBTQ+ community.[19]

Aboriginal land and language rights have been another focus of civic activism, rewarded in 2016 when incoming President Tsai Ing-wen, apologised for 'centuries of pain and mistreatment'. As previously noted, Taiwan has sixteen recognised indigenous tribes, making up around 580,000 people, or 2.5 per cent of the population. They trace their presence on the island back thousands of years. The president herself has aboriginal ancestry – her grandmother was from the Paiwan tribe, one of the biggest. In 2017, parliament passed a law aiming to promote and preserve indigenous languages. It designated sixteen indigenous languages as national languages of Taiwan and boosted their teaching.[20] The same year, Tsai also moved to recognise ancestral land. Her government's Council of Indigenous Peoples declared 1.8 million hectares – about half of Taiwan's total land area – to be traditional territory. Around 90 per cent of this was public land that indigenous people could claim, and the development of which would require their consent.[21] Some would have liked the law to go further and include land now in private hands, and there have been legal setbacks – in May 2021, the Bunun tribe lost an eight-year fight over hunting rights.[22]

Nonetheless, the reforms mark a significant step forward, both in terms of legal protections and more broadly in Taiwan's embrace of indigenous culture and identity.

Women's rights and the environment are other areas where civic movements have had a big and growing impact. Because Taiwan is not a member of the UN, it is not included in the UN Development Programme's Gender Inequality Index. As a result, Taipei does a self-assessment using the UN's criteria of reproductive health, empowerment and the labour market. In 2021 it placed itself sixth in the world and the highest in Asia.[23] Even allowing for a bit of generosity with the figures it awards itself, that is a striking achievement. The latest UN ranking for China, in 2019, was thirty-ninth.[24] In President Tsai Ing-wen, Taiwan has a female leader; across the Taiwan Strait, Xi Jinping heads a seven-strong politburo standing committee, all grey middle-aged men. Beneath them the twenty-five-member politburo has at the time of writing just a single woman. The ratio improves lower down the Communist Party ranks, but not by much.

Taiwan's environmental activists targeted nuclear power, and succeeded in pressuring the government into mothballing a fourth nuclear power plant.[25] President Tsai's administration is now intent on phasing out nuclear power completely by 2025, and sharply increasing the share of renewables. Taiwan's dependence on nuclear energy for electricity generation has fallen from over 50 per cent in 1985 to only 12.7 percent in 2020, according to Taiwan Power Company data.[26]

Taiwan's new activism can best be seen as a form of civic nationalism, underpinned by a determination to defend the democratic system they have created and its liberal values. Wu'er Kaixi describes Taiwan as 'anti-nationalist' because it stands in opposition to the narrow and dangerous way nationalism is being defined by the Chinese Communist Party. He sees diversity and liberalism as cornerstones of Taiwanese democracy – an inclusive and freewheeling mix of cultures, ethnicities and religions that include Buddhism, Taoism, Christianity and Confucianism. It is a sharp contrast to the strident and often xenophobic nationalism of Xi Jinping's China, which is based on narrow ethnicity and grievance, where religion is effectively outlawed, and where Xi has overseen a severe crackdown on civil society. The Communist Party sees ethnic and cultural differences as a threat to be eliminated – as seen at its most egregious in the Orwellian 're-education' camps of Xinjiang, Wu'er Kaixi's ancestral home.

Before the rise of civic activism in Taiwan there was a considerable amount of soul searching about whether young people in particular cared sufficiently to be willing to defend their democracy in the event of Chinese aggression. As we have seen, young people have been a particular target of Communist Party disinformation, as well as economic inducements to do business or study in China. In America, some strategists have questioned the wisdom of providing open-ended commitments to Taiwan's defence if the island cannot be relied upon to stand up for itself. The rise of civic activism suggests young Taiwanese are willing to stand up for what they believe in – and attitudes on the island have been profoundly influenced by events 450 miles to the southwest.

The Communist Party's repression of Hong Kong's democracy movement was one of the factors that lifted support for Tsai Ing-wen at the 2020 presidential election. The campaign for that vote took place at a time when large and at times violent protests were taking place in the former British colony. The more harshly Hong Kong's Beijing-appointed government cracked down, the more Tsai's support rose.[27] For many young people in Taiwan, the events in Hong Kong provided a political awakening. Some travelled there and took part in the protests, others showed their support by helping those who fled settle in Taiwan. 'Hong Kong today, Taiwan tomorrow' became a popular refrain among young people to draw attention to the way their fates were linked.[28]

The Hong Kong protests began in response to a law that would have allowed Hong Kong people to be extradited and face trial in Party-controlled courts on the mainland. They soon embraced broader calls for greater democracy – calls that were stubbornly resisted by Beijing. In June 2020, China imposed a national security law on the territory, snuffing out its limited freedoms and autonomy. In doing so, it tore up a mini-constitution that had been agreed at the time of the 1997 handover from Britain and was enshrined in an international treaty. Beijing moved quickly to crush the democracy movement, shutting down pro-democracy newspapers and jailing activists and critics. It marked the death of 'one country two systems', a formula designed to give Hong Kong a degree of autonomy – and the end of Beijing's dream of using that as a model for Taiwan. 'With their lives, blood and tears, the young people of Hong Kong have demonstrated for us that one country, two systems is not feasible,' Tsai Ing-wen told her last campaign rally.[29]

'They are dirty words now,' said Wu'er Kaixi, for whom the repression in Hong Kong has been particularly painful. 'I have shed more tears in the last two years than in my entire life, watching Hong Kong, every time. It just makes you so emotional. I think I am sharing a strong sentiment of Taiwanese people too, especially younger generation,' he said. Until 2019, Hong Kong was the only place in China to commemorate the 1989 Tiananmen Square massacre. Every year tens of thousands joined a 4 June vigil in memory of those who were killed, turning the city's Victoria Park into a sea of candles. Now the vigil has been banned, and the Hong Kong Alliance in Support of Patriotic Democratic Movements of China, which organised the vigil, was forced to disband. The group and three of its leaders were charged with inciting subversion.[30] Hong Kong University ordered the removal of a sculpture commemorating those killed in and around Tiananmen Square. The sculpture, depicting dozens of torn and twisted bodies, had been on display at the university for two decades.[31] When a museum dedicated to Tiananmen was forced to close, it took its exhibits online, only for the website to be blocked.[32]

Not only has the ongoing repression in Hong Kong generated widespread revulsion in Taiwan, but it is also seen as further evidence (should it be needed) that Beijing simply cannot be trusted. The impact on Taiwanese politics has been far-reaching, according to Wu'er Kaixi, undermining those arguing for engagement with Beijing. Few on the island now want anything to do with China politically. 'Beijing is not lending a hand for those people advocating on their behalf by being a major bully,' he said.

Monitoring precisely how the people of Taiwan think about China and their own identity has generated quite an industry on the island, and national identity is one of the most studied topics in Taiwanese political science.[33] A July 2021 poll by National Chengchi University's Election Study Center found that those self-identifying as Taiwanese and Chinese or solely as 'Chinese' had dropped to a record low.[34] The poll showed that almost two-thirds of the public regard themselves as Taiwanese, while just over 30 per cent regard themselves as a mixture of Taiwanese and Chinese. Only 2.7 per cent identify solely as Chinese. Polls gauging attitudes to independence are more complicated since a vast majority (more than 70 per cent) regard Taiwan as a sovereign state already.[35] Other polls have found support for independence at all-time highs, while the numbers advocating unification have slumped. One poll for the Taiwanese Public Opinion Foundation found 54 per cent supporting outright Taiwanese independence and just 12.5 per cent for unification. Almost a quarter supported the 'status quo', which is often described as de facto independence.[36] Young people in particular identify more strongly as Taiwanese – as many as 90 per cent of those aged eighteen to twenty-nine. The young are also stronger advocates of formal independence.[37] These polls are not without their critics, who point to the difficulty of interpretation. For instance, is the rejection of Chinese identity a rejection of China per se, or merely a rejection of China in its current communist form? Are the respondents distancing themselves from Chinese ethnicity or Chinese politics? Yet when polls are examined over three decades they show clear trends: a drastic decline in those supporting unification and a slower, but steady rise in those favouring formal independence and self-identifying as Taiwanese.[38] None of which will come as comfortable reading for the Chinese Communist Party.

The American political scientist Samuel Huntington wrote that a democracy can be considered consolidated once it has survived two changes of ruling party during the transition period – the so-called 'two-turnover rule'.[39] Taiwan has survived three: in 2000 (KMT to DPP), 2008 (DPP to KMT) and 2016 (KMT to DPP). Taiwan's elections are noisy, passionate events with a high level of participation. The island's democratic transformation came about not as a result of some revolutionary upheaval, but by peaceful means, through reforming existing political institutions, and was initiated by the ruling party at that time. One of the trickiest challenges now is addressing the crimes and injustices of the martial law period, and even further back in the case of Taiwan's indigenous people – a process that President Tsai Ing-wen has accelerated.

The National Chiang Kai-shek Memorial Hall stands in the heart of Taipei surrounded by 240,000 square metres of parkland. It was built in traditional Chinese style after the Generalissimo's death in 1975 and opened to the public in 1980. It contains a 6.3-metre-tall seated bronze statue of Chiang, and a museum features memorabilia including cars, his favourite books and food. Activists have long regarded the memorial as an affront to democracy and to the many victims of Chiang's brutal rule. It became the focus of regular protests and occasional vandalism. In September 2021, the government's Transitional Justice Commission (TJC) announced plans to remove the statue and turn the park into a public space that would host exhibitions examining the country's authoritarian past and its transition to democracy.[40] The TJC was set up in 2018 by Tsai Ing-wen's government to review injustices committed in the martial law period between 1949 and 1987 when Chiang and his son Chiang Ching-kuo were in power – the period dubbed the 'White Terror'. Hundreds of other statues and memorials to the former dictator have been quietly removed from schools and public buildings and put on display in a park close to his mausoleum in Taoyuan, where the weathered busts are treated as historical and cultural heritage rather than political totems, according to city officials.[41]

There is no more chilling a symbol of that period than Green Island, a six-square-mile islet off Taiwan's wild southeastern coast. It housed two notorious prisons, able to hold 2,000 mostly political prisoners. An estimated 20,000 are estimated to have been incarcerated on the island over almost four decades of arbitrary arrests, disappearances, torture and executions. One of the prisons became known as Oasis Villa, an Orwellian moniker that belied the horrors that took place behind its tall walls. The prison consisted of a hexagonal central building, from which radiated four lines of cells. It's not clear if the 'Oasis' name came from the prisoners – a grim expression of irony – or their captors, but the name stuck and is carved into a rock nearby. The prisons are now a museum, renamed in 2018 as the Green Island White Terror Memorial Park, when they became part of the National Human Rights Museum. Visitors are able to enter the tiny cells and read the fading propaganda slogans of Chiang's nationalist government – 'With bitterness all around you the only salvation is repentance', 'Destroy the communists and recover the mainland' and 'Staunchly anti-communist' are among them.[42] The museum hosts regular art and cultural exhibitions – among them Taiwan's first Human Rights Arts Festival. In the prison yard Tsai Hai-ru, a sixth generation Taiwanese artist erected a 3D sculpture of the Chinese character *qing*, which translates as clean or purge. The steel character bears scarred holes, slashed as if by lightning. 'I hope that political victims and their families will write down their words of pain, regret, thoughts or remorse on a piece of paper and insert it in the openings,' Tsai said.[43]

Those who lost relatives during this period are beginning to find answers to painful questions. In 1953, Huang Wen-kung was accused of anti-government activities, hauled away from his five-month pregnant wife and jailed. The night before he was executed he wrote a letter to his unborn daughter Huang Chun-lan, telling her, 'My most beloved Chun-lan, I was arrested when you were still in your mother's womb. Father and child cannot meet. Alas, there's nothing more tragic than this in the world.'[44] Almost six decades later, the letter was among some 300 of his papers unearthed in government archives. 'As soon as I read the first sentence, I cried,' Huang Chun-lan told the BBC. 'I finally had a connection with my father. I realised not only do I have a father, but this father loved me very much.' Her experience unleashed a wave of requests for access to documents, and the Transitional Justice Commission has been tasked with speeding up the opening of political archives.

There is a lot that remains unknown about both the White Terror and the killings and the crackdown that immediately followed the 2-28 rebellion in 1947. Groups representing the families of victims are increasingly impatient for answers. 'We demand the truth be clarified and those who were responsible be made accountable, with their names listed in official records and textbooks,' says Yang Chen-long, head of the Memorial Foundation of 2-28.[45] The foundation runs a museum in Taipei, and among the exhibits is a cigarette packet on which are scrawled the words, 'Don't be sad, I die for the residents of our city. I die with no regret.' They were written by Pan Mu-chi, a doctor and local politician, who opposed Chiang Kai-shek. The packet was smuggled out of jail to his family shortly before he was executed by firing squad. His blood-stained shirt is also part of the exhibition. 'We don't want revenge, we want justice,' said his son, who is among those demanding Chiang's image should no longer be displayed in Taiwan out of respect for those who died.

Many of these measures have faced opposition from the KMT, which was of course the party of Chiang. After he died it was his son Chiang Ching-kuo (the former head of the secret police) and then Lee Teng-hui, who ushered in democratic change. However, many in today's party would prefer not to rake over the past. For her part, President Tsai Ing-wen said, 'The goal of transitional justice is "reconciliation not political vendetta"; this is the principle that the government will insist on, as only when the people face the past together can the country move toward the future in unity.'[46] On the seventy-fourth anniversary of the 2-28 incident, Tsai pledged that Taiwan would 'face its past with honesty'.[47]

It serves to further underscore the pace and extent to which Taiwan and China are moving rapidly in opposite directions. The Chinese Communist Party attempts to airbrush the Tiananmen Square massacre from history, as well as Mao Zedong's responsibility for millions of deaths during the disastrous Great Leap Forward and Cultural

Revolution. As long as the Party derives its legitimacy from Mao, he remains untouchable, and Xi Jinping draws inspiration from Mao as he constructs his own cult of personality. President Tsai used the thirty-first anniversary of the Tiananmen Square massacre in 2020 to highlight the sharp difference between her government's determination to confront its difficult past and China's distortion of history. 'Around the world, there are 365 days in a year. Yet in China, one of those days is purposely forgotten each year,' she tweeted. 'There were once days missing from our calendar, but we've worked to bring them to light. I hope one day China can say the same.'[48]

In 2021, Taiwan became a refuge for another group fleeing Communist Party repression – foreign journalists. By one estimate more than twenty journalists shifted from Beijing to Taipei after China expelled or put other pressure on them for writing articles critical of repression in Hong Kong and Xinjiang, or of the Party's cover-up of the coronavirus outbreak in Wuhan. This included journalists from the *New York Times*, the *Wall Street Journal*, *Washington Post* and BBC. With Hong Kong also becoming an increasingly inhospitable place to work, Taipei was the location of choice for covering China from afar.[49] In Taiwan they joined a thriving and noisy local media scene, comprising hundreds of newspapers, TV and radio stations – complemented and turbo-charged by one of the world's highest levels of internet penetration. Much of the local media is politically partisan, and in recent years Beijing has sought to exert influence over media owners, many of whom have business interests in China, but it still ranks among the most free in Asia. In its annual ratings of political rights and civil liberties in 2021, Freedom House gave Taiwan a four out of four for freedom of expression.[50] The Washington DC-based NGO gave Taiwan an overall 'freedom' rating of 94 out of 100, higher than both the US (83) and Britain (93).[51] China, where the expulsion of foreign journalists was accompanied by the elimination of the last vestiges of home-grown independent journalism, was given zero out of four for freedom of expression and nine out of 100 overall.[52]

Taiwan's leaders are aware that their democracy is a form of defence, that it would be hard for the United States or its allies to abandon a like-minded liberal democracy in the face of Chinese aggression. Democracy has been described as a form of 'firewall' against external threats.[53] However, it is Taiwan's critical role in the world's high-tech economy that also concentrates the minds of Western leaders.

# Chapter 11

# *Chips with Everything: A Taiwanese Lynchpin in the Global Economy*

'In the world of semiconductors,
this is the center of the universe.'

*Financial Times, March 2021*

My nineteenth-floor room in the W Hotel in central Taipei provided a grandstand view of the storm. Gusting wind and torrential rain came in violent bursts, racing along the streets below, engulfing the surrounding buildings. It retreated briefly, and then roared back, angrier than ever, pounding against my window. For a while I could see nothing, a complete whiteness beyond the thick glass, but the storm's terrifying shriek was louder than ever. The window rattled and the building seemed to sway.

When the storm eased, I ventured gingerly outside. The roads were littered with uprooted trees, branches, signposts – even bikes and motorcycles which had been ripped away from stands, their locks being no match for the wind. This was Typhoon Soudelor, which hit Taiwan in August 2015, and was the strongest storm in the world that year. It packed winds of up to 100 miles per hour, with gusts approaching 130 miles per hour, and killed at least eight people on the island. Around 400 others were injured, mostly from flying debris, and for a while more than 3 million households were without power after the storm brought down electricity lines.[1] The sheer volume of rain was astounding – in parts of northern Taiwan over twelve inches fell in just twenty-four hours.

That experience came back to me five years later, when Taiwan's typhoons dried up, and in so doing opened the eyes of the world to the critical importance of the island to the digital world and the global economy. Historically, Taiwan has been hit by three or four typhoons per year, and they account for half the island's annual rainfall. So while they are frightening for those caught up in them, they would reliably fill the country's reservoirs year after year.[2] In 2020, for the first time in almost half a century there was not a single typhoon, and by early 2021 Taiwan was facing a severe drought. As the water levels in reservoirs across the country fell perilously low, President Tsai Ing-wen called on residents to conserve water. Rationing was introduced, farmers were ordered to stop irrigating their fields, there were power outages, and military aircraft were dispatched to carry out cloud seeding.[3]

The drought triggered debate about Taiwan's long-term vulnerability to climate change, but the government also had more immediate concerns. It urgently sought to limit the impact on the island's critical high-tech industries. Water supplies from Taipei were diverted to reservoirs around Hsinchu, a tech hub on the coast southwest of the capital. An emergency desalination plant was also rushed into service to supply the area's water-hungry factories. The government battled to keep the production lines going, aware that a shutdown would not only damage the Taiwanese economy, but could potentially bring key sectors of the global economy to their knees.

The Hsinchu Science Park is home to Taiwan Semiconductor Manufacturing Co. Ltd (TSMC), the world's largest contract chip manufacturer, which makes almost all the world's most advanced chips. Chip-making is particularly water-intensive, and huge amounts are used throughout the manufacturing process – in cleaning the thin silicon wafers that form the basis of the chips, in etching the patterns on them, polishing the layers and the constant rinsing. Although TSMC recycles much of what it uses, its Hsinchu facilities still consumed 63,000 tons of water a day in 2019, or more than 10 per cent of the supply from two local reservoirs.[4] By May 2021 the company was reportedly spending millions of dollars to truck in water to its thirsty plants.[5] That month the government warned that if the drought did not break it would have to cut water supplies to Hsinchu as well as to Taichung, another chip-making hub, by 17 per cent.[6]

Even before the drought, there was a global shortage of chips, and Taiwan had been under diplomatic pressure to step up production. Worldwide lockdowns due to Covid-19 had led to an unanticipated surge in demand for gadgets ranging from gaming systems to smartphones, personal computers and other electronics for those stuck inside. Companies upgraded their digital systems and broadband providers upped their speeds to accommodate those working from home – all fuelling demand for semiconductors. The global car industry, increasingly dependent on electronic components, found itself badly wrongfooted. Early in the pandemic, car makers reduced their orders for chips, anticipating a fall-off in car sales, but when demand snapped back they could not get the chips they needed and many were forced to cut production. The chip crunch was estimated to cost car makers more than $210 billion in sales in 2021, with global production falling by more than 7 million units.[7] It was reported that Apple might have to slash the production of its new iPhone 13 because of chip shortages, which had already started to affect production of Macs and iPads.[8]

Companies worldwide found themselves anxiously watching the weather forecasts for Taiwan. At the end of May, their prayers were answered when Tropical Depression Choi-wan swept in, bringing heavy rain to the northern and central portions of the island.[9] With that rain came a reprieve for the semiconductor industry, but the experience had provided a wake-up call about the centrality of Taiwan to the most advanced sectors of the world economy.

In a March 2021 profile of TSMC, the *Financial Times* described the chip-maker as 'possibly the most important company in the world that few people have heard of', saying of its latest fabrication plant, 'In the world of semiconductors, this is the centre of the universe.'[10] It was not an over-statement. The company has become a lynchpin of the global economy. 'Twenty years ago there were 20 foundries [worldwide], and now the most cutting-edge stuff is sitting on a single campus in Taiwan,' Peter Hanbury, a partner at Bain & Company in San Francisco, told the newspaper. The industry measures the size and performance of chips in nanometres – which is units of one billionth of a metre. Smaller means more efficient, with lower energy costs and higher speeds. The chips used in cars are typically 28–65nm, and here TSMC has an estimated global market share of around 65 per cent. The most advanced chips on the market in early 2022 were 5nm, and this is the cutting edge where TSMC dominates, with 90 per cent of the market. As of 2021, it was pouring $100 billion into a three-year investment programme to maintain that lead, planning new fabrication plants – or 'fabs' as the industry calls them – that aim to begin production of 3nm chips in 2022, and with plans for 2nm, according to some reports.[11] The huge investment costs make it very difficult for others to compete, and in 2021 the only other company worldwide capable of commercially producing the most advanced chips was South Korea's Samsung Electronics, though America's Intel was racing to catch up.[12]

TSMC was founded in 1987, the year that martial law was lifted in Taiwan, by a Chinese-born and American-educated entrepreneur called Morris Chang. When he retired in 2018, aged eighty-six, President Tsai Ing-wen awarded him the Order of Propitious Clouds, one of the country's most prestigious medals, for his contribution to the nation.[13] He spent his early years in China and Hong Kong, before moving to the United States after the communists seized power in Beijing in 1949. A keen bridge player and reader of Shakespeare, he was educated at Harvard University and then the Massachusetts Institute of Technology, after which he spent nearly three decades working in the US, much of that time at Texas Instruments.[14]

TSMC prospered by being at the forefront of a major change in the tech industry – the separation of chip design from chip manufacturing. Until a little over a decade ago, tech companies bought chips off the shelf, now they want them made to order.[15] In other words, you won't see TSMC's name on the label of its most advanced chips, because it makes them for the better-known companies that design them and then contract out production. It was an approach pioneered by Apple, which in 2012 handed Chang a contract to make custom-chips for the iPhone. Apple reportedly liked the way Chang did business, making trade-secret protection one of his priorities, and requiring guests to seal the USB ports of their laptops when they visited his premises.[16] Chips built by TSMC went on to power the iPhone 6, the best-selling smartphone of all time, and Apple remains the Taiwanese company's biggest client. The separation of design from production has spawned its own multi-billion-dollar chip design industry, much of it centred on Silicon Valley. The US also produces many of the specialist tools for producing, programming and testing chips, though it largely abandoned manufacturing to its Asian rivals.

In 2021, TSMC had a market value of more than half a trillion dollars, and was the world's eleventh most valuable company – though even that probably understates its importance to the global economy.[17] It is hugely profitable – with a net income of $6.5 billion in the three months to the end of September 2021 alone, with gross profit margins soaring towards 50 per cent as the global shortage forced up prices. It is headquartered on a sprawling science park in Hsinchu, but has other facilities in Taichung in central Taiwan and Tainan in the south. It also has facilities in China and the United States. The US is its largest market, while China is number two, but growing fast. For many years it managed the geopolitics well, making itself indispensable to both countries. Now both have the jitters about their chip supplies.

The Biden administration has described the shortage of chips as a national security issue, and vowed to boost America's own manufacturing capabilities. The US accounted for some 37 per cent of global semiconductor manufacturing in the 1990s, but this had fallen to 12 per cent by 2021, as the production end of the business was contracted out to companies such as TSMC.[18] Biden pledged to spend $52 billion over five years to help boost domestic chip production. America's Intel, once synonymous with microchip production, is investing heavily in its own new fabrication plants in the US.[19]

In China, the government is making its own efforts to become self-sufficient in chips, pouring billions into Shanghai-based Semiconductor Manufacturing International Corporation (SMIC), the country's largest foundry. However, in spite of being a massive consumer of chips, China's chip-making abilities are years behind that of America or Taiwan. Estimates vary, but at the high end the 'chip-gap' is reckoned to be up to a decade, and even then China is chasing a fast-moving target.[20] Its attempts to catch up are hampered by tightening US export restrictions that bar access to equipment needed for building cutting-edge chip production facilities. China's semiconductor industry also faced a chronic shortage of talent, according to a report published by the China Institute for Educational Finance Research at Peking University.[21] As a result, China increased its efforts to poach engineers away from Taiwan, which became another source of tension.

TSMC is expanding overseas. It is building a new 5nm fab in Arizona after coming under pressure from President Trump, and is extending a facility in Nanjing, China, though only for the production of less advanced 28nm chips. It is planning another in Japan and possibly the EU, and is under pressure from anxious customers to go further in internationalising its production. Both the EU and Japan have pledged to spend billions of dollars to boost their domestic chip industry. Yet the dominance of TSMC and of the island of Taiwan is unlikely to be challenged any time soon. Like democracy, control of top-end chip-making is regarded by the government as a form of protection. Some 97 per cent of the company's assets are based on the island, including its most advanced fabrication facilities, and some 90 per cent of its staff are located there.[22] Its latest fab, to make 3nm chips, 1/20,000th of the width of a human hair, is being built in southern Taiwan and will cover 160,000 square metres, the size of twenty-two football fields.[23] Others have described chip production as a 'silicon shield' because the impact on the global economy in the event of conflict would be unthinkable. Taiwan has been described as 'potentially the most critical point of failure for the entire semiconductor value chain'.[24] This at a time that the global demand for chips is soaring, and will continue to do so. With the growth of the Internet of Things (IoT), all manner of everyday devices will carry an element of computing power. Global chip sales were $440 billion in 2020 and are projected to grow over 5 per cent annually.[25]

There is a joke among Taiwan's residents about the best place to go should the worst happen and China invades. Perhaps run to the hills, is one suggestion. No, comes the answer, the best place to head for is a factory run by TSMC, which are so vital they can't possibly be touched.[26] In October 2021, after China sent record numbers of warplanes close to Taiwan, the island's Minister of Economic Affairs Wang Mei-hua spelt out the risks to the global economy. 'Taiwan has helped foster a great chip manufacturing ecosystem with three decades of efforts against the backdrop of globalization,' he said. 'The global community should take Taiwan's security more seriously so Taiwan can continue to provide stable service to everyone and be a very good partner to everyone.'[27] In early 2022, a Washington think tank conducted a war game which began with the failure of Taiwanese semiconductor foundries as a result of a suspected cyber attack. The scenario, played out by researchers at the Center for a New American Security, triggered an international confrontation between China and the US.[28] It was a reminder, if one were needed, that no territorial dispute on the planet has a higher potential cost to outsiders.

The neo-Gothic National Liberal Club at Whitehall Place in London is one of the grandest of the capital's private members' clubs. It was established by William Gladstone in 1882, and in the 'smoking room' there is a portrait of the former British prime minister leaning on an axe, along with a chest made from an oak tree he felled. Gladstone intended for the club to be more accessible and adventurous than its stuffier rivals and it quickly gained a radical, even bohemian reputation – members would end their evening meal by diving into the Thames, according to one early biography of the place.[29] On the evening of 5 October 2021, the Thames was off-limits, but there was a mood of defiance, a faint hint of the illicit, that founders might well have found familiar as guests crowded into the wood-panelled Gladstone Library to raise their glasses to the future of Taiwan.

A small stage had been erected between pillars, flanked by the flags of the UK and Taiwan. Servers manoeuvred gingerly through the crowd with trays of drinks and canapés, their masks the only reminder of the onerous Covid-19 restrictions, in place in London for much of the previous eighteen months, but now lifted. The event was to mark Taiwan's National Day, which falls on 10 October, and was hosted by Kelly Hseih. He goes by the official title of Representative to the United Kingdom, and heads the Taipei Representative Office in the UK. He is Taiwan's ambassador, and the representative office is an embassy in all but name, but Britain dare not call them either. This is another example of the warped diplomatic protocols that underpin the 'One China Policy' that we have already met in several guises. Members of the British parliament were there to show their support, including from the ruling Conservative Party – though careful to stress they were present as backbenchers and not representatives of the government. The event had a particular edge because it took place during a period of intense military harassment of Taiwan by Chinese warplanes, and Hseih was warmly applauded when he reminded his guests of the democratic values Taiwan shares with Britain, and declared that Taiwan would not be intimidated.

Some of the loudest applause came when Hseih announced that Taiwan's economy had reached an important milestone – that Gross National Product (GDP) per head had now surpassed $30,000. That compares with just $154 in 1952 and $5,350 in 1987, the year that martial law was lifted.[30] The economy was pushed over that threshold thanks to strong growth during the Covid-19 pandemic, which Taiwan contained so well. In 2020, Taiwan was the fastest growing economy in Asia, outstripping China, thanks to surging technology sales, which made up half the country's exports.[31] As of August 2021, Taiwan was the twenty-first wealthiest country in the world in terms of nominal GDP, while 'ease of business' indexes gave it a ranking ranging from sixth (Heritage Foundation) to fifteenth (World Bank).[32] Taiwan is now ranked by the World Bank as a high income economy. Its journey to the $30,000 per capita milestone is impressive in itself, but has also been achieved in a reasonably equitable way. The relative distribution of income within a population is usually measured by what is called the Gini coefficient. Low inequality countries score between 0.25 and 0.35, and medium inequality between 0.35 and 0.5. High inequality is any score over 0.5. In 2021, Taiwan was awarded a 33.6, which placed it amid the world's more equal societies – and was considerably better than nominally-Communist China with 38.5.[33] Some observers have attributed Taiwan's success in the fight against coronavirus to this relative wealth equality, which includes a universal healthcare system, launched in 1995, and one of the early fruits of democratisation.[34]

Taiwan is roughly the size of Belgium or Netherlands, but the comparison is misleading, because most of the population, together with industry and agriculture, are squeezed into the flat and fertile western third of the island. The east is rugged, mountainous and sparsely populated. The population is heavily urbanised, well educated, digitally connected and tech-savvy. There are very high penetrations of mobile phones and the internet. What Taiwan does not have is an abundance of natural resources, but that did not prevent the island quickly joining the post-Second World War ranks of what were dubbed the 'Tiger Economies', alongside Singapore, South Korea and Hong Kong. The foundations of Taiwan's economic success were laid during its martial law period, when the country's authoritarian leaders built an export-led economy around textiles, electronics and other manufactured goods. Between 1951 and 1987 it grew at an average annual rate of 8.9 per cent.[35] The period from 1952 to 1980 saw Taiwan top the global league as the fastest growing economy.[36]

Building high-technology industry was an early priority, and to that end the Hsinchu Science Park – home to TSMC – was established in 1978, and quickly grew into one of Asia's leading tech hubs. The ruling nationalist party, the KMT, had its own business empire, and the lines between business and politics were constantly blurred – a legacy that continues to bedevil politics in the democratic era, with the KMT facing demands to account for and return assets the DPP claims were improperly acquired. Growth slowed as the economy matured, averaging 4.5 per cent between 1992 and 2012, but Taiwan continued to be a big beneficiary of globalisation, its economy highly dependent on international trade. By the end of that period it was the world's nineteenth largest trader. Some 94 per cent of the world's motherboards and laptops were produced on the island, and in Acer and Asus it had its own global brands.[37] It became the world leader in the production of liquid crystal display screens. A strong service sector also emerged, and the island became a regional centre for banking, insurance and other business services.

Taipei's soaring ambition to be at the heart of innovation is symbolised in the post-modernist Taipei 101 skyscraper, which for five years was officially the world's tallest building (in 2009, the Burj Khalifa in Dubai took the title). It still claims to be the tallest green building in the world because of its environmental friendliness. Its 101 floors represent the renewal of time and the binary numerals of computer code. It is also designed to symbolise prosperity and good fortune, though observers less attuned to notions of feng shui have likened it to a stack of luncheon boxes.[38] It is also seen as a symbol of inclusiveness, becoming something of an icon for the LGBTQ+ community – the tower emits a different colour for each day of the week, covering the rainbow.[39]

During the Covid-19 pandemic Taiwan became a place of refuge for dozens of American tech entrepreneurs, many of them ethnic Taiwanese, who came to the island to explore new ventures, boosting its nascent tech start-up scene.[40] They included Steve Chen, co-founder of YouTube, and Susan Wu, an investor who was involved in the early stages of some of the world's biggest consumer tech companies, including Twitter, Reddit and Stripe. Chen said he planned to launch a global internet start-up from Taiwan, praising the high quality of the island's engineers, even compared with Silicon Valley, where he lived for twenty years.[41] Wu, who holds an employment gold card, a government initiative that aims to attract top talent from abroad, passed on advice from her time in Silicon Valley. All of which will have been music to the ears of Audrey Tang, Taiwan's digital minister. Nurturing a dynamic start-up scene has become a government priority, and the pandemic gave that ambition an unexpected lift. As of April 2021, Taiwan had only one unicorn – that is, a start-up valued at $1 billion or more – compared with 288 in the US and 133 in China, according to Statista.[42] The message from the likes of Chen and Wu is that there's no reason why the island should not aspire to be Asia's Silicon Valley.

***

For most of the martial law period Taiwan had no ties with China. There was no bilateral trade and visits were forbidden. That began to change in the 1980s as Taiwan moved towards democracy and China under Deng Xiaoping began its policy of reform and opening, creating special economic zones that offered favourable terms to foreign investors. They were especially welcoming to overseas Chinese, with one of the earliest zones based in Shenzhen, just across the border from Hong Kong. Initially there were four such zones, but by the end of 1984 this had expanded to fourteen. They included Xiamen, the city in Fujian province directly facing Taiwan, which was designed to attract Taiwanese investment. Taipei was cautious at first – in 1986 investment in China totalled just $20 million.[43] However, investment surged after 1990 when new Taiwanese regulations allowed investment via third-party countries. Mostly it (and a growing number of business people) travelled via Hong Kong, investment reaching $9.9 billion in 1993 and $40 billion in 1996 – around 5 per cent of Taiwan's GDP at that time.[44]

China quickly became the biggest destination for Taiwanese investment, outpacing the flow of investment to Southeast Asia. Taiwanese entrepreneurs entering China were known as *Taishang* (which translates roughly as 'Taiwan business'), and their numbers exploded. The opening of China coincided with the newly democratic government of Taiwan tightening labour and environmental standards at home, pushing up costs. Taiwanese manufacturers saw China, with its cheap labour, lax regulations and cultural familiarity, as a better alternative, and were soon setting up factories in China at breakneck pace, shifting their more labour intensive and dirtier production across the Taiwan Strait.[45] The Communist Party welcomed the savvy *Taishang*, who brought with them business know-how and global connections. Perhaps the best known *Taishang* is Terry Gou, the founder of Foxconn, also known as Hon Hai Precision Industries, which is now the world's largest contract electronics manufacturer. Gou set up the company in 1974 in a gritty Taipei suburb called Tucheng with a $7,500 loan from his mother and a shed where he started making plastic channel-changing knobs for black-and-white televisions.[46] He opened his first factory in China in Shenzhen in 1988, and Foxconn is now the largest exporter and largest private employer in China – by some estimates it has more than a million workers. This colossal workforce is spread across a series of sprawling facilities that resemble small cities. Working conditions in the factories came under scrutiny in 2010 after a series of suicides among workers.[47] Arguably Foxconn's most important client is Apple, for whom it assembles most of the world's iPhones and iPads. One factory complex alone, in Zhengzhou, Henan province, can churn out an estimated 500,000 iPhones per day and has been dubbed 'iPhone City'.[48]

By the time of the 2008 presidential election in Taiwan, the Taiwanese economy was becoming increasingly integrated with that of China. The KMT's Ma Ying-jeou argued that this had lifted the island's economy, and he won the presidency on a promise of still closer economic ties, even while the two sides of the Strait were moving further apart politically. During the campaign he spoke of a common Chinese market and argued that closer trade cooperation was important for the island's future prosperity. He was good to his word, and soon after being elected he quickly restored direct links across the Taiwan Strait. Shortly before Christmas 2008, an eighty-minute passenger flight from Shenzhen in China to Taiwan marked the beginning of the first regular cross-Strait service since the end of the civil war in 1949.[49] There was to be no more troublesome changing of planes in Hong Kong and Macao, and within weeks, more than 100 direct passenger flights and dozens of cargo flights were crossing the Strait, linking twenty-one Chinese cities with eight in Taiwan. The two sides also signed agreements to allow direct shipping, and for a major expansion of Chinese tourists, who by 2010 were the biggest source of overseas visitors to Taiwan. Chinese students were also allowed to study on the island.[50] In total, Ma signed more than twenty economic and technical agreements with China, including in 2010 a landmark Economic Framework Cooperation Agreement (EFCA) designed to eliminate trade barriers and cut tariffs on goods traded across the Strait.[51]

When Ma was elected for a second term as president in 2012, it seemed like his policies of greater economic integration with China would continue. Growing political contacts with Beijing culminated in a November 2015 meeting between Ma and China's leader Xi Jinping in Singapore, the first time leaders from the two sides of the Taiwan Strait had met since the end of the civil war in 1949.[52] But far from being applauded, Ma faced fierce criticism at home. He was ridiculed when he said Xi had assured him that the hundreds of missiles based in China's coastal provinces were not targeted at Taiwan. His popularity went into freefall, and his China policies faced a growing backlash. Taiwanese identity was becoming more deeply rooted, and civil society was increasingly vocal. As we have seen, attempts to conclude a free-trade agreement in services triggered the Sunflower Movement, which occupied parliament and succeeded in halting the deal and with it any further integration. There was widespread and growing unease about Taiwan's increased economic dependence on China, which was by then Taipei's biggest trading partner and investment destination. Between 1 and 2 million Taiwanese were based in China, working or studying. There was a growing realisation – which we are now seeing in many other parts of the world – that economic dependence on China had created dangerous vulnerabilities. Beijing was explicit that it viewed economic integration, and the wooing of Taiwanese businesses, as a stepping stone and a tool for taking political control of the island. Courting Taiwanese investment and talent might originally have been seen by Deng Xiaoping as a means of modernising China's economy, but under Xi it became a tool of coercion and control.

When the Taiwanese electorate had the audacity (in Beijing's eyes) to turf Ma out of office in 2016 and elect as president Tsai Ing-wen of the DPP, Beijing responded with military drills close to the coastal city of Xiamen. Taiwan's fears about dependency seemed to be borne out when China restricted the flow of tourists in a bid to cripple the island's important tourism industry. 'If there is no peace and stability in the Taiwan Strait, Taiwan's new authority will find the sufferings of the people it wishes to resolve on the economy, livelihood and its youth will be as useless as looking for fish in a tree,' growled the *Xinhua* state news agency in a rather mangled commentary.[53]

In early 2021, pineapples became the latest weapons of economic warfare used by China against Taiwan, followed a few months later by apples. China was by far the biggest market for both, and Beijing declared that its move was to prevent plant disease since Taiwanese pest control was inadequate. Few believed that, and it was left to the Party's reliably pugnacious *Global Times* to spell out the real reason. 'Unfortunately, the current secessionist policies of the DPP authority will certainly continue to make Taiwan products less appealing to the mainlanders,' it growled.[54] President Tsai Ing-wen appealed to the Taiwanese public to buy the fruit. She launched a 'freedom pineapple' campaign that succeeded in finding alternative markets, one of the biggest being Japan, which took up much of the slack.[55] It was a small gesture by Japan, but as we shall see in the next chapter, part of a far broader Japanese reassessment of its security interests in the region, which has been forced upon it by Beijing's growing aggression.

Beijing wielded the carrot, as well as the stick. Even while it was restricting fruit and tourists, it offered incentives to lure more Taiwanese business people to China, promising to make investment and employment easier in a range of projects from 5G to civil aviation.[56] Taipei warned businesses that this was a trap. Huang Tien-lin, an adviser to the president called the measures and the earlier trade deal a 'sugar-coated poison pill'. Writing in the *Taipei Times*, he said, they 'are aimed at enticing Taiwanese professionals, businesses and students to move to China, hollowing out Taiwan's talent pool'.[57]

Taiwanese business people are regarded by the Communist Party as pawns in a larger game, and this was seen in November 2021 when Beijing hit the Far Eastern Group, a Taiwan-based conglomerate, with substantial interests in China, with fines of $13.9 million. This was ostensibly for environmental, land use, health and safety, and other violations, but Chinese officials and state media made clear that it was punishment for the group's role as a donor to the DPP.[58] The company's chairman responded by saying he does not support independence from China. The fine was seen as evidence of the Communist Party's increased willingness to punish companies and entrepreneurs who do not toe its line, and came shortly after warning that it would hold supporters of independence criminally liable.[59]

In an effort to reduce Taiwan's dependence, President Tsai stepped up her New Southbound Policy, a programme aimed at diverting the attention of Taiwanese companies to Australasia and Southeast Asia. Her government also launched a three-year incentive plan for Taiwanese companies to move back from China. In 2019, the year before Covid-19 distorted global trade patterns, these seemed to be meeting with some success, with investment in China falling by over half.[60] President Donald Trump's imposition of tariffs on Chinese goods also influenced the decisions of many Taiwanese companies. Giant Manufacturing, the world's biggest maker of mountain and racing bikes, moved most production of bikes for the US market out of China to its home base in Taiwan. 'The era of "Made in China" and supplying globally is over,' said Bonnie Tu, the company's chairwoman.[61] It also announced that it was building a factory in Hungary to service the European market. 'Moving production close to your market is a trend,' Tu said.

In spite of these efforts, Taiwanese companies remain deeply embedded in the Chinese economy. Total Taiwanese investment in China in the two decades since 1991 was close to $200 billion. Cross-Straits trade reached a record in 2020, when China accounted for nearly 44 per cent of Taiwan's exports, with a strong trade surplus in Taiwan's favour.[62] Taiwan provides many of the high-tech inputs (including chips) for goods assembled in China (including in Taiwanese-owned factories) – and the 2020 figure was no doubt inflated by the effects of Covid-19. The pandemic saw a surge in demand for goods made in China, the first big economy to bounce back. The nature of Taiwan's exports to China does give the island some protection from punitive action, because China lacks the ability to produce many of the components Taiwan supplies, and disrupting this trade or targeting Taiwanese businesses would also damage the Chinese economy. The Taiwanese technology giants also became caught up in the growing geopolitical rivalry between the US and China. The Trump administration's imposition of trade restrictions on sales to China of both semiconductors and the tools to make them effectively asked them to choose sides. It also made Taiwan's high-tech trade even more important to Beijing. Pineapples and apples are far less complicated.

In 2021, Taiwan tightened laws to prevent China from stealing key technology and poaching talent, amid concerns that Beijing had stepped up its economic espionage against the island.[63] The revisions would require people who have received government money for developing sensitive technology to seek permission before travelling to China. The government also told Taiwan recruitment companies to remove all listings for jobs in China, especially those involving critical industries such as integrated circuits and semiconductors. 'China has become more aggressive in poaching and targeting top Taiwanese chip talent to help build a self-sufficient supply chain,' the Labour Ministry warned.[64] As the chip war intensified, the justice ministry's Investigations Bureau, Taiwan's main counter-intelligence agency, set up a special task force to root out clandestine Chinese operations on the island. Taiwan accused Beijing of setting up front companies to poach technology and talent, and the Bureau revealed that 27 had been raided and dozens more were under investigation.[65]

Taiwan's government revealed that semiconductor companies were also among the most prominent targets of cyberattacks from across the Strait. In this increasingly tense atmosphere, one regional neighbour in particular has become increasingly outspoken in defence of Taiwan, words that are increasingly being matched by deeds. That neighbour is Japan. Tokyo, in recent decades, has been the epitome of geopolitical caution, but increasingly sees its own security as inexorably linked to that of Taiwan.

## Chapter 12

# *Japan: Asia's Quiet Achiever Steps Out of the Shadows*

> 'If a major problem occurred in Taiwan, it would not be going too far to say that it could be an existential threat [for Japan] . . . In such a case, Japan and the United States will have to work together to defend Taiwan.'
>
> *Taro Aso, Japan's deputy prime minister, July 2021*

The debate in the National Diet, Japan's parliament, in June 2021 would not usually have attracted much international attention. It was about the country's handling of the Covid-19 pandemic, and Prime Minister Yoshihide Suga listed Taiwan alongside Australia and New Zealand as 'countries' that had taken strict measures to combat the virus. When opposition leader Yukio Edano joined the debate, he also used the word 'country' when referring to Taiwan. Cue Chinese outrage at such 'erroneous' remarks. Beijing immediately lodged a diplomatic protest. 'China demands that Japan make an immediate clarification to undo the harm already caused, and guarantee a similar incident will never happen again,' fumed Wang Wenbin, a Chinese Foreign Ministry spokesman.[1] No such guarantee came, and Japan's Foreign Minister Toshimitsu Motegi committed the same offence when discussing his government's donation of Covid-19 vaccine doses to Taiwan, which followed Beijing's attempts to block the island from gaining access to shots from elsewhere. Japanese leaders are usually extremely cautious in their diplomacy and careful with their choice of words, especially as regards China. So when officials began to describe Taiwan as a country, this was no mere slip of the tongue – Tokyo was sending a message.

Over the following weeks, the message became more explicit. 'We have to wake up' in the face of an 'aggressive' China, said Deputy

Defence Minister Yasuhide Nakayama. 'We have to protect Taiwan as a democratic country.'[2] Beijing reacted with outrage, describing his remarks as 'highly sinister, dangerous and irresponsible'.[3] Soon after, Taro Aso, Japan's finance minister and deputy prime minister, explicitly linked the security of Taiwan to the security of Japan. 'If a major problem occurred in Taiwan, it would not be going too far to say that it could be an existential threat [for Japan],' he told a fundraising event. 'In such a case, Japan and the United States will have to work together to defend Taiwan.'[4]

Japan's annual defence review is usually quite an anodyne document. However, in 2021, the 'Defense of Japan' review also directly linked Japan's security to that of Taiwan. 'Stabilizing the situation surrounding Taiwan is important for Japan's security and the stability of the international community. Therefore, it is necessary that we pay close attention to the situation with a sense of crisis more than ever before,' the report states.[5] The front cover of the review carried a drawing of a fully armed samurai warrior on charging steed, as opposed to the previous year's pink cover and illustration of Mount Fuji and white cherry blossoms.[6] 'International society needs to pay greater attention to the survival of Taiwan,' said Defence Minister Nobuo Kishi, when the report was published.[7]

For the first time, the US and Japanese defence ministers agreed to 'closely cooperate' in the event of conflict over the island. It was revealed that the US and Japan had significantly expanded their military planning and were conducting war games and joint military exercises geared towards conflict over Taiwan. These reportedly began during the last year of the Trump administration, and continued under Joe Biden. They included top-secret tabletop war games and joint exercises in the South China Sea and East China Sea. If conflict does break out between China and the US over Taiwan, it seems inevitable that Japan will be involved because key American bases are located in Japan – bases that might well be targeted by Beijing. But Japan's new assertiveness and its greater willingness to criticise, following decades of avoiding offending Beijing, is primarily motivated by a reassessment of China's ambitions and Tokyo's own security.

Japan historically was the first of the great powers to recognise the strategic importance of Taiwan, the 'cork in the bottle' of the South China Sea, controlling access between Southeast Asia and Northeast Asia.[8] Japan is acutely aware that keeping shipping lanes open is essential to its national survival. Its reappraisal of policy towards Taiwan and China over the summer of 2021 was all the more dramatic, since it represented such a stark break from the cautious policy of previous decades. Tokyo was deeply unnerved by the prospect of Taiwan falling under the control of an increasingly hostile and aggressive Beijing – and at the same time Japanese officials concluded that China's imperial ambitions in north Asia are unlikely to stop at Taiwan.

Taiwan lies just seventy miles west of the Japanese island of Yonaguni, from where it can be seen on a clear day. 'I can see that Taiwan is very close, right on the opposite shore,' said Japan's defence minister, Nobuo Kishi, during a visit to a recently established military base on Yonaguni in May 2021. 'The peace and stability of Taiwan is linked to the peace and prosperity of the region and the international community,' he added.[9] Until recently the tiny Japanese outpost, the country's westernmost point, was perhaps best known for its giant moths and a fiery local liquor. But it has taken on a greater strategic importance as Japan's closest inhabited land not only to Taiwan, but also to the Senkakus, a string of tiny islands controlled by Japan, but claimed by China. These islets, which China calls the Diaoyu Islands, sit around a hundred miles north of Yonaguni. The Yonaguni garrison, equipped with early warning radar and other sensors is tasked with keeping tabs on Beijing's growing activities in the area.

The Senkakus have become yet another flashpoint as China pursues its territorial claims with ever increased aggression. They comprise five uninhabited islands and three rocky outcrops, over which Japan has exercised effective control since 1895, apart from a period after the end of the Second World War when the US controlled the territory. Historically they seem to have been used largely as navigation markers, with no one nation exercising any meaningful sovereignty. It wasn't until the 1970s, with talk of potential oil and gas reserves, that China began to assert historic rights to the area. Beijing's claims have become particularly shrill over the past decade, especially under Xi Jinping. His strident nationalism has targeted Japan, which has become the main bogeyman of the Communist Party's 'patriotic education' drive. Chinese children are fed a relentless xenophobic diet of wartime atrocities, with the Senkakus becoming a proxy for these animosities. There were a record number of incursions into Japanese waters around the islands in 2021, with armed Chinese coastguard vessels entering on an almost daily basis. Defence Minister Kishi warned, 'We can never accept [China's] unilateral attempts to alter the status quo by force.'[10] On one occasion, four Chinese ships reportedly harassed Japanese fishing boats before being warned off by Japanese patrol ships amid mounting tension in the area.[11] China also dramatically increased the frequency and complexity of combat air patrols near the islands and over the East China Sea more generally, forcing Japan to scramble its own fighters in response.[12]

The Senkakus sit just north of a chain of Japanese islands called the Ryukyu (also known as the Nansei Islands), which stretch some 750 miles southwest from Japan's main landmass to tiny Yonaguni. The biggest of these islands is Okinawa, which hosts 26,000 US military personnel, around half of the total American force in Japan. The Ryukyus are strategically important because they form a natural boundary between the East China Sea and the rest of the Pacific Ocean, through which much of China's expanding navy must transit to get away from its coastal waters. For decades, Japan had little meaningful military presence on the Ryukyus, but that is now changing in response to the frequency and forcefulness of Chinese military incursions. Tokyo is now looking to exert tighter control over the 'choke points' through these islands, which could limit the Chinese navy's freedom of action if conflict were to break out.[13]

The most important 'choke point' is a 150-mile channel which runs between the islands of Miyako and Okinawa, through which Chinese warships routinely pass. This is the deepest of any strait in the Ryukyus, and therefore also thought to be a key submarine transit point. Tokyo has started to install anti-ship missile batteries all along the islands, including on Miyako, and is planning to install air defence units. This would create what has been characterised as a 'gauntlet' of overlapping missile fire through which Chinese ships would need to battle to get out to the open sea.[14] It has also been reported that Japan has invested heavily in underwater listening capability, including an underwater sonar array to detect submarines, strung along the Ryukyu archipelago. This has been installed with US cooperation. Yonaguni is the western end of this, with a 'branch' line to the Senkaku Islands. The system has been described by an officer of the Taiwanese Military Intelligence Bureau as the US Navy's 'Fish Hook Undersea Defense Line'.[15]

In his first call as president with Japan's then Prime Minister Yoshihide Suga, Joe Biden assured Suga that US security guarantees under the US–Japan mutual defence treaty apply to the Senkaku Islands.[16] The call was designed as a demonstration not only of America's commitment to its ally after the uncertainties of the Trump era, but also as a warning to China that Washington will take a strong line against its aggressive territorial claims

Japan does not have an army, it has a Self-Defence Force (SDF). It looks like an army, is equipped like one, and has a budget only a little shy of that of Britain's military. It is in other words, an army in all but name – and a more formidable one than that of most other countries. It is not called an army because of Japan's pacifist constitution, written by the country's American occupiers after the Second World War, which states that 'The Japanese people forever renounce war as a sovereign right of the nation and the threat or use of force as a means of settling international disputes.' It goes on to state that 'land, sea, and air forces, as well as other war potential, will never be maintained'.[17]

Broadly speaking, chasing away Chinese aircraft and hunting submarines, at which Japan excels, are acts of self-defence; hitting back in response to aggression is not – under Japan's defence treaty with Washington, that is the job of its US ally. However, in recent years, Japan's leaders have pushed to have the SDF look and behave more like a normal military. They have interpreted the constitutional limits more broadly and have passed laws to allow Japan to provide logistical support and other aid to allies and to use its weapons in a wider range of circumstances.[18] The SDF has taken part in UN peacekeeping missions, and the government set up a National Security Council to develop and oversee defence and security policies. The maritime SDF is now the second largest navy in Asia after China. The SDF's ground forces have established their first unit of marines since the Second World War, and Japan has sharply increased defence spending, which was expected to reach a record 5.4 trillion yen ($48 billion) in 2022. Tokyo is acquiring some of the latest American kit, including F-35 advanced stealth fighter jets and new destroyers equipped with the Aegis missile interceptor system.[19] It is also developing its own stealth fighter. Furthermore, Japan is earmarking more money for weapon systems that target drones, as well as for artificial intelligence, hypersonic weapons and cyber and space capabilities. This is likely to take defence spending over a guideline of 1 per cent of GDP it set itself in 1976. This is a significant milestone, but spending is still only a fifth of that of

China. *Izumo*, Japan's largest warship, officially described as a helicopter destroyer focusing on anti-submarine warfare, has been modified to carry up to twelve of the new F-35s, further blurring the lines between defence and offence. Similar modifications are due to take place on the *Kaga*, the *Izumo*'s sister ship. They will become formidable aircraft carriers in all but name.[20] US-operated stealth fighter jets, will also use the reinforced Japanese carriers, a landmark in cooperation between the two forces.[21]

Then there is Japan's potential nuclear weapons capability. The country has been described as a latent nuclear power because it has the skills, the technology and the materials to quickly develop nuclear weapons should it so desire. Before the Fukushima power plant disaster, which followed the 2011 Tohoku earthquake and tsunami, Japan had fifty-four operating nuclear reactors. They generated more than a third of the nation's electricity – and a huge plutonium stockpile. Some Western strategists calculate that Japan could build a device in as little as six months, giving it the shortest 'break out' time in the world. Japan's leaders have at times been happy to encourage that sort of speculation, which in itself is a form of deterrence both to keep China at bay and to keep America engaged in the region. This has been described as the 'bomb in the basement' strategy – a 'nuclear hedging strategy that would enable a quick-start nuclear-weapons programme, should circumstances dramatically change for the worse'.[22] In 2016, as vice-president to Barack Obama, Joe Biden said in an interview that he had warned Xi Jinping that Japan had the capacity to acquire nuclear weapons 'virtually overnight'. The context then was North Korea's nuclear ambitions, and Biden's efforts to get Xi to exert his influence on Pyongyang, but Biden's warning remains as pertinent as ever.

It is generally accepted that the security situation in Northeast Asia would need to deteriorate drastically for Tokyo to take that route, as would the credibility of America's security umbrella – a promise that any attack on Japan would trigger a retaliatory attack from the United States. Yet Tokyo's confidence in that commitment has wavered, particularly during the presidency of Donald Trump. He called the security treaty with Japan unfair and reportedly considered cancelling it altogether. During his election campaign, he suggested that it might even serve Japanese (and South Korean) interests if both countries developed their own nuclear weapons.[23]

The main factor holding back a more militarised Japan is the public's overwhelming attachment to pacifism. Japan is the only country to have been attacked by nuclear weapons during war, in Hiroshima and Nagasaki in 1945, and public opinion is overwhelmingly opposed to their acquisition and use. Public opposition has also so far prevented the Japanese government from scrapping altogether the constitutional ban on an offensive military and on going to war. Some 54 per cent of the public are opposed even to the smallest constitutional change, according to opinion polls.[24] Though in another poll at the end of 2020, 86 per cent of respondents said China posed a threat to Japan. During the October 2021 national election, Japan's ruling Liberal Democratic Party, which was returned to power, made an unprecedented pledge to double defence spending.[25] For more than seven decades, Japan has not fired a shot in anger, and so far the changes have been cautious – but step by step change is happening, and China is the primary reason for it.

The strong pacifist mood among Japanese people is strikingly at odds with the way the country is portrayed in China's virulent nationalist propaganda and education material. It is ironic that for the more hawkish of Japan's leaders who argue for a more robust military stance, the Chinese Communist Party in its aggressive behaviour is their greatest ally. The Party is forever accusing Japan of renewed militarism. That is far from being the case, but could well become a self-fulfilling prophecy for which the Party would only have itself to blame. It is remarkable that as a threat to peace, China has overshadowed that traditional Northeast Asia bogeyman, North Korea, though the two threats are more closely connected than is often appreciated.

Happy villagers sing and play, a proud mother cradles her baby. The backdrop is a simple village hut and a canopy of trees. It's an idyllic country scene, but it doesn't last, because the Japanese are on the march. Cue ominous music and panic in the village. Japanese soldiers, bayonets fixed, storm onto the stage, shooting and stabbing. They torch the hut and the baby is ripped from its mother's back and tossed into the flames. Thus unfolds the plot of the 'revolutionary opera', *Sea of Blood*. It's pretty dramatic stuff, but completely lost on my two North Korean minders, a Mr Li and a Mr Bak, who sleep through it. Their job is to watch me, but also I suspect to watch each other, and they are failing on both counts. It had been a long day, and they'd probably seen it countless times before.

I made several visits to North Korea between 2004 and 2008, and as my trip to the opera demonstrated, the hermit kingdom could easily outdo China in terms of demonising Japan, which colonised Korea between 1910 and 1945. Back then, Pyongyang was unequalled in sheer paranoia. A growing number of Chinese tourists were visiting the country, and trade was building across their shared border. With greater social and economic liberalism at home, younger Chinese visitors I interviewed found the place creepy and faintly amusing, some of the older tourists who remembered Mao found it nostalgic. There was much talk of 'China-style reforms', as Pyongyang experimented with modest farmers markets, and a free-ish market in basic consumer goods, mostly Chinese.

At the time, Beijing was chairing a series of seemingly endless and ultimately fruitless talks aimed at ridding North Korea of nuclear weapons. For both Washington and Tokyo, North Korea was then the chief regional villain, seen in both capitals as by far the main security challenge in Northeast Asia. Japanese citizens had been kidnapped by the North, and while America watched Pyongyang's missile tests from afar, those same missiles overflew Japan or splashed down in nearby waters. China's cooperation in pressuring North Korea was deemed essential for curtailing Pyongyang's nuclear ambitions. China was the North's economic lifeline, so the argument went, and the only country with serious leverage. The problem of course was that this cut both ways, and Beijing's perceived leverage with Pyongyang also gave it leverage over the US. Washington came under pressure to appease China by playing down concerns about other aspects of Communist Party behaviour in order to keep it engaged on North Korea. (Similar arguments are made about climate change, to which we shall return later.)

The assumption among China watchers was that Beijing was primarily concerned with stability on its border, and had a shared interest in curtailing the maverick behaviour of the totalitarian Kim Dynasty. Beijing encouraged that view. The Party knew that North Korea gave it leverage with the West and was keen to portray itself as an honest broker. It also sought to reduce expectations by stressing that there were limits to its influence. In this way, it was able to play both sides. Party hardliners have always seen North Korea as primarily a buffer state against US influence in the region, and do not want to see it collapse in a way that might bring America and its South Korean ally closer to China's border. The Party also has a strong emotional attachment to the North, having fought with it against American-led UN forces during the 1950 to 1953 Korean War. The two countries have a mutual defence treaty, signed in 1961, and committing them to come to each other's military support in the event of an attack. This makes Pyongyang China's only treaty ally, but there have been doubts about whether it would ever be honoured. However, in July 2021, on the sixtieth anniversary of its signing, the two sides reaffirmed the treaty. The Chinese Foreign Ministry said it would 'always be valid', while North Korean leader Kim Jong-un said the two countries were 'staunchly advancing towards a bright future by smashing the high-handedness and desperate manoeuvres of hostile forces'.[26] The well-worn slogan that the two countries are 'as close as lips and teeth' seemed more apt than ever.

Over the years of fruitless nuclear negotiations, Western diplomats largely suppressed their doubts as to whether China was acting in good faith, but those doubts have grown with mounting evidence of Chinese sanctions-busting. In December 2020, a month before Joe Biden was inaugurated as president, Washington accused China of 'flagrant violations' of its obligations to enforce UN sanctions on North Korea and warned of US measures against China-based individuals and entities.[27] The US observed ships carrying prohibited coal or other sanctioned goods from the North to China on 555 separate occasions. 'It's not particularly disguised or hidden,' said one official.[28] Satellite images also showed oil tankers openly smuggling fuel from Chinese ports to North Korea.[29] In February 2021, officials from the US and other G7 countries reportedly delivered a formal diplomatic complaint to Beijing and the Chinese mission to the United Nations documenting China's failures to enforce sanctions.[30] A UN panel of experts responsible for monitoring sanctions on North Korea on behalf of the Security Council reported that millions of dollars of cryptocurrency stolen by North Korean hackers were being laundered through over-the counter cryptocurrency brokers in China.[31] Beijing responded by denying the accusations and saying that while it didn't agree with sanctions it was doing its best to enforce them. That line became more difficult when the US provided the panel with satellite images of Chinese coastguard vessels looking on while coal was transferred from North Korean vessels to Chinese-flagged ships.[32]

China insisted that the presence of its patrol boats was 'completely normal'. It pressured the UN panel to place the photograph in a confidential annex of the September 2021 report, though the incident is described in the text. At the time China was facing a looming energy crisis and was scouring the world for coal supplies. Still, it's hard not to conclude that the West has reached the limits of what can be expected from China, and that Beijing has leveraged the North Korean situation for its own benefit. In so doing it has introduced a dangerous new element into the region's already combustible mix.

During his presidency, Donald Trump held three high-profile summit meetings with North Korea's leader Kim Jong-un, but achieved no breakthrough other than a brief pause in missile tests.[33] Trump was accused of ignoring his Japanese and South Korean allies. Biden has tried to involve both on North Korean policy, which a White House spokeswoman described as a 'calibrated practical approach', steering clear of any noisy Trump-style pursuit of a grand bargain.[34] After a period of relative quiet, North Korea tested more missiles in January 2022 than in the whole of 2021, including its first intermediate-range missile for five years, but the reaction from the US was low key. The US State Department repeated a past statement saying the US harboured no hostile intent and urging the North to return to dialogue.[35]

Analysts have characterised Biden's policy as a 'holding action', downgrading his attention to Pyongyang so that he can sharpen America's focus on China.[36] He no longer wants North Korea to be the centre of attention, and does not want publicly to dwell on Kim Jong-un. Covid-19 has helped with that, since the North was quieter while it fought to keep the virus at bay. It closed its land border to China in an effort to insulate itself from the pandemic, claiming implausibly to have had not a single case. The shutting down of overland trade was likened to 'self-sanctions' and resulted in a sharp contraction of the economy and fears of yet another famine.[37]

As much as Biden would like to park his North Korean policy in order to concentrate on China, Kim rather likes being the centre of attention, and China and North Korea are inextricably linked. One sign of this is the resurrection by the CCP of Korean War propaganda, which has increased as relations between China and the United States have plummeted to their worst in decades. The Party calls the conflict the 'war to resist American aggression and aid Korea', and in October 2021, *The Battle at Lake Changjin*, a gory chest-thumping nationalist epic, broke box-office records in China. The film was commissioned by the Party's propaganda department and timed to coincide with the one hundredth anniversary of the founding of the Party. It depicts the People's Liberation Army's 'volunteers' defeating the villainous Americans in one of the major battles of the war. 'Resist American aggression and aid Korea – protect your home and country!' the volunteers cry as they wade through the deep snow.[38] The Party's *Global Times* was quick to draw contemporary parallels – 'Observers said the movie's success shows the national feeling displayed in the film echoes the rising public sentiment in safeguarding national interests in front of provocations, which has great implications for today's China–US competition,' it declared.[39] Police reportedly arrested a leading social media commentator who questioned the film's depiction of a war during which China is estimated to have lost between 200,000 and 900,000 soldiers.[40] The estimates vary widely because no official casualty count has ever been published by Beijing. Little open discussion has been allowed, and CCP propaganda ignores the fact that the war began with an invasion by the North, and the US-led force that responded fought under the UN flag and was multinational.

The year before *The Battle at Lake Changjin* came out, China marked the seventieth anniversary of the war with a series of documentaries, *Heroic Sons and Daughters*, which portrayed the conflict as a defensive struggle against unprovoked American aggression. A Mao-era film, *Battle on Shangganling Mountain*, was resurrected, in which evil and depraved American troops with prosthetically enlarged noses are defeated by brave and patriotic Chinese soldiers. As the trade war with the US intensified, state media encouraged people to once again demonstrate the 'spirit of Shangganling'.[41] During the Mao era, the Korean War was a staple part of Communist Party propaganda and popular culture, but it later fell into disuse. It was dusted down and wheeled out from time to time when US relations were under strain, but has now been resurrected by Xi Jinping as a symbol of resistance to the US.

Not only has Xi generally embraced more war-like rhetoric, but he has presented war as a legitimate instrument of statecraft – far more so than was the case with his immediate predecessors. Evidence of this is seen in the increasingly bellicose language of Communist Party publications, in which the willingness to go to war is seen as an expression of pride and self-confidence. Xi told an Army Day celebration that the PLA should be ready to fight and win wars: 'No one should expect us to swallow bitter fruit that is harmful to our sovereignty, security or development interests,' he said.[42]

***

South Korea has been cautious in its dealings with Beijing, its biggest trading partner, seeking to strike a balance between its economic interests and its security alliance with the United States. However, attitudes towards China have been hardening – and once again it is Beijing's behaviour that is the root cause. This came to a head in 2020 with a bizarre spat over kimchi, a fiery Korean dish made from fermented cabbage, chilli and garlic. After lobbying by Beijing, the International Standards Organization published new rules on pao cai, a kimchi-like dish produced in China, which Chinese state-owned media promptly hailed as an 'international standard for the kimchi industry led by China'.[43] There was outrage on South Korean social media, accusing China of cultural theft.

Kimchi became a vehicle for all manner of pent-up frustration at China. It followed controversies over claims on Chinese social media that Yun Dong-ju, a Korean poet and independence activist during the Japanese colonial era, was Chinese, and the use in a Chinese mobile game of a traditional Korean costume, which the game presented as being Chinese.[44] There had already been anger after Beijing imposed sanctions on South Korean products in response to the 2016 installation of a missile defence system at the request of the United States. The purpose of the system was to defend the South from an attack from the North, but Beijing claimed it threatened its own security. South Korea suffered a $7.5 billion loss when Beijing hit a swathe of industries, from tourism to entertainment, while state media stirred up a wave of anti-Korean vandalism and assault in China. South Korea's economic dependence was brutally exposed, as was China's willingness to leverage it. It was a familiar pattern.

A July 2021 opinion poll found that 72 per cent of South Koreans saw China as a military threat. They also found strong support for the US, which has around 28,500 troops in South Korea. A separate survey by the Pew Research Center found that negative views of China among South Koreans reached an all-time high of 75 per cent in 2020, compared with 31 per cent in 2002.[45] In May 2021, amid this growing anti-Chinese sentiment, a $1 billion project to build a Korea–China cultural town, dubbed 'Chinatown' by opponents, was cancelled after 650,000 people signed an online petition against the project in Gangwon province.[46] Two months earlier, a $28 million historical television drama series was scrapped after its second episode after producers were accused of distorting Korean history by using Chinese-style props, including Chinese liquor and food, such as dumplings, mooncakes and century eggs.[47] Beijing's 2022 Winter Olympics provoked more angry accusations of cultural appropriation after a woman from China's Korean minority wore a traditional Korean hanbok dress while carrying the Communist Chinese flag during the opening ceremony.[48] A Chinese flag was ripped up outside the Chinese embassy in Seoul after two young South Korean speed skaters were disqualified from a semi-final that China went on to win.[49]

Xi Jinping's glorification of China's role in the Korean War, also stoked popular outrage in Seoul. However, the South Korean government itself remained cautious, its comments low key, merely saying that it had made the 'necessary communication to the Chinese side'. After their first summit meeting in May 2021, South Korean President Moon Jae-in and President Biden issued a joint statement in which they recommitted to their mutual defence treaty an 'ironclad alliance'. 'President Biden affirms the US commitment to provide extended deterrence using its full range of capabilities,' the statement said.[50] They also specifically mentioned Taiwan, emphasising the importance of peace and stability in the Taiwan Strait, which brought a sharp warning from Beijing that they were 'playing with fire'.[51] Against this background of growing popular resentment towards Beijing, relations with China became a significant issue during the March 2022 presidential election campaign in South Korea. The winner, Yoon Suk-yeol, from the conservative opposition, promised stronger ties with the US and Japan and a more robust line towards Beijing. That should help Joe Biden in his efforts to keep Japan and South Korea in sync on North Korea – but especially on China. That aim has been complicated by the mutual animosity of his two allies.

Relations between Seoul and Tokyo have suffered over Japan's Second World War atrocities and disagreements over compensation for wartime Korean labourers and up to 200,000 'comfort women', the women and girls forced into sexual slavery by Japan's military before and during the war.[52] The two countries also have their own territorial disputes over islands in the Sea of Japan which are occupied by South Korea and claimed by Japan.[53] Washington is keen to have them both concentrate on the strategic challenge from China. Seoul has been slower to respond, though the caution of the South Korean government in its dealings with Beijing is increasingly out of sync with the national mood in the country. Still, the security focus in Northeast Asia is changing – and that is more a result of China's aggressive behaviour than it is of Washington's cajoling of its allies.

Xi Jinping was scheduled to visit Japan for the first time in spring 2020, but the visit was delayed because of the Covid-19 pandemic. No new date was set, and a majority of Japanese would rather it be called off completely.[54] Japan and China mark the fiftieth anniversary of the normalisation of bilateral diplomatic relations in 2022, but with tensions high it is unlikely to be greeted in Tokyo with any great enthusiasm. The October 2021 election in Japan returned the Liberal Democratic Party to power with a new prime minister, Fumio Kishida, and new top diplomat in Yoshimasa Hayashi, both of whom have in the past been regarded as cautious on China. Hayashi was chairman of the Japan–China Friendship Parliamentarians' Union, a group of lawmakers seeking good relations with Beijing – a post from which he quickly resigned.[55] Both are strong supporters of the US alliance and have significantly hardened their stance towards Beijing since taking office – being soft on China is no longer a political option in Japan.

Japan has been described as the 'quiet achiever' of Asia. It is the largest investor in infrastructure in the region, while inciting few of the worries attached to China.[56] While China's Belt and Road Initiative attracted the headlines, with a stock of investment in unfinished projects in Indonesia, Malaysia, Philippines, Thailand and Vietnam worth $159 billion in 2021, Japan quietly stumped up $259 billion.[57] Japan has been described as the region's 'stealth superpower', 'large enough to be helpful, but not so large to attract fear and anxiety'.[58] In spite of its wartime record, Japan regularly tops polls as the most respected country in Asia, especially among the young. *Modern Diplomacy*, an online platform, labels Japan the 'titan of soft power', from its technology to its cuisine, the country attracts the sort of respect that most others (and China in particular) can only dream about.[59] The Global Soft Power Index 2021, compiled by Brand Finance, ranks Japan top in Asia and second globally.[60]

While the UK, US and EU have talked about challenging China's BRI with their own investment programmes, Japan has quietly got on with the job through such initiatives as the 'Partnership for Quality Infrastructure' and the 'Free and Open Indo-Pacific', aided by proximity and a close familiarity with Asian markets.[61] When Donald Trump withdrew from the Trans-Pacific Partnership, a free-trade agreement,

Japan stepped forward to fill the void, championing the pact, as it has the Comprehensive Economic Partnership, an Asian trade deal concluded in 2020. Both are seen by Tokyo as important economic and diplomatic pillars in the region, designed to counter Beijing's influence. Japan is also at the heart of an evolving network of military alliances, quietly expanding military ties and consultations with almost every country in the region.[62] It is an enthusiastic member of the revitalised Quadrilateral Security Dialogue (the 'Quad'), comprising the US, India, Japan and Australia, and has strengthened bilateral military ties with both India and Australia. When the British aircraft carrier, HMS *Queen Elizabeth* and its battle group visited the region in summer 2021, the Japanese navy was at hand to join the military exercises.

## CHAPTER 13

# *The Muddled China Policy of 'Global Britain'*

'I'm not going to tell you the UK government is going to pitchfork away every overture from China. Of course not. China is a gigantic part of our economic life and will be for a long time – for our lifetime.'

*Boris Johnson, October 2021*

The British and Japanese submarines played a game of cat and mouse in the depths of the Sea of Japan, taking it in turns to assume the role of the Chinese adversary. The exercise, described as the first of its kind, took place in mid-September 2021 and involved a nuclear-powered submarine from the Royal Navy and a Japanese diesel-electric vessel.[1] Few details were made available – it was one of the more sensitive drills that took place during the deployment to the region of Britain's new aircraft carrier, the HMS *Queen Elizabeth* and its strike group. The group also exercised with the *Izumo*, the modified Japanese carrier – 'deepening our co-operation and enhancing the interoperability between our armed forces', according to Commodore Steven Moorhouse, commander of the British strike group.[2] The war games ended with a fly-past by stealth fighters from the British and Japanese carriers.

HMS *Queen Elizabeth* is the largest and most powerful vessel ever constructed for the Royal Navy.[3] Its strike group, comprising eight ships, one submarine, thirty-two aircraft and 3,700 personnel, left Portsmouth in May 2021 with plans to visit forty nations.[4] The Royal Navy described it as 'the largest concentration of maritime and air power to leave the UK in a generation'.[5] It was sent on its way by Boris Johnson, who appeared on the bridge of the £3 billion carrier wearing a zipped-up navy-blue windcheater, with a round patch featuring the symbol of the carrier and the words 'PRIME MINISTER'. For Johnson, the eight-month, 26,000-mile voyage was to be a symbol of the new post-Brexit 'Global Britain', strutting out on the world stage. He wanted Britain to play a bigger role in the strategically important Indo-Pacific region, but to critics, 'Global Britain' was an empty slogan. They argued that Britain should concentrate its dwindling defence resources closer to home, and that the voyage of the *Queen Elizabeth* was a pointless and expensive exercise in battleship diplomacy, a reckless exercise in post-imperial nostalgia. Others suggested that Britain's diplomacy would be better served by stuffing the carrier's holds with Covid-19 vaccines for nations along the route who were struggling to control the virus.[6] 'This is a piece of diplomatic theatre, not a military strategy,' said Lord Peter Ricketts, a former UK national security adviser.[7] The strike group included a Dutch frigate and a US destroyer, and on the deck of the British carrier were ten US F-35B lightning jets, outnumbering the UK's eight. Some 250 of the carrier's 1,600 crew members were from the US Marine Corps. To critics, this underscored the limits of Britain's armed forces and the absurdity of the mission; to supporters it was a demonstration of how allies could work together, a sign of solidarity and strength.[8]

The carrier strike group exercised with the Indian navy in the Bay of Bengal, a 'muscular expression of the closer defence partnership' between the two countries, according to Commodore Moorhouse. As his ships prepared to enter the South China Sea, which is claimed in almost its entirety by China, he told the *Times of India* that freedom of navigation was the root of maritime law. 'As the UK defence secretary Ben Wallace recently said, we do so [enter the South China Sea] in a spirit of confidence, not confrontation. And just as we respect China, so we expect China to respect us in return.'[9] The group – or elements of it – also held drills with the navies of Singapore, South Korea and Vietnam. It took part in the Bersama Gold 2021 exercise, alongside forces from Malaysia, Singapore, Australia and New Zealand. The five nations comprise the Five Power Defence Arrangement (FPDA), originally formed in 1971 for the defence of Malaysia and Singapore and one of the world's oldest non-binding military pacts. Singapore's defence minister, Ng Eng Hen, described the FPDA as a 'stabiliser for the region' that remained relevant, even as security challenges changed.[10] Although few were saying so directly, it was another example of an old pact being freshened up and repurposed to face an increasingly aggressive China.

On 27 September 2021, HMS *Richmond*, a frigate from the carrier strike group, sailed through the narrow and sensitive Taiwan Strait, separating Taiwan from China. The ship was shadowed by Chinese air and naval forces, and in a statement the PLA's Eastern Theatre Command warned, 'This kind of behaviour harbours evil intentions and damages peace and stability in the Taiwan Strait.'[11] Chinese state media ridiculed Britain's 'second rate' navy. 'The UK's attempt to use an aircraft carrier strike group to project its strength and show its might to China is completely beyond its ability,' said the Party's *Global Times*.[12] At one point it suggested the PLA might make an example of the British. 'To execute one is an example to a hundred,' it warned in an editorial. 'To be precise, if the UK wants to play the role of bullying China in the region, it is demeaning itself. And if there is any real action against China, it is looking for a defeat.'[13] As the *Queen Elizabeth* and its support vessels prepared to leave the South China Sea, the Ministry of Defence announced that from late 2021 it would permanently assign two offshore patrol vessels to the region.[14]

Theatre or not, most commentators viewed the *Queen Elizabeth* carrier strike group as Britain's response to the new geopolitics of the region. Yet when he sent off the strike group from Portsmouth, Boris Johnson struck a curiously ambiguous tone, referring to 'our friends in China' and even appeared apologetic, saying that although the mission was designed to uphold the international law of the sea, 'We don't want to antagonise anybody.'[15] That same ambiguity was evident when Britain struck a deal with Australia and the US to help Australia build nuclear submarines. The AUKUS pact is clearly designed to deter China, but in interviews after it was signed Johnson went out of his way to avoid directly saying so.[16] He insisted that he was a 'Sinophile' and later told MPs that the deal was 'not intended to be adversarial towards any other power'.[17] It seemed like a curious way to deter, almost as if Johnson had not quite made up his mind what all this activity was for. Rather like Voldemort, the main antagonist in the Harry Potter films, it seemed like he dare not utter the name of China or Xi Jinping in relation to his defence strategy – the Chinese leader became 'Xi Who Must Not Be Named'.

Similar ambiguities were evident in a March 2021 'Integrated Review of Security, Defence, Development and Foreign Policy', which identified the 'geopolitical and economic centre of gravity moving eastward towards the Indo-Pacific' as the most significant of global trends.[18] The review designated China as 'the biggest state-based threat to the UK's economic security' and a 'systemic competitor', but it also described Beijing as an 'important partner in tackling global challenges like pandemic preparedness, diversity and climate change'. It emphasised the importance of economic ties, saying, 'We will continue to pursue a positive economic relationship, including deeper trade links and more Chinese investment in the UK.' Incredibly, the review did not even mention Taiwan. The contradictions were not lost on Lord Peter Ricketts, the UK's former national security adviser. 'A kind way of putting it would be that this is a policy of strategic ambiguity,' he said. 'A less kind way would be to say the government isn't able to tell us where the balance is going to lie between a competitor challenge [with China], an adversarial relationship and one where we are needing them economically.'[19]

In October 2021, the Science Museum was the backdrop for another attempt by 'Global Britain' to assert itself, and another display of ambiguity. It was the venue of a 'global investment summit' for 200-odd international business leaders, followed by a reception with the Royal Family at Windsor Castle. Plenty of thought had gone into the choreography, but government thinking on China was as muddled as ever. In an interview with Bloomberg ahead of the summit, Boris Johnson was pressed on what sort of investment he welcomed from China. 'Investment in stuff that drives jobs and growth in this country,' he replied rather vaguely, before adding 'I'm not going to tell you the UK government is going to pitchfork away every overture from China. Of course not. China is a gigantic part of our economic life and will be for a long time – for our lifetime.'[20] At the same time he said Britain would not be naive about its critical national infrastructure, citing 5G next-generation telecoms networks, from which Britain had excluded the Chinese telecoms giant Huawei, and nuclear power, where Britain was trying to extricate itself from a Chinese partnership. His words were echoed by his international trade secretary, Anne-Marie Trevelyan, who said Britain was not uneasy about Chinese investment in most parts of the economy. 'For everything that's in a non-strategic area, we welcome investment from all those who understand the value and importance of working here,' she said.[21]

The problem of course is how to define 'strategic'. At the time of the summit (and in the run up to COP26, an international climate change conference held in Glasgow in autumn 2021) the government announced that Huaneng, a Chinese state-owned power company is to invest in a battery storage project described as a 'major new milestone for battery storage in the UK'.[22] The facility is expected to be built alongside an existing project in Minety, Wiltshire, which involves Huaneng and CNIC, a Chinese state-owned investment company, and is touted as the largest lithium-ion storage facility in Europe.[23] At the same time Envision, a Shanghai-based manufacturer of wind turbines, announced a big expansion of its electric vehicle battery plant in Sunderland. At the time of writing this was Britain's only 'Gigafactory', as such factories have been dubbed, making these key components for the future of motoring. 'The electric car has become the starting point for the green industrial revolution,' said Zhang Lei, the billionaire owner of Envision, when he announced the expansion.[24] Zhang is also a member of the National People's Congress (NPC), China's rubber-stamp parliament, and the Chinese People's Political Consultative Conference, a Communist Party advisory body.[25] Chinese entities are quickly establishing an outsize role in British battery projects, giving them a powerful grip on a technology considered vital for our 'green' future – though they do not appear to come under the government's definition of 'strategic'. As we have seen elsewhere in this book, this is only part of China's tightening grip on the global battery supply chain, which extends from mineral extraction and processing to the production of the batteries and electric vehicles themselves.

An Australian company, Peak Rare Earths, is planning to build a $165 million rare earth refinery on Teesside to extract a compound critical for powerful magnets used in wind turbines and electric cars – an investment that was seen as an important step for the UK towards lessening dependence on Beijing for these key minerals. In January 2022, it was reported that the company is no longer so Australian, having sold a 20 per cent stake to Shenghe Resources, the Chinese rare earths giant we met in Greenland in Chapter 5.[26]

At least nuclear power is now recognised as 'strategic'. Under a 2015 deal, agreed at the height of David Cameron's so-called 'golden era' of relations, China's state-owned nuclear group CGN was to build its own nuclear power station in Bradwell on the Essex coast in exchange for financially backing two French-led projects in Britain.[27] This, in spite of CGN being accused by the US government of stealing American technology for military use and being placed on the US 'entity list', which effectively bans US companies from doing business with it. Washington warned against partnering with the company. By 2022, the first French project, at Hinkley Point in southwest England, was well under way and well over budget. It is expected to cost more than £22 billion and CGN has a 33 per cent stake. The second French project, at Sizewell in Suffolk, has yet to begin construction. As is so often the way with Chinese investment, Beijing's goals were strategic, with Bradwell as the real prize – the first Chinese-designed plant outside its own borders, which Beijing saw as a springboard for international sales of its technology. In summer 2021, the government said it was looking for ways of removing CGN from the Sizewell project and scrapping Bradwell, but it was unclear how it was going to fill the funding hole or manage the fallout with Beijing.[28]

The Cameron 'golden era' that spawned the nuclear deal is now dead, though it is not clear precisely what it has been replaced with. Britain needed considerable prodding from the United States before it barred Huawei from Britain's 5G networks, and sought to remove China from the country's nuclear infrastructure. Britain has been a popular and welcoming destination for Chinese investment, which has been valued at £134 billion. Almost 200 British companies are either controlled by Chinese investors or count them as minority shareholders – from the energy, defence, infrastructure, property and transport sector, to healthcare, schools and technology.[29] Chinese companies have invested in the Leadenhall Building in the City, otherwise known as the 'Cheesegrater', as well as Pizza Express, Thomas Cook, Wolves and Southampton football clubs, and a company that builds black cabs. A Chinese sovereign wealth fund holds minority stakes in Thames Water and Heathrow Airport, while China's National Offshore Oil Corporation (CNOOC) is responsible for around a quarter of UK North Sea oil production. Chinese entities have also bought stakes in the National Grid's gas distribution arm, and Global Switch, one of the world's largest cloud data providers. Chinese venture capital firms built stakes in a number of emerging British tech companies, including Oxford Nanopore, the gene-sequencing company, and Immunocore, a cancer specialist. The risks in this type of investment came to light in 2020 when Chinese shareholders sought to take control of Imagination, a Hertfordshire-based designer of mobile graphics processors, flouting assurances that they would be passive investors. On this occasion the government blocked the attempted boardroom coup.[30]

While Huawei has been excluded from 5G, the company remains deeply embedded in earlier generation telecoms networks and has extensive research tie-ups throughout British academia. Other Chinese tech companies are being welcomed with little scrutiny into sensitive corners of the British economy. Take Hikvision, the world's biggest manufacturer of surveillance cameras and a leader in the marriage of those cameras with artificial intelligence, which includes facial recognition and gait recognition – identifying the unique way an individual walks. There are even cameras able to read emotions. Hikvision has close links to the Communist Party, is an enabler of Xi Jinping's dystopian surveillance state and has been blacklisted by the US government for facilitating repression in Xinjiang. The UK Parliament Foreign Affairs Committee has called for the company to be banned from Britain. Yet an estimated 1.2 million Hikvision cameras are being used in the UK by airports, local councils, hospitals – even on buses and in schools.[31] More than half of London's councils own Chinese surveillance cameras.[32] They are widely used by government departments – it was a Hikvision camera in the UK's health department that captured former Health Minister Matt Hancock kissing an aide, images which were leaked and led to the end of his job and his marriage. The leak of the images was blamed on a disgruntled employee – but it is deeply troubling that surveillance tech made by a Communist Party-linked entity was being used at the heart of government.[33]

UK intelligence agencies reportedly pushed for curbs on 'smart cities' technology supplied by China, fearing it could facilitate surveillance, espionage, sabotage or the theft of sensitive data.[34] 'Smart cities' is the umbrella term used for the surveillance cameras, sensors and other 'intelligent' systems that will supposedly keep our future cities ticking over – but collect a chilling amount of data in the process. In a May 2021 blog post highlighting the potential dangers, Ian Levy, the technical director of the National Cyber Security Centre (NCSC), a branch of GCHQ, invoked *The Italian Job* to make his point about the vulnerabilities. In the 1969 film, Michael Caine stars as Charlie Croker, leader of a cockney gang who rob a lorry full of gold bullion by shutting down Turin's traffic control system and causing gridlock.[35]

In January 2022, a new National Security and Investment Act (NSIA) came into force in the UK, empowering ministers to block company takeovers deemed harmful to national security. The bill was watered down during its passage, raising the threshold above which an overseas stake must be examined from 15 per cent to 25 per cent.[36] This will sharply reduce the number of deals facing scrutiny, and the rules were criticised as too cumbersome and missing too many small but worrying investments.[37] The government insisted it had a great deal of discretion as to how the rules were exercised – but discretion cuts both ways. A few months before the law came into force, ministers waved through the acquisition by a Chinese company of Newport Wafer Fab, the UK's largest producer of semiconductors, only ordering a probe after the intervention of senior Conservative backbenchers.[38]

The problem with Johnson's attempt to separate pricklier political issues from economic relations is that this is not a distinction China makes. As we have seen, under Xi Jinping, China has stepped up the use of trade, investment and market access as tools of coercion. It is not just a question of Britain protecting narrowly defined 'strategic' parts of the economy, but of avoiding an over-dependence on China more broadly. This can be in trade, tech or supply chains, which Beijing has not hesitated to weaponise against others. China does not have private companies in the sense they are understood in the West. All companies are beholden to the Party and exist at its pleasure. Several laws require them to assist the Party on demand. Within China, tech companies are an integral part of the surveillance state. The Communist Party is never far from the boardroom, whatever the share certificate says, and the Party is adept at spotting strategically important acquisitions.

University research tie-ups have also come under greater scrutiny. In May 2021, the UK government announced the establishment of a Research Collaboration Advice Team (RCAT) to offer universities advice about protecting their work from 'hostile activity'.[39] 'This new team will give universities and institutions access to the latest advice on safe collaboration with international partners and protections against those who seek to harm the UK,' said Business Secretary Kwasi Kwarteng. His move followed growing concern over partnerships with Chinese research institutions and companies, and the threat of espionage and IP theft, but university vice-chancellors grumbled that government guidance lacked clarity, and critics claimed the RCAT was insufficiently robust.

The Cameron–Osborne 'golden era' acted like a giant starting pistol for Britain's increasingly business-orientated universities to chase Chinese cash. Research collaborations between the UK and China increased by 115.6 per cent between 2013 and 2019. There were 15,623 such tie-ups in 2019, making China Britain's biggest research partner after the US and Germany, and the fastest growing.[40] It seemed like easy money, and UK universities scrambled for it with little regard to due diligence. By 2021 Chinese Communist Party-linked entities were deeply embedded in Britain's universities. A report from the think tank Civitas claimed that half of the UK's twenty-four Russell Group universities, usually considered the UK's leading research institutions, had relationships with universities or companies linked to China's military.[41] A February 2022 investigation by *The Times* newspaper revealed that British universities had accepted £240 million from Chinese institutions, many with links to the military. It suggested the number of research collaborations between scientists in the UK and Chinese institutes with deep connections to the country's defence forces has tripled to more than 1,000 in six years.[42]

The UK's security agencies gave a stark warning about the risks of collaborating with countries such as Russia and China. Hostile state actors were targeting British universities to steal research and intellectual property 'which could be used to help their own military, commercial and authoritarian interests', said the Centre for the Protection of National Infrastructure.[43] Huawei alone was working with thirty-five UK institutes and universities, including funding advanced facilities at Cambridge, Edinburgh, Surrey and Imperial College London.[44] It was allowed to buy a small stake in Oxford Sciences Innovation, a company that commercialises research from Oxford University, giving the Chinese telecoms maker access to some of the most promising early stage technology developed by academics in Britain.[45]

Cambridge University, which came in for particular scrutiny for its links with China, in 2021 announced its own guidelines for students and academics working on projects with countries that 'do not share the UK's commitment to democracy and the rule of law', as vice-chancellor Stephen Toope described it.[46] Toope, who was scheduled to step down in September 2022, is a human rights lawyer by training, yet has been a strong advocate of strengthening ties with Beijing. One of the first places he visited after becoming vice-chancellor in 2017 was the Chinese embassy in London, where he posed for photographs with Ambassador Liu Xiaoming, and the two men discussed collaboration in furthering the 'golden era' of China–UK relations, according to the embassy website.[47] Shortly afterwards, Toope told *Xinhua*, 'There will be more opportunities to engage actively with China, a country with an extraordinarily growing influence which a university like Cambridge must pay attention to.'[48]

On Toope's watch, Cambridge accepted millions of pounds from the Chinese government to set up a 'smart cities' research centre in the city of Nanjing. It described the Cambridge University-Nanjing Centre of Technology and Innovation, as its 'most ambitious' Chinese collaboration to date, and its first overseas enterprise of this scale. 'The innovations emerging from this Centre will enable the development of "smart" cities in which sensors can enable sustainable lifestyles, improve healthcare, limit pollution and make efficient use of energy,' Toope said, as he stood shoulder to shoulder with Nanjing's Communist Party boss at a September 2019 ground-breaking ceremony for the new centre.[49] Perhaps fully connected cities brimming with cameras and sensors will improve urban lifestyles, but in Xi Jinping's China that same technology is enabling hitherto unseen levels of surveillance and repression.

The Nanjing tie-up was driven by Cambridge's Engineering Department, which also announced in 2021 that it had received a 'generous gift' from the Chinese company Tencent to help fund research into futuristic quantum computers.[50] In a statement on its website, the department said, 'Founded in 1998, Tencent uses technology to enrich the lives of Internet users.' This and other phrases were lifted directly from Tencent's publicity material.[51] A little due diligence would have revealed that Tencent is closely linked to the Communist Party and its security agencies. Its ubiquitous WeChat app (Weixin in China), the 'app for everything', as it is often called, is a key component of the surveillance state – censoring, pumping out disinformation and spying on users.[52]

In March 2022, Prince Charles formally opened the new home of the Cambridge Institute for Sustainable Leadership. It is housed in the city's old telephone exchange, which has been turned into the ultimate low-energy building at a cost of £12.8 million. The building is called Entopia (a play on energy and utopia) and was named by Zhang Lei, the entrepreneur and Communist Party adviser who we met earlier. His company, Envision, provided just under half the funds.[53] When work on the building began a year earlier, Toope described it as 'the most sustainable premises in the University of Cambridge Estate'. It coincided with the National People's Congress, of which Zhang is a member, overwhelmingly endorsing a law to neuter Hong Kong's electoral system, snuffing the last life out of democracy in the former British colony.

Huawei is also busy building what is described as Cambridge's 'first 5G mobile private network' within the university-owned Cambridge Science Park. It is part of a partnership to accelerate the digitisation of the park. Partners gain access to 'our state of-the-art equipment and markets including China and beyond', said Huawei Vice-President Victor Zhang.[54] In other words, the company that was barred on national security grounds from participation in Britain's national 5G infrastructure was handed contracts to provide that same technology and more to what is touted as a home for some of Britain's most innovative new companies. Cambridge University has a £200 million joint venture to develop the science park with Tuspark an offshoot of China's Tsinghua University.[55] It is apparently unperturbed by Xi Jinping's intense crackdown on academic freedom, including the persecution of prominent Tsinghua law professor Xu Zhangrun. He was barred from teaching and detained after criticising Xi Jinping's 'cult of personality' and his handling of the Covid-19 pandemic.[56] Tsinghua University is Xi Jinping's alma mater and senior Tsinghua academics are regarded as the ideological architects of the Communist Party's efforts to eradicate the Uyghur culture in Xinjiang. Hu Angang who heads the university's Institute of Contemporary China Studies, co-authored an influential book with senior Party official Hu Lianhe, that argued for a single 'state-race'. 'Any nation's long-term peace and stability is founded upon building a system with a unified race (a state-race) that strengthens the state-race identity and dilutes ethnic group identity,' they wrote.[57]

The area around Cambridge aspires to become the next Silicon Valley, Europe's answer to the Californian high-tech start-up scene, and Huawei aspires to be at the heart of it. The Cambridge version has been dubbed 'Silicon Fen' after the nearby wetlands. It is an area on the outskirts of the city that is home to more than 5,000 companies, employing 68,000 people, many attracted by the proximity to the world-class research of the university and the technical spin-outs it is producing.[58] On 25 June 2020, Huawei was given planning permission to build a £1 billion research campus in 'Silicon Fen'. It was the same day that the Trump administration listed Huawei among firms owned or backed by the Chinese military.[59] 'It's the perfect location for this integrated innovation campus. Through close collaboration with research institutes, universities, and local industry, we want to advance optical communications technology for the industry as a whole, while doing our part to support the UK's broader Industrial Strategy,' said Victor Zhang.[60]

Jesus College Cambridge has two China-focused centres: a China Centre established in 2017 and a UK–China Global Issues Dialogue Centre, established the following year. They were both creatures of the 'golden era', designed primarily to ingratiate the college with China. Both initially embarked on programmes of China-friendly events that largely steered clear of topics such as Xinjiang, Hong Kong, Taiwan and human rights in general. Their websites borrowed language from Communist Party handouts, dripping with jargon about China's 'extraordinary transformation' and its 'rejuvenation' under the leadership of the Party. The Dialogue Centre was set up with money from the Chinese government's National Development and Reform Commission (NDRC), a planning agency, and has accepted sponsorship from Huawei. Both centres have sought to reinvent themselves in the light of growing criticism – the Dialogue Centre dropping the word 'China' from its title, the China Centre adopting a more varied programme, and both have changed the language of their websites.[61] Though as recently as November 2020, Professor Peter Nolan, director of the China Centre, cautioned students against discussing China's human rights abuses in Xinjiang and Hong Kong, saying it might not be 'helpful in advancing mutual understanding', warning that 'We have a lot of mainland students.' He made the comments to a meeting of an advisory committee of the China Centre that was discussing forthcoming events, a transcript of which was obtained by the openDemocracy website and shared with *The Sunday Times*.[62] In August 2021, Nolan was one of the first visitors to the Chinese embassy in London to meet new ambassador, Zheng Zequang. They sat sipping water beside large flags of the UK and China and below a giant painting of galloping horses, depicting the 'liberation' of Tibet. The two men 'had an in-depth exchange of views on outstanding global and regional issues'.[63]

'Leadership training' for Chinese corporate bosses and Party officials, often one and the same thing, has also been a lucrative business for Jesus College. Its Chinese Executive Leadership Programme 'each year brings CEOs from China's largest firms to the University of Cambridge for a three-week training programme, taught by a combination of academics and the leaders of international firms', according to the college's website.[64]

Events in Hong Kong have been especially tricky for Cambridge University. When students from the territory demanded that Wolfson College strip Hong Kong Chief Executive Carrie Lam of her honorary fellowship in the light of the crackdown against the pro-democracy movement, Wolfson initially refused.[65] Only after a draconian security law was imposed in 2020, did it say that it was 'considering' her position. Lam eventually took the decision out of Wolfson's wavering hands, cutting her ties with the college.[66] Hong Kong students who protested in Cambridge faced intimidation, threats and surveillance from mainland Chinese students. Mainlanders are the biggest single group of international students at the university, more than 1,300 strong, and an important source of revenue. One Wolfson student from Hong Kong, Ulysses Chow, in his third year at the time, said he no longer felt safe after being bombarded with online abuse and even a death threat to his mother.[67]

Hong Kong students are particularly wary of the Chinese Students and Scholars Association (CSSA), which depicts itself as a social, cultural and welfare organisation. In reality it works in tandem with, and is at least partly funded by, the Chinese embassy. It is the embassy's eyes and ears on British campuses, keeping tabs on Chinese students, and mobilising them to hound perceived enemies and critics. In 2011, the CSSA was briefly disbanded by Cambridge after accusations of electoral interference by the embassy and bribery by its favoured candidate for president. It has since come under increasingly close scrutiny internationally, but at Cambridge it is heavily indulged by the colleges, according to Hong Kong students.

The examples above are numerous and wide-ranging – but they barely scratch the surface, so embedded are Chinese Communist Party-linked entities in British academia. Cambridge has strongly denied that accepting Chinese money impinges in any way on academic freedom. It insists that its research is 'subject to ethics governance and export control regulations', and that it has a 'robust system for reviewing strategic relationships and donations'.[68] For some academics, the mere act of outsiders scrutinising partnerships and examining how innovations are applied by partners is seen as a grubby affront to academic freedom. The lack of transparency about donations and other tie-ups is worthy of the Communist Party itself. Cambridge is especially prickly, not welcoming scrutiny. It is not the only university implicated, far from it, but arguably has a special responsibility as the top-ranked university in Britain.

As I have argued elsewhere in this book, in China the Communist Party is never far from the lab or the lecture theatre or the boardroom, whatever the share certificate says, or a researcher's nominal affiliation.

Supposedly commercial enterprises enjoy subsidies, hidden and open, and are deployed by the Party in a strategic manner. Research bodies are similarly encumbered since by law innovations must be shared with the security apparatus and the military. Xi Jinping has tightened this requirement by having 'civil–military fusion' written into the constitution. Beijing is adept at picking off know-how it sees as strategically important, and no doubt regards British academia as a rich and gullible repository. 'National security' is often difficult to assess, and the bodies established by the UK government to provide advice and to examine business investment and academic collaboration hardly seem equipped for the task.

In January 2022, MI5, Britain's domestic intelligence agency, sent an 'interference alert' to House of Commons Speaker Sir Lindsey Hoyle, which he then passed on to MPs. It warned that Christine Lee, a London-based Anglo-Chinese solicitor, was 'knowingly engaged in political interference activities on behalf of the United Front Work Department of the Chinese Communist Party'.[69] Lee was accused of attempting to influence several MPs from the Labour, Lib Dems and Conservative parties through donations or 'donations in kind'. The biggest were to Labour MP Barry Gardiner, who received tens of thousands of pounds. Lee's son was a volunteer diary manager for Gardiner, who generally took a pro-Beijing line while he was in Jeremy Corbyn's shadow cabinet. The Brent North MP said the donations were fully declared, and he had been 'liaising with our security services for a number of years about Christine Lee'. He said he made MI5 fully aware 'of her engagement with my office and the donations she made to fund researchers in my office in the past'.

Perhaps the biggest surprise was that Lee's activities came as a surprise at all. The Chinese Communist Party operates a vast and growing influence operation in Britain, which has pretty much been allowed free rein. Influence is of course the stuff of all diplomacy, but China has persistently crossed the line between influence on the one hand, and infiltration and interference on the other. The United Front Work Department (UFWD) is an opaque organisation, responsible for coordinating these operations. It is run from a large, nameless compound next to Party headquarters in Beijing, and much of its work is covert, using front organisations or individuals to funnel money and favours in an effort to promote the Party's interests and shape opinion in its favour. Mao Zedong once described 'united front' work as a 'magic weapon', and it has been a particular priority of Xi Jinping, who has overseen a massive expansion of its activities.

Lee, who is affiliated with the Chinese Overseas Friendship Association, made a £5,000 donation to the local party association of Liberal Democrat leader Sir Ed Davey while he was energy secretary in the coalition government led by David Cameron. A spokesman for the party said Sir Ed was 'shocked by these revelations'. When she was prime minister, Theresa May presented Lee with an award for 'promoting engagement, understanding and cooperation between the Chinese and British communities in the UK'. She reportedly targeted members of the now disbanded parliamentary group, Chinese in Britain. Payments came from Hong Kong and China, but were made covertly to disguise the origin of the money. No action was taken against Lee because Britain has no laws against political influence activities that fall short of espionage. MI5's interference alert was only the second it has ever issued, and that it felt the need to sound the alarm is testament to its concern about just how thoroughly compromised British institutions have become.

The UFWD operates in parallel with China's conventional espionage agencies. The word *Qingbao* in Chinese means both 'intelligence' and 'information', and it neatly encapsulates the unique nature and breadth of a vast system that combines formal and informal techniques, both overt and covert. There is often a fine line between theft and the voluntary transfer of know-how, and, as we have seen with British universities, China has pushed the latter to the limit. Over the years, the CCP has built a comprehensive system for spotting and acquiring foreign technologies by multiple means.

Two months before Lee was unmasked as an agent of influence, Richard Moore, the head of Britain's Secret Intelligence Service MI6, warned that 'Chinese intelligence services are highly capable and continue to conduct large-scale espionage operations against the UK and our allies. This includes targeting those working in government, industries, or on research of particular interest to the Chinese state. They also monitor and attempt to exercise undue influence over the Chinese diaspora.'[70]

In a September 2021 report, the House of Lords International Relations and Defence Committee described UK policy on China as a 'strategic void'.[71] It said that while ambiguity sometimes has advantages, much more clarity was needed on dealings with Beijing. The report warned on China's possible 'weaponisation of trade, investment and the supply of raw materials', and said: 'Increased economic co-operation must not be at the cost of upholding the UK's values, including human rights and labour protection. The Government must not sit on the fence over these issues.'[72]

Seven former foreign secretaries, covering both major political parties in the UK, joined forces to urge the British government to take the lead in coordinating an international response to China's repression in Hong Kong. They argued that as the former colonial power and co-signatory to the 'one country two systems' agreement that China has now dismantled, Britain has a special moral and legal obligation.[73] Others have urged the government to sanction Hong Kong leaders accused of human rights abuses and to extend visa rights, particularly for Hong Kong students and young people who had been at the forefront of the protest movement.[74] During a parliamentary exchange in September 2021, Boris Johnson was accused of failing in his duty and challenged to take 'meaningful action', including sanctions. Johnson said he found the accusation 'a bit bizarre', claiming that Britain has stood up for human rights. He cited a visa scheme open to British National (Overseas) passport holders and their immediate dependents that allows for 300,000 Hong Kong residents to come to the UK. He told parliament, 'I think it is very important that we continue to engage with our Chinese partners, but to engage very firmly on the points that we care about, whether it is human rights in Hong Kong, democracy in Hong Kong or the treatment of the Uyghurs.'[75]

Johnson's government in March 2021 joined the EU, Canada and the US in sanctioning for the first time senior officials in Xinjiang for 'gross human rights violations' against the Uyghurs, for which China retaliated with sanctions of its own, including against five British MPs who had been critical of China.[76] The British parliament passed a non-binding resolution that, for the first time, described China's persecution of the Uyghurs as 'crimes against humanity and genocide'.[77] Then Foreign Secretary Dominic Raab accused China of 'industrial scale' abuses, but the government shied away from using the term genocide – at least not in public.

In November 2021, *The Times* reported that Liz Truss, who succeeded Raab as foreign secretary, had privately accused China of committing genocide. She reportedly did so in a testy conversation with Caroline

Wilson, the UK ambassador to China, who urged a less confrontational approach to Beijing. Wilson reportedly asked why Britain could not treat China 'like we treat the French', to which Truss retorted, 'Because the French aren't committing genocide.' The call, confirmed by two sources, took place while Truss was still in her old role as international trade secretary and is said to have ended abruptly.[78] She was said to be 'personally appalled' by the persecution of the Uyghurs. She was also more wary of China's unfair trade practices and economic coercion. During a visit to India shortly after she became foreign secretary, she said: 'The way I would put it is that, of course, we trade with China. It's an important trading partner of the UK. But it's important that we don't become strategically dependent.'[79] The conversation with Ambassador Wilson was almost certainly leaked by allies of Truss to emphasise her more hardline stance on China – a stance that is considerably more hawkish than that of her predecessor Raab or of Boris Johnson.

By early 2022, a tug of war was raging within the British government over China policy and strategy. The more dovish wing was led by chancellor Rishi Sunak, who argued for a reset in relations, starting with the revival of a major trade summit that had been suspended amid tensions over Covid and Hong Kong. 'The debate on China lacks nuance,' he said. While a source close to Sunak asserted: 'Like it or not you can't ignore the China trade opportunity.'[80] That sentiment seemed to have the support of the prime minister. One former Downing Street official even suggested Johnson's decision to ban Huawei from Britain's 5G networks lacked conviction, and had only been made under pressure from the US and his own backbenchers.[81]

Truss heightened her rhetoric on Hong Kong, urging China to uphold freedom of speech, after the mass removal of district councillors deemed insufficiently loyal to Beijing. That earned her a sharp rebuke from the Chinese embassy for her 'irresponsible' remarks.[82] The criminalisation of political activity and the elimination of the last vestiges of freedom in Hong Kong continued apace. Hong Kong's prisons were filling with political prisoners – by late 2021 an estimated 10,000 people had been arrested in connection with the pro-democracy protests, though court proceedings had only begun against a quarter of them.[83] As with all such regimes, there were times when the repression teetered on the brink of farce. During the Hong Kong marathon in October 2021, runners were ordered to cover up tattoos, slogans or logos or be banned from the race. One male runner was told to cover with a bandage a tattoo on his leg reading 'Hong Kong add oil' – a common Cantonese phrase of support. A woman was stopped from running after organisers took issue with a 'Hong Kong' logo on her shorts. The marathon was sponsored by the British bank Standard Chartered.[84]

The two buildings are at opposite ends of London and very different in character, but they both speak to Beijing's influence and ambition – and the ability of determined people to push back. The first, in Wapping in the east of the city, is the grand former home of the Royal Mint, which China has bought and plans to transform into its biggest embassy in Europe. The second, on a modern business park in Chiswick, west London, is the new European headquarters of China Global Television Network (CGTN), the international arm of the Communist Party's propaganda channel.

At the handover ceremony for the Royal Mint site in March 2018, ambassador Liu Xiaoming proclaimed, 'It is the new face of China in the new era, to write a new chapter for a China–UK golden era.'[85] The Georgian building, constructed in 1809, will be at the heart of a vast embassy complex, a 'new landmark for London' and a 'welcoming public face for China', according to Liu. Its sale to Beijing was brokered on behalf of the UK government by one of Boris Johnson's closest aides, Sir Edward Lister (since ennobled as Baron Udny-Lister). Johnson was foreign secretary at the time, and it was later revealed that Lister was being paid both by the property firm representing Beijing and the developer that sold the site for £255 million.[86] Ambassador Liu personally thanked Lister for his 'effort' in securing the deal.[87] The government insisted that Johnson's trusted adviser had declared his interests in the appropriate way and there were no conflicts of interest.[88] When Johnson became prime minister, he appointed Lister as his Chief Strategic Adviser and then interim Chief of Staff after the departure of Dominic Cummings. One former Downing Street aide described him as 'a strong Sinophile voice in Johnson's ear'.[89] He left government in April 2021 and later that year became a senior adviser to the chairman of HSBC.[90]

Tower Hamlets is one of Britain's poorest and most diverse boroughs. It is also nearly 40 per cent Muslim, the largest proportion of any borough in Britain, and the East End of London has a long history of fighting oppression and tyranny. The 1936 Battle of Cable Street, less than a mile from the Royal Mint, stopped Oswald Mosley's blackshirt fascists marching through what at the time was the predominantly Jewish Whitechapel district.[91] Soon after the Royal Mint deal was done John Biggs, the mayor of Tower Hamlets, wrote to Liu that 'reports about the situation in Xinjiang are of huge concern to our diverse borough'. Liu hit back that such reports are 'all lies fabricated by a few irresponsible politicians and media from the West'.[92] Councillors also raised concerns about repression in Hong Kong and the practical issue of road closures and disruption from anticipated protests. Liu angrily demanded that local councillors stop trying to disrupt his plans. In March 2021, the local council voted to consider changing the names of roads and buildings in the surrounding area. Tiananmen Square, Uyghur Court, Hong Kong Road and Tibet Hill were among the suggestions to 'assert support for the freedom and diversity of our borough'.[93]

CGTN's European production centre is a 30,000-square-foot, state-of-the-art facility occupying an entire floor of a new building in Chiswick Park, west London. It is at the forefront of a vast worldwide expansion of China's state-owned media, which China's leaders have described as the 'eyes, ears, tongue and throat of the Communist Party'.[94] Complaints soon came rolling in. Ofcom, the UK government's broadcast regulator, found CGTN repeatedly broke its impartiality rules during coverage of the Hong Kong pro-democracy protests. The Chinese broadcaster was also sanctioned for airing forced confessions on multiple occasions. These included those of British private investigator Peter Humphrey and his wife Yu Yingzeng, who were imprisoned on charges of illegally trading in personal information. Humphrey later described how he had been drugged and locked into an iron chair while cameras shot his 'confession' through the bars of his cage.[95] Confessions made under duress have always been a feature of communist China, but have increased under Xi Jinping, broadcast and amplified by propaganda outlets at home and abroad.

In February 2021, CGTN was stripped of its licence to broadcast in the UK when an Ofcom investigation found the network is controlled directly by the Chinese Communist Party. That seemed to somewhat state the obvious, but was still a big step for Ofcom, whose rules state that a broadcaster should not be under direct political control.[96] Beijing retaliated by banning the BBC from broadcasting in China, even though the BBC was already restricted to international hotels, and business and residential compounds for foreigners, and was regularly blacked out when carrying critical reports.[97] CGTN fought back, and in August 2021, it announced that it was back on the air in the UK having found a loophole. Under the European Convention on Transfrontier Television (ECTT), of which the UK remains a member, CGTN has the right to air in the UK using a licence from any country bound by that agreement. It secured an authorisation from the French TV regulator, the Conseil supérieur de l'audiovisuel (CSA), though it is unclear how long this will last since the CSA is also investigating CGTN for rule breaking.[98] By the end of 2021, it has yet to find a platform willing to take its programming and was exploring streaming services that do not require a broadcast licence.[99]

The story of these two buildings, in Chiswick and Tower Hamlets, does hold some hope for those wishing to see the Chinese Communist Party held to account. But, as we have seen, British policy on China lacks clarity. At the time of writing there is still considerable tension within government over how tough to be towards China. The result is an ambiguous message. The experience of CGTN and the Royal Mint demonstrate that China has considerable ambition and sway, that it is persistent – and in the battle for influence, it sees Britain as very much in play.

When Boris Johnson was looking for advice on the economic opportunities for 'Global Britain' he turned to former Australian Prime Minister Tony Abbott, appointing him as a special trade envoy. Abbott was once a strong supporter of engagement with China, signing a free-trade deal with Beijing during his time as prime minister between 2013 and 2015. During a visit to the UK, he said he would not sign such a deal today. 'I think it's been a hell of a wake-up call,' he said.[100] He shared a platform in London with Liz Truss, then Britain's secretary of state for international trade. 'The Beijing government sees trade as a strategic weapon to be turned on and off, like a tap, to reward friends and to punish foes,' he warned. He described China as a far more formidable adversary than the Soviet Union, 'because it's been increasingly embedded inside the global economy and can bring economic as well as military pressure to bear against its targets', he said.[101] He was speaking from bitter experience.

## CHAPTER 14

# *Standing up to China: Lessons from Aussie 'Scumbags' and 'Tiny, Crazy' Lithuanians*

'Clearly, Canberra is increasingly unhinged and in way over its head by taking such a suicidal attack on not just China but also its own economic interests.'

*Global Times, April 2021*

It was a remarkable speech even by the standards of China's aggressive 'wolf warrior' diplomats. 'History will prove that it is wise and visionary to be China's friend,' Wang Xining told his audience of Australian business people. Then came the warning – those who 'deliberately vilify' China are 'scum' who will be 'cast aside in history', he barked. 'Their children will be ashamed of mentioning their names in the history.' The deputy head of mission at the Chinese embassy in Canberra was speaking at a Lunar New Year dinner in the Australian capital in March 2021. The Chinese version of the speech includes the characters for *bài lèi*, which translate as 'degenerate' or 'scum' (or 'scumbag' as outraged Australians rendered it), though in an English-language transcript the embassy removed the offending word.[1] It was only the latest in a fuselage of insults and threats fired at Australia – with Chinese officials describing the country as 'sick' and in need of medicine, and peddling 'ignorance and bigotry'. State media published a cartoon depicting Australia as a gormless kangaroo puppet controlled by America.[2] It described the country as 'gum stuck on the bottom of China's shoe' and a 'giant kangaroo that serves as a dog of the US'.[3]

Australia's offence? To call for an independent inquiry into the origin of Covid-19, which first emerged in the Chinese city of Wuhan in December 2019. When Australia began its push for an inquiry, in

April 2020, China's Ambassador Jingye Cheng, threatened a boycott of the country's goods. 'Maybe the ordinary people will say "Why should we drink Australian wine? Eat Australian beef?"' Cheng said.[4] When Australia stood firm, accusing Beijing of 'economic coercion', China followed up its threats by launching a trade war, targeting up to A$19 billion dollars in Australian exports.[5] China is Australia's biggest trading partner, taking more than a third of the country's exports, mostly resources, though Beijing initially targeted barley, beef, cotton, coal, wine and seafood.[6] It hit them with hefty tariffs or other spurious technical restrictions, which effectively blocked their import to China. Beijing warned its students and tourists against travelling to a 'racist' country. China had become Australia's biggest source of both international students and foreign visitors at the time, though the immediate impact was blunted by the Covid-19 pandemic, which closed Australia's and China's borders. 'Clearly, Canberra is increasingly unhinged and in way over its head by taking such a suicidal attack on not just China but also its own economic interests,' the *Global Times* growled.[7] Beijing has used trade as a weapon many times and in many places over the years, but what made the Australian boycott stand out was its sheer size, equivalent to around 10 per cent of Australia's exports, with little attempt to dress it up as anything other than a punishment for 'hurting the feelings of the Chinese people'. While other trade boycotts have also been designed to punish, the connection was rarely made so explicit.

Australia was hit by a series of cyberattacks against political and private sector organisations that the government said were carried out by a 'sophisticated state-based cyber actor'.[8] The targets included all levels of government, industry, political organisations, education, health, essential service providers and operators of other critical infrastructure. The attacks continued intermittently over several months, during which the email systems of Australia's federal parliament, the parliament of mineral-rich Western Australia and a leading broadcaster were breached. Cybersecurity experts said there was little doubt about who carried out the waves of attacks, following the digital trail to groups linked to the Chinese state.[9]

The Chinese embassy in Canberra raised the stakes further by handing over a list of additional grievances that included just about any and every criticism of China that had been made by Australian politicians, media and think tanks. The 'offences' included criticising China's island-building and other aggressive behaviour in the South

China Sea, its repression in Hong Kong and Xinjiang, and its intimidation of Taiwan. To this were added Australian accusations of cyber spying against Beijing, Canberra's exclusion of Huawei from Australia's 5G networks and its siding with the US more broadly. Beijing also complained about new anti-foreign interference laws Australia had introduced to push back against Chinese influence in Australian politics, business and academia. It attacked 'unfriendly and antagonistic media' and think tanks. It was quite a list, fourteen grievances in total, contained in a document produced by the Chinese embassy. 'China is angry. If you make China the enemy, China will be the enemy,' the document warned.[10]

The grievances were echoed by the Foreign Ministry in Beijing, where spokesperson Zhao Lijian said Australia needed to 'squarely face the crux of the current setback in bilateral relations, take China's concerns seriously and take concrete actions to correct its mistakes'.[11] Beijing was in effect seeking to muzzle Australia by extending internationally the intolerance of dissent it practices at home – telling Canberra to 'shut-up' as the price for doing business. Australian political leaders gave it short shrift. 'Australia will always be ourselves,' said Prime Minister Scott Morrison. 'We will always set our own laws and our own rules according to our national interests – not at the behest of any other nation.'[12] Former Prime Minister Malcolm Turnbull was a little more direct, describing the list as 'truly one of the nuttiest things I've ever seen'.[13]

While Canberra's call for an independent Covid-19 inquiry sent relations plummeting, political and trade ties had already begun to sour, likened by one commentator to Hemingway's description of bankruptcy – gradually then suddenly.[14] Canberra was forced to confront a fundamental question: Had Australian businesses and politicians for too long allowed themselves to be gripped by a dangerous 'gold rush' mentality towards Beijing that not only blinded them to the thuggish reality of Xi Jinping's China, but had created an over-dependence that was now coming back to haunt them?

Darwin is Australia's northern-most city, the wettest, smallest and most isolated on the continent. *Crocodile Dundee*, the 1986 action comedy that turned Paul Hogan into the face of Australia, was filmed in the Kakadu National Park, just to the east of the city. To many metropolitan Australians sitting in Sydney or Melbourne little has changed. In their eyes it remains a rough outback city, a home of rednecks and marauding man-eating crocodiles. It was always an unfair stereotype. And these days the capital of the Northern Territory is an increasingly vibrant, multicultural city. More than a third of the population was born overseas and it has the largest indigenous population of any city in Australia. While it might be isolated from the rest of the country, it is far closer to Asia's major cities and sea routes, offering the quickest access to the South China Sea and beyond. It is, in other words, of enormous strategic importance.

In recent years, Darwin has been promoted as Australia's front door to Asian markets, a potential export hub for agricultural produce and resources. Since 2011, US marines have rotated in and out of the city, conducting exercises and training with the Australian Defence Force for up to six months a year. The marines are based not far from Darwin port, through which transits ammunition, equipment and fuel. In addition, the port regularly supports Australian exercises and hosts visits from foreign navies. Yet in 2015, the government of the Northern Territory sold the port to China. To be precise, it sold a ninety-nine-year lease to a Chinese company called Landbridge Group for A$506 million (£270 million). US President Barack Obama rebuked Australian Prime Minister Malcolm Turnbull for going ahead with the deal without even consulting him.[15] There were plenty of red flags: Landbridge is an opaque nominally private company based in the port city of Rizhao in China's Shandong province, and has close links to the Communist Party. Australian reporters who descended on Rizhao in an effort to discover more about the company and its reclusive owner, Ye Cheng, found themselves staring into a black hole. They dubbed Ye the 'invisible billionaire', since he has almost no public profile.[16] To long-time China-watchers the opacity was very familiar, as were the links with the Party. Ye was a member of a Party advisory body, and he was once described by the authorities as one of the 'top ten individuals caring about the development of national defence'. Landbridge is among a number of companies to have established armed militia units to support the military in the event of war or major emergencies, according to an official military newspaper.[17] All companies in China are required to do the Communist Party's bidding, whatever the share register says. They cannot say no, not if they want to stay in business. Yet, at the time the Australian Strategic Policy Institute was a lonely voice pointing out that Landbridge was little more than a Communist Party front.[18]

The deal went ahead, structured in such a way that it escaped scrutiny by the Foreign Investment Review Board. The Northern Territory chief minister welcomed his new 'private sector partner'. Fears over the deal were 'alarmist nonsense' said Dennis Richardson, secretary of the Department of Defence. The Northern Territory had been trying to attract investment to the port for some time and its chief minister accused critics of the deal of 'spreading xenophobia and fear'.[19]

This was the time of peak 'China mania' in Australia. The Darwin deal was representative of that era, rather in the manner of Britain's nuclear deal with Beijing. Australia's economy was booming – a quarter of a century without a recession, largely on the back of a fast-growing China, which was snapping up iron ore, coal, liquified natural gas and other resources just about as fast as Australia could get them out of the ground. Chinese money poured into Australian assets, with acquisitions ranging from energy companies, gas pipelines, port facilities in New South Wales, dairy processors and cattle stations, to waterfront mansions and country estates – with few questions asked. China was soon to surpass New Zealand as the biggest source of foreign tourists, and Chinese students were generating billions of dollars for Australian universities.

A free-trade deal was agreed at the end of 2014, which promised lower Chinese tariffs on agriculture, dairy and wine, and improved access to China for Australian banking and other professional services. At the time, Prime Minister Tony Abbott lauded the trade deal as his government's biggest achievement. He hosted Xi Jinping in Canberra in November 2014 and Xi addressed the federal parliament, telling senators and MPs that 'Australia is a country of dynamism and innovation'. Abbott responded: 'We have become a model of how two peoples and two countries can complement each other.'[20]

Fast forward seven years and Abbott had become one of China's biggest critics, and China's embassy in Canberra was denouncing him as 'a failed and pitiful politician'.[21] Darwin port was back in the news, but for very different reasons. The government announced a Department of Defence review of the 2015 agreement, armed with new powers not only to scrutinise deals that could impact on national security, but to impose new conditions or even reverse those that have already been approved.[22] During a visit to the Northern Territory, Prime Minister Scott Morrison said he would heed any advice 'about the national security implications of any piece of critical infrastructure'.[23] The port was now described as a 'critical strategic asset for Australia', suitable for developing a major naval hub. Darwin port had become a dramatic symbol of how rapidly and dramatically times had changed. Rather like a regretful drunk waking with a bad hangover, Australia was attempting to come to terms with its over-indulgence of Beijing, and to rectify the damage to its security – but also to its democratic and civic institutions.

With hindsight, the free-trade agreement at the end of 2014 and the Darwin port deal marked the high point of Australia's love affair with China. By then there were aspects of its partner's behaviour that were already generating disquiet. At that time, Australian diplomacy was frequently described as a balancing act between the burgeoning economic relationship with China and its security partnership with the United States, with whom Canberra is a treaty ally. Canberra thought it could avoid hard choices and enjoy the best of both worlds, a policy that Hugh White, an Australian defence analyst, describes as 'systematic duplicity'.[24] There was a growing realisation that China's rise was far from benign and presented a growing threat to Australia's sovereignty. Concern was focused initially on Beijing's influence in the Australian economy and the level of dependence on China's giant market, but the loudest wake up call came in the form of a political influence buying scandal.

The ink was barely dry on the free-trade agreement, when the country was shaken by revelations that politicians and political parties had received donations from business people linked to the Chinese Communist Party in an effort to shape policy towards China.[25] One Labor Party senator, after accepting money, called on Australia to respect China's territorial claims in the South China Sea and tried to stop his foreign affairs spokesman from meeting pro-democracy activists in Hong Kong.[26] It was also revealed that the senator had tipped off his CCP-linked patron that he might be under surveillance by security agencies.[27] The revelations led in 2018 to a package of new laws to tighten rules on political funding and influence operations. 'We will not tolerate foreign influence activities that are in any way covert, coercive or corrupt. That is the line that separates legitimate influence from illegitimate interference,' said then Prime Minister Malcolm Turnbull, when he introduced the bill.[28] That warning was echoed by Australian spy chiefs: 'The level of threat we face from foreign espionage and interference activities is currently unprecedented,' said Mike Burgess, director-general of the Australian Security Intelligence Organisation. 'It is higher now than it was at the height of the Cold War.'[29] The laws ban foreign political donations and require foreign lobbyists to register. They also criminalise covert, deceptive or threatening actions that are intended to interfere with democratic processes or provide intelligence to overseas governments. These laws represent the most robust push-back to date by a Western democracy against Chinese interference, and are designed to include actions that previously fell short of definitions of espionage – a yawning gap that still exists in UK legislation.

The activities of Chinese Communist Party-linked groups within Australia's universities, think tanks and civic organisations also came under scrutiny. A student group connected to the Chinese embassy was accused of intimidating critics on the country's campuses and seeking to stifle debate on issues sensitive to the Communist Party, such as Taiwan, Tibet, Hong Kong and Xinjiang. Universities had become highly dependent on fees from Chinese students who numbered around 160,000 before the Covid-19 pandemic – around 40 per cent of international students. A 2019 report from the Centre for Independent Studies described Chinese students as the 'cash cows' of Australian universities. It found that Australia's seven top-ranked universities were generating more than A$2 billion from Chinese students, which represented between 12 per cent and 23 per cent of total revenues. The highest figure was from the University of Sydney, which took in more than half a billion Australian dollars.[30]

In a later report, Human Rights Watch (HRW) said the Chinese government maintains surveillance of mainland and Hong Kong students, and found an 'atmosphere of fear' among pro-democracy activists, who feared their activities in Australia could result in relatives at home being punished or interrogated.[31] One Chinese activist, who uses the pseudonym Horror Zoo, told the BBC how she organised a protest in Melbourne against the Communist Party's early cover-up of the Covid-19 outbreak in Wuhan and the hounding of doctors who tried to sound the alarm. She was photographed by nationalist students, and received threats when the pictures were posted online. 'People say they want to kill me,' she told the broadcaster. She said police visited her parents in China, frightening her mother, who had no idea about her daughter's activism.[32]

HRW also said tutors and lecturers were coming under increasing pressure. More than half of a sample who teach China studies or Chinese students said they self-censored, while academics perceived to be critical of the Communist Party were harassed in person or online. Some said they had been asked by university management to steer clear of sensitive issues. It is an open policy of Xi Jinping to use students studying abroad to promote the Party's interests, and nearly all the academics interviewed for the report pointed to a marked increase in nationalism among their students since Xi came to power. Research collaboration also came under scrutiny, as did the activities of Confucius Institutes, Chinese government-funded organisations that ostensibly promote language and culture, but were accused of peddling propaganda and stifling debate. There are thirteen of them on Australian campuses.

The Communist Party also targeted Australia's large 1.2 million strong Chinese diaspora, lavishing money on community organisations, and taking effective control of most Chinese-language media.[33] Party front organisations provided news outlets with content and favours, and channelled direct and indirect funding. As in other Chinese communities worldwide, WeChat became an indispensable tool for migrants to keep abreast of friends and relatives at home, but it has also become a potent tool of Communist Party censorship, surveillance and disinformation, providing a distorted view of reality for those for whom English is not their first language.[34]

By the time Covid-19 emerged in Wuhan, Australia–China relations were fast heading to the rocks. Wang Xining, China's deputy ambassador to Australia – who would later make the 'scumbags' remark – likened the call for an independent inquiry to the betrayal of Julius Caesar by the assassin Brutus. It was 'approximately identical to Julius Caesar in his final day when he saw Brutus approaching him. "Et tu, Brute?",' he told the National Press Club in Canberra.[35] Many Australian economists were prepared to heed China's warnings, urging Canberra to be 'realistic' in its dealings with Beijing because its giant market could not be replaced. 'There are no other options that come anywhere near to making up China's numbers,' warned Professor Jane Golley, a China economy specialist at the Australian National University.[36] She said she found the calls to turn away from China 'depressing'. 'I wonder if the man on the street who reads the headline and thinks we need to diversify from China – I always wonder if they think through what that could mean and how it might lead to them or their children not having jobs in the future.' It was a familiar refrain, heard in many forms in other Western countries – in effect, telling politicians to stop posturing, hold their noses and reap the supposed economic rewards of China trade. Yet, as China heaped on the economic pressure, Australia stood firm – and the economy seemed none the worse for it.

The smugglers were loading two powerful speedboats off a pier in the small village of Lau Fau Shan in Hong Kong's northwest when the marine police swept in. There were four smugglers, and though taken by surprise they still managed to escape in one of their specially adapted boats, its multiple outboard motors giving it more than enough power to outrun the police, speeding across Deep Bay and to mainland China beyond. But they were forced to abandon most of their valuable cargo on the pier, and police and customs officials were soon sifting through the contraband – Styrofoam boxes packed with almost 600kg of flaming red Australian rock lobsters, with a street price of around US$25,000.[37] Live rock lobsters had been a staple delicacy at Chinese wedding banquets and other up-scale parties, and China had been by far Australia's main market for them – until they were targeted as part of Beijing's trade sanctions. An export market estimated to be worth more than half a billion US dollars a year to Australia vanished overnight. That's when the smuggling began. Hong Kong is still treated as a separate customs territory, and in the months following the China ban imports of Australian rock lobsters into the territory increased fiftyfold – most of it destined for illicit backdoor channels to the mainland.

China also targeted wine, and direct exports to what had been the biggest market for Australian winemakers dried up after being hit with crippling tariffs as high as 212 per cent. But once again Hong Kong picked up some of the slack, with imports of Australian wine to the territory more than doubling in the months that followed the ban, the extra almost certainly destined for China's backdoor. As Beijing slapped restrictions on trade with Australia, so the former British colony appeared to be returning to its roots as a black-market hub, a centre for the sort of grey China trade on which it had once thrived.[38]

The backdoor into China came as a welcome relief to Australian winemakers and lobster catchers. Vineyards also found some relief in a big increase in exports to Britain, where home wine racks were well stocked during Covid-19 lockdowns. Like other sectors hit by Beijing, they scrambled to find alternative markets. Barley growers found new buyers in Asia and Latin America, while coal was diverted to India,

Europe and Latin America. By one estimate the value of exports to China of goods which faced tariffs or other barriers fell by about A$11.7 billion (US$9 billion) a year. But the value of exports of these same commodities to the rest of the world increased by A$13.4 billion.[39] Furthermore, the overall value of exports to China reached an all-time *high*, thanks to Beijing's addiction to Western Australian iron ore, where prices surged by more than a third between 2019 and 2021.[40] Australia accounts for 60 per cent of China iron ore imports, and while Beijing grumbled about the price it was having to pay, it had no alternative in the short term. While restricting exotic crustaceans and pinot noir imports might irritate guests at wedding banquets, the Party couldn't jeopardise the iron ore imports that power its real economy.

Overall, the Australian economy was remarkably resilient. An emboldened Canberra launched formal complaints at the World Trade Organization against China over the wine and barley duties.[41] Australia ripped up agreements signed under China's Belt and Road Initiative. The Chinese embassy reacted with fury, accusing Canberra of being 'unreasonable and provocative', while one Australian analyst pointed out, 'There is not much they can do to Australia anymore. Once you've thrown the kitchen sink at someone, in a tactical sense the Australian government is liberated to do whatever the hell it wants.'[42]

Prime Minister Scott Morrison announced a sharp increase in defence spending, up 40 per cent over the next decade and focused on the Indo-Pacific region. He said Australia needed to prepare for a post-Covid world that is 'poorer, more dangerous and more disorderly'. Australia signed up to a security pact with the US and UK which will allow Australia to build nuclear-powered submarines for the first time. It moved to revitalise regional 'medium power' military relationships with Japan and India and joined discussions over ways of expanding the role of the 'five eyes' intelligence gathering alliance comprising Australia, Canada, New Zealand, the UK and US. Australia also spoke more forcefully about Chinese disinformation campaigns that seek to undermine democracies, it suspended its extradition treaty with Hong Kong over China's imposition of a draconian security law in the city, and filed a declaration with the United Nations rejecting China's maritime claims in the South China Sea.[43] It also moved to counter Chinese influence in the Pacific, where Canberra has long cultural and political ties. It stepped up support and engagement with island states, offering Covid-19 vaccines as an alternative to Chinese donations.[44] It sought to block a Chinese firm from buying Digicel Pacific, the dominant telecoms operator in the South Pacific.[45]

The pushback against China seemed to catch the national mood. In 2021, an annual poll by the Lowy Institute, a foreign-policy research group, found public sentiment towards Beijing had soured sharply and China had become the least trusted country by Australians. Some 84 per cent of those polled said they trusted China not at all or not very much.[46] When asked to weigh up whether China was more of a security threat or more of an economic partner, nearly two-thirds identified it as a threat.[47] It was hard not to conclude that China had shot itself in the foot, and the experience was watched particularly closely from the other side of the world – from the shore of the Baltic Sea.

Lithuania knows what it's like to live next door to a bully. It was the first of the old Soviet states to escape the clutches of the disintegrating USSR when it declared independence in 1990. In Vladimir Putin's Russia, it now has a growling, resentful and intimidating neighbour. It is therefore not at all surprising that the tiny Baltic state made common cause with Taiwan and demonstrates a backbone towards Beijing that has been woefully missing elsewhere in Europe.

In November 2021, it joined Australia in Beijing's doghouse when it allowed Taiwan to open a diplomatic mission in Vilnius, the Lithuanian capital, which for the first time in Europe carries the name 'Taiwan'. Most of its other de facto embassies use the name of its capital 'Taipei' in the title out of fear of upsetting China. The 'Taiwanese Representative Office in Lithuania' provoked predictable tantrums from Beijing. It was an 'extremely egregious act', barked the Chinese Foreign Ministry. 'We demand that Lithuania immediately correct its wrong decision.'[48] The Party's *Global Times* called Lithuania a 'crazy, tiny country full of geopolitical fears', and warned it 'will eventually pay a price for its evil deed'.[49]

China withdrew its ambassador from Vilnius and threw out Lithuania's top diplomat from Beijing. The Lithuanian embassy in China was bombarded with threatening calls, many targeting local Chinese staff.[50] In December 2021, Lithuania pulled out all its remaining diplomats, fearing for their safety after Beijing demanded they hand back their diplomatic IDs.[51] China suspended rail freight to the country, and imposed a de facto trade embargo.

Lithuania is a tiny country, Beijing was right on that front. Its population is a little under 3 million, compared with China's 1.4 billion, and its economy is 1/270th the size of China's, but it wasn't about to go grovelling to Beijing for forgiveness in the manner of so many larger countries over the years. Not only did it double down, but it rather seemed to be enjoying itself. Lithuania's Foreign Ministry said the country was interested in expanding economic and cultural cooperation with Taiwan. 'Freedom-loving people should look after each other,' said Minister of Foreign Affairs Gabrielius Landsbergis, announcing a donation of 20,000 doses of AstraZeneca Covid-19 vaccine to Taiwan after China sought to block the island's access to global supplies.[52] Beijing is especially wary of Landsbergis, who is the grandson of Vytautas Landsbergis, who led the country to independence in 1990, a move that hastened the demise of the Soviet Union.

Lithuania also left the '17+1 group', a diplomatic forum through which China seeks to exert influence over eastern and central European countries, and which was widely seen as an attempt to split the EU.[53] The Lithuanian government urged people to throw away their Chinese mobile phones and avoid buying new ones. A report by the country's National Cyber Security Centre said a top-end phone made by Xiaomi had in-built tools able to censor 449 terms, including 'Free Tibet', 'Long live Taiwan independence' or 'democracy movement'. The list, which could be updated remotely from China, was included in the phone's internet browser. Although the capability had been switched off in European models, it could be remotely activated at any time. The report also found flaws in a Huawei phone that made it vulnerable to cyberattack.[54] The government also blocked the use of Chinese baggage-screening technology at Lithuanian airports over national security fears.[55] It banned Huawei from its telecoms infrastructure, and proposed Chinese investment in Klaipeda, Lithuania's only seaport and a key transit point for NATO forces, was also put on hold after Lithuania's president called it a national security risk.[56]

In a non-binding resolution supported by three-fifths of its members, the Lithuanian parliament described China's treatment of its Uyghurs in Xinjiang as 'genocide', called for a UN investigation of detention camps and urged the European Commission to review relations with Beijing. It also called on China to abolish a national security law in Hong Kong, and to let observers into Tibet and begin talks with the Dalai Lama.[57] Lithuania is one of the few countries in the world where Tibet's spiritual leader remains a welcome guest.

Beijing's heavy-handed interference was grating well before the spat over Taiwan's diplomatic mission. In September 2019, the Lithuanian government lodged a formal complaint with China's embassy in Vilnius, accusing diplomats of disrupting protests in the city in support of the Hong Kong democracy movement. The Lithuanian Foreign Ministry said Chinese diplomats acted 'in violation of public order' after protesters were jostled and attempts were made to rip away their megaphones.[58] Later that year, Lithuanians were appalled when a Chinese visitor posted online a video of herself removing a cross supporting Hong Kong that had been planted on the Hill of Crosses, a national independence shrine. A photo, also uploaded, showed another cross defaced with the words, 'Hope all cockroaches rest in peace' – cockroaches being a derogatory term used against the protesters in Hong Kong.[59] The Hill, located near the northern Lithuanian city of Šiauliai, is covered with tens of thousands of wooden crosses, effigies and rosaries and is regarded as a symbol of faith, hope and freedom. It is in many ways a narrative of war, uprising and struggles, and the tradition of planting crosses is believed to date back to an 1831 rebellion against the Russians. During the Soviet occupation, the authorities made several unsuccessful attempts to level the hill, but the crosses kept coming back. It is easy to understand why the vandals, likely Chinese tourists pumped up by the Communist Party's nationalist propaganda, caused such outrage.

Arguably, Lithuania could afford to thumb its nose at Beijing, because direct China trade is small – China accounts for only 1 per cent of Lithuania's total exports, according to Economy Minister Aušrinė Armonaitė.[60] Hardest hit were companies relying on China-made electronic components who reportedly received near identical letters claiming power shortages had made it difficult to fulfil orders.[61] Beijing sought other, indirect ways to apply pressure, demanding that multinational companies sever ties with Lithuania or face being shut out of the China market.[62] This represented a sharp escalation in Beijing's use of economic coercion – in effect prescribing where companies operating in China could source their components. Foreign Minister Landsbergis appealed to the European Union for support. In a letter to the Commission, he wrote, 'A strong reaction is necessary at the EU level in order to send a signal to China that politically motivated economic pressure is unacceptable and will not be tolerated.'[63]

***

Australia and Lithuania are on opposite sides of the globe. One a medium-size Pacific power, the other a small but plucky European state, a member of both the EU and NATO. They both have plenty of attitude, which is perhaps why the Chinese Communist Party wanted to make an example of them – to punish them both for having the audacity to cross China and to send a message to others to think twice before causing offence to Xi Jinping. At the time of writing, not only have both stood firm, but Beijing's tactics are backfiring. 'Sometimes it's quite the opposite – the pressure increases resilience rather than breaks the country,' Landsbergis said. He described his country as a 'canary in the coal mine' for how China pressures smaller countries that don't bend to its will.[64] The same expression was used by Heino Klinck, US deputy assistant secretary of defense for East Asia in the Trump administration, to describe Australia. 'It's not just about Australia. It's just that the Chinese have decided if they can put the Aussies back into a box, that sends a message to everyone else,' he said.[65] In a February 2022 visit to Australia, US Secretary of State Antony Blinken said that Australia 'set an incredibly powerful example' for the world.[66] Instead of striking fear into the hearts of other would-be transgressors, the treatment of Australia and Lithuania appeared to galvanise critics and inspire others to stand up to coercion from China.

Defiance spread across central and eastern Europe, partly because China's promised investment in the region had not materialised, and partly because China's bullying triggered memories of their own Cold War history as client states of the USSR. Taiwan's Foreign Minister Joseph Wu was warmly welcomed in Slovakia and the Czech Republic. 'Like Taiwan, countries in Central and Eastern Europe have gone through the shackles of authoritarian regimes and uphold the shared values of democracy, freedom, human rights, and the rule of law,' he said in a statement that was opportunistic but captured the growing sentiment – a sentiment echoed by Miloš Vystrčil, the speaker of the Czech Senate, who said, 'We know very well from our own history what it's like to live with a big brother behind your back.'[67] Slovenia's Prime Minister Janez Janša described China's treatment of Lithuania as 'terrifying' and 'ridiculous' and announced that his country was also looking to strengthen diplomatic ties with Taiwan.[68] Even Greece, once one of Beijing's staunchest defenders in Europe began to cool. Athens said that promised investment in Piraeus port, in which a Chinese state-owned company acquired a controlling stake in 2016, had not been forthcoming and the company had damaged the marine environment.[69]

China sought to apply pressure on Lithuania through the EU, which has traditionally been cautious about confronting Beijing. However, in Brussels too, the mood is changing. The European Parliament froze any consideration of a massive investment deal with Beijing over China's repression in Xinjiang.[70] The parliament also overwhelmingly backed a resolution urging the EU to upgrade its ties with Taiwan. 'Strategic autonomy' is becoming the latest foreign policy catchphrase in Brussels, which translates as less dependence on Chinese supply chains, more scrutiny of inbound investment and speaking out more robustly on human rights. The EU also proposed new 'anti-coercion' regulation designed to combat non-European Union countries wielding undue pressure on any of the bloc's members, which would seem tailor-made for defending Lithuania.[71] The regulation would empower the EU to impose trade or investment restrictions on China. That would be a big step for the cautious eurocrats, but the direction of travel in Brussels is clear enough.

Germany has been especially careful not to upset Beijing, since the China market is particularly important for German manufacturers, especially its car makers. Continental, a German car parts giant was reportedly among the companies pressured to stop using components manufactured in Lithuania.[72] German big business reportedly put pressure on Vilnius to back down, the German-Baltic Chamber of Commerce suggesting some companies might otherwise have to leave Lithuania.[73] However, the German government backed an EU complaint against China at the World Trade Organization, alleging unfair trade practices – with UK, US and of course Australia joining the consultation process. The WTO complaints process can be agonisingly slow, but the fact it was launched at all was enormously symbolic. There is cautious optimism that Germany's new government, which took office at the end of 2021, will be more robust on China than was the administration of Angela Merkel. The 'traffic light' coalition of Social Democrats, Greens and Free Democrats has as its foreign minister Annalena Baerbock, the co-leader of the Greens, who pledged to take greater account of human rights in Germany's foreign affairs.

By most definitions, diplomacy is a two-way process of give and take. In the era of Xi Jinping, China's diplomats don't see it that way, rigidly glued to an ever-hardening Party line that sees no space for compromise. They see rules and agreements as tactical concessions that can be discarded as needs be. Diplomacy is reduced to what has been described as 'displays of performative anger'. Peter Martin, in his study of 'wolf warrior' diplomacy, characterises Chinese diplomacy as a 'combination of outrage with another common negotiating ploy: the insistence that responsibility for the health of diplomatic relations belongs entirely to the other side.'[74]

Lithuania and Australia illustrate Communist Party bullying at its most stark. Over the years, most countries (and companies and politicians and celebrities) have fallen meekly into line in the face of coercion. China bullies because it can, and because it works – or at least it has in the past. Lithuania and Australia are the vanguard of a new assertiveness. In January 2022, Lithuania's Foreign Minister Gabrielius Landsbergis stood side by side with his Australian counterpart Marise Payne at Government House in Canberra and joked that they were members of an 'exclusive club'. They warned that more nations would be targeted if like-minded countries did not challenge Beijing's coercive practices. Landsbergis was visiting to open his country's first embassy in Australia.[75] Their willingness to face down Beijing's tantrums could well be turning points in the global pushback against China. In both cases, the actions of the Communist Party have been counterproductive, further damaging China's international standing. Both countries in their own way provide warnings about Beijing's coercion as well as object lessons in how to deal with it.

In an August 2021 debate hosted by La Trobe University in Melbourne, former Australian Prime Minister Malcolm Turnbull said Beijing had tried to make an example of Australia, 'to come down hard on us to make us more compliant'. He said that the strategy had 'completely and utterly backfired', and he warned those still advocating engagement: 'You engage, you start getting into one bit of sucking up, and then more sucking up, and then sycophancy will be required.'[76] For its part, Lithuania described its experience as a 'wake-up call' for fellow Europeans. 'If you want to defend democracy you have to stand up for it,' said Vice-Minister of Foreign Affairs Arnoldas Pranckevičius.[77]

The Communist Party is quick to accuse Western countries, the US in particular, of seeking to contain China's rise, to prevent it taking up its rightful place in the world. Lithuania and Australia illustrate that it is not China's rise that is the issue, but the nature of that rise, and the way Beijing chooses to exercise its new power. The global pushback is not being guided by some dark conspiratorial hand of the type the Party tends to see behind all its setbacks, but is the result of its own behaviour. It has overplayed its own repressive hand. The court of Xi Jinping is an arrogant and deeply insecure place, which may well have reached the peak of its power. The Party could well be facing precisely the sort of decay and decline that it routinely wishes on the West, though in the short term could be all the more dangerous for it.

# Chapter 15

## *Peak China: The Future of the Chinese Communist Party*

'We have to step up combat readiness exercises, joint exercises and confrontational exercises to enhance servicemen's capabilities and preparation for war.'

*Xi Jinping, October 2018*

When world leaders gathered in Glasgow in autumn 2021 for COP26, the UN's 'make or break' climate change summit, the most notable absence was Xi Jinping. He stayed in China, where his urgent priority was massively ramping up the production and import of coal to solve a severe energy crunch, described as the worst in a decade.[1] Half of the country's provinces were rationing electricity, factories had closed, and there were regular blackouts. Old coal mines were rapidly brought back into production and output ramped up at existing ones. China scoured the globe for supplies, which included the sanctions-busting purchases from North Korea. There were a number of reasons for the crisis, including flooding in coal producing regions, but most can be traced to policy missteps. These ranged from an economic bounce-back after Covid that relied (as always) on energy-hungry construction and heavy industry, to self-defeating energy subsidies.[2] Coal prices in China reached an all-time high in October 2021, up 260 per cent since the beginning of the year, before falling back on government intervention.[3]

China is the world's biggest polluter, responsible for 27 per cent of global emissions of greenhouse gases at the time, burning more coal than the rest of the world combined.[4] It was opening new coal-fired power stations and increasing emissions at an annual rate that was greater than the savings each year of the rest of the world put together.[5] As of autumn 2021, it was building new coal plants at more than sixty locations across the country. Beijing pledged that its greenhouse gas emissions would peak before 2030 and the country would reach carbon neutrality before 2060, but these 'peak carbon' pledges were light on detail and heavy on caveats.

In the run-up to the Glasgow summit, Xi said China would no longer finance coal-powered plants internationally. This was presented as a concession and eagerly embraced as such by the West, desperate for signs of Beijing's cooperation.[6] It was no such thing. Construction had already dried up because of the soaring price of coal and the fall in price of renewables, as well as concern over debt among the recipients of Beijing's largesse. China is a world leader in renewables, generating more energy from solar power than any other country, and claims to have bold ambitions to ramp this up. It is also seeking to corner the global market in many green technologies, but the fact remains that it is addicted to coal.[7] In 2021, fossil fuels accounted for 85 per cent of energy used, and coal represents 57 per cent of that. It has given few details of how it intends to kick the coal habit – rendering its climate pledges largely meaningless.

Beijing made it clear that it sees climate change as a geopolitical tool. John Kerry, the US climate envoy, hoped it could be a stand-alone issue of global concern, divorced from prickly bilateral tensions. Wang Yi, China's foreign minister, told him to forget it, that climate cooperation could not be separated and the US should 'cease containing and supressing China in the world'.[8] China has long used its cooperation on climate change (and on North Korea) as leverage, bargaining chips to get concessions elsewhere, or to blunt criticism of its human rights abuses or other aspects of its international behaviour, but rarely has this been stated so bluntly.

It was further evidence that China is not a serious partner. Not only is the Communist Party a serial breaker of rules and agreements, it approaches issues from a perspective of narrow self-interest. Concessions are tactical, to be discarded as needs be. As the Party's *Global Times* put it, 'China has already announced its own climate road map and will stick to its own pace.'[9] At the end of the Glasgow meeting, China's representative was instrumental in watering down the final pact that agreed to accelerate efforts to 'phase down' instead of 'phase out' coal use.[10]

It is true that the world will only achieve its climate goals if China acts to reduce its greenhouse-gas emissions, but Beijing will do so in its own way and at its own speed, prioritising its economy. China is very susceptible to the impact of climate change and climate-related disasters, such as the catastrophic flooding that hit Henan province in summer 2021, and these are more likely to force its hand than Western pressure or any desire to be a good global citizen.[11] In the meantime, the broader message Xi Jinping was sending to Glasgow was that cooperation with the United States and its allies would be on Xi's terms or not at all.[12]

There was a growing bunker mentality in the Zhongnanhai leadership compound in Beijing as the Party followed a 'zero-Covid' policy just as the most of the rest of the world was learning to live with the virus. Xi had not left China since before the pandemic and played an increasingly desperate game of Whac-A-Mole with the virus. The approach was about politics as much as health, with 'victory' over the virus a key plank of the cult of Xi. Entire cities were locked down following the detection of just a handful of cases.[13] More than 30,000 visitors were locked inside Shanghai's Disneyland theme park after a single customer tested positive, with everyone required to undergo a test before being allowed to leave.[14] Armed police paraded shackled and hooded rule-breakers through the streets of one city, placards around their necks in a public shaming reminiscent of the Cultural Revolution.[15] The enforcement of the rules were so zealous that in the city of Xian, a man complaining of chest pains was refused entry to hospital because he lived in a medium risk district. He died of a heart attack. An eight-month pregnant woman lost her baby after being refused treatment because her Covid test was invalid.[16]

With its borders sealed, Xi sought to further insulate China against the infiltration of dangerous foreign ideas and values, as if they were as infectious as any virus.[17] In November 2021, this insularity, as well as sabre-rattling over Taiwan, combined to trigger a bizarre online panic. The Chinese internet was gripped with rumours of war after a seemingly innocuous instruction to households to stock up on necessities for winter. The notice was likely related to Covid-19 outbreaks and ongoing power shortages, but in the febrile world of China's social media the PLA was on the march.[18]

The self-isolation came at a time when the Party faced a raft of economic problems that raised the intriguing possibility that while we may not be seeing 'peak carbon' any time soon, we could be witnessing peak China. The Communist Party may be facing the sort of decline it so frequently wishes on the West, and as with the climate, the impact could be dangerous and unpredictable. China faces multiple and growing problems linked to an unsustainable economic model.

In September 2021, the country's property bubble began to burst. A Shenzhen-based property developer called Evergrande was no longer able to pay debts of more than $300 billion, and the meltdown quickly spread to other property firms.[19] By one estimate Evergrande, the world's most indebted developer, had taken deposits for more than 1.6 million apartments, bought off-plan, and riot police were deployed outside the company's Shenzhen headquarters to keep buyers at bay. 'Evergrande, give back my money I earned with blood and sweat!' yelled one who managed to force his way into the lobby.[20] Foreign bond holders, fearful they would not be repaid, began to circle the personal assets of Hui Ka Yan, Evergrande's billionaire chairman. Pictures of his $45 million superyacht, 'Event', dwarfing everything else in Hong Kong's Gold Coast yacht club, featured prominently in the financial press.[21] Investigators sought to unravel the complex web of companies through which he managed assets that included at least three private jets worth $236 million and two mansions on Hong Kong's Peak worth an estimated $204 million combined.[22]

Hui was well connected, rubbing shoulders with tycoons in Hong Kong and Communist Party leaders in Beijing, with whom he celebrated the Party's 100th anniversary in July 2021. Two decades of frenzied construction saw entire new cities sprouting across the country, built on rampant speculation – vast and empty 'ghost cities', metropolises with all the trappings of urban life, but without the people. By one estimate, China has 65 million empty apartments, almost enough to give one each to the entire population of Britain.[23] While many buyers over the years were genuine owner-occupiers, demand was driven by speculators who believed prices would just keep on rising. Now the speculators were fading away and there were simply not enough young people to buy all those apartments, and the millions more under construction.[24]

Banks fell over themselves to lend to the developers and to the buyers, and by late 2020, property-related lending accounted for an astonishing 39 per cent of bank loans, according to Guo Shuqing, chairman of the China Banking and Insurance Regulatory Commission, and the Party chief at the central bank. He described the property market as a 'grey rhino' – a very obvious, but ignored threat.[25] Soon after his comments, the regulator tightened lending rules, which precipitated

Evergrande's problems. Guo hoped he could slowly let the air out of the bubble, but an awful lot is riding on that hope. Property is the main driver of the economy, with property and related goods and services accounting for almost a third of GDP.[26] A large proportion of local government income comes from selling land to the property developers. There was already concern about hidden local government debts because of the widespread use of opaque financing vehicles. By one estimate, outstanding local government debt is worth 44 per cent of GDP, but nobody knows for sure, since the financial system is so lacking in transparency.[27]

A crash would hit the Chinese economy hard. The Party was terrified of the instability that might result, and hoped it could muddle through, bailing out firms and shuffling distressed assets onto state-owned banks and other pliable entities. But even if it manages the pace at which the air leaves the bubble, the economy could still face years of relative economic stagnation. The property sector is in many ways a microcosm of the wider economy – a scary combination of eye-watering debt, lack of transparency and diminishing returns on wasteful investment.

The property crisis came as the Party was targeting some of the country's biggest tech companies, curbing the power and activities of firms including e-commerce giants Alibaba and Pinduoduo, ByteDance (the company behind TikTok), TenCent and ride-hailing platform Didi Chuxing. Leading entrepreneurs abandoned formal management roles at the head of the companies they founded.[28] In some ways the assault was puzzling, since the Communist Party already exerts tight control over nominally private tech companies, which play a key role in censorship and surveillance on the Party's behalf. New data protection and competition rules were cited, as were amorphous new Party slogans about the 'disorderly expansion of capital' and nurturing 'common prosperity' – the latter generally understood to refer to efforts to reduce China's yawning wealth gap.[29] The crackdown was typically arbitrary and without due process and essentially boiled down to the Party asserting greater control, particularly over technology and data, and a further centralisation of power around Xi Jinping. The former Party boss of Hangzhou, a hub for e-commerce, was expelled from the Party and faced corruption charges, accused of colluding with private companies to support their 'disorderly expansion'.[30] Xi wants China to become the world centre for innovation. However, neutering China's most dynamic firms hardly seems the best way of achieving this – especially with China increasingly cut off from the Western know-how it has so easily been able to steal, copy or otherwise acquire in the past. A 2021 assessment from Peking University, which was subsequently censored, spelt out the challenges the country faces. China is 'following [the United States] in most fields, running side by side in a few, and leading in very few,' it stated.[31] As we have seem, in chip production China is years behind its rivals, and while it has made great strides in artificial intelligence, the only real field it leads in is surveillance. No great surprise there.

The crackdown wiped hundreds of billions of dollars off the value of the companies and rattled foreign investors asked whether China was now 'uninvestable'.[32] In October 2021, LinkedIn, the only major Western social media network still operating in China, announced that it was pulling out, leaving behind a jobs-only version of the site. The company, which had previously been willing to censor on the Party's behalf, announced: 'We're facing a significantly more challenging operating environment and greater compliance requirements in China.'[33] Two weeks later, Yahoo said that it too was heading for the exit, citing an 'increasingly challenging business and legal environment'.[34]

It has sometimes seemed that Western companies were willing to endure any indignity for a slice of the mythical China market, and Beijing has extracted a high price for market access. Now they were having to navigate increasingly tense geopolitics, sanctions and counter-sanctions, and a Communist Party armed with a rash of new security, data and cyber laws empowering it to take out through the front door what it used to steal from the back. Supply chains, already under strain from Covid-19 lockdowns, were coming under closer scrutiny amid accusations of forced labour in Xinjiang. The number of foreigners employed in China's two largest cities declined sharply. Over the decade to 2021, the number of expatriates in Shanghai, China's financial centre, fell by 20 per cent to around 163,000. The decline in Beijing was even steeper, falling by 40 per cent to about 63,000.[35] There were a number of reasons for this, and anecdotal evidence suggests it has accelerated since the Covid-19 pandemic closed China's borders. However, the broader reason is that China was becoming a far more hostile place for Western business and foreigners in general.

Hong Kong used to be a bolthole, a place with the rule of law and free expression, an island of sanctuary from the harder edges of doing business in the mainland. Now 'one country two systems' is dead, and the Party is rounding up critics as enthusiastically in Hong Kong as elsewhere in China. Here too an expat exodus was underway – an American Chamber of Commerce survey in May 2021 found that 42 per cent of those questioned were considering leaving the city.[36]

Longer-term challenges are also mounting. The country is aging rapidly, and there is no sign that the Party has grasped the challenges of a looming demographic crisis that is more acute than anywhere else in the world – and largely of its own making. The number of births to Chinese women under thirty fell by half between 2015 and 2020, to reach its lowest level in more than 60 years.[37] There were fewer births in 2021 than in 1961, when the Great Leap Forward resulted in widespread famine and death. China's population was expected to start shrinking from 2022. The number of marriages in China halved in the seven years to 2022, which also indicates extremely low birth rates ahead. Much of this is a legacy of its brutal family planning policies, which have also left the balance of the sexes skewed heavily towards men. The one-child policy has now been scrapped, but that has done nothing to raise the birth rate, with women now choosing to have fewer children. By some estimates, by mid-century as many as a third of Chinese will be more than 65 years old.[38] The Communist Party insists it can innovate its way through the crises, and move away from a labour-intensive economy. Others see extreme strains ahead, on growth and also on the country's overwhelmed hospitals and under-funded pension system.

The Party's legitimacy in the eyes of many Chinese people lies in its ability to deliver economic progress and stability. If this is the case, then life could become more perilous for Xi Jinping. He has made many enemies, purging rivals in his ruthless accumulation of power, much of it under the guise of curbing corruption. In 2021, ahead of key Party meetings expected to rubber-stamp his bid for power for life, he targeted the country's domestic security apparatus. Among those swept up were senior officials, including a former deputy minister, who had acted as Xi's enforcers in the early part of his rule. [39]

Xi has squandered China's soft power globally. A survey by the Pew Research Center in early summer 2021 found negative views of China and Xi at, or close to, all-time highs in nearly every one of the seventeen advanced economies it surveyed.[40] The mood is also darkening in many nations which have received Chinese investment under the Belt and Road Initiative. In truth, China has never been much loved, the relationship was primarily transactional. The apparent generosity of 'no-strings' finance is turning out to be no such thing.

For several weeks in late 2021 protesters filled the streets of Pakistan's port city of Gwadar, chanting '*Gwadar ko haq do!*' ('Give Gwadar Rights!'). They blocked roads into the city and burned tyres. They threatened to blockade the Chinese-owned port, which increasingly resembled a fortified compound. They demanded the end of illegal trawling that was devastating the local fishing industry and claimed they had no access to water, electricity and other basic necessities that had been promised by Beijing. They also demanded an end to the heavy security, including numerous checkpoints, that was disrupting everyday life.[41] The militarisation of the city followed a series of terrorist attacks on Chinese staff and assets in Pakistan, including a bomb attack on a bus that killed nine Chinese engineers working on a dam project, and a blast at a hotel in which China's ambassador was staying.[42] Baluchistan, where Gwadar is located, has a long-simmering and often violent separatist movement, which seized on the growing Chinese presence as a threat to Baloch identity.

Gwadar port, on which state-owned China Overseas Port Holding Company was handed a forty-year lease, was touted as the next Singapore – 'Pakistan's largest infrastructural project since independence', as the Port Authority described it.[43] It occupies a strategic position on the Arabian Sea, opposite Oman, near the mouth of the Persian Gulf, and is the hub for Chinese investment in Pakistan, dubbed the China–Pakistan Economic Corridor (CPEO), into which China is sinking billions of dollars. The CPEO is part of Beijing's Belt and Road Initiative, and its pipes, roads and railways across Pakistan will give China another outlet to the sea. In early 2022, China pushed Pakistan to fence off the entire area and turn it into a high-security zone, a demand Islamabad has so far resisted, fearing it will further inflame Baloch anger.

Gwadar is only the latest of China's BRI projects to face difficulties. As we have seen, the economic 'corridor' to the sea in Myanmar is overshadowed by an intensifying civil war, and Beijing's lithium mining interests in Congo have been targeted by violent protesters. Wariness is fuelled by the Communist Party's deeply ingrained habit of smothering, intimidating and bullying. It is intensified by the whiff of corruption. There is a growing realisation that the primary purpose of the BRI's opáque projects is to benefit Chinese companies and workers, and to further Beijing's geopolitical interests. In many cases, such as in eastern Europe and Greece, the anger is down to Beijing's failure to deliver on promises. As one frustrated union leader in Piraeus, who had previously supported China's purchase of the Greek port, put it: 'They haven't spent a dime here; even when they need to change a lamp, they bring it from China.'[11]

The BRI could never live up to the original hype, and what was once hailed as an ambitious tool for geopolitical engineering and influence-building is looking like an exercise in hubris and over-reach. The Party's march down its new silk roads has created a complex web of interests and assets in volatile regions it may struggle to defend. Although Beijing has tried to spread the boundaries of its largesse far and wide, it has always felt more comfortable in the company of the most dictatorial and rapacious of regimes. Yet there is a danger in coddling thugs and thieves, especially when it comes to getting your money back. Some twenty-three BRI countries are 'significantly or highly vulnerable to debt distress', according to a study by the Center for Global Development.[45] In late 2021, Xi Jinping announced that funding for Africa was to be cut by a third over the next three years.[46] China's lending worldwide was already declining, as the debt strain on its clients was exacerbated by the economic fallout from the Covid-19 pandemic.[47]

Calculating the precise level of Chinese international lending and grant giving is difficult because it is shrouded in secrecy. Official figures need to be treated with caution. In September 2021 AidData, a research group, identified 13,427 projects worth $843 billion across 165 countries in every major world region over an eight-year period.[10] Chinese lending has frequently been analysed from the perspective of 'debt-trap diplomacy', the ability of Beijing to leverage the debt for influence and control. However, debt is double-edged, and the sums involved so vast, that it could be as big a problem for China and its over-stretched banks as for the borrowing countries. Beijing has no experience of managing an international debt crisis, which could not only severely damage its lenders but could further undermine China's standing if it seeks to impose arduous terms or seize assets pledged as collateral.

China also holds around $1.06 trillion of US debt in the form of Treasury bonds, which is around 15 per cent of the total owned by foreign countries. There have been suggestions that this could be used as a weapon if tensions with Washington escalated further. If Beijing started to sharply sell off the debt, it would likely lead to a steep fall in the value of the US dollar and push up American borrowing costs. However, this would destabilise the international financial system, which would also cause severe damage to China – not least in those massive loans to BRI countries. All of which highlights a bigger issue for Beijing: as much as China might resent it, the dollar remains the lynchpin of the international financial system, and Beijing is integrated into (and highly dependent on) that system.

There is another paradox here – one that affects China's territorial ambitions. Over three decades China has massively expanded and modernised its military, a prime purpose being the taking of Taiwan and deterring American intervention. However, over that same time, China has become the world's largest creditor, fully integrated into the world economy. Beijing is especially exposed to the massive jolt to the global financial system that would surely follow any conflict over Taiwan – and that is before any punitive financial sanctions from the West in response to Chinese aggression have been applied.

The Chinese Communist Party has become an instrument of belligerent ethnic nationalism, built around the cult of Xi Jinping. Xi's much-vaunted 'Chinese Dream' is a chauvinistic vision of recovering stolen greatness, underpinned by grievance and victimhood. It harks back to a largely mythical age when China's dominance was the natural order of things. It is an ideology of expansion and obedience by destiny, and it is complemented by a dark and paranoid world view that sees enemies and conspiracies at every turn – where every criticism is regarded as an affront to national dignity. This underpins the many examples we have explored in this book.

There are many echoes of Hitler's Germany in Xi Jinping's China – not least the chilling 're-education camps' of Xinjiang, which are the largest mass incarceration of an ethnic group since the Nazis. Yet a more accurate comparison may be with pre-World War I Germany of Kaiser Wilhelm II.[49] Wilhelm oversaw a meteoric rise in his country's economic and military power, which he sought to turn into global political clout through the acquisition of colonies and the expansion of the German empire. 'No one can dispute with us the place in the sun that is our due,' he said in a speech in Hamburg in 1911, three years before the outbreak of war in Europe.[50] This vision harked back to the days of supposed national greatness, and was complemented by an acute paranoia and resentment that Germany's rightful rise was being held back by foreign powers. He was frustrated that the world would not simply bend to his will, and was convinced that Germany was being encircled by hostile powers determined to thwart his ambitions. However, as with contemporary China, encirclement was of Wilhelm's own making. His military build-up, imperial ambitions and growing economic strength alienated and alarmed his neighbours, who took countervailing measures.

The precise causes of the First World War have been much pored over by historians, but Wilhelm was under pressure to use his modernised military to launch a pre-emptive war while Germany was comparatively strong. He feared that the balance of power in Europe could shift away from Berlin by the 1920s. Much the same arguments have been made by strategists in Beijing, where the paranoia of encirclement is at its most acute along its sea border, notably around the South China Sea. The most obvious 'break-out' point for China is Taiwan, which Beijing regards as its own territory by historic right, but is also of enormous strategic importance for access to the oceans and controlling trade routes. China's military build-up and modernisation has been at its most relentless in this region, but Western powers are responding by stepping up their presence, bolstering and reinvigorating regional alliances and strengthening Taiwan's defences.

China's relative power advantages will not last, and Xi Jinping, like Kaiser Wilhelm, is under pressure to use his military edge before it is countered. He is also aware that with each year he delays, the island is slipping further from him. It has long been assumed that Beijing would be patient, with 2049, the century of the Party's seizure of power, often cited as a target date for 'unification'. Xi Jinping has given it greater urgency, making the 'recovery' of Taiwan central to his 'Chinese Dream' of national rejuvenation. 'It's necessary to strengthen the mission . . . and concentrate preparations for fighting a war,' Xi said on a visit to the PLA's Southern Theatre Command, which monitors the South China Sea. 'We have to step up combat readiness exercises, joint exercises and confrontational exercises to enhance servicemen's capabilities and preparation for war.'[51] Many around Xi argue that a declining America does not have the will to fight, and now is the time to humiliate the US and cement China's position as the pre-eminent regional power.

Though more sober minds in Beijing will be aware that to try and to fail in a project so central to the Party's identity would spell the end of Xi and possibly of the Party itself. Like Kaiser Wilhelm before him, an increasingly isolated Xi may be over-estimating his capacity for wise political judgement.

It is inconceivable that Western democracies would abandon Taiwan in the face of a Chinese invasion – or even a blockade. The issue of Taiwan's defence has become a key concern of America's foreign policy establishment. There is a growing view that 'strategic ambiguity' and even the 'One China Policy' itself are obsolete, and that a more explicit security guarantee might have a better deterrence effect than leaving Beijing guessing. It is accepted that to allow Taiwan to be swallowed by China would not only be a blow to democratic values, but would irreversibly alter the global balance of power.

The US is building more flexibility into its evolving strategy. The public disclosure in October 2021 of a small number of US military trainers on the island is one sign of this.[52] As we have seen, much thought is also going into hardening Taiwan's defences, not by trying to match China weapon by weapon, but through asymmetrical warfare – small, low cost but lethal kit from armed drones to mobile coastal cruise missiles and smart mines that would dramatically raise the cost of attack. This has been dubbed the 'porcupine strategy'.[53]

The revitalised alliances focused on countering China include the Quad, the grouping that brings together Japan, Australia, India and the United States, and the Five Eyes intelligence gathering network that comprises the UK, US, Australia, Canada and New Zealand. The new AUKUS pact will not only transfer US and UK nuclear submarine technology to Australia, but commits the three countries to work together on strategic technologies, including quantum computers and artificial intelligence.[54] The NATO alliance, which for decades countered the Soviet Union and then Russia, is also shifting its focus towards China.[55] The Quad may become the core of a loose and shifting coalition, with others participating as needs arise and interests dictate. The AUKUS pact, which was broadly welcomed in the Indo-Pacific region, could also be expanded. This more flexible structure may be a more effective way of countering China and encouraging the involvement of more Asian countries, who are wary of large and rigidly structured alliances.[56] Western patrols in the region have become more regular and the US was reportedly restructuring and dispersing some of its forces in the area to reduce response times.[57]

In early 2022, the Biden administration was preparing a broad new economic strategy for the Indo-Pacific region, with the aim of working more closely with friendly nations on issues including digital trade, supply chains and green technology. The G7 forum of advanced democratic countries launched a multi-billion dollar international investment fund aimed at countering Beijing's economic influence in lower-income countries.[58] The EU and UK announced separate funds with similar aims. British Foreign Secretary Liz Truss said it would operate to high standards over transparency, property rights and personal freedoms: 'That will help those countries get the infrastructure and other finance they need to develop in a way that doesn't have the strings attached or the opacity of other finance offers,' she said in a thinly veiled swipe at China's BRI.[59] It is too early to judge what this means in practice, how much money will be forthcoming and how effective it will be. However, it is recognition that pushing back against China requires more than beefed up military alliances – and, as we have seen, Japan has been an exemplar in this.

In late 2021, the Women's Tennis Association suspended its lucrative tournaments in China after accusations of sexual assault were made by Chinese tennis star Peng Shuai against a retired Communist Party leader and her subsequent disappearance. 'This is bigger than business. Women need to be respected and not censored,' said WTA chairman Steve Simon.[60] Serena Williams, Novak Djokovic, Andy Murray and Naomi Osaka were among tennis stars expressing support for Peng. In a November 2021 post to her Weibo social media account, Peng alleged that Zhang Gaoli, a former vice-premier and member of the seven-strong Standing Committee of the Party's Politburo, the country's highest ruling group, had assaulted her. The post was removed by censors within twenty minutes, and Peng's account was blocked. In a desperate effort to close down the conversation, the censors added 'tennis' to a list of banned words.

For more than two weeks, nothing was seen or heard of Peng. Then state media released a screenshot of an email (the cursor could still be seen), supposedly from her to Simon, in which she said she was safe and her earlier abuse allegations were untrue. Simon said it only raised more concerns. 'I have a hard time believing that Peng Shuai actually wrote the email we received or believes what is being attributed to her,' he said.[61] He also questioned the credibility of a subsequent series of staged photos and videos of Peng. During the 2022 Winter Olympics, in a tightly controlled interview with the French sports magazine *L'Équipe*, she said it had all been an 'enormous misunderstanding'. She also met the Olympic Committee President Thomas Bach, who was accused of being a prop for Communist Party propaganda. It is highly unlikely that Peng will be allowed to communicate freely while she remains in China.

In standing up to the Communist Party, the tennis fraternity demonstrated something altogether too rare in dealings with China – a backbone, a willingness to put concern for human rights ahead of the lucrative Chinese market. It was a remarkable moment. For its part, the Party had grown so used to bullying those who do business in China, that it seemed to be genuinely taken aback, and struggled for a response. The staged videos were clunky and amateur – on one a voice could be heard giving cues. It made the Communist Party look thuggish and absurd in equal measure.

School teachers will tell you that bullies behave the way they do because they think they can get away with it. Their targets are usually those they believe to be weaker, and appeasement only encourages them. Sometimes they are seeking attention, trying to make themselves feel more important. Bullying can also be a symptom of insecurity. Strategies for dealing with a bully include standing up for yourself, recognising your own self-worth, avoiding the bully where you can and joining forces with friends as a means of deterrence. For educators, these are some of the basic rules of the playground – and they are not a bad place to start for policy makers grappling with China.

Like all bullies, dictatorships are good at showing off their perceived strengths and hiding their weaknesses. James Schlesinger, who served as US secretary of defense at the height of the Cold War with the USSR, cautioned against what he called 'ten-foot-tall syndrome' – the proclivity to exaggerate the strength and intellect of their Soviet counterparts, without accounting sufficiently for its vulnerabilities.[62] China is a serious global threat, perhaps more so than the Soviet Union ever was, but the Communist Party has weaknesses. It is not ten feet tall, far from it, and is facing mounting challenges – largely of its own making.

For decades Western democracies showed considerable forbearance, as well as gullibility and greed, as they clung almost desperately to a belief that China's rise was benign when mounting evidence suggested the opposite. Xi Jinping has long accused the West, and Washington in particular, of seeking to 'contain' China. Until recently that was an absurd accusation; the West aided and abetted China's rise. It is the Communist Party by its own behaviour that has made an enemy – or at least an adversary – of the West. Containment, an old Cold War term, is coming back into vogue, as Western strategists explore ways of blunting China's expansion and influence. As we have seen, China's over-reach has created multiple vulnerabilities, which in turn should provide opportunities to push back – if liberal democracies and those who share those values are willing and confident enough to assert their interests. It wasn't long ago that Xi Jinping was boasting of creating a new China-centric world order. The irony is that by his repression and aggression he is breathing new life into the old one, forcing Western allies together and spurring the creation of other alliances and initiatives to counter Beijing.

China's vulnerabilities are not lost on some of Xi Jinping's more perceptive colleagues. In a December 2021 speech to a Beijing symposium, Cui Tiankai, a former ambassador to the US, took a swipe at 'wolf warrior' diplomacy. 'In principle, we should not fight a war we are not prepared for, a war we are not sure of winning, a war of anger and attrition,' he said. 'Every ounce of our people's gains has been hard-won, and we must not allow them to be plundered by anyone or suffer losses due to our own carelessness, laziness and incompetence.'[63] It was remarkable as much for the fact he was able to make it, as it was for the content.

Kaiser Wilhelm II's ambitions culminated in the First World War, and some scholars have argued that historically there is always a high risk of war between an established and an emerging power. That is too fatalistic. As we have seen, it is not the fact of China's rise, but the nature of that rise, and the way Beijing is exercising its new power that is the issue. There are dangers ahead in the Taiwan Strait, but taking on China does not come down to military deterrence alone. For more than three decades, Beijing eroded Western power by multiple means short of warfare. In many ways, the roles are now reversed. China is now an established power – an overstretched and overbearing power, vulnerable to the very 'war by other means' in which it so excelled as underdog.

One of the key documents of the last Cold War was the 'long telegram', written by George Kennan, an American diplomat, who also formulated the policy of containment. Kennan was number two at the US embassy in Moscow in 1946 when he sent the telegram to Washington explaining why there could be no normal peacetime relationship with the Soviet Union. Many in Washington were still struggling to understand the motives and behaviour of Joseph Stalin, their wartime ally. There has been a similar sense of confusion in Western capitals about the behaviour of Xi Jinping, and in re-reading Kennan's telegram, it is remarkable how so many of his observations about Stalin's USSR can be applied to Xi Jinping's China today. He writes of the Kremlin's 'neurotic view of the world', its sense of insecurity and its view of the West as 'evil, hostile and menacing'. He describes an atmosphere of secretiveness and conspiracy, the disrespect for objective truth, and he warns, 'Our first step must be to apprehend, and recognise for what it is, the nature of the movement with which we are dealing.' That is as fundamental in dealing with China today as it was when Kennan formulated the policy for dealing with the USSR.

## Epilogue

# *The Long Shadow of the Ukraine War*

'We are both on the front line against authoritarianism . . . The reaction here is very strong because it is a mirror image of what might happen to Taiwan in the future.'

*Joseph Wu, Taiwan's Minister of Foreign Affairs, in an interview with the author, May 2022*

Nowhere watched the Russian invasion of Ukraine more closely than Taiwan. It might be half a world away, but in the early months of 2022 it seemed chillingly close. A resentful and aggressive dictator seeking to crush his democratic neighbour was a wake-up call for Taipei – and the resilience and courage of the Ukrainian people was an inspiration. When Russian tanks rolled into Ukraine, Taiwan immediately put its own forces on heightened alert. It rushed out a handbook on civil defence detailing how to find bomb shelters and water and food supplies via smartphone apps, as well as tips for preparing emergency first aid kits. 'We are both on the front line against authoritarianism,' said Foreign Minister Joseph Wu when I met him in the Taiwanese capital in May 2022. 'The reaction here is very strong because it is a mirror image of what might happen to Taiwan in the future.' Buildings, including the iconic Taipei 101 skyscraper, were lit-up in the blue and yellow of the Ukrainian flag and angry protesters gathered outside Russia's representative office in Taipei. Taiwan joined sanctions against Moscow and US$33 million was quickly raised to help Ukrainian refugees. Taiwan's president, Tsai Ing-wen, gifted one month of her salary.

My meeting with Wu coincided with China carrying out large-scale military exercises off the east coast of Taiwan, involving the aircraft carrier *Liaoning*. 'They keep circling in that area,' Wu said. 'Non-stop for two weeks, and it is very threatening.' For many Taiwanese, China's grey-zone tactics – its toolkit of military intimidation, economic pressure, disinformation and cyber-attacks – had become background noise, something they'd got used to. Surely Xi Jinping would never actually invade. Yet much the same had been said about Putin. 'The way decisions are made in an authoritarian system, especially in highly authoritarian China, can become very dangerous,' Wu said. Ukraine was a stark warning that autocracies have their own dynamic, especially when they are driven by an almost messianic vision of restoring national greatness.

The Ukraine war accelerated Taiwan's efforts to re-think its own defence and adopt the 'porcupine strategy' – the doctrine of asymmetric warfare, designed to frustrate a much bigger and seemingly more powerful adversary. As we have seen, the tools of the porcupine are small, mobile and highly resilient weapon systems, from drones to smart mines and precision missiles. To Foreign Minister Wu, Ukraine's repelling of Russia's attempt to take Kyiv, and the sinking of the *Moskva*, the flagship of the Black Sea Fleet, were examples of this doctrine in action. He cautioned that it was early days in the Ukraine war, but Kyiv's tactics were right out of the porcupine playbook. 'We can learn from them about how to defend ourselves against a major military power.' He was also surprised and encouraged by Ukraine's ability to rally a global alliance of support – and the alliance's unity of purpose and unprecedented sanctions. 'This is good for Taiwan in the sense that if China wants to attack Taiwan, we hope the democracies can also unite together in reacting to the Chinese aggression,' he said. 'The international community is paying attention to Taiwan.'

The man most closely associated with the 'porcupine strategy' in Taiwan is Admiral Lee Hsi-min, although that's not the way he describes it. 'I don't like the term. I never use it,' he told me as a torrential rainstorm drummed against tall windows behind us. It created a backdrop of smudgy neon and flickering headlights that resembled a scene from the movie *Blade Runner*. He called his strategy the Overall Defense Concept (ODC), and he developed it when he was head of the armed forces between 2017 and 2019. 'You know, the concept is almost the same as Ukraine is doing now,' he told me. 'You should re-define winning of the war. Don't try to destroy the enemy totally in the battlefield, you just make the enemy fail to accomplish their mission. If you are very robust, and make your enemies believe it is impossible to take over Taiwan, then you are safe.'

Lee realised that Taiwan could never match China's vast military spending or the PLA's numerical advantage in big weapon systems, a gap that was growing. In 2022, Taiwan's defence budget was US$16.8 billion, while Beijing was spending an estimated US$287.8 billion.[1] Taiwan had to be smarter. Admiral Lee sought to combine the island's natural geographic advantages with small, lethal and highly mobile weapons, including fleets of micro missile assault boats equipped with stinger missiles based in small fishing ports, easily hidden and immune from long-range missile systems. 'You have to establish highly survivable systems, so you need a large number of small precision, mobile weapons,' he said. The ODC was an exercise in deterrence by denial, with a simple message: 'You cannot conquer me, take over Taiwan . . . you cannot swallow me.' The aim was to make the island 'indigestible' by massively raising the cost to China of any attempt to invade. However, it was initially a hard sell to the military. 'All officers want to have big toys,' he said, 'because they are symbols of military power.' Now he felt vindicated. 'When people ask who has benefited from Ukraine war, I make a joke, I say "me", because I was criticised years ago.' Initially, Lee did not think Russia would invade Ukraine, 'because it is an irrational decision. It would not benefit Russia . . . but I was wrong'. Like Wu, he sees this as a warning. 'It doesn't matter if it makes sense or not . . . So the lesson for Taiwan is don't think it's impossible for war to happen here.'

Three months after the Russian invasion, the ODC was the talk of Taiwan's defence establishment. The Ukraine war was far from over and Russia appeared to have re-focused its grinding assault on the more limited objective of capturing the eastern Donbas region, but Taiwanese strategists still saw parallels and opportunities. 'The Taiwan Strait is actually the highway for the Chinese army, where they are most vulnerable,' according to Su Tzu yun, a research fellow at the Institute for National Defense and Security Research in Taipei, a military-linked research group. To Su, it was the equivalent of the highway into Kyiv along which the Russians were repulsed, though potentially even more treacherous for the vast invasion force of up to 2 million Chinese soldiers that would be required for an invasion of Taiwan. 'That's our opportunity,' Su told me. 'First there are anti-ship missiles, second naval minefields, then tiny UAVs [unmanned aerial vehicles – drones], micro UAVs, kamikaze UAVs.'

In the early weeks of the Ukraine war, there was an assumption among Western strategists that the Russian invasion of Ukraine might give

China pause for thought over Taiwan – that it had made the island safer in the short term. Beijing was shocked by the tough Western sanctions on Russia and the unified and re-invigorated Western alliance, having regularly derided liberal democracies as a spent force. The early incompetence of the Russian military also stung, because tactically and organizationally it has many similarities to the PLA. In Taipei they were cautious. 'We might have a breathing space,' Joseph Wu said, 'but they are learning [from Ukraine] so they can improve their military activities, and if they think they have overcome the difficulties of the Russian military, they might be tempted to use force.'

The Russian invasion coincided with a severe downturn in the Chinese economy, resulting from Xi Jinping's zero-Covid policy, his fanatical attempt to completely eliminate the virus, even as most of the world was learning to live with the less severe but more infectious Omicron variant. By May 2022, an estimated 327.9 million people in 40 cities in China faced some degree of restriction.[2] Shanghai, home to 26 million and China's business capital, was strictly locked down for two months, strangling business activity. The authorities imposed a de-facto international travel ban forbidding Chinese citizens from going abroad for 'non-essential' reasons.[3] Foreign investors were turning their backs. The often brutal enforcement of lockdowns triggered online anger the likes of which had not been seen since the first outbreak in Wuhan at the end of 2019. Xi was boxed in because of low vaccination rates among the elderly and the lower effectiveness of Chinese vaccines. As the economy slumped, rumours swirled about his future. In Taiwan, which was opening up and learning to live with Omicron, this was seen as a potentially dangerous time. Perhaps Xi needed a distraction, so the thinking went, and what better distraction than Taiwan, maybe the seizure of an offshore island, such as Kinmen. 'Authoritarianism always tries to create an external crisis when there are domestic issues,' said Wu.

Beijing ordered a comprehensive 'stress test' to study the ability of the Chinese economy to withstand Russian-style sanctions. Banks and regulators were told to come up with a plan to make the economy more resilient.[4] The sanctions imposed on Moscow amounted to the most comprehensive set of coordinated punitive measures ever seen. The barring of Russian lenders from the SWIFT international payments system and the blocking of half of Moscow's $630 billion of foreign exchange and gold reserves held abroad particularly rattled Beijing. A party directive ordered senior officials to shed property or other assets abroad to prevent them being seized should there be a conflict.[5]

Beijing doubled down on its backing for Moscow, voting against the (successful) suspension of Russia from the UN Human Rights Council and later opposing an investigation by the council into possible war crimes by Russian troops.[6] Beijing blamed NATO and America for provoking Russia. 'U.S. has inescapable responsibilities for Ukraine crisis,' thundered the *People's Daily*,[7] while the military newspaper, the *PLA Daily*, ran a series on the 'despicable role by the United States and the West in the Ukrainian crisis'.[8] Communist Party members across the country were summoned to screenings of a Party-produced documentary on the collapse of the Soviet Union, which was depicted as a tragedy, with Putin portrayed as a hero for restoring Russian pride.[9] The two countries reiterated their pledge to build a 'just, democratic world order' – a euphemism for displacing the US-led global system with one more favourable to them.[10] In late May 2022, Russian and Chinese strategic bombers carried out a joint exercise over the Sea of Japan to coincide with a visit to Tokyo by US President Joe Biden.[11]

Initially, at least, Xi's public support for Putin did not extend to openly breaking Western sanctions, which Chinese tech and energy companies largely observed out of fear of attracting secondary penalties. Xi seethed in resentment at the sanctions, which he seemed to regard as a greater evil than Russian aggression. He was calculating that they would soon fray, along with Western unity, and to this end put considerable effort into trying to drive a wedge between Europe and America, and between European nations, a strategy that has worked well enough in the past. He publicly called on Europe to act more independently of the US over Ukraine.[12] Xi craved stability in a year when a crucial Communist Party congress was expected to extend his rule for another five years and open the way for him to remain leader for life. However, he wasn't about to abandon his good friend Putin. The two men had too much in common, and in any case if Russia was weakened by war and sanctions, that would increase its dependence on China and reinforce Beijing's position as the senior partner – even at the cost of being seen globally as an accessory to Russia's barbarity.

The Communist Party angrily dismissed comparisons between Taiwan and Ukraine, repeating its dubious claim that Taiwan is just a renegade province and already part of China, as if aggression in this context would be somehow different. Nevertheless, Beijing was watching Ukraine closely. 'From a technical point of view, the Ukraine issue can indeed be seen as a rehearsal for a Taiwan Strait crisis,' said Jin Canrong of Renmin University in Beijing and a Party adviser. 'This is a very good learning opportunity. China can learn a lot from it, such as how to fight militarily, what pressure may be encountered politically, how to relieve that pressure, and so on.'[13] Military strategists noted that Washington avoided direct military conflict with Russia out of fear of nuclear escalation and pressed for a faster build-up of China's nuclear arsenal. Ukraine was also seen in Beijing as a useful 'strategic distraction', drawing Washington's attention away from the Indo-Pacific region and back to Europe.

The American Institute in Taipei sits fortress-like on a hillside in Neihu, a suburb in the north-east of the capital. It is a solid, sprawling and imposing slab of concrete, surrounded by tall walls – an embassy in all but name. It cannot be called that because of the 'One China policy', which prohibits formal diplomatic relations. In practice, relations are thriving, and in the early months of 2022, the Institute was busy with a stream of visits from members of Congress and retired (and semi-retired) officials, as Washington re-calibrated its policy towards China and Taiwan. The US is Taiwan's principal arms supplier, and although US arms companies benefit from the sale of big-ticket items to Taipei, the Biden administration strongly supported the 'porcupine strategy'. During a visit to Japan, President Biden also said that the US would be willing to use force to defend Taiwan against China.[14] It was the third time he had made such comments. The White House denied that it represented a change in policy, though to outsiders the long-standing policy of 'strategic ambiguity' towards Taiwan's defence was starting to look a good deal less ambiguous. That was welcomed by the Taiwanese government, though Foreign Minister Wu insisted that the island was not relying on it. 'We want to show to the international community that we are willing, and we are determined to defend ourselves,' he said. While Admiral Lee says: 'The only thing you can rely on is yourself.'

As a result of Russia's aggression against Ukraine, liberal democracies found their voice. It reinvigorated security structures and political alliances that had seemed to be struggling for direction and relevance. There was a new confidence, unity and sense of purpose that belied the image of a divided and decaying West in terminal decline, so central to the world view of Xi Jinping (and Putin). When Xi sought to lecture the EU about distancing itself from America, he was told bluntly that China's reputation too was now at stake.[15] Biden's five-day visit to Asia in late May 2022 marked another step towards redrawing geopolitics, moving beyond terms like 'the West' and towards a broader notion of 'autocracy *vs* democracy'. By this definition, the Ukraine war is an opening salvo. And while Russia should not be underestimated, CIA director Bill Burns warned that Xi's China was the 'biggest geopolitical challenge we face over the long term as a country'.[16]

No country has welcomed this re-definition of world affairs more than Japan, whose transformation in security terms has been remarkable. It was now explicitly linking its own security to that of Taiwan. During a visit to London, the Japanese prime minister, Fumio Kishida, stressed the importance of a strong international response to Russia's aggression in deterring possible Chinese action against Taiwan. 'Ukraine may be east Asia tomorrow,' he warned.[17] Kishida signed a defence partnership with the UK, which will see the two militaries exercising and operating together.[18] On the eve of his UK visit, Kishida also confirmed plans to double Japan's defence budget to around £86 billion, breaking restrictions imposed after the Second World War.[19] Change was also afoot in South Korea, under a new more hawkish president, Yoon Suk-yeol. He angered China by joining a NATO cyber defence group, becoming its first Asian member. 'If South Korea takes a path of turning hostile against its neighbours, the end of this path could be a Ukraine,' growled Hu Xijin, one of China's more prominent and pugnacious commentators.[20] Washington moved to involve its allies more closely in contingency planning over Taiwan. It explored with the UK and EU more ways to engage diplomatically with Taipei, and more generally draw the island closer as a fellow democracy.[21] In a major foreign policy speech, British Foreign Secretary Liz Truss said, 'We must ensure that democracies like Taiwan are able to defend themselves.'[22] Taiwan's Foreign Minister Wu described these comments as 'probably the strongest we can find in Europe when it comes to Taiwan'.

Even Hollywood seemed to take notice. When the movie *Top Gun: Maverick* opened in Taipei, audiences erupted in cheers and applause – not at the daredevil stunts of Tom Cruise, but at his iconic leather jacket on which the Taiwanese flag had been reinstated. As we saw in chapter 8, when a trailer for the movie, a remake of the 1986 classic, was first released, the jacket had been altered. The moviemakers removed the flag, which had been among several patches on the back of the original jacket – apparently to appease Chinese censors. Tencent, a Chinese tech company, was one of the original financial backers of the movie, which had high hopes for the China market. However, Tencent reportedly pulled out, fearing that supporting a film about the US military would anger the Communist Party. Hopes for the China market were much reduced and the flag came back. It's probably too early to say Hollywood is developing a backbone – *Top Gun: Maverick* was careful to keep its adversary anonymous – but in Taipei in late May 2022 the symbolism was powerful.

Putin's unprovoked aggression generated soul-searching in Western democracies about how they had allowed themselves to become so dependent on Russian hydrocarbons. The EU estimated it will cost nearly €200 billion over five years to secure energy independence from Russia.[23] Western companies scrambled to disengage – a messy and expensive process. It raised broader questions about the danger of dependency – particularly on China, which is far more central to the world economy than Russia. Possibly with this in mind (and after considerable dithering), the UK announced it was using its new National Security and Investment Act to examine the takeover of Newport Wafer Fab, the country's largest semiconductor plant by a Chinese company – a case examined earlier in this book.[24] The government also introduced a new national security law aimed at closing gaping holes in current legislation covering cyber-spying and foreign influence operations. At the time of writing, it is unclear how attempts to identify foreign agents of influence will work in practice. Universities pressed to have their financial tie-ups with China exempted.[25] They argued that simply taking money does not turn them into lobbyists for a foreign state. As this book has sought to demonstrate, there is often a fine line, and transparency is the essential starting point. If there is one overriding lesson from the Ukraine war it must surely be that over-dependency on tyrants is foolhardy in the extreme – whether that tyrant is in Moscow or Beijing.

The Touat bookstore and café sits in a narrow alleyway in Taipei's government district, rows of the city's ubiquitous scooters lined up outside. 'Stand with Ukraine' is written in large letters across the front window. A Ukrainian flag flutters nearby and a notice board is plastered with Post-it notes in Chinese and English – 'Justice will prevail', Go Ukraine! We are with you', 'Stop Putin's imperialism', 'Putin – arsehole'.

The bookstore is a hub for Taipei's non-governmental organisations (NGOs), the thriving civil society movement we met earlier in this book, and its shelves strain with books ranging from indigenous rights to the battle for freedom in Tibet, Xinjiang and Hong Kong. This is where I met Lin Hsinyi, a veteran of many of these battles. It was the third anniversary of the legalisation of same-sex marriage, and she showed me photographs on her phone of protesters gathered outside the nearby parliament building to mark the occasion. 'It was a long fight and we passed it. But it wasn't easy.' She was now campaigning to have the death penalty abolished, which still sits on Taiwan's statue book, a hangover from a more oppressive past. She was also on the board of the bookshop, which occupies part of a block that under military rule was a detention centre. 'It's an ideal location. There are many ghosts,' she told me.

Like many Taiwanese, Lin Hsinyi was shocked by Russia's aggression and moved by the courage of young Ukrainians. 'Before, I really didn't think about it. But it made me think, if there was a war, what would I do?' She signed up for a civil defence training course – one of many designed to teach basic first aid and survival skills which have filled rapidly since the start of the Ukraine conflict. 'I want to be trained. I want to be able to help myself and to help others,' she said, telling me she was particularly taken by the leadership of Ukraine's president Volodymyr Zelensky. 'What he said was really inspiring. I would not run away from China. I would fight for my country.' It is a widely held sentiment. Opinion polls since the Ukraine invasion show a sharp increase in the number of people willing to fight for their country in the event of a Chinese invasion – more than one in seven according to one survey.[26]

The invasion of Ukraine was extensively covered in the lively Taiwanese media. Wang Jui-ti, a 35-year-old Taiwanese citizen, became an instant celebrity when he signed up for Ukraine's foreign legion, the International Legion of Territorial Defense of Ukraine, and began posting from the front line. 'I want to do my part to defend basic human values,' he said. The broad mood change was noticed by Audrey Tang, the digital minister we met earlier in this book, who is a former activist. 'A lot of people are now saying, "what can we do during an escalation of tension? We don't need to wait for the ministry of defence or really anyone to tell us what to do. We should be just preparing ourselves".' Nor is it lost on Admiral Lee, the architect of the 'porcupine strategy', who sees in this enthusiasm the makings of a revamped territorial defence body. 'We should attract a lot of youngsters who are patriotic, who love their country, love their city, love their community, but are reluctant to join the military,' he told me. 'They would come together twice a year, no uniform, but would receive basic training with light weapons such as grenade guns, javelin, stinger, micro UAVs [drones] – mobile survivals skills, hit and run.'

Russia's aggression provided a stark warning. 'We should thank Ukraine. It's good for Taiwan,' my taxi driver said to me during our drive back to the airport. Then he asked if I thought China would still invade. I said I wasn't sure. It was a question I heard frequently in Taipei – and after Ukraine they realised they cannot afford to wait for an answer. They have to be prepared.

Taipei, June 2022

# *Notes*

## Introduction: China's New Cold War

1 BBC Online, 'Huawei executive Meng Wanzhou freed by Canada arrives home in China', 25 September 2021. https://www.bbc.com/news/world-us-canada-58690974

2 Christian Paas-Lang, 'Michael Kovrig and Michael Spavor arrive in Canada after nearly 3-year detention in China', CBC, 25 September 2021. https://www.cbc.ca/news/politics/spavor-kovrig-in-canada-1.6189640

3 Nathan Vanderklippe, '365 days of detention in China: What life is like for Canadians Michael Spavor and Michael Kovrig', *The Globe and Mail*, 9 December 2019. https://www.theglobeandmail.com/world/article-michael-kovrig-michael-spavor-china-detained-canadians-huawei/

4 David E. Sanger and William J. Broad, 'China's Weapon Tests Close to a "Sputnik Moment" US General Says', *New York Times*, 27 October 2021. https://www.nytimes.com/2021/10/27/us/politics/china-hypersonic-missile.html?referringSource=articleShare

5 Demetri Sevastopulo, 'China conducted two hypersonic weapons tests this summer', *Financial Times*, 21 October 2021. https://www.ft.com/content/c7139a23-1271-43ae-975b-9b632330130b

6 Demetri Sevastopulo, Kathrin Hille and Sylvia Pfeifer, 'What China's hypersonic test launch reveals about the global arms race', *Financial Times*, 21 October 2021. https://www.ft.com/content/f647d654-e870-4829-8dc2-90c98985c034

7 Sanger and Broad, *New York Times*, 27 October 2021.

8 Demetri Sevastopulo, 'China plans to quadruple nuclear weapons stockpile, Pentagon says', *Financial Times*, 3 November 2021. https://www.ft.com/content/d1225e37-30ef-4fa7-99a9-e5994ebe2aba

9 Robert D. Blackwill and Philip Zelikow, 'The United States, China,

and Taiwan: A Strategy to Prevent War', Council on Foreign Relations, Council Special Report No. 90, February 2021, p. 5.

10 The full transcript of President Biden's 21 September address to the UN General Assembly, 'Remarks by President Biden Before the 76th Session of the United Nations General Assembly', can be accessed via the White House website. https://www.whitehouse.gov/briefing-room/speeches-remarks/2021/09/21/remarks-by-president-biden-before-the-76th-session-of-the-united-nations-general-assembly/

11 Larisa Brown, 'Boris Johnson warns Tories of cold war with China', *The Times*, 16 March 2021. https://www.thetimes.co.uk/article/uk-builds-up-nuclear-arsenal-to-counter-cyber-threat-cl96v0wbb

12 Sian Elvin, 'We don't want a war with China, says Boris Johnson', *Metro*, 14 June 2021. https://metro.co.uk/2021/06/14/boris-johnson-tells-nato-summit-nobody-wants-war-with-china-14767744/

13 Yew Lun Tian and Ryan Woo, 'Xi warns against foreign bullying as China marks party centenary', Reuters, 1 July 2021. https://www.reuters.com/world/china/beijing-set-celebrate-centenary-chinas-communist-party-2021-06-30/

14 BBC Online, 'CCP 100: Xi warns China will not be "oppressed" in anniversary speech', 1 July 2021. https://www.bbc.com/news/world-asia-china-57648236

15 Tom Mitchell, 'Xi lays groundwork for third term by adopting Mao and Deng's power ploy', *Financial Times*, 8 November 2021. https://www.ft.com/content/71b165a6-052d-4d7d-9006-e2e757f40d98

16 Demetri Sevastopulo and Tom Mitchell, 'Xi-Biden agreement on nuclear talks clouded by "deep distrust"', *Financial Times*, 17 November 2021. https://www.ft.com/content/968c299c-83b4-42e5-8d65-8078beec6c7c

17 Julian Borger, 'Biden-Xi virtual summit: leaders warn each other over future of Taiwan', *The Guardian*, 16 November 2021. https://www.theguardian.com/us-news/2021/nov/16/xi-biden-virtual-summit-us-china-conflict-taiwan-hong-kong

18 Reuters, 'Factbox: Moscow-Beijing partnership has "no limits"', 4 February 2022. https://www.reuters.com/world/china/moscow-beijing-partnership-has-no-limits-2022-02-04/

19 George Orwell's 19 October 1945 essay for *Tribune* magazine, 'You and the Atom Bomb', can be accessed via the website of the Orwell Foundation. https://www.orwellfoundation.com/the-

orwell-foundation/orwell/essays-and-other-works/you-and-the-atom-bomb/

20 A full transcript of Richard Moore's 30 November 2021 speech to the International Institute for Strategic Studies can be accessed via the UK government website. https://www.gov.uk/government/speeches/cs-speech-to-the-international-institute-for-strategic-studies

## Chapter 1: The Taiwan Strait: The Most Dangerous Place on Earth

1 For a more detailed analysis of the events of 1958, also known as the Second Taiwan Strait Crisis, see GlobalSecurity.org. https://www.globalsecurity.org/military/ops/quemoy_matsu-2.htm

2 The US government's classified documented history of the 1958 Kinmen crisis, written by Morton Halperin and obtained by Daniel Ellsberg, can be accessed at https://archive.org/details/The1958TaiwanStraitsCrisisADocumentedHistory_201712/page/n3/mode/2up

3 Nick Aspinwall, '6km from China, Taiwan's Kinmen charts its own path', *The Diplomat*, 4 September 2018. https://thediplomat.com/2018/09/6-km-from-china-taiwans-kinmen-charts-its-own-path/

4 Agence France-Presse, 'China is Angry with Taiwan', *The ASEAN Post*, 31 October 2020. https://theaseanpost.com/article/china-angry-taiwan

5 Ian Easton, 'Why a Taiwan invasion would look nothing like D-Day', *The Diplomat*, 26 May 2021. https://thediplomat.com/2021/05/why-a-taiwan-invasion-would-look-nothing-like-d-day/

6 Liu Zhen, 'China's military gives glimpse of updated long-range rocket system', *South China Morning Post*, 9 January 2021. https://www.scmp.com/print/news/china/military/article/3117041/chinas-military-gives-glimpse-updated-long-range-rocket-system

7 Minnie Chan, 'PLA showcases missiles in New Year's Eve "warning for Taiwan"', *South China Morning Post*, 7 January 2021. https://www.scmp.com/news/china/military/article/3116674/pla-showcases-missiles-new-years-eve-warning-taiwan

8 Felix K. Chang, 'China's Anti-Ship Ballistic Missile Capability in the South China Sea', Foreign Policy Research Institute analysis, 24

May 2021. https://www.fpri.org/article/2021/05/chinas-anti-ship-ballistic-missile-capability-in-the-south-china-sea/

9 Kathrin Hille and Demetri Sevastopulo, 'Chinese warplanes simulated attacking US carrier near Taiwan', *Financial Times*, 30 January 2021. https://www.ft.com/content/e6f6230c-b709-4b3d-b9a2-951516e52360

10 James T. Areddy, 'China Has Built Mock-Ups of US Aircraft Carrier, Warships in the Desert', *Wall Street Journal*, 8 November 2021. https://www.wsj.com/articles/china-has-built-mock-ups-of-u-s-aircraft-carrier-warships-in-the-desert-11636403790

11 Oriana Skylar Mastro, 'The Taiwan Temptation. Why Beijing Might Resort to Force', *Foreign Affairs*, July/August 2021. https://www.foreignaffairs.com/articles/china/2021-06-03/china-taiwan-war-temptation

12 Agence France-Presse (via France24), 'China sends largest incursion of jets into Taiwan defence zone in months', 24 January 2022. https://www.france24.com/en/live-news/20220124-china-sends-largest-incursion-of-jets-into-taiwan-defence-zone-in-months

13 Brin Hioe, 'What Do Taiwanese Think of China's Record-Setting Incursions Into Taiwan's ADIZ?' *The Diplomat*, 6 October 2021. https://thediplomat.com/2021/10/what-do-taiwanese-think-of-chinas-record-setting-incursions-into-taiwans-adiz/

14 Helen Davidson, 'Taiwan reports record Chinese incursions into its air defence zone', *The Guardian*, 4 October 2021. https://www.theguardian.com/world/2021/oct/04/taiwan-reports-record-chinese-incursions-into-its-air-defence-zone

15 Reuters, 'Taiwan reports largest incursion yet by Chinese military aircraft', *The Guardian*, 26 March 2021. https://www.theguardian.com/world/2021/mar/26/taiwan-reports-incursion-by-20-chinese-military-aircraft?CMP=Share_iOSApp_Other

16 Didi Tang, 'China fortifies three military airbases facing Taiwan', *The Times*, 15 October 2021. https://www.thetimes.co.uk/article/39c2c0e6-2daa-11ec-a1c0-649c1183346f?shareToken=53ee708ed9fe3a235ceb9efa1bc0c313

17 Brad Lendon, 'China flanks Taiwan with military exercises in air and sea', CNN, 8 April 2021. https://edition.cnn.com/2021/04/07/asia/china-taiwan-military-surrounded-intl-hnk-scli-ml/index.html

18 John Feng, 'China Military's Taiwan Invasion Force conducts

Amphibious Beach Assault Drills', *Newsweek*, 26 May 2021. https://www.msn.com/en-us/news/world/china-military-s-taiwan-invasion-force-conducts-amphibious-beach-assault-drills/ar-AAKp7wp

19 Liu Xuanzun, 'PLA Army helicopters switch role from support to main force in cross-sea operations', *Global Times*, 23 December 2020. https://www.globaltimes.cn/page/202012/1210819.shtml

20 'Facing up to the Chinese threat', *Taipei Times* editorial, 19 March 2021. https://www.taipeitimes.com/News/editorials/archives/2021/03/19/2003754089

21 Liu Zhen, 'Xi Jinping tells Chinese army to step up combat readiness as budget rise is blamed on security threats', *South China Morning Post*, 26 May 2020. https://www.scmp.com/news/china/military/article/3086175/xi-jinping-tells-chinese-army-step-preparations-combat-budget

22 Helen Davidson, 'China could invade Taiwan in next six years, top US admiral warns', *The Guardian*, 10 March 2021. https://www.theguardian.com/world/2021/mar/10/china-could-invade-taiwan-in-next-six-years-top-us-admiral-warns?CMP=Share_iOSApp_Other

23 Agence France-Presse, 'China threat to invade Taiwan is "closer than most think", says admiral', *The Guardian*, 23 March 2021. https://www.theguardian.com/world/2021/mar/23/taiwan-china-threat-admiral-john-aquilino

24 Demetri Sevastopulo and Kathrin Hille, 'US fears China is flirting with seizing control of Taiwan', *Financial Times*, 27 March 2021. https://www.ft.com/content/3ed169b8-3f47-4f66-a914-58b6e2215f7d?shareType=nongift

25 John Feng, 'US can "resist" Chinese Force or Coercion Against Taiwan: State Department', *Newsweek*, 8 April 2021. https://www.newsweek.com/us-can-resist-chinese-force-coercion-against-taiwan-state-department-1581872

26 Kathrin Hille, 'China flies record number of fighter jets towards Taiwan', *Financial Times*, 15 June 2021. https://www.ft.com/content/64778dbb-1b99-425b-b09f-80dd2eb622f1?shareType=nongift

27 Michael Peel and Lauren Fedor, 'NATO warns China's military ambitions threaten global order', *Financial Times*, 15 June 2021. https://www.ft.com/content/f454033a-9975-4efd-92eb-9cf63306af7f?shareType=nongift

28 'The most dangerous place on earth', *The Economist*, 1 May 2021.

https://www.economist.com/leaders/2021/05/01/the-most-dangerous-place-on-earth

29 Johnson Lai, 'Former President Lee Teng-hui, Who Helped Birth Taiwan's Democracy, Dies', *The Diplomat*, 31 July 2020. https://thediplomat.com/2020/07/former-president-lee-teng-hui-who-helped-birth-taiwans-democracy-dies/

30 For a detailed analysis of the events of 1996, see Barton Gellman, 'US and China nearly came to blows in '96', *Washington Post*, 21 June 1998. https://www.washingtonpost.com/archive/politics/1998/06/21/us-and-china-nearly-came-to-blows-in-96/926d105f-1fd8-404c-9995-90984f86a613/

31 For a more detailed overview of the evolution of the 'One China Policy', see Kerry Brown and Kalley Wu Tzu-hui, *The Trouble with Taiwan: History, the United States and a Rising China* (London: Zed Books, 2019).

32 J. Michael Cole, 'Taiwan Between the Extremes of War and Abandonment', a MacDonald Laurier Institute Commentary, September 2020. https://macdonaldlaurier.ca/files/pdf/20200922_Cole_COMMENTARY_FWeb.pdf

33 Robert D. Blackwill and Philip Zelikow, 'The United States, China, and Taiwan: A Strategy to Prevent War', Council on Foreign Relations, Council Special Report No. 90, February 2021.

## Chapter 2: The South China Sea: The Biggest Territorial Grab Since the Second World War

1 Richard Lloyd Parry, 'Philippine's minister fires four-letter salvo at China over disputed reef', *The Times*, 4 May 2021. https://www.thetimes.co.uk/article/ba82e564-acc5-11eb-9dc9-5a05c2885d62?shareToken=ab9845c7af6542dc5e123610ecfbe5e6

2 Neil Arwin Mercado, 'Lacson pushes for review of PH-China diplomatic ties amid WPS incursions', *Inquirer*, 4 May 2021. https://globalnation.inquirer.net/195808/lacson-pushes-for-review-of-ph-china-diplomatic-ties-amid-wps-incursions

3 Samir Puri and Greg Austin, 'What the Whitsun reef incident tells us about China's future operations at sea', International Institute for Strategic Studies analysis, 9 April 2021. https://www.iiss.org/blogs/analysis/2021/04/whitsun-reef-incident-china

4 Gordon G. Chang, 'China And The Biggest Territory Grab Since World War II', Forbes, 2 June 2013. https://www.forbes.com/sites/gordonchang/2013/06/02/china-and-the-biggest-territory-grab-since-world-war-ii/?sh=6e5d5d202c35
5 'China allows PH banana, pineapple exports ahead of Duterte visit', ABS-CBN News, 8 October 2016. https://news.abs-cbn.com/business/10/08/16/china-allows-ph-banana-pineapple-exports-ahead-of-duterte-visit
6 The full UNCLOS ruling can be accessed via the website of the Permanent Court of Arbitration in the Hague. https://pca-cpa.org/en/cases/7/
7 'Arbitration award more shameless than worst predicted', *Global Times*, 12 July 2016. https://www.globaltimes.cn/content/993855.shtml
8 Patricia Lourdes Viray, 'Philippines rejects talks not based on arbitral ruling; China warns of confrontation', *Philippines Star*, 19 July 2016. https://www.philstar.com/headlines/2016/07/19/1604466/philippines-rejects-talks-not-based-arbitral-ruling-china-warns-confrontation
9 BBC Online, 'Philippines' Duterte tells Obama to "go to hell"', 4 October 2016. https://www.bbc.com/news/world-asia-37548695
10 BBC Online, 'Duterte in China. Xi lauds "milestone" Duterte visit', 20 October 2016. https://www.bbc.com/news/world-asia-37700409
11 John Feng, 'Philippines Duterte Says Court Ruling Against China is Trash to Be Thrown Away', *Newsweek*, 6 May 2021. https://www.newsweek.com/philippines-duterte-says-court-ruling-against-china-trash-thrown-away-1589183
12 Jamaine Punzalan, 'Enrile digs up US role in Scarborough loss to China', ABS-CBN News, 17 May 2021. https://news.abs-cbn.com/news/05/17/21/enrile-duterte-us-china-sea
13 Brad Lendon and Steve George, 'The long arm of China's new maritime law risks causing conflicts with US and Japan', CNN, 3 September 2021. https://edition.cnn.com/2021/09/03/china/coast-guard-law-mic-intl-hnk/index.html
14 See Commander Harry Harris's address to the Australian Strategic Policy Institute in Canberra, 31 March 2015, as published by the US Pacific Fleet. https://www.cpf.navy.mil/leaders/harry-harris/speeches/2015/03/ASPI-Australia.pdf
15 Jeremy Page, Carol E. Lee and Gordon Lubold, 'China's President

Pledges No Militarization in Disputed Islands', *Wall Street Journal*, 25 September 2015. https://www.wsj.com/articles/china-completes-runway-on-artificial-island-in-south-china-sea-1443184818

16 Matthew Southerland, 'China's Island Building in the South China Sea: Damage to the Marine Environment, Implications, and International Law', US–China Economic and Security Review Commission, Staff Research Report, 12 April 2016. https://www.uscc.gov/sites/default/files/Research/China%27s%20Island%20Building%20in%20the%20South%20China%20Sea_0.pdf

17 Tom Phillips, 'Images show "significant" Chinese weapon systems in South China Sea', *The Guardian*, 15 December 2015. https://www.theguardian.com/world/2016/dec/15/images-show-significant-chinese-weapons-systems-in-south-china-sea

18 Frances Mangosing, 'New photos show China is almost nearly done in its militarization of the South China Sea', *Inquirer*, 5 February 2018. https://www.inquirer.net/specials/exclusive-china-militarization-south-china-sea/

19 Toru Takahashi, 'What Beijing really wants from South China Sea code of conduct', *Nikkei Asia*, 12 August 2019. https://asia.nikkei.com/Spotlight/Comment/What-Beijing-really-wants-from-South-China-Sea-code-of-conduct

20 Christopher P. Cavas, 'UK Progress, Pacific tensions, Key Naval Conference', *Defence News*, 14 September 2015. https://www.defensenews.com/digital-show-dailies/dsei/2015/09/15/uk-progress-pacific-tensions-key-naval-conference/

21 For a more detailed analysis of trade through the South China Sea, see the database maintained by China Power, 'How Much Trade Transits the South China Sea', updated 25 January 2021. https://chinapower.csis.org/much-trade-transits-south-china-sea/

22 Ibid.

23 David Uren, 'Southeast Asia will take a major economic hit if shipping is blocked in the South China Sea', *The Strategist*, 8 December 2020. https://www.aspistrategist.org.au/southeast-asia-will-take-a-major-economic-hit-if-shipping-is-blocked-in-the-south-china-sea/

24 Anders Corr, 'China's $60 Trillion Estimate of Oil and Gas in The South China Sea: Strategic Implications', *The Journals of Political Risk*, 23 January 2013. https://www.jpolrisk.com/

chinas-60-trillion-estimate-of-oil-and-gas-in-the-south-china-sea-the-strategic-implications/

25 Radio Free Asia, 'Washington Tells Southeast Asian Nations to oppose China's "coercion" in Disputed Sea', 1 August 2019. https://www.rfa.org/english/news/china/asean-southchinasea-08012019172640.html

26 Li Xiaokun and Liu Xiaoli, 'Ancient Book "provides ironclad proof of Chinese ownership"', *China Daily*, 24 May 2016. http://www.chinadaily.com.cn/china/2016-05/24/content_25433846.htm

27 John Sudworth, 'South China Sea: the mystery of missing books and maritime claims', BBC Online, 19 June 2016. https://www.bbc.com/news/world-asia-china-36545565

28 'China Museum Of The South China Sea / Architectural Design Research Institute of SCUT', ArchDaily, 16 November 2019. https://www.archdaily.com/928029/the-south-china-sea-museum-architectural-design-research-institute-of-scut

29 Max Walden, 'Peaceful explorer or war criminal: Who was Zheng He, China's Muslim symbol of diplomacy?' ABC News of Australia, 21 September 2019. https://www.abc.net.au/news/2019-09-22/zheng-he-chinese-islam-explorer-belt-and-road/11471758

30 Xi Jinping, *The Governance of China*, vol. II (Beijing: Foreign Languages Press 2017), p. 554.

31 Andrew S. Erickson, 'The South China Sea's third force: understanding and countering china's maritime militia', testimony before the House Armed Services Committee, Seapower and Projection Forces Subcommittee Hearing on Seapower and Projection Forces in the South China Sea, 21 September 2016. https://docs.house.gov/meetings/AS/AS28/20160921/105309/HHRG-114-AS28-Wstate-EricksonPhDA-20160921.pdf

32 Philip Wen, 'South China Sea: sleepy port is base for Beijing's "little blue men"', *The Sydney Morning Herald*, 12 July 2016. https://www.smh.com.au/world/south-china-sea-sleepy-port-town-is-base-for-beijings-little-blue-men-20160630-gpv84r.html

33 Ibid.

34 Andrew S. Erickson's Congressional testimony.

35 Andrew S. Erickson, Joshua Hickey and Henry Holst, 'SURGING SECOND SEA FORCE. China's Maritime Law-Enforcement Forces, Capabilities, and Future in the Gray Zone and Beyond', Naval War College review, vol. 72, no.2 (Spring 2019), pp. 10–34.

36 Ibid., p. 12.

37 The Jamestown Foundation, 'Early Warning Brief: Introducing the "New, New" China Coast Guard', *China Brief*, vol. 21, issue 2, 25 January 2021. https://jamestown.org/program/early-warning-brief-introducing-the-new-new-china-coast-guard/

38 Ryan D. Martinson, 'Gauging the real risks of China's new coastguard law', *The Strategist*, 23 February 2021. https://www.aspistrategist.org.au/gauging-the-real-risks-of-chinas-new-coastguard-law/

39 Kawashima Shin, 'China's Worrying New Coast Guard Law', *The Diplomat*, 17 March 2021. https://thediplomat.com/2021/03/chinas-worrying-new-coast-guard-law/

40 Didi Tang, 'Xi unveils three new warships in warning to Taiwan', *The Times*, 26 April 2021. https://www.thetimes.co.uk/article/xi-unveils-three-new-warships-in-warning-to-taiwan-xf2cz50kq

41 Liu Xuanzun and Guo Yuadan, '3 new world-class warships commissioned together, shoring up "nuke retaliation, S. China Sea security, island seizing"', *Global Times*, 24 April 2021. https://www.globaltimes.cn/page/202104/1221970.shtml

42 Ralf Jennings, 'Expansion of Naval Base Seen Giving China More Power in Disputed Asian Sea', *VOA News*, 15 January 2021. https://www.voanews.com/east-asia-pacific/voa-news-china/expansion-naval-base-seen-giving-china-more-power-disputed-asian

43 The Chinese video of the battle for Johnson South Reef is still available to view on YouTube. https://www.youtube.com/watch?v=uq30CY9nWE8

44 For a more detailed analysis of the February 1979 border war see David Shambaugh's book, *Where Great Powers Meet: America and China in Southeast Asia* (New York: Oxford University Press, 2021), pp. 49–52.

45 Rachel Zhang, 'South China Sea: what are rival claimants building on islands and reefs?' *South China Morning Post*, 7 March 2021. https://www.scmp.com/news/china/diplomacy/article/3124309/south-china-sea-what-are-rival-claimants-building-islands-and

46 Robert D. Kaplan, *Asia's Cauldron: The South China Sea and the End of a Stable Pacific* (New York: Random House, 2014), p. 59.

47 Alexander L. Luving, 'South China Sea: Who Occupies What in the Spratlys?', *The Diplomat*, 6 May 2016. https://thediplomat.com/2016/05/south-china-sea-who-claims-what-in-the-spratlys/

48 Reuters, 'Chinese ships intruded into Malaysian waters 89 times

in four years, report says', 14 July 2020. https://www.reuters.com/article/us-malaysia-china-southchinasea-idUSKCN24F17U

49 Reuters, 'Malaysia protests "suspicious" Chinese air force activity over South China Sea', *The Guardian*, 2 June 2021. https://www.theguardian.com/world/2021/jun/02/malaysia-protests-suspicious-chinese-air-force-activity-over-south-china-sea

50 Bhavan Jaipragas, 'South China Sea: Chinese coastguard ships, warplanes, engaged in "parallel escalation" off Malaysia, US think tank says', *South China Morning Post*, 8 July 2021. https://www.scmp.com/print/week-asia/politics/article/3140263/south-china-sea-chinese-coastguard-ships-warplanes-engage

51 Euan Graham, 'Aerial manoeuvres in the South China Sea', International Institute for Strategic Studies analysis, 9 June 2021. https://www.iiss.org/blogs/analysis/2021/06/aerial-manoeuvres-south-china-sea

52 Sebastian Strangio, 'Affirming Trump-Era Policy, US Warns China Over South China Sea', *The Diplomat*, 21 July 2021. https://thediplomat.com/2021/07/affirming-trump-era-policy-us-warns-china-over-south-china-sea/

53 Alex Vivona, 'Water Wars: No One in the Mood for Compromise in the South China Sea', Lawfare, 7 July 2021. https://www.lawfareblog.com/water-wars-no-one-mood-compromise-south-china-sea

54 Dzirhan Mahadzir, '6 Naval Task Groups from U.S, U.K., India, Japan and Australia Underway in Pacific', *USNI News*, 30 August 2021. https://news.usni.org/2021/08/30/6-naval-task-groups-from-u-s-u-k-india-japan-and-australia-underway-in-pacific

## Chapter 3: Southeast Asia: Paying Tribute to the Emperor

1 Associated Press, 'Chinese influx transforming Myanmar's quintessential city', *Myanmar Times*, 2 May 2018. https://www.mmtimes.com/news/chinese-influx-transforming-myanmars-quintessential-city.html

2 Myat Pyae Phyo, 'CCTV Contract with Huawei Will Guard Against Spying: Chief Minister', *The Irrawaddy*, 18 July 2019. https://www.irrawaddy.com/news/burma/cctv-contract-huawei-will-guard-spying-mandalay-chief-minister.html

3 Thant Myint-U, *Where China Meets India: Burma and the New Crossroads of Asia* (London: Faber & Faber, 2012), p. 70.

4 Gray Sergeant, 'Is China's hidden hand behind the Myanmar coup?' *The Spectator*, 4 February 2021. https://www.spectator.co.uk/article/is-china-s-hidden-hand-behind-the-myanmar-coup-

5 Sai Wunna, 'November voters list had millions of errors: Tatmadaw', *Myanmar Times*, 14 January 2021. https://www.mmtimes.com/news/november-voters-list-had-millions-errors-tatmadaw.html

6 Dominic Oo, 'China's interests going up in flames in Myanmar', *Asia Times*, 16 March 2021. https://asiatimes.com/2021/03/chinas-interests-going-up-in-flames-in-myanmar/

7 'Myanmar locals urged not to be incited by West as 32 Chinese factories in Yangon suffer from attacks', *Global Times*, 15 March 2021. https://www.globaltimes.cn/page/202103/1218466.shtml

8 'Chinese-Made Drones Reportedly Monitor anti-Regime Protests in Myanmar', *The Irrawaddy*, 10 April 2021. https://www.irrawaddy.com/news/burma/chinese-made-drones-reportedly-monitor-anti-regime-protests-myanmar.html

9 Reuters, 'Analysis: "Chinese business, Out!" Myanmar anger threatens investment plans', 11 March 2021. https://www.reuters.com/article/us-myanmar-politics-china-analysis-idUSKBN2B31C2

10 'Deadly Attack on Pipeline Station Spotlights China's High Stakes in Myanmar', *The Irrawaddy*, 6 May 2021. https://www.irrawaddy.com/news/burma/attack-oil-and-gas-pipelines-china-off-take-station-spotlight-stakes-junta-regime-protect-protesters-arson-attack-strategic-investment-unsc-support.html

11 For a detailed overview of China's investment in Myanmar, see Lucas Myers's analysis for the Wilson Center, published 26 May 2020, 'The China-Myanmar Economic Corridor and China's Determination to See It Through'. https://www.wilsoncenter.org/blog-post/china-myanmar-economic-corridor-and-chinas-determination-see-it-through

12 Sebastian Strangio, *In the Dragon's Shadow: Southeast Asia in the Chinese Century* (New Haven and London: Yale University Press, 2020), p. 150.

13 Oliver Slow, Win Zar Ni Aung and Ei Ei Mon, 'Left behind by the Letpaduang copper mine', *Frontier Myanmar*, 5 June 2019. https://www.frontiermyanmar.net/en/left-behind-by-the-letpadaung-copper-mine/

14 Tom Daly and Min Zhang, 'China's metals imports from Myanmar show trade contortions amid post-coup protest', Reuters, 20 April 2021. https://www.reuters.com/article/us-china-economy-trade-myanmar-idUSKBN2C70S9
15 Human Rights Watch, '"Give Us a Baby and We'll let you go". Trafficking of Kachin "brides" from Myanmar to China', 21 March 2019. https://www.hrw.org/report/2019/03/21/give-us-baby-and-well-let-you-go/trafficking-kachin-brides-myanmar-china
16 Monish Tourangbam and Pawan Amin, 'China's Dynamic Grip on Myanmar. Beijing's influence in Myanmar permeates multiple levels of engagement between two neighbors', *The Diplomat*, 7 May 2019. https://thediplomat.com/2019/05/chinas-dynamic-grip-on-myanmar/
17 Laura Zhou, 'China promises to support Myanmar peace talks with rebel groups', *South China Morning Post*, 12 January 2021. https://www.scmp.com/print/news/china/diplomacy/article/3117408/china-promises-support-myanmar-peace-talks-rebel-groups
18 Antoni Slodkowski and Yimou Lee, 'Through reclusive Wa, China's reach extends into Suu Kyi's Myanmar', Reuters, 28 December 2016. https://www.reuters.com/article/myanmar-wa-china/through-reclusive-wa-chinas-reach-extends-into-suu-kyis-myanmar-idINKBN14H1VA?edition-redirect=in
19 Alex Willemyns, 'Cambodia and China: Rewriting (and Repeating) History', *The Diplomat*, 15 January 2018. https://thediplomat.com/2018/01/cambodia-and-china-rewriting-and-repeating-history/
20 'Hun Sen's Cambodia slides into despotism', *Financial Times* editorial, 7 September 2017. https://www.ft.com/content/50f36eb4-93cb-11e7-a9e6-11d2f0ebb7f0
21 Reuters, 'Cambodia suspends annual military drill with the United States', 16 January 2017. https://www.reuters.com/article/us-cambodia-usa-idUSKBN1501YK
22 Matt Blomberg, 'Chinese scammers enslave jobless teachers and tourists in Cambodia', *Thomson Reuters Foundation News*, 16 September 2021. https://news.trust.org/item/20210916120210-olp4a
23 *Xinhua* news agency, 'Cambodia-China expressway cooperation project expected to be completed ahead of schedule:

minister', 21 June 2021. http://www.xinhuanet.com/english/2021-06/21/c_1310019865.htm

24 For a full mapping of the location of mass burial pits, prisons and much more relating to the Khmer Rouge genocide, see the website of the Yale University's Cambodian Genocide Program. https://gsp.yale.edu/case-studies/cambodian-genocide-program

25 Daphne Psaledakis and Prak Chan Thul, 'US imposes sanctions on Chinese firm over Cambodia project', Reuters, 15 September 2020. https://www.reuters.com/article/usa-china-cambodia-sanctions/u-s-imposes-sanctions-on-chinese-firm-over-cambodia-project-idINKBN2670BJ

26 Jeremy Page, Gordon Lubold and Rob Taylor, 'Deal for Naval Outpost in Cambodia Furthers China's Quest for Military Network', *Wall Street Journal*, 22 July 2019. https://www.wsj.com/articles/secret-deal-for-chinese-naval-outpost-in-cambodia-raises-u-s-fears-of-beijings-ambitions-11563732482

27 Ian Storey, 'China's Missteps in Southeast Asia: Less Charm, More Offensive', Jamestown Foundation's *China Brief*, vol. 10, issue 25, 17 September 2010. https://jamestown.org/program/chinas-missteps-in-southeast-asia-less-charm-more-offensive/

28 For a fuller examination of the way China's imperial past colours and shapes contemporary policy, see Howard W. French, *Everything Under the Heavens: How the Past Helps Shape China's Push for Global Power* (New York: Vintage Books, 2018).

29 These observations were part of a lecture given by Bilahari Kausikan to Singapore's Institute of Policy Studies on 30 March 2016, and published in the *Straits Times* two days later. https://www.straitstimes.com/opinion/pavlovian-conditioning-and-correct-thinking-on-the-south-china-sea

30 Martin Stuart-Fox, *A Short History of China and Southeast Asia: Tribute, Trade and Influence* (Crow's Nest, NSW: Allen & Unwin, 2003), p. 34.

31 'In no region is China's influence felt more strongly than in South-East Asia', *The Economist*, 27 February 2021. https://www.economist.com/briefing/2021/02/27/in-no-region-is-chinas-influence-felt-more-strongly-than-in-south-east-asia

32 Milton Osbourne, 'Chinese dams and the Mekong drought', *The Interpreter* (a publication of Australia's Lowy Institute), 11 August 2020. https://www.lowyinstitute.org/the-interpreter/chinese-dams-and-mekong-drought

33 Bryan Eyler, Regan Kwan and Courtney Weatherby, 'How China Turned Off the Tap on the Mekong River', Stimson Center Research paper, 13 April 2020. https://www.stimson.org/2020/new-evidence-how-china-turned-off-the-mekong-tap/
34 Strangio, *In the Dragon's Shadow*, p. 59.
35 *The Economist*, 27 February 2021.
36 Ibid.
37 Sterling Seagrove, *Lords of the Rim: The Invisible Empire of the Overseas Chinese* (London: Bantam Press, 1995).
38 *The Economist*, 27 February 2021.

## Chapter 4: Brawling on the Roof of the World

1 Amy Kazmin and Tom Mitchell, 'Brutal details emerge of deadly China-India border clash', *Financial Times*, 17 June 2020. https://www.ft.com/content/572ecd74-af77-400e-aa0a-6012dec260a6
2 'PLA Xinjiang Military Command commemorates Galwan Valley martyrs', *Global Times*, 16 June 2021. https://www.globaltimes.cn/page/202106/1226310.shtml
3 Debanish Achom, 'Australian Journalist to NDTV on China's Attempts to Hide Galwan Deaths', NDTV, 3 February 2022. https://www.ndtv.com/india-news/galwan-clash-australian-journalist-anthony-klan-of-the-klaxon-to-ndtv-on-chinas-attempt-to-hide-casualties-2747075
4 Didi Tang, 'China turns Ladakh battleground with India into a "microwave oven"', *The Times*, 17 November 2020. https://www.thetimes.co.uk/article/china-turns-ladakh-battleground-with-india-into-a-microwave-oven-6tlwtrtzz
5 'India and China have their first deadly clashes in 45 years', *The Economist*, 18 June 2020. https://www.economist.com/asia/2020/06/18/india-and-china-have-their-first-deadly-clashes-in-45-years
6 Ian Hall, 'India-China: Pressure at altitude', *The Interpreter*, 18 June 2020. https://www.lowyinstitute.org/the-interpreter/india-china-pressure-altitude
7 Jeff M. Smith, 'The Galwan Killings Are the Nail in the Coffin for China and India's Relationship', *Foreign Policy*, 26 June 2020. https://foreignpolicy.com/2020/06/26/galwan-border-china-india-war-conflict/

8 'Galwan Valley: A year after the violent clash', *Indian Express*, 14 June 2021. https://indianexpress.com/article/india/galwan-valley-clash-timeline-india-china-disengagement-7358554/
9 Benjamin Parkin, 'India to curb Chinese bids for state contracts', *Financial Times*, 24 July 2020. https://www.ft.com/content/5f9de846-c210-42f7-af72-36e677ace3ad
10 Amy Kazmin, Tom Mitchell and Katrina Manson, 'India re-thinks strategic ties following border clashes with China', *Financial Times*, 18 June 2020. https://www.ft.com/content/47d40de6-42a9-4d45-833c-c5dc76cd4fa2
11 'Malappuram Summit: Mutton, Lobster in Dinner For Xi Jinping Hosted by PM Narendra Modi; Check Full Menu', Latestly, 11 October 2019. https://www.latestly.com/india/news/malappuram-summit-mutton-lobster-in-dinner-for-xi-jinping-hosted-by-pm-narendra-modi-check-full-menu-1262617.html
12 Sadanand Dhume, 'India, Like the US, Has Grown Impatient With China', *Wall Street Journal*, 22 July 2021. https://www.wsj.com/articles/india-china-modi-xi-new-dehli-beijing-11626983609
13 Sahil Joshi and Divyesh Singh, 'Mega Mumbai power outage may be result of cyber attack, final report awaited', *India Today*, 20 November 2020. https://www.indiatoday.in/india/story/mumbai-power-outage-malware-attack-1742538-2020-11-20
14 ANI, 'Maharashtra issues advisory regarding cyber attacks from China', 23 June 2020. https://www.aninews.in/news/national/general-news/maharashtra-issues-advisory-regarding-cyber-attacks-from-china20200623203741/
15 Recorded Future, 'China-Linked Group RedEcho Targets the Indian Power Sector Amid Tightened Border Tensions', 28 February 2021. https://www.recordedfuture.com/redecho-targeting-indian-power-sector/
16 'Mumbai Power Outage in October May Have Been Result of "cyber sabotage": Anil Deshmukh', *The Wire*, 2 March 2021. https://thewire.in/government/mumbai-power-outage-october-cyber-sabotage-anil-deshmukh-china
17 David Rising, 'Suspected Chinese hack targets Indian media, gov't', *The Seattle Times*, 22 September 2021. https://www.seattletimes.com/nation-world/report-suspected-chinese-hack-targets-indian-media-govt/
18 Eric Bellman and Rajesh Roy, 'India suspects China May Be

Behind Major Mumbai Blackout', *Wall Street Journal*, 1 March 2021. https://www.wsj.com/articles/india-suspects-china-may-be-behind-major-mumbai-blackout-11614615383

19 David E. Sanger and Emily Schmall, 'China Appears to Warn India: Push Too Hard and the Lights Could Go Out', *New York Times*, 28 February 2021. https://www.nytimes.com/2021/02/28/us/politics/china-india-hacking-electricity.html

20 Long Xingchun, 'India to invite trouble playing Taiwan card', *Global Times*, 18 October 2020. https://www.globaltimes.cn/content/1203786.shtml

21 For a useful account of Tezpur during this period, see Ankush Saikia, 'The Evacuation of Tezpur: A family recounts the story of its flight during the India-China war of 1962', *Hindustan Times*, 21 August 2017. https://www.hindustantimes.com/india-news/the-evacuation-of-tezpur-a-family-recounts-the-story-of-its-flight-during-the-indo-china-war-of-1962/story-mnBG9scHj4WXrSpMmCIPVJ.html

22 Tora Agarwala, 'Seema – the untold story of how Tezpur rose to defend itself from the Chinese', *The Indian Express*, 30 March 2019. https://indianexpress.com/article/north-east-india/assam/seema-the-untold-story-of-how-tezpur-rose-to-defend-itself-from-the-chinese-5649842/

23 Bertil Lintner, 'Behind China's threat to support insurgency in India', *Asia Times*, 30 October 2020. https://asiatimes.com/2020/10/behind-chinas-threat-to-support-insurgency-in-india/

24 Bertil Lintner, *China's India War: Collision Course on the Roof of the World* (New Delhi: Oxford University Press, 2018), p. 269.

25 Thant Myint-U, *Where China Meets India*, p. 225.

26 Lintner, *China's India War*.

27 Ibid., pp. 10–11.

28 Amy Kazmin and Charles Clover, 'India and China end Himalayan border stand-off', *Financial Times*, 28 August 2017. https://www.ft.com/content/2d9fb42c-8bce-11e7-a352-e46f43c5825d

29 Robert Barnett, 'China is Building Entire Villages in Another Country's Territory', *Foreign Policy*, 7 May 2021. https://foreignpolicy.com/2021/05/07/china-bhutan-border-villages-security-forces/

30 Anbarasan Ethirajan, 'Why Bhutan's Sakteng wildlife sanctuary is disputed by China', BBC News, 25 November 2020. https://www.bbc.com/news/world-asia-55004196

31 Brabim Karki, 'Nepal needs Coronavirus vaccines as India and the west fall short', *South China Morning Post*, 1 June 2021. https://www.scmp.com/print/comment/opinion/article/3135446/nepal-needs-chinese-coronavirus-vaccines-india-and-west-fall-short

32 Tsering Shakya and Ashok Gurung, 'Was Nepal a Soft Power Victory for China?' *Foreign Policy*, 1 May 2015. https://foreignpolicy.com/2015/05/01/nepal-china-earthquake-aid-taiwan-power/

33 Michael Bristow, 'China encroaching along Nepal border – report', BBC online, 8 February 2022. https://www.bbc.co.uk/news/world-asia-60288007

34 Rajeswari Pillai Rajagopalan, 'The China-Pakistan Partnership Continues to Deepen', *The Diplomat*, 9 July 2021. https://thediplomat.com/2021/07/the-china-pakistan-partnership-continues-to-deepen/

35 Thomas Kika, 'China Sends Bomber Planes to India Border in "warning" to Country', *Newsweek*, 16 November 2021. https://www.newsweek.com/china-sends-bomber-planes-indian-border-warning-country-1649746

36 Hannah Ellis-Petersen, 'Tensions remain high as hopes dashed for breakthrough in India-China stalemate', *The Guardian*, 18 July 2021. https://www.theguardian.com/world/2021/jul/18/tensions-remain-high-as-hopes-dashed-for-breakthrough-in-china-and-india-stalemate

37 'Indian border troops' bravado will backfire', *Global Times*, 8 September 2020. https://www.globaltimes.cn/content/1200226.shtml

38 Minnie Chan, 'China's military steps up training along disputed Indian border', *South China Morning Post*, 26 June 2021. https://www.scmp.com/print/news/china/military/article/3138824/chinese-military-steps-training-along-disputed-indian-border

39 Amy Kazmin and Christian Shepherd, 'Himalayan border tension is a recipe for disaster', *Financial Times*, 6 September 2020. https://www.ft.com/content/1ffe2b85-42aa-4f0b-b4ae-d49e198c9259

40 Amber Wang, 'India joint South China Sea drills shows concern about Beijing, experts say', *South China Morning Post*, 4 September 2021. https://www.scmp.com/print/news/china/diplomacy/article/3147526/indias-joint-south-china-sea-drills-show-concern-about-beijing

41 Sanjeev Miglani, 'India's Modi phones Dalai Lama on birthday,

sign of friction with Beijing', Reuters, 6 July 2021. https://www.reuters.com/world/china/indian-pm-modi-greets-dalai-lama-birthday-rare-phone-call-2021-07-06/

42 Indrani Bagchi, 'China most distrusted nation, says survey of Indian youth', *Times of India*, 15 August 2021. https://timesofindia.indiatimes.com/world/china/china-most-distrusted-nation-says-survey-of-indian-youth/articleshow/85340235.cms

43 Max Walden and Bang Xiao, 'Chinese social media blows up over official Communist Party post mocking India's COVID-19 catastrophe', ABC News, 3 May 2021. https://www.abc.net.au/news/2021-05-04/chinese-social-media-blows-up-over-india-s-covid-19-catastrophe/100112266

## Chapter 5: From the Frozen Arctic to the Digital World: The Frontiers of China's New Cold War

1 Ryan Castilloux, 'Rare Earth Elements: Market Issues and Outlook', Adamas Intelligence, Q2 2019. http://www.adamasintel.com/wp-content/uploads/2019/07/Adamas-Intelligence-Rare-Earths-Market-Issues-and-Outlook-Q2-2019.pdf

2 Keith Bradsher, 'China is Blocking Minerals, Executives Say', *New York Times*, 23 September 2010. https://www.nytimes.com/2010/09/24/business/energy-environment/24mineral.html

3 Zhenhua Lu and Sarah Zheng, 'US moves to reduce reliance on Chinese rare earths exports after Beijing threatens to cut supplies', *South China Morning Post*, 5 June 2019. https://www.scmp.com/news/china/diplomacy/article/3013227/us-moves-reduce-reliance-chinese-rare-earth-exports-after

4 Sun Yu and Demetri Sevastopulo, 'China targets rare earth export curbs to hobble US defence industry', *Financial Times*, 16 February 2021. https://www.ft.com/content/d3ed83f4-19bc-4d16-b510-415749c032c1

5 Harry Dempsey, 'US enticed by Greenland's rare earth resources', *Financial Times*, 20 August 2019. https://www.ft.com/content/f418bb86-bdb2-11e9-89e2-41e555e96722

6 The 2016 documentary, *Kuannersuit; Kvanefjeld* was commissioned by Nuclear Culture, a group that explores nuclear issues through art. It can be viewed on Vimeo. https://vimeo.com/214697146

7 For a detailed forensic analysis of the 2016 deal between Greenland Minerals and Shenghe, see Jinchang Lulu's blogpost, 'More on Shenghe's Greenland Deal'. https://jichanglulu.tumblr.com/post/151328982186/more-on-shenghes-greenland-deal

8 See the Greenland Minerals company announcement of 23 January 2019, 'Shenghe Resources and China National Nuclear Corporation (CNNC) Co-invest in Processing Facilities For Treatment of Rare Earth Minerals in China'. https://wcsecure.weblink.com.au/pdf/GGG/02068532.pdf

9 CNNC's full mission statement and other company details can be accessed via its website: https://en.cnnc.com.cn/2016-02/01/c_49164.htm

10 Ana Swanson, 'Trump Bars Investments in Chinese Firms with Military Ties', *New York Times*, 3 June 2021. https://www.nytimes.com/2020/11/12/business/economy/trump-china-investment-ban.html

11 Stacy Meichtry and Drew Hinshaw, 'China's Greenland Ambitions Run Into Local Politics, U.S. Influence', *Wall Street Journal*, 8 April 2021. https://www.wsj.com/articles/chinas-rare-earths-quest-upends-greenlands-government-11617807839

12 Eva Dou, 'A New Cold War? China declares Itself a "Near-Arctic State"', *Wall Street Journal*, 26 January 2018. https://www.wsj.com/articles/a-new-cold-war-china-declares-itself-a-near-arctic-state-1516965315?mod=article_inline

13 Jeremy Greenwood, 'Is China worried about an Arctic choke-point?' Brookings Institution, 22 September 2021. https://www.brookings.edu/blog/order-from-chaos/2021/09/22/is-china-worried-about-an-arctic-choke-point/

14 Drew Hinshaw and Jeremy Page, 'How the Pentagon Countered China's Designs on Greenland', *Wall Street Journal*, 10 February 2019. https://www.wsj.com/articles/how-the-pentagon-countered-chinas-designs-on-greenland-11549812296?mod=article_inline

15 Timothy J. Jorgensen, '50 years ago a B-52 crashed in Greenland . . . with four nuclear bombs on board', *Air Force Times*, 23 January 2018. https://www.airforcetimes.com/news/your-air-force/2018/01/23/50-years-ago-a-b-52-crashed-in-greenland-with-4-nuclear-bombs-on-board/

16 Martin Pengelly, 'Trump confirms he is considering attempt to buy

Greenland', *The Guardian*, 18 August 2019. https://www.theguardian.com/world/2019/aug/18/trump-considering-buying-greenland

17 Gordon Lubold, 'U.S. Holds Talks Over Economic, Security Arrangements With Greenland', *Wall Street Journal*, 28 October 2020. https://www.wsj.com/articles/u-s-holds-talks-over-economic-security-arrangements-with-greenland-11603927474?mod=article_inline

18 Harry Dempsey, 'US enticed by Greenland's rare earth resources', *Financial Times*, 20 August 2019. https://www.ft.com/content/f418bb86-bdb2-11e9-89e2-41e555e96722

19 Kevin McGwin, 'Greenland joins EU minerals group', *Arctic Today*, 9 July 2021. https://www.arctictoday.com/greenland-joins-eu-minerals-group/?wallit_nosession=1

20 Rosie Birchard, 'NATO chief: Melting Arctic ice could heat up geopolitics', *Deutsche Welle*, 22 March 2021. https://www.dw.com/en/nato-chief-melting-arctic-ice-could-heat-up-geopolitics/a-56954283

21 Reuters, 'Greenland bans uranium mining, halting rare earths project', 10 November 2021. https://www.reuters.com/world/americas/greenland-bans-uranium-mining-halting-rare-earths-project-2021-11-10/

22 Esmaric Iannucci, 'Greenland Minerals looking for solutions to uranium issues', *Mining Weekly*, 12 November 2021. https://www.miningweekly.com/article/greenland-minerals-looking-for-solutions-to-uranium-issues-2021-11-12

23 Reuters, 'Greenland strips Chinese mining firm of license to iron ore deposit', 22 November 2021. https://www.reuters.com/markets/commodities/choose-side-china-tells-taiwan-firms-it-punishes-conglomerate-2021-11-22/

24 These figures and more are available in an Institute for Energy Research report, 'China Dominates the Global Lithium Battery Market', published 9 September 2020. https://www.instituteforenergyresearch.org/renewable/china-dominates-theglobal-lithium-battery-market/

25 Ibid.

26 Dionne Searcey, Michael Forsythe and Eric Lipton, 'A Power Struggle over Cobalt Rattles the Clean Energy Revolution', *New York Times*, 7 December 2021. https://www.nytimes.com/2021/11/20/world/china-congo-cobalt.html

27 Ibid.

28 International Energy Agency, 'The Role of Critical Minerals in Clean Energy Transition', Flagship Report, May 2021. https://www.iea.org/reports/the-role-of-critical-minerals-in-clean-energy-transitions

29 Neil Hume, 'China's magnesium shortage threatens global car industry', *Financial Times*, 19 October 2021. https://www.ft.com/content/1611e936-08a5-4654-987e-664f50133a4b?shareType=nongift

30 Eric Onstad, 'Exclusive – China's Nanhua plans London Metal Exchange debut', Reuters, 19 September 2018. https://www.reuters.com/article/uk-metals-lme-nanhua-exclusive-idUKKCN1LZ23I

31 Reuters, 'China unveils vision of "Polar Silk Road" across Arctic', 26 January 2018. https://www.reuters.com/article/us-china-arctic-idUSKBN1FF0J8

32 These quotes are taken from Xi Jinping's 14 May 2017 speech at the opening ceremony of the Belt and Road Forum for International Cooperation, as reprinted in *The Governance of China*, vol. II (Beijing: Foreign Language Press, 2017), pp. 553–66.

33 Bruno Maçães, 'At the crossroads of the new Silk road', *The Guardian*, 29 January 2019. https://www.theguardian.com/commentisfree/2018/jan/29/at-the-crossroads-of-the-new-silk-road#maincontent

34 Simon Mundy, 'China backed port sparks Sri Lanka sovereignty fears', *Financial Times*, 23 October 2017. https://www.ft.com/content/f8262d56-a6a0-11e7-ab55-27219df83c97

35 John Hurley, Scott Morris and Gailyn Portelance, 'Examining the Debt Implications of the Belt and Road Initiative from a Policy Perspective', Center for Global Development, March 2018. https://www.cgdev.org/sites/default/files/examining-debt-implications-belt-and-road-initiative-policy-perspective.pdf

36 Howard W. French, *China's Second Continent: How a Million Migrants are Building a New Empire in China* (New York: Alfred A. Knopf, 2014).

37 Joan Tilouine and Ghalia Kadiri, 'A Addis-Abeba, le siège de l'Union africaine espionné par Pékin', *Le Monde*, 26 January 2018. https://www.lemonde.fr/afrique/article/2018/01/26/a-addis-abeba-le-siege-de-l-union-africaine-espionne-par-les-chinois_5247521_3212.html

38 African Business Central, 'Huawei looks to Africa to cut network deals', 26 March 2016. https://www.africanbusinesscentral.

com/2016/03/25/huawei-looks-to-africa-to-cut-network-deals/

39 See Huawei's corporate brochure, *Huawei Safe City Solution*. https://e.huawei.com/en/material/industry/safecity/044042f765c04a518e3e25c87fea5133

40 Jonathan Hillman and Maesea McCalpin, 'Watching Huawei's "safe cities"', Center for Strategic and International Studies, 4 November 2019. https://csis-prod.s3.amazonaws.com/s3fs-public/publication/191030_HillmanMcCalpin_HuaweiSafeCity_layout_v4.pdf?X6hq2FMWVTX9qK68Z7wK1QXRS4l.Zgip

41 Scott Reeves, 'China Looks to Challenge US Dollar With New Digital Yuan', *Newsweek*, 4 September 2021. https://www.newsweek.com/china-looks-challenge-us-dollar-new-digital-yuan-1582547

42 Roula Khalaf and Helen Warrell, 'UK spy chief raises fears over China's digital renminbi', *Financial Times*, 11 December 2021. https://www.ft.com/content/128d7139-15d6-4f4d-a247-fc9228a53ebd?shareType=nongift

43 Alan Gross, Madhumita Murgia and Yuan Yang, 'Chinese tech groups shaping UN facial recognition standards', *Financial Times*, 2 December 2019. https://www.ft.com/content/c3555a3c-0d3e-11ea-b2d6-9bf4d1957a67

44 Joel Gunter, 'China committed genocide against Uyghurs, independent tribunal rules', BBC Online, 9 December 2021. https://www.bbc.com/news/world-asia-china-59595952

45 'China's global power damps criticism of Uighur clampdown', *Financial Times*, 23 December 2019. https://www.ft.com/content/51a1bf9a-2015-11ea-92da-f0c92e957a96

46 Ben Westcott, 'Pakistan PM Imran Khan refuses to condemn China's Xinjiang crackdown', CNN, 22 June 2021. https://edition.cnn.com/2021/06/22/asia/imran-khan-xinjiang-axios-intl-hnk/index.html

47 Maria Abi-Habib, 'China's Belt and Road Plan in Pakistan Takes a Military Turn', *New York Times*, 19 December 2018. https://www.nytimes.com/2018/12/19/world/asia/pakistan-china-belt-road-military.html

48 Catherine Putz, '2020 Edition: which countries Are For or Against China's Xinjiang Policies?' *The Diplomat*, 9 October 2020. https://thediplomat.com/2020/10/2020-edition-which-countries-are-for-or-against-chinas-xinjiang-policies/

49 Associated Press, 'Exclusive: Diplomats say China puts squeeze on Ukraine', 25 June 2021. https://apnews.com/article/united-nations-china-europe-ukraine-health-a0a5ae8f735b92e39c623e453529cbb9
50 BBC Online, 'Nike, H&M face China fury over Xinjiang cotton "concerns"', 25 March 2021. https://www.bbc.com/news/world-asia-china-56519411
51 BBC Online, 'Intel apologises to China over supplier advice', 23 December 2021. https://www.bbc.co.uk/news/business-59769393?at_medium=RSS&at_campaign=KARANGA
52 Reuters, 'Intel deletes mention of Xinjiang in letter after China backlash', *The Guardian*, 11 January 2022. https://www.theguardian.com/world/2022/jan/11/intel-deletes-mention-of-xinjiang-in-letter-after-china-backlash
53 The full video of the 16 April 2019 interview with Herbert Diess, headlined 'VW boss "not aware" of China's detention camps' is available via the BBC News website. https://www.bbc.com/news/av/business-47944767
54 Jon Sudworth, 'China Muslims: Volkswagen says "no forced labour" at Xinjiang plant', BBC Online, 12 November 2020. https://www.bbc.com/news/world-asia-china-54918309
55 Timothy Garton Ash, 'VW's dilemma in Xinjiang shows how the west is headed for an ethical car crash in Xinjiang', *The Guardian*, 28 July 2021. https://www.theguardian.com/commentisfree/2021/jul/28/vw-dilemma-xinjiang-west-ethical-car-crash
56 Tom Mitchell and Primrose Riordan, 'China rushes through bill tightening ban on abiding by western sanctions', *Financial Times*, 11 June 2021. https://www.ft.com/content/78883da1-ea26-45d6-9012-3c09d53aef42
57 Frank Tang, 'China's new financial court given jurisdiction to handle lawsuits against overseas firms', *South China Morning Post*, 17 March 2021. https://www.scmp.com/print/economy/china-economy/article/3125830/chinas-new-financial-court-given-jurisdiction-handle-lawsuits
58 Michael Martina, 'Chinese Embassy lobbies US businesses to oppose China bills – sources', Reuters, 13 November 2021. https://www.reuters.com/business/exclusive-chinese-embassy-lobbies-us-business-oppose-china-bills-sources-2021-11-12/
59 Steve Stecklow and Jeffrey Dastin, 'Special Report: Amazon partnered

with Chinese propaganda arm', Reuters, 18 December 2021. https://www.reuters.com/world/china/amazon-partnered-with-china-propaganda-arm-win-beijings-favor-document-shows-2021-12-17/

60 *Xinhua* news agency, 'Chinese premier holds dialogue with British business leaders', 7 July 2021. http://www.xinhuanet.com/english/2021-07/07/c_1310046391.htm

61 James Anderlini, 'Western companies in China succumb to Stockholm syndrome', *Financial Times*, 5 May 2021. https://www.ft.com/content/51e1a437-3aca-42ed-8403-2a05b338622b

62 'Data scandal taints IMF and World Bank', *Financial Times*, 23 September2021.https://www.ft.com/content/5e8356be-bf80-4736-9b09-c7c77a9ca9a7?shareType=nongift

63 'China makes inroads in the Solomon Islands', *The Economist*, 27 February 2021. https://www.economist.com/asia/2022/04/02/china-makes-inroads-in-the-solomon-islands

64 Robert D. Blackwill and Jennifer M. Harris, *War by Other Means: Geoeconomics and Statecraft* (London: Harvard University Press, 2017).

## Chapter 6: Disinformation, Spying and Sabotage: The Cyber Panda Bears Its Claws

1 Helen Davidson, 'Chinese media in fake news claims over Swiss scientist critical of the US', *The Guardian*, 11 August 2021. https://www.theguardian.com/world/2021/aug/11/chinese-media-fake-news-claims-swiss-scientist-wilson-edwards-critical-of-us

2 The Swiss embassy tweet together with some priceless responses (and memes) can be found at https://twitter.com/SwissEmbChina/status/1425042973289504770

3 Muyi Xiao, Paul Mozur and Gray Beltran, 'Buying Influence: How China Manipulates Facebook and Twitter', *New York Times*, 20 December 2021. https://www.nytimes.com/interactive/2021/12/20/technology/china-facebook-twitter-influence-manipulation.html

4 Thomas Rid, *Active Measures: A Secret History of Disinformation and Political Warfare* (London: Profile Books, 2020).

5 Ibid., p. 12.
6 For a good overview of Russia's cyber activities during the 2016 US presidential election, see Timothy Summers, 'How the Russian government used disinformation and cyber warfare in 2016 election – an ethical hacker explains', *The Conversation*, 27 July 2018. https://theconversation.com/how-the-russian-government-used-disinformation-and-cyber-warfare-in-2016-election-an-ethical-hacker-explains-99989
7 Jessica Brandt and Bret Shafer, 'How China's "wolf warrior" diplomats use and abuse Twitter', Brookings Institute Tech Stream, 28 October 2018. https://www.brookings.edu/techstream/how-chinas-wolf-warrior-diplomats-use-and-abuse-twitter/
8 'China pushes back against critics of its policies in Xinjiang', *The Economist*, 8 May 2021. https://www.economist.com/china/2021/05/08/china-pushes-back-against-critics-of-its-policies-in-xinjiang?frsc=dg%7Ce
9 Jennifer Rankin, 'EU says China behind "huge wave" of Covid-19 disinformation', *The Guardian*, 10 June 2020. https://www.theguardian.com/world/2020/jun/10/eu-says-china-behind-huge-wave-covid-19-disinformation-campaign
10 Anna Schecter, 'China launches new Twitter accounts, 90,000 tweets in Covid-19 info war', NBC News, 20 May 2020. https://www.nbcnews.com/news/world/china-launches-new-twitter-accounts-90-000-tweets-covid-19-n1207991
11 BBC Online, 'Coronavirus: Twitter removes more than 170,000 pro-China accounts', 12 June 2020. https://www.bbc.com/news/business-53018455
12 Lily Kou, 'Google deletes 2,500 China-linked YouTube channels over disinformation', *The Guardian*, 6 August 2021. https://www.theguardian.com/technology/2020/aug/06/google-deletes-2500-china-linked-youtube-channels-over-disinformation
13 'China pushes back against critics of its policies in Xinjiang', *The Economist*, 8 May 2021. https://www.economist.com/china/2021/05/08/china-pushes-back-against-critics-of-its-policies-in-xinjiang
14 Newley Purnell, 'Facebook Staff Fret Over China's Ads Portraying Happy Muslims in Xinjiang', *Wall Street Journal*, 2 April 2021. https://www.wsj.com/articles/facebook-staff-fret-over-chinas-ads-portraying-happy-muslims-in-xinjiang-11617366096

15 Albert Zhang, Jacob Wallis and Zoe Meers, 'Strange bedfellows on Xinjiang: The CCP, fringe media and social media platforms', Australian Strategic Policy Institute, 30 March 2021. https://s3-ap-southeast-2.amazonaws.com/ad-aspi/2021-03/Strange%20bedfellows.pdf?VersionId=mOh5mC5B_a08J6ntNwTC2q6GdjtWz4di

16 Brenda Goh, 'Twitter locks account of China's US embassy over its defence of Xinjiang policy', Reuters, 21 January 2021. https://www.reuters.com/article/us-china-twitter-idUSKBN29Q03O

17 Agence France-Presse, 'China's YouTube army of foreign fans takes on Western "lies" about human rights abuses', *South China Morning Post*, 12 September 2021. https://www.scmp.com/print/news/china/politics/article/3148458/chinas-youtube-army-foreign-fans-takes-western-lies-about-human

18 Holly Chik and Eduardo Baptista, 'The China-based foreigners defending China from Xinjiang genocide claims', *South China Morning Post*, 30 March 2021. https://www.scmp.com/print/news/china/politics/article/3127611/china-based-foreigners-defending-beijing-xinjiang-genocide

19 Morgan Ortagus's 30 May 2021 tweet and the reply can be seen at https://twitter.com/spokespersonchn/status/1266741986096107520?lang=en

20 Reuters, 'In China, bemusement and scorn over unresolved US election', 4 November 2020. https://www.reuters.com/article/us-usa-election-china-reaction-idUSKBN27K1EF

21 'China mocks "beautiful sight" of US Capitol chaos', *The Standard*, 7 January 2021. https://www.thestandard.com.hk/breaking-news/section/4/162885/China-mocks-%22beautiful-sight" of US Capitol-chaos

22 Oliver Laughland and Peter Beaumont, 'Atlanta massage parlour shootings leave eight dead, including six Asian women', *The Guardian*, 17 March 2021. https://www.theguardian.com/us-news/2021/mar/16/atlanta-massage-parlor-shootings

23 Michael Sisak and Karen Matthews, 'Video shows vicious attack of Asian American woman in NYC', Associated Press, 31 March 2021. https://apnews.com/article/65-year-old-asian-woman-assaulted-nyc-street-692b82db37efae29d12e7fa638eb2e1d

24 The cartoon, 'Aiming at Asians', was originally published in the *Global Times* on 20 March 2021. https://www.globaltimes.cn/page/202103/1218915.shtml

25 The CGTN cartoon, 'Is there also a vaccine for racism', posted on 24 March 2021, can be accessed at https://twitter.com/CGTNOfficial/status/1374551542037053443/photo/1
26 Brandt and Shafer, 'How China's "wolf warrior" diplomats use and abuse Twitter'.
27 Chinese Foreign Ministry spokesman Zhao Lijian has set the tone for much of the online 'wolf warrior' rhetoric employed by Chinese diplomats. For this tweet – and many in a similar vein – see Zhao's Twitter feed. https://twitter.com/zlj517/status/1376518976373620738?lang=en
28 Fan Anqi, 'Chinese Consulate General in NY warns of anti-Asian violence amid rising "racist terror"', *Global Times*, 20 March 2021. https://www.globaltimes.cn/page/202103/1219653.shtml
29 Brandt and Shafer, 'How China's "wolf warrior" diplomats use and abuse Twitter'.
30 Masha Borak, 'Chinese Twitter bots are clearly fake, but they still might be influential', *South China Morning Post*, 10 December 2019. https://www.scmp.com/print/abacus/tech/article/3041354/chinese-twitter-bots-are-clearly-fake-they-might-still-be-influential
31 Erika Kinetz, 'Army of fake fans boost China's messaging on Twitter', Associated Press, 28 May 2021. https://apnews.com/article/asia-pacific-china-europe-middle-east-government-and-politics-62b13895aa6665ae4d887dcc8d196dfc
32 Chris Vallance, 'Wikipedia blames pro-China infiltration for bans', BBC Online, 16 September 2021. https://www.bbc.com/news/technology-58559412
33 Amnesty International, 'Nowhere Feels Safe: Uighurs Tell of a China-Led Intimidation Campaign Abroad', 21 February 2020. https://www.amnesty.org/en/latest/research/2020/02/china-uyghurs-abroad-living-in-fear/
34 Shira Ovide, 'WeChat Unites and Divides in America', *New York Times*, 6 October 2020. https://www.nytimes.com/2020/10/06/technology/wechat-unites-and-divides-in-america.html
35 Richie Koch, 'TikTok and the privacy perils of China's first international social media platform', ProtonMail blog, 23 July 2020. https://protonmail.com/blog/tiktok-privacy/
36 Charlie Osborne, 'TikTok agrees to pay $92 million to settle teen class action privacy laws', *ZDNet*, 26 February 2021. https://www.zdnet.com/article/tiktok-agrees-to-pay-92-million-to-settle-teen-privacy-class-action-lawsuit/

37 Fergus Ryan, Audrey Fritz and Daria Impiombato, 'TikTok and WeChat: Curating and Controlling global information flows', International Cyber Policy Centre, Australian Strategic Policy Institute, Report No. 37/2020. https://s3-ap-southeast-2.amazonaws.com/ad-aspi/2020-09/TikTok%20and%20WeChat.pdf?7BNJWaoHImPVE.6KKcBP1JRD5fRnAVTZ
38 Ibid., pp. 17–21.
39 'In the West, China holds growing sway over Chinese language media', *The Economist*, 23 September 2021. https://www.economist.com/china/2021/09/23/in-the-west-china-holds-growing-sway-over-chinese-language-media
40 Office of the National Counterintelligence Executive, *Foreign Spies Stealing US Economic Secrets in Cyberspace*, October 2011. https://www.hsdl.org/?view&did=720057
41 Josh Rogin, 'NSA Chief: Cybercrime constitutes the "greatest transfer of wealth in history"', *Foreign Policy*, 9 July 2012. https://foreignpolicy.com/2012/07/09/nsa-chief-cybercrime-constitutes-the-greatest-transfer-of-wealth-in-history/
42 Adam Segal, 'How China is preparing for cyberwar', *Christian Science Monitor*, 20 March 2017. https://www.csmonitor.com/World/Passcode/Passcode-Voices/2017/0320/How-China-is-preparing-for-cyberwar
43 Barack Obama, *Promised Land* (New York: Crown, 2020), p. 474.
44 Zolan Kanno-Youngs and David E. Sanger, 'US Accuses China of Hacking Microsoft', *New York Times*, 19 July 2021. https://www.nytimes.com/2021/07/19/us/politics/microsoft-hacking-china-biden.html
45 Dustin Voltz and Aruna Viswanatha, 'Biden Administration Blames Hackers Tied to China for Microsoft Cyberattack Spree', *Wall Street Journal*, 19 July 2021. https://www.wsj.com/articles/biden-administration-to-blame-hackers-tied-to-china-for-microsoft-cyberattack-spree-11626692401
46 Dmitri Alperovitch and Ian Ward, 'How Should the US Respond to the SolarWinds and Microsoft Exchange Hacks?' Lawfare, 12 March 2021. https://www.lawfareblog.com/how-should-us-respond-solarwinds-and-microsoft-exchange-hacks
47 'China's Hackers Crack Devices at Tianfu for US$1.5M in Prizes', Dark Reading, 15 October 2021. https://www.darkreading.com/vulnerabilities-threats/china-s-hackers-crack-devices-at-tianfu-cup-for-1-5m-in-prizes

48 J. D. Work, 'China Flaunts its Offensive Cyber Power', War on the Rocks, 22 October 2021. https://warontherocks.com/2021/10/china-flaunts-its-offensive-cyber-power/

49 The 6 December 2021 Microsoft statement on shutting down Nickel, 'Protecting people from recent cyber attacks', written by Tom Burt, Corporate Vice President, Customer Security and Trust, can be accessed via the Microsoft website. https://blogs.microsoft.com/on-the-issues/2021/12/06/cyberattacks-nickel-dcu-china/

50 Insikt Group, 'Chinese State-Sponsored Cyber Espionage Activity Supports Expansion of Regional Power and Influence in Southeast Asia', Recorded Future, 8 December 2021. https://go.recordedfuture.com/hubfs/reports/cta-2021-1208.pdf

51 Krebs on Security, 'FBI Raids Chinese Point-of-Sale Giant PAX Technology', 26 October 2021. https://krebsonsecurity.com/2021/10/fbi-raids-chinese-point-of-sale-giant-pax-technology/

52 Graham Allison, Kevin Klyman, Karina Barbesino and Hugo Yen, 'The Great Tech Rivalry: China vs The US', Harvard Kennedy School, Belfer Center for Science and International Affairs, December 2021. https://www.belfercenter.org/sites/default/files/GreatTechRivalry_ChinavsUS_211207.pdf

53 Martin Farrer, 'China more "brazen and damaging" than ever, says FBI director', *The Guardian*, 1 February 2022. https://www.theguardian.com/world/2022/feb/01/china-more-brazen-and-damaging-than-ever-says-fbi-director

54 National Cyber Security Centre, *Annual Review 2021: Making the UK the safest place to live and work online*, 17 November 2021. https://www.ncsc.gov.uk/news/record-number-mitigated-incidents

55 Charlie Mitchell, 'Russia-based group DarkSide behind Colonial Pipeline attack', *The Times*, 11 May 2021. https://www.thetimes.co.uk/article/russia-based-group-behind-colonial-pipeline-cyber attack-llmkhxbm2

56 Eric Tucker, 'Microsoft Exchange hack caused by China, US and allies say', Associated Press, 20 July 2021. https://apnews.com/article/microsoft-exchange-hack-biden-china-d533f5361cbc3374fdea58d3fb059f35

## Chapter 7:
## The Awkward Dance of the Panda and the Bear

1 Tony Munroe, Andrew Osborn and Humeyra Pamuk, 'China, Russia partner up against West at Olympics summit', Reuters, 4 February 2022. https://www.reuters.com/world/europe/russia-china-tell-nato-stop-expansion-moscow-backs-beijing-taiwan-2022-02-04/

2 Anton Troianovski and Steven Lee Myers, 'Putin and Xi Show United Front Amid Rising tensions with U.S.'., *The New York Times*, 15 December. https://www.nytimes.com/2021/12/15/world/asia/china-russia-summit-xi-putin.html

3 Anastasia Lyrchikova, Putin and Xi cement partnership in face of Western pressure', Reuters, 15 December 2021. https://www.reuters.com/world/china/russia-says-xi-backs-putin-push-western-security-guarantees-2021-12-15/

4 Tass Russian News Agency, Putin-Xi virtual summit concludes, running a little over an hour', 15 December 2021. https://tass.com/world/1376009

5 Daniel R Coats, US Director of National Intelligence, *Worldwide Threat Assessment of the US Intelligence Community*, 29 January 2019. https://www.dni.gov/files/ODNI/documents/2019-ATA-SFR---SSCI.pdf

6 Laura Zhou, 'Ready, set, fire: China and Russia get back to testing reach other's military tactics', *South China Morning Post*, https://www.scmp.com/print/news/china/diplomacy/article/3144092/ready-set-fire-china-and-russia-get-back-testing-each-others

7 Catherine Wong, 'China–Russia military drill makes room for combined force against US', *South China Morning Post*, 13 August 2021. https://www.scmp.com/print/news/china/diplomacy/article/3145010/china-russia-military-drill-makes-room-combined-force-against

8 Brett Forrest, Ann M. Simmons and Chao Deng, 'China and Russia Military Cooperation Raises Prospect of New Challenge to American Power', *The Wall Street Journal*, 2 January 2022. https://www.wsj.com/articles/china-russia-america-military-exercises-weapons-war-xi-putin-biden-11641146041

9 Richard Lloyd Parry, 'China and Russia send warships between Japanese Islands,' *The Times*, 19 October 2021. https://www.the

times.co.uk/article/8211756a-30d7-11ec-afd6-aa3ee2eb8a34?shareToken=0387f43d89575121325ea0a1e180225c

10 Maryann Xue, 'Explainer. China's arms trade: which countries does it buy from and sell to?', *South China Morning Post*, 4 July 2021. https://www.scmp.com/print/news/china/military/article/3139603/how-china-grew-buyer-major-arms-trade-player

11 Andrei Soldatov and Irina Borogan, 'Putin brings China's Great Firewall to Russia in cybersecurity pact', *The Guardian*, 29 November 2016. https://www.theguardian.com/world/2016/nov/29/putin-china-internet-great-firewall-russia-cybersecurity-pact

12 Richard Spencer and Didi Tang, 'China woos Assad to win a foothold in the Middle East', *The Times*, 20 July 2021. https://www.thetimes.co.uk/article/4ecca64e-e8a6-11eb-984b-57a44d13e8d6?shareToken=75cf071446fff3b249aa1b4fbdb4c390

13 Eric Cheung and Ben Westcott, 'Chinese officials and Taliban meet in Tianjin as US exits Afghanistan', CNN, 29 July 2021. https://edition.cnn.com/2021/07/29/china/china-taliban-tianjin-afghanistan-intl-hnk/index.html

14 Liu Xin and Liu Caiyu, 'US leaves chaos, destruction in Afghanistan', *Global Times*, 31 August 2021. https://www.globaltimes.cn/page/202108/1232914.shtml

15 Didi Tang, 'China offers to help the Taliban to re-build Afghanistan', *The Times*, 27 October 2021. https://www.thetimes.co.uk/article/china-offers-to-help-taliban-rebuild-afghanistan-8j8g9995c

16 Raffaello Pantucci, 'How China Became Jihadis' New Target', *Foreign Policy*, 22 November 2021. https://foreignpolicy.com/2021/11/22/china-jihadi-islamist-terrorism-taliban-uyghurs-afghanistan-militant-groups/

17 BBC Online, 'Chinese engineers killed in Pakistan bus blast', 14 July 2021. https://www.bbc.com/news/world-asia-57837072

18 Laura Zhou, 'China conducts anti-terror drills with Tajikistan as Afghan spillover worries grip central Asia', *South China Morning Post*, 18 August 2021. https://www.scmp.com/news/china/diplomacy/article/3145532/china-conducts-anti-terror-drill-tajikistan-afghan-spillover

19 Amy Mackinnon, 'Central Asia Braces for Fallout of US Pullout from Afghanistan', *Foreign Policy*, 16 July 2021. https://foreignpolicy.com/2021/07/16/central-asia-us-afghanistan-withdrawal-impact/

20 Reuters, 'China to build outpost for Tajikistan special forces near Afghan border', 28 October 2021. https://www.reuters.com/world/asia-pacific/china-build-outpost-tajikistan-special-forces-near-afghan-border-2021-10-28/
21 Mackinnon, *Foreign Policy*, 16 July 2021.
22 Peter Hopkirk, *The Great Game: On Secret Service in High Asia* (Oxford: Oxford University Press, 1990), p. 2.
23 Bruni Maçães, 'New Western frontier, conquered by China', *Politico*, 20 June 2016. https://www.politico.eu/article/khorgas-china-kazakhstan-new-silk-road-trade/
24 Henry Ruehl, 'The Khorgos hype on the Belt and Road', *The Diplomat*, 27 September 2019. https://thediplomat.com/2019/09/the-khorgos-hype-on-the-belt-and-road/
25 Rachel Zhang, 'China looks to Turkmenistan for more gas as it cuts Australian supplies', *South China Morning Post*, 21 May 2021. https://www.scmp.com/news/china/diplomacy/article/3133084/china-looks-turkmenistan-more-gas-it-cuts-australian-supplies
26 For a good analysis of the area, and of its importance in Uyghur culture in particular, see Rachel Harris and Ablet Kamalov's 'Nation, religion and social heat: heritaging Uyghur *mäshräp* in Kazakhstan', Central Asian Survey, 25 January 2021, 40:1, 9-33, DOI: 10.1080/02634937.2020.1835825
27 David Brophy, 'Manchu memorials to the martyrs of Kashgar', Sinoturcica, 28 December 2015. http://www.sinoturcica.org/manchu-memorials-to-the-martyrs-of-kashgar/
28 Nathan Vanderklippe, '"Everyone was silent, endlessly mute": Former Chinese re-education instructor speaks out', *The Globe and Mail*, 2 August 2018. https://www.theglobeandmail.com/world/article-everyone-was-silent-endlessly-mute-former-chinesere-education/
29 Catherine Putz, '2 More Ethnic Kazakhs Who Fled Xinjiang Won't Be Deported', *The Diplomat*, 22 January 2020. https://thediplomat.com/2020/01/2-more-ethnic-kazakhs-who-fled-xinjiang-wont-be-deported/
30 Temur Umarov, 'Can Russia and China Edge the United States out of Kazakhstan?' Carnegie Moscow Center, 3 August 2021. https://carnegiemoscow.org/commentary/85078
31 Reuters, 'China, Kazakhstan to ink deals worth $30 billion on

Saturday', 7 September 2013. https://www.reuters.com/article/us-kazakhstan-china-deals-idUSBRE98608320130907

32 Reuters, 'Dozens protest against Chinese influence in Kazakhstan', 4 September 2019. https://www.reuters.com/article/us-kazakhstan-china-protests-idUSKCN1VP1B0

33 Jacob Mardell, 'China's Weak Spot. Beijing isn't winning hearts and minds in its immediate neighbourhood', Politico, 12 February 2020. https://www.politico.eu/article/china-beijing-weak-spot-corona virus-central-asia-kazakhstan-kyrgyzstan-diplomacy/

34 Reuters, 'Kazakhstan summons Chinese ambassador in protest over article', 14 April 2020. https://www.reuters.com/article/us-kazakhstan-china-idUSKCN21W1AH

35 NATO Review, 'Monitoring contamination in Kazakhstan', 1 September 2001. https://www.nato.int/docu/review/articles/2001/09/01/monitoring-contamination-in-kazakhstan/

36 Anna Sorokina, 'How many cosmodromes does Russia have?' *Russia Beyond*, 6 December 2021. https://www.rbth.com/science-and-tech/334487-russian-cosmodromes-space

37 KPMG, 'Private equity market in Kazakhstan', May 2019, p. 23. https://assets.kpmg/content/dam/kpmg/kz/pdf/2019/09/KPMG-Private-Equity-Market-in-Kazakhstan-ENG-2019.pdf

38 Ivan Nechepurenko, Valerie Hopkins and Andrew E. Kramer, 'Russia Sends Troops to Kazakhstan to Help Quell Uprising', *New York Times*, 6 January 2022. https://www.nytimes.com/live/2022/01/06/world/kazakhstan-protests

39 Reuters, 'Putin, before vote, says he'd reverse Soviet collapse if he could', 2 March 2018. https://www.reuters.com/article/us-russia-election-putin-idUSKCN1GE2TF

40 Michael S. Gerson, 'The Sino-Soviet Border Conflict: Deterrence, Escalation, and the Threat of Nuclear War in 1969', Center for Naval Analyses, US Department of Defense, November 2010, pp. 33–4. https://www.cna.org/cna_files/pdf/d0022974.a2.pdf

41 For a more detailed analysis of this period, see Adeeb Khalid's *Central Asia: A New History from Imperial Conquests to the Present* (Princeton and Oxford: Princeton University Press, 2021), pp. 397–417.

42 John Hurley, Scott Morris and Gailyn Portelance, 'Examining the Debt Implications of the Belt and Road Initiative from a Policy Perspective', Center for Global Development, Policy Paper 121,

March 2018. https://www.cgdev.org/sites/default/files/examining-debt-implications-belt-and-road-initiative-policy-perspective.pdf

43 'Living in Debt: To Whom and How Much Does Tajikistan Owe?' Central Asian Bureau for Analytical Reporting, 17 February 2021. https://cabar.asia/en/living-in-debt-to-whom-and-how-much-does-tajikistan-owe

44 Hurley, et al.

45 Vladimir Rozanskij, 'Tajikistan, "part of Chinese empire"', *PIME Asia News*, 26 January 2021. https://www.asianews.it/news-en/Tajikistan,-'part-of-the-Chinese-empire'-52169.html

46 Eleanor Albert, 'The Shanghai Cooperation Organization', Council on Foreign Relations Backgrounder, 14 October 2015. https://www.cfr.org/backgrounder/shanghai-cooperation-organization

47 Reid Standish, 'China's Central Asian Plans Are Unnerving Moscow', *Foreign Policy*, 23 December 2019. https://foreignpolicy.com/2019/12/23/china-russia-central-asia-competition/

48 Kunal Purohit, 'India, Russia ties see a revival as China, Afghanistan, Central Asia dominate bilateral agenda', *South China Morning Post*, 28 December 2021. https://www.scmp.com/week-asia/politics/article/3161295/india-russia-ties-see-revival-china-afghanistan-and-central-asia

49 Lindsey Kennedy and Nathan Paul Southern, 'Central Asia Is Turning Back to Moscow', *Foreign Policy*, 7 November 2021. https://foreignpolicy.com/2021/11/07/central-asia-russia-china-development-security-belt-and-road/

50 Human Rights Watch, 'China: Mongolian Mother-Tongue Classes Curtailed', 4 September 2020. https://www.hrw.org/news/2020/09/04/china-mongolian-mother-tongue-classes-curtailed

51 Antonio Graceffo, 'China's Crackdown on Mongolian Culture', *The Diplomat*, 4 September 2020. https://thediplomat.com/2020/09/chinas-crackdown-on-mongolian-culture/

52 Reuters, 'China says hopes Mongolia learned lessons after Dalai Lama visit', 24 January 2017. https://www.reuters.com/article/us-china-mongolia-dalailama-idUSKBN158197

53 Charlie Campbell, '"We Face Very Tough Challenges." How Mongolia Typifies the Problems Posed to Small Countries by China's Rise', *Time*, 13 April 2021. https://time.com/5953518/mongolia-china-russia-problems/

54 Ibid.

55 Dan Levin, 'Genghis Khan Rules Mongolia Again, in a PR campaign', *New York Times*, 2 August 2009. https://www.nytimes.com/2009/08/03/world/asia/03genghis.html
56 'The IMF bails Mongolia out – again', *The Economist*, 25 February 2017. https://www.economist.com/asia/2017/02/25/the-imf-bails-mongolia-out-again
57 Antonio Graceffo, Khangal Odbayar and Enkhjin Erdenetulga, 'Mongolian traders in disarray as China's zero-covid policy chokes business', *bne INTELLINEWS*, 15 December 2021. https://www.intellinews.com/mongolian-traders-in-disarray-as-china-s-zero-covid-policy-chokes-business-230137/
58 Nikola Mikovic, 'Russia eyes Mongolia as a shortcut to China', *Asia Times*, 2 July 2021. https://asiatimes.com/2021/07/russia-eyes-mongolia-as-a-shortcut-to-china/
59 Sidharth Shekar, 'Russia's Vladivostok celebration irks Chinese diplomat, says "in the past it was our Haishenwai"', *TimesNowNews.com*, 3 July 2020. https://www.timesnownews.com/international/article/after-galwan-valley-china-lays-claim-on-russia-s-vladivostok-calling-it-haishenwai/615563
60 An excellent description of the area and the mood of the people on both sides of the border is provided by travel writer Colin Thubron, in his book, *The Amur River. Between Russian and China* (London: Chatto & Windus 2021)
61 Ivan Tselichtchev, 'Chinese in the Russian Far East: a geopolitical timebomb?', *South China Morning Post*, 8 July 2017. https://www.scmp.com/week-asia/geopolitics/article/2100228/chinese-russian-far-east-geopolitical-time-bomb
62 Reuters, 'West concerned by closer Russia-China ties, top NATO general says', 3 February 2021. https://www.reuters.com/article/us-usa-russia-china-military-idUSKBN2A32KK
63 Tom Miller, *China's Asian Dream. Empire Building Along the New Silk Road* (London: Zed Books 2019), p. 91)
64 Bloomberg, 'China Pushes Conspiracy Theory About U.S. Labs in Ukraine', 8 March 2022. https://www.bloomberg.com/news/articles/2022-03-08/china-pushes-russia-conspiracy-theory-about-u-s-labs-in-ukraine
65 Edward Wong and Julian E Barnes, 'China Asked Russia to Delay Ukraine War Until After Olympics, US Officials Say', *The New York Times*, 22 March 2022. https://www.nytimes.com/2022/03/02/us/politics/russia-ukraine-china.html

## Chapter 8:
## Target Taiwan: The Chinese Anaconda Tightens Its Grip

1 David Victor, 'John Cena Apologises to China for Calling Taiwan a Country', *New York Times*, 25 May 2021. https://www.nytimes.com/2021/05/25/world/asia/john-cena-taiwan-apology.html
2 Jesse Johnson, '"Top Gun" sequel, co-produced by China's Tencent, drops Japanese and Taiwanese flags', *Japan Times*, 20 July 2019. https://www.japantimes.co.jp/news/2019/07/20/asia-pacific/top-gun-sequel-appears-remove-japanese-taiwanese-flags/
3 Sui-Lee Wee, 'Giving in to China, US Airlines Drop Taiwan (In Name at Least)', *New York Times*, 25 July 2018. https://www.nytimes.com/2018/07/25/business/taiwan-american-airlines-china.html
4 Abha Bhattarai, 'China asked Marriott to shut down its website. The company complied', *Washington Post*, 18 January 2018. https://www.washingtonpost.com/news/business/wp/2018/01/18/china-demanded-marriott-change-its-website-the-company-complied/
5 Tom Barnes, 'China destroys 30,000 maps because they don't list Taiwan and state in north India as its territory', *Independent*, 26 March 2019. https://www.independent.co.uk/news/world/asia/china-maps-destroyed-taiwan-arunachal-pradesh-india-territory-disputed-south-tibet-a8840836.html
6 Sidney Leng, 'Off the charts: why China publishers don't want maps in their books', *South China Morning Post*, 19 May 2018. https://www.scmp.com/news/china/economy/article/2146876/charts-why-chinese-publishers-dont-want-maps-their-books
7 'A cartographic clash between the LSE and its Chinese students', *The Economist*, 13 April 2019. https://www.economist.com/britain/2019/04/13/a-cartographic-clash-between-the-lse-and-its-chinese-students
8 Reuters, 'China criticises NBC Universal for showing "incomplete map" during Olympic opening ceremony', NBC News, 24 July 2021. https://www.nbcnews.com/news/olympics/china-criticizes-nbc-universal-showing-incomplete-map-during-olympic-opening-n1274905
9 AFP, 'Taiwan pulls out of HK event', *Taipei Times*, 7 August 2021. https://www.taipeitimes.com/News/taiwan/archives/2021/08/07/2003762181
10 Patrick Brzeski, 'Venice Sparks Political Controversy With Taiwan

Films Name Change', *The Hollywood Reporter*, 3 September 2021. https://www.hollywoodreporter.com/movies/movie-news/venice-film-fest-political-controversy-taiwan-movies-name-change-1235007855/

11 Rana Siu Imboden, 'China Is Choking Civil Society at the United Nations', *Foreign Policy*, 27 September 2021. https://foreignpolicy.com/2021/09/27/china-is-choking-civil-society-at-the-united-nations/

12 Yimou Lee and Ben Blanchard, 'Taiwan says China blocked deal with BioNTech for Covid-19 shots', Reuters, 26 May 2021. https://www.reuters.com/world/china/taiwan-says-china-blocked-deal-with-biontech-covid-19-shots-2021-05-26/

13 Yimou Lee, 'Taiwan says request to drop the word "country" preceded BioNTech vaccine deal collapse', Reuters, 27 May 2021. https://www.reuters.com/world/asia-pacific/taiwan-says-request-drop-word-country-preceded-biontech-vaccine-deal-collapse-2021-05-27/

14 Helen Davidson, 'Taiwan accuses China of interfering in Covid vaccine deals', *The Guardian*, 27 May 2021. https://www.theguardian.com/world/2021/may/27/taiwan-president-accuses-china-interfering-covid-vaccine-deals

15 Reuters, 'Taiwan suggests China to blame after deal for 5m Covid vaccine doses is put on hold', *The Guardian*,17 February 2021. https://www.theguardian.com/world/2021/feb/17/taiwan-china-pressure-covid-vaccine-deal-biontech

16 Jesus Jiménez and Annie Karni, 'The United States sends 2.5 million doses of Moderna's vaccine to help Taiwan battle its first major outbreak', *New York Times*, 19 June 2021. https://www.nytimes.com/2021/06/19/world/us-taiwan-vaccine.html

17 Ann Wang, 'Taiwan welcomes US vaccine aid, bolstering its COVID fight', Reuters, 20 June 2021. https://www.reuters.com/world/asia-pacific/forces-good-will-prevail-taiwan-welcomes-massive-us-vaccine-aid-2021-06-20/

18 Keoni Everington, 'Signs on Grand Hotel, Taipei 101, thank US for 2.5 million Moderna jabs', *Taiwan News*, 21 June 2021. https://www.taiwannews.com.tw/en/news/4228383

19 Joyu Wang and Chao Deng, 'Tech Firms to Buy Covid-19 Vaccines on Behalf of Taiwan Government', *Wall Street Journal*, 12 July 2021. https://www.wsj.com/articles/tech-firms-to-buy-

covid-19-vaccines-on-behalf-of-taiwans-government-11626020496

20 Christian Shepherd and Primrose Riordan, 'Delta outbreak piles pressure on China's homegrown vaccines', *Financial Times*, 10 August 2021. https://www.ft.com/content/dd7ca21d-d779-45d8-aca5-c8f86f94f15e?shareType=nongift

21 Emma Graham-Harrison, 'China denies offer of "vaccine diplomacy" deal to Paraguay', *The Guardian*, 24 March 2021. https://www.theguardian.com/society/2021/mar/24/china-denies-offer-of-covid-vaccine-diplomacy-deal-to-paraguay

22 Tung Cheng-Chia and Alan H. Yang, 'How China is remaking the UN in its image', *The Diplomat*, 9 April 2020. https://thediplomat.com/2020/04/how-china-is-remaking-the-un-in-its-own-image/

23 Jonathan Calvert and George Arbuthnott, 'China, the WHO and a power grab that fuelled a pandemic', *The Sunday Times*, 14 August 2021. https://www.thetimes.co.uk/article/china-the-who-and-the-power-grab-that-fuelled-a-pandemic-3mt05m06n

24 Javier C. Hernández and Chris Horton, 'Taiwan's Weapon Against Coronavirus: An Epidemiologist as Vice-President', *New York Times*, 9 May 2020. https://www.nytimes.com/2020/05/09/world/asia/taiwan-vice-president-coronavirus.html

25 Reuters, 'China berates New Zealand over support for Taiwan at WHO', 11 May 2020. https://www.reuters.com/article/us-china-taiwan-new-zealand-mofa-idUSKBN22N18E

26 Nectar Gann and Steve George, 'Chinese state media sets sights on Taiwan as US' Afghan retreat stokes nationalism', CNN, 18 August 2021. https://edition.cnn.com/2021/08/18/china/china-afghanistan-taiwan-mic-intl-hnk/index.html

27 'Afghanistan today, Taiwan tomorrow? US treachery scares DPP', *Global Times*, 16 August 2021. https://www.globaltimes.cn/page/202108/1231635.shtml

28 'Afghan abandonment a lesson for Taiwan's DPP', *Global Times* editorial, 16 August 2021. https://www.globaltimes.cn/page/202108/1231636.shtml

29 'Tsai says Taiwan needs to be stronger', *Taipei Times*, 19 August 2021. https://www.taipeitimes.com/News/front/archives/2021/08/19/2003762844

30 Kathrin Hille, 'Taiwan's unity cracks under Chinese disinformation onslaught', *Financial Times*, 29 June 2021. https://www.

ft.com/content/f22f1011-0630-462a-a21e-83bae4523da7?shareType=nongift

31 Yimou Lee, David Lague and Ben Blanchard, 'Special Report – China launches "grey zone" warfare to subdue Taiwan', Reuters, 10 December 2021. https://www.reuters.com/article/hongkong-taiwan-military-idUSKBN28K1GS

32 Eleanor Olcott, 'China deploys hulking sand dredgers to crank up pressure on Taiwan', *Financial Times*, 27 May 2021. https://www.ft.com/content/aac6840f-26cf-410d-9e48-ed0e921bf32a?shareType=nongift

33 Audrey Tang and Joseph Wu, 'Why Taiwan seeks Israel's help to combat cyber security threats – opinion', *Jerusalem Post*, 26 July 2021. https://www.jpost.com/opinion/why-taiwan-seeks-israels-help-to-combat-cybersecurity-threats-opinion-674983

34 Yimou Lee, 'Taiwan says China behind cyberattacks on government agencies, emails', Reuters, 19 August 2020. https://www.reuters.com/article/us-taiwan-cyber-china-idUSKCN25F0JK

35 Mercedes Hutton, 'Mainland Chinese tourists stay away from Taiwan, but the self-ruled island doesn't seem to mind', *South China Morning Post*, 23 October 2019. https://www.scmp.com/magazines/post-magazine/travel/article/3034071/mainland-chinese-tourists-are-staying-away-taiwan

36 'Military and Security Developments Involving the People's Republic of China 2020', annual report to Congress, Office of the Secretary of Defense, p. i. https://media.defense.gov/2020/Sep/01/2002488689/-1/-1/1/2020-DOD-CHINA-MILITARY-POWER-REPORT-FINAL.PDF

37 Helen Warrell and Michael Peel, 'Senior NATO officer warns of China's "shocking" military advances', *Financial Times*, 25 June 2021. https://www.ft.com/content/8a0b3975-1938-4815-af3b-22b5d3e6aca4?shareType=nongift

38 Peter R. Mansoor, 'Strategic Ambiguity and the Defense of Taiwan', a Hoover Institution briefing paper, 30 June 2021. https://www.hoover.org/research/strategic-ambiguity-and-defense-taiwan

39 Department of Defense annual report to Congress, 2020, p. 119.

40 Brendan Taylor, *Dangerous Decade: Taiwan's Security and Crisis management* (Oxford: Routledge, 2019), p. 10.

41 The Stockholm International Peace Research Institute (SIPRI) military expenditure database is regularly updated and can be accessed via its website. https://www.sipri.org/databases/milex

42 'Taiwan eyes jet fighter buy amid modest hike in 2022 defence spending', Reuters, 26 August 2021. https://www.reuters.com/world/asia-pacific/taiwan-proposes-4-hike-defence-spending-2022-2021-08-26/

43 Department of Defense annual report to Congress, 2020, pp. 113–14.

44 Oriana Skylar Mastro, 'The Taiwan Temptation: Why Beijing Might Resort to Force', *Foreign Affairs*, July/August 2021. https://www.foreignaffairs.com/articles/china/2021-06-03/china-taiwan-war-temptation

45 Ian Easton, *The Chinese Invasion Threat: Taiwan's Defense and America's Strategy in Asia* (Manchester: Eastridge Books, 2019).

46 See Avery Goldstein, 'First Things First. The Pressing Danger of Crisis Instability in US-China Relations', International Security, vol. 37, no. 4 (Spring 2013), pp. 49–89 for a fuller discussion of C4ISR.

47 Easton, p. 143.

48 Taylor, p. 111.

49 BBC Online, 'China–Taiwan tensions: Xi Jinping says "reunification must be fulfilled"', 9 October 2021. https://www.bbc.com/news/world-asia-china-58854081

50 Nicola Smith, 'Mines and speedboats: How Taiwan plans to repel a Chinese invasion', *The Telegraph*, 9 November 2021. https://www.telegraph.co.uk/world-news/2021/11/09/mines-speedboats-taiwan-plans-repel-chinese-invasion/

51 Helen Davidson and Julian Borger, 'China could mount full-scale invasion by 2025, Taiwan defence minister says', *The Guardian*, 6 October 2021. https://www.theguardian.com/world/2021/oct/06/biden-says-he-and-chinas-xi-have-agreed-to-abide-by-taiwan-agreement

## Chapter 9: The Myth of 'One China': Why Taiwan is an Independent Country

1 A very good and far more detailed examination of the life of Koxinga can be found in Jonathan Manthorpe's excellent history, *Forbidden Nation: A History of Taiwan* (New York: St Martin's Griffin, 2009).

2 China Travel's online guide to Xiamen is a typical example of the

way China has twisted the Koxinga narrative for its own propaganda purposes. https://www.chinatravel.com/xiamen

3 Manthorpe, pp. 84–5.

4 Ibid., p. 84.

5 Ibid., p. 86.

6 John Grant Ross, *Formosan Odyssey: Taiwan, Past and Present* (Camphor Press, 2014).

7 Helen Davidson, 'Families plead for Hong Kong activists accused of trying to flee by speedboat', *The Guardian*, 30 September 2020. https://www.theguardian.com/world/2020/sep/30/we-want-our-son-back-families-of-detained-hong-kong-activists-left-in-the-dark?share=twitter

8 BBC Online, 'Hong Kong boat activists; China jails group for up to three years', 30 December 2020. https://www.bbc.com/news/world-asia-china-55481425

9 'Contested Legacy', *The Economist*, 27 July 2012. https://www.economist.com/analects/2012/07/27/contested-legacy

10 This quote is taken from the cover blurb for Ross's *Formosan Odyssey*.

11 'Naval Air: Hull Humber 16 Replaces Shi Lang', StrategyPage, 14 September 2014. https://www.strategypage.com/htmw/htnavai/articles/20120914.aspx

12 Kyoshi Ito, *Taiwan – 400 Years of History and Outlook*, translated and edited by Walter Chen, is available in abridged form at https://docplayer.net/3822139-History-of-taiwan-dr-kiyoshi-ito-walter-chen.html

13 Gerrit van der Wees, 'Has Taiwan Always Been Part of China?' *The Diplomat*, 1 December 2020. https://thediplomat.com/2020/12/has-taiwan-always-been-part-of-china/

14 Ibid.

15 The quote is taken from *Small Sea Travel Diaries: Yonghe's Records of Taiwan* (Taipei: SMC Publishing, 2004), as referenced in John Grant Ross, *Taiwan in 100 Books* (Manchester: Camphor Press, 2020), p. 38.

16 Manthorpe, p. 101.

17 Ross, *Formosan Odyssey*, p. 170.

18 Kerry Brown and Kalley Wu Tzu-Hui, *The Trouble with Taiwan: History, the United States and a Rising China* (London: Zed Books, 2019).

19 Dafydd Fell, *Government and Politics in Taiwan* (Abingdon: Routledge, 2018), p. 12.
20 Chas W. Freeman Jr, 'Interesting Times: The Strategic Significance of Taiwan to the United States: An Historical Appreciation', a paper written in 1969 and published as a supplement to Freeman's book, *Interesting Times: China, America, and the Shifting Balance of Prestige* (Just World Books, 2013). https://chasfreeman.net/books-and-publications/supplementary-texts-interesting-times/strategic-significance-of-taiwan/
21 'Civil Affairs Handbook. Taiwan (Formosa)', Office of the Chief of Naval Operations, Navy Department, OPNAV 50E-12, 15 June 1944.
22 Hsiao-ting Lin, *Accidental State: The United States, and the Making of Taiwan* (Cambridge, Massachusetts and London: Harvard University Press, 2016).
23 George Kerr, *Formosa Betrayed* (Manchester: Camphor Press, 2018).
24 Ibid., p. 109.
25 Ibid., pp. 103–4.
26 Fell, p. 15.
27 Kerr, p. 429.
28 Manthorpe, p. 194.
29 Ibid., p. 195.
30 President Truman's full statement on Korea and the despatch of the 7th fleet, can be accessed via the Harry S. Truman Library Museum website. https://www.trumanlibrary.gov/library/public-papers/173/statement-president-situation-korea
31 Ibid.
32 Agence France-Presse, '70 years after Taiwan's "White Terror", relatives of victims still seeking justice', *South China Morning Post*, 26 February 2017. https://www.scmp.com/print/news/china/policies-politics/article/2074156/70-years-after-taiwans-white-terror-relatives-victims
33 Manthorpe, p. 185.
34 Kerr, p. 88.
35 Michael Turton and Brian Benedictus, 'US Policy and International Law: Taiwan's Friend', *The Diplomat*, 17 July 2014. https://thediplomat.com/2014/07/us-policy-and-international-law-taiwans-friend/

36 Ibid.
37 Kerr, p. 534.
38 Hu Ching-hui, 'Most Hokla, Hakka have aboriginal genes, study finds', *Taipei Times*, 21 November 2007. http://www.taipeitimes.com/News/front/archives/2007/11/21/2003388825
39 Linda van der Horst, 'The Evolution of Taiwanese Identity', *The Diplomat*, 10 June 2016. https://thediplomat.com/2016/06/the-evolution-of-taiwanese-identity/
40 Kathrin Hille and Robin Kwong, 'Obituary: Lee Teng-hui, former Taiwan president, 1923–2020', *Financial Times*, 30 July 2020. https://www.ft.com/contentc8050b09-baf9-41eb-8aa0-6c00109ca219
41 Lily Kou, 'Lee Teng-hui, Taiwan's "father of democracy" dies aged 97', *The Guardian*, 30 July 2020. https://www.theguardian.com/world/2020/jul/30/lee-teng-hui-taiwan-father-of-democracy-first-president-dies-aged-97

## Chapter 10: Why Taiwan Matters

1 Anne Quito, 'Taiwan is using humor as a tool against coronavirus hoaxes', *Quartz*, 5 June 2020. https://qz.com/1863931/taiwan-is-using-humor-to-quash-coronavirus-fake-news/
2 Emma Graham-Harrison and Helen Davidson, 'How Taiwan triumphed over Covid as the UK faltered', *The Guardian*, 24 March 2021. https://www.theguardian.com/world/2021/mar/24/how-taiwan-triumphed-over-covid-as-uk-faltered
3 Craig Silverman, 'Chinese Trolls Are Spreading Coronavirus Disinformation in Taiwan', *Buzzfeed News*, 5 March 2020. https://www.buzzfeednews.com/article/craigsilverman/chinese-trolls-coronavirus-disinformation-taiwan
4 Vincent Chao, 'Vaccine Donations to Taiwan Strengthened Democratic Partnerships', *Newsweek*, 25 June 2021. https://www.newsweek.com/vaccine-donations-taiwan-strengthened-democratic-partnerships-opinion-1603366
5 Chun Han Wong and Philip Wen, 'Taiwan Turns to Facebook and Viral Memes to Counter China's Disinformation', *Wall Street Journal*, 3 January 2020. https://www.wsj.com/articles/taiwan-turns-to-facebook-and-viral-memes-to-counter-chinas-disinformation-11578047403

6 V-Dem Institute, 'Democracy Facing Global Challenges', V-Dem Annual Democracy Report 2019. https://www.v-dem.net/static/website/files/dr/dr_2019.pdf
7 Richard C. Bush, *Difficult Choices: Taiwan's Quest for Security and the Good Life* (Washington DC: Brookings Institution Press, 2021), p. 237.
8 Lin Chia-nan, 'False information on the rise in Taiwan: academic', *Taipei Times*, 28 September 2019. http://www.taipeitimes.com/News/taiwan/archives/2019/09/28/2003723046
9 Maeve Whelan-Wuest and Victoria Welborn, 'Canary in a Digital Coalmine', National Democratic Institute, 26 May 2020. https://www.ndi.org/our-stories/canary-digital-coal-mine
10 Chen Yu-fu and Kayleigh Madjar, 'Beware Chinese face-swap app: official', *Taipei Times*, 8 February 2021. https://www.taipeitimes.com/News/front/archives/2021/02/08/2003751971
11 'Chinese nationalist taunt hits YouTube heights', *Taipei Times*, 24 October 2021. https://www.taipeitimes.com/News/taiwan/archives/2021/10/24/2003766676
12 Jake Chung, 'PROFILE: Audrey Tang: 100% made in Taiwan', *Taipei Times*, 28 August 2016. http://www.taipeitimes.com/News/taiwan/archives/2016/08/28/2003654031
13 Ann Scott Tyson, 'The web's a threat to democracy? Think again, Taiwan says', *Christian Science Monitor*, 8 April 2020. https://www.csmonitor.com/World/Asia-Pacific/2020/0408/The-web-s-a-threat-to-democracy-Think-again-Taiwan-says
14 Andrew Leonard, 'How Taiwan's Unlikely Digital Minister Hacked the Pandemic', *Wired*, 23 July 2020. https://www.wired.com/story/how-taiwans-unlikely-digital-minister-hacked-the-pandemic/
15 Chris Horton, 'The simple but ingenious system Taiwan uses to crowdsource its laws', *MIT Technology Review*, 21 August 2018. https://www.technologyreview.com/2018/08/21/240284/the-simple-but-ingenious-system-taiwan-uses-to-crowdsource-its-laws/
16 Newcomb, *The Diplomat*, 5 July 2021.
17 Staś Butler, 'EU Disinformation Committee Heads to Taiwan', *The Diplomat*, 2 November 2021. https://thediplomat.com/2021/11/eu-disinformation-committee-heads-to-taiwan/
18 Tom Capon, 'The modern gay history of Taipei, Asia's most LGBTI-friendly city', *Gay Star News*, 26 October 2018. https://

www.gaystarnews.com/article/the-modern-gay-history-of-taipei-asias-most-lgbti-friendly-city/

19 Vincent Ni and Helen Davidson, 'Outrage over shutdown of LGBTQ WeChat accounts in China', *The Guardian*, 8 July 2021. https://www.theguardian.com/world/2021/jul/08/outrage-over-crackdown-on-lgbtq-wechat-accounts-in-china

20 Helen Davidson, 'Healing words: Taiwan's tribes fight to save their disappearing languages', *The Guardian*, 9 June 2021. https://www.theguardian.com/world/2021/jun/09/healing-words-taiwans-tribes-fight-to-save-their-disappearing-languages

21 Reuters, 'Taiwan's indigenous people take land rights fight to the heart of the capital', *South China Morning Post*, 11 June 2018. https://www.scmp.com/news/china/society/article/2150209/taiwans-indigenous-people-take-land-rights-fight-heart-capital

22 BBC Online, 'Taiwan's indigenous groups lose court fight for hunting rights', 7 May 2021. https://www.bbc.com/news/world-asia-57023554

23 'Taiwan No. 1 in Asia, world No. 6 for gender equality', *Taipei Times*, 9 January 2021. https://www.taipeitimes.com/News/taiwan/archives/2021/01/09/2003750242

24 The full UNDP Gender Inequality Index can be accessed via the organisation's website. http://hdr.undp.org/en/composite/GII

25 Reuters, 'Taiwan to halt construction of fourth nuclear power plant', 27 April 2014. https://www.reuters.com/article/taiwan-nuclear-idUKL3N0NJ08C20140427

26 Fan Cheng-hsiang, Kuo Chien-shen and Lee Hsin-Yin, 'REFERENDUMS 2021: Nuclear plant will be reactivated if people vote for it: premier', Central News Agency, 9 November 2021. https://focustaiwan.tw/politics/202111090013

27 Jamil Anderlini, 'China's dream of using Hong Kong as a model for Taiwan's future is dead', *Financial Times*, 11 January 2011. https://www.ft.com/content/15d992f4-33a1-11ea-9703-eea0cae3f0de

28 Sarah A. Topol, 'Is Taiwan Next?' *New York Times Magazine*, 5 August 2021. https://www.nytimes.com/2021/08/04/magazine/taiwan-china.html

29 Mari Saito, Yimou Lee and David Lague, 'The leader who's standing up to China', Reuters, 24 December 2021. https://www.reuters.com/investigates/special-report/taiwan-china-tsai/

30 Clifford Lo and Cat Wang, 'National security law: three leaders, group behind Tiananmen vigil in Hong Kong charged with inciting subversion against state power', *South China Morning Post*, 9 September 2021. https://www.scmp.com/news/hong-kong/law-and-crime/article/3148114/national-security-law-hong-kong-police-search-june-4

31 Alexander Solum, 'Tiananmen statue creator accuses HK university of "mafia" tactics', Reuters, 13 October 2021. https://www.reuters.com/world/asia-pacific/tiananmen-statue-creator-slams-mafia-tactics-by-hong-kong-university-2021-10-13/

32 Reuters, 'In Hong Kong, access to online museum about Tiananmen Square appears blocked', NBC News, 2 June 2021. https://www.nbcnews.com/news/world/hong-kong-access-online-museum-about-tiananmen-square-appears-blocked-n1280411

33 Dafydd Fell, *Government and Politics in Taiwan* (Abingdon: Routledge, 2018).

34 Chien Hui-ju and Jake Chung, 'Survey shows "Chinese" identity at a record low', *Taipei Times*, 24 July 2021. https://www.taipeitimes.com/News/taiwan/archives/2021/07/24/2003761369

35 Fang-Yu Chen, Austin Wang, Charles K. S. Wu and Yao-Yuan Yeh, 'What Do Taiwan's People Think About Their Relationship to China?' *The Diplomat*, 29 May 2020. https://thediplomat.com/2020/05/what-do-taiwans-people-think-about-their-relationship-to-china/

36 Jason Pan, 'Independence support spikes: survey', *Taipei Times*, 23 June 2020. https://www.taipeitimes.com/News/taiwan/archives/2020/06/23/2003738708

37 Jason Pan, 'Survey finds 85 percent define as Taiwanese', *Taipei Times*, 11 December 2020. https://www.taipeitimes.com/News/taiwan/archives/2020/12/11/2003748533

38 Fell, pp. 149–70.

39 Samuel P. Huntington, *The Third Wave: Democratization in the Late Twentieth Century* (University of Oklahoma Press, 1993).

40 Lawrence Chung, 'Taiwan's Chiang Kai-shek Memorial set to lose authoritarian symbols and giant statue of former KMT leader', *South China Morning Post*, 9 September 2021. https://www.scmp.com/print/news/china/politics/article/3148034/taiwans-chiang-kai-shek-memorial-hall-set-lose-authoritarian

41 Agence France-Presse, 'Taiwan has its answer to unwanted,

divisive statues', *Taipei Times*, 27 August 2017. http://www.taipeitimes.com/News/taiwan/archives/2017/08/27/2003677269

42 For a more detailed description of the Green Island prisons and their history, see the website of the National Human Rights Commission. https://www.nhrm.gov.tw/en/history_74.html

43 Thomas Bird, 'Taiwan's brutal White Terror period revisited on Green Island: confronting demons inside a former prison', *South China Morning Post*, 1 August 2019. https://www.scmp.com/print/magazines/post-magazine/long-reads/article/3020894/taiwans-brutal-white-terror-period-revisited

44 Cindy Sui, 'Taiwan Kuomintang: Revisiting the White Terror years', BBC Online, 13 March 2016. https://www.bbc.com/news/world-asia-35723603

45 Agence France-Presse, '70 years after Taiwan's "White Terror", relatives of victims still seeking justice', *South China Morning Post*, 26 February 2017. https://www.scmp.com/print/news/china/policies-politics/article/2074156/70-years-after-taiwans-white-terror-relatives-victims

46 Yeh Hung-ling, 'Taiwan passes act promoting transitional justice', *Taiwan Democracy Bulletin*, 11 December 2017. https://bulletin.tfd.org.tw/tag/yeh-hung-ling/

47 Ching-Tse Cheng, 'Freedom and democracy cannot be traded: Taiwan president', *Taiwan Times*, 28 February 2021. https://www.taiwannews.com.tw/en/news/4138665

48 See President Tsai Ing-wen's Twitter feed from 4 June 2020. https://twitter.com/iingwen/status/1268370481469521920?lang=en

49 Eleanor Olcott, 'Taiwan seizes chance to host foreign reporters kicked out of China', *Financial Times*, 20 April 2021. https://www.ft.com/content/ab588fed-fc21-4b19-b601-538d87d79db3

50 The Taiwan section of the 'Freedom in the World 2021' report from Freedom House can be accessed at https://freedomhouse.org/country/taiwan/freedom-world/2021

51 The full 'Freedom in the World 2021' rankings from Freedom House can be accessed at https://freedomhouse.org/countries/freedom-world/scores

52 The China section of the 'Freedom in the World 2021' report from Freedom House can be accessed at https://freedomhouse.org/country/china/freedom-world/2021

53 J. Michael Cole, *Black Island: Two Years of Activism in Taiwan* (CreateSpace Independent Publishing Platform, 2015), p. 104.

## Chapter 11:
## Chips with Everything: A Taiwanese Lynchpin in the Global Economy

1 Austen Ramzy, 'Typhoon Soudelor Kills 6 in Taiwan and Leaves Millions Without Power', *New York Times*, 8 August 2015. https://www.nytimes.com/2015/08/09/world/asia/typhoon-soudelor-kills-6-in-taiwan-and-leaves-millions-without-power.html

2 Alice (Ting-Yu) Liang, Leo Oey, Shiming Huang and Simon Chou, 'Long-term trends of typhoon-induced rainfall over Taiwan: In situ evidence of poleward shift of typhoons in western North Pacific in recent decades', *Journal of Geophysical Research Atmospheres*, vol. 22, Issue 5, pp. 2750–65. https://agupubs.onlinelibrary.wiley.com/doi/10.1002/2017JD026446

3 Reuters, 'Taiwan to ration water for 1 million households, tech hub unaffected', 24 March 2021. https://www.reuters.com/article/us-taiwan-drought-idUSKBN2BG1AM

4 Raymond Zhong and Amy Chang Chien, 'Drought in Taiwan Pits Chip Makers Against Farmers', *New York Times*, 8 April 2021. https://www.nytimes.com/2021/04/08/technology/taiwan-drought-tsmc-semiconductors.html

5 Huang Tzu-ti, 'Taiwan's TSMC reportedly spending US$28.6 million on water', *Taiwan News*, 21 May 2021. https://www.taiwannews.com.tw/en/news/4207661

6 Reuters, 'Drought-hit Taiwan plans more water curbs for chip hubs', 19 May 2021. https://www.reuters.com/technology/amid-drought-taiwan-plans-more-water-curbs-chip-hub-hsinchu-2021-05-19/

7 'Shortages related to semiconductors to cost the auto industry $210 billion in revenues this year, says new AlixPartners forecast', AlixPartners press release, 23 September 2021. https://www.alixpartners.com/media-center/press-releases/press-release-shortages-related-to-semiconductors-to-cost-the-auto-industry-210-billion-in-revenues-this-year-says-new-alixpartners-forecast/

8 Debby Wu, 'Apple Set to Cut iPhone Production Goals Due to Chip Crunch', Bloomberg, 21 October 2021. https://www.bloomberg.com/news/articles/2021-10-12/apple-poised-to-slash-iphone-production-goals-due-to-chip-crunch

9 Reuters, 'Heavy rain brings Taiwan's chip makers a reprieve just as tougher drought measures were due to hit', *South China*

*Morning Post*, 31 May 2021. https://www.scmp.com/news/china/article/3135490/heavy-rain-brings-taiwans-chip-makers-reprieve-just-tougher-drought

10 Kathrin Hille, 'TSMC: how a Taiwan chipmaker became a lynchpin of the global economy', *Financial Times*, 24 March 2021. https://www.ft.com/content/05206915-fd73-4a3a-92a5-6760ce965bd9?shareType=nongift

11 'How TSMC has mastered the geopolitics of chipmaking', *The Economist*, 1 May 2021. https://www.economist.com/business/2021/04/29/how-tsmc-has-mastered-the-geopolitics-of-chipmaking?frsc=dg%7Ce

12 Charlie Campbell, 'Inside the Taiwan Firm That Make's the World's Tech Run', *Time*, 1 October 2021. https://time.com/6102879/semiconductor-chip-shortage-tsmc/

13 'TSMC Founder receives Order of Propitious Clouds', *Taipei Times*, 15 September 2018. http://www.taipeitimes.com/News/taiwan/archives/2018/09/15/2003700456

14 Yang Jie, Stephanie Yang and Asa Fitch, 'The World Relies on One Chip Maker in Taiwan, Leaving Everyone Vulnerable', *Wall Street Journal*, 19 June 2021. https://www.wsj.com/articles/the-world-relies-on-one-chip-maker-in-taiwan-leaving-everyone-vulnerable-11624075400

15 'Chipmaking is being redesigned. Effects will be far-reaching', *The Economist*, 21 January 2021. https://www.economist.com/business/2021/01/23/chipmaking-is-being-redesigned-effects-will-be-far-reaching

16 *The Economist*, 1 May 2021.

17 Jie, Yang and Fitch, *Wall Street Journal*, 19 June 2021.

18 Cheng Ting-fang and Lauly Li, 'TSMC founder chides US plan for full chip supply chain onshore', *Financial Times*, 2 November 2021. https://www.ft.com/content/a629a648-d824-4c41-92ee-475905f5d6f8?shareType=nongift

19 Kif Leswing, 'Intel is spending $20 billion to build two new chip plants in Arizona', CNBC, 23 March 2021. https://www.cnbc.com/2021/03/23/intel-is-spending-20-billion-to-build-two-new-chip-plants-in-arizona.html

20 Yvette To, 'China chases semiconductor self-sufficiency', East Asia Forum, 22 February 2021. https://www.eastasiaforum.org/2021/02/22/china-chases-semiconductor-self-sufficiency/

21 Che Pen, 'China's semiconductor industry faces a growing talent

shortage as Beijing aims for global dominance in chip manufacture', *South China Morning Post*, 18 October 2021. https://www.scmp.com/print/tech/tech-war/article/3152782/chinas-semiconductor-industry-faces-growing-talent-shortage-beijing

22 *The Economist*, 1 May 2021.

23 Hille, *Financial Times*, 24 March 2021.

24 Bloomberg, 'The World Is Dangerously Dependent on Taiwan for Semiconductors', Supply Chain Brain, 26 January 2021. https://www.supplychainbrain.com/articles/32482-the-world-is-dangerously-dependent-on-taiwan-for-semiconductors

25 Campbell, *Time*, 1 October 2021.

26 Helen Davidson and Martin Farrer, 'Chips with everything: how one Taiwanese company drives the world economy', *The Guardian*, 19 May 2021. https://www.theguardian.com/world/2021/may/19/chips-with-everything-how-one-taiwanese-company-drives-the-world-economy

27 Debby Wu and Argin Chang, 'Taiwan Says Peace Crucial to Chip Supply as China Pressure Grows', Bloomberg, 4 October 2021. https://www.bloomberg.com/news/articles/2021-10-04/taiwan-says-peace-crucial-to-chip-supply-as-china-pressure-grows

28 Julian E. Barnes, 'How the Computer Chip Shortage Could Incite a US Conflict with China', *New York Times*, 26 January 2022. https://www.nytimes.com/2022/01/26/us/politics/computer-chip-shortage-taiwan.html

29 Robert Steven, *The National Liberal Club: Politics and Persons* (London: Robert Holden, 1925).

30 For fuller historic figures, see the website of the Taiwan government's Statistical Bureau. https://eng.stat.gov.tw/point.asp?index=1

31 Yen Nee Lee, 'Asia's top-performing economy in 2020 could grow even faster this year', CNBC, 22 February 2021. https://www.cnbc.com/2021/02/23/taiwan-asias-top-performing-economy-in-2020-could-grow-faster-in-2021.html

32 For a useful thumbnail sketch of Taiwan's economy, see Asia Fund Managers August 2021 country report. https://www.asiafundmanagers.com/int/taiwan-economy/

33 The website of the World Population Review carries an interactive map showing the latest Gini Coefficient by country for 2021. https://worldpopulationreview.com/country-rankings/gini-coefficient-by-country

34 Jules Quartly, 'The Gini in Taiwan's Bottle', *Taiwan Business*

*TOPICS*, a publication of the American Chamber of Commerce in Taiwan, 19 November 2020. https://topics.amcham.com.tw/2020/11/taiwan-gini-coefficient/

35 Dafydd Fell, *Government and Politics in Taiwan* (Abingdon: Routledge, 2018), p. 17.

36 Scott L. Kastner, 'Cross-Strait Tension and Taiwan's Economic Vitality', in Steve Tsang (ed.), *The Vitality of Taiwan: Politics, Economics, Society and Culture* (Basingstoke: Palgrave Macmillan, 2012), p. 122.

37 Joshua P. Meltzer, 'Importance of the trans-pacific partnership', Brookings Policy Paper, 24 February 2014. https://www.brookings.edu/research/taiwans-economic-opportunities-and-challenges-and-the-importance-of-the-trans-pacific-partnership/

38 Greg Rodgers, 'Overview of Taipei 101 Tower', tripsavvy.com, 5 March 2019. https://www.tripsavvy.com/taipei-101-tower-facts-1458242

39 Vivian Hsiao, 'Taipei 101 "rainbow lights" earn praise of inclusiveness', *The China Post*, 11 December 2020. https://chinapost.nownews.com/20201211-1914610

40 Kathrin Hille, 'Covid-19 brings wave of US tech entrepreneurs to Taiwan', *Financial Times*, 12 April 2021. https://www.ft.com/content/423b3ef3-6223-499a-ae3a-d79ade8be9a5?shareType=nongift

41 Akito Tanaka, 'YouTube co-founder Steve Chan bets on Taiwan for next start-up', *Nikkei Asia*, 21 May 2021. https://asia.nikkei.com/Editor-s-Picks/Interview/YouTube-co-founder-Steve-Chen-bets-on-Taiwan-for-next-startup

42 See the Statista website for the latest comparative figures on unicorns worldwide. https://www.statista.com/statistics/1096928/number-of-global-unicorns-by-country/

43 Kerry Brown, Justin Hempson-Jones and Jessica Pennisi, 'Investment Across the Taiwan Strait. How Taiwan's Relationship with China Affects its Position in the Global Economy', Royal Institute of International Affairs, November 2010. https://www.kerry-brown.co.uk/wp-content/uploads/2020/01/website-8.pdf

44 Ibid., p. 13.

45 'Dancing with the Dragon: An Economic History of Taiwan's China Policy', Berkeley Economic Review, 27 October 2020. https://econreview.berkeley.edu/dancing-with-the-dragon-an-economic-history-of-taiwans-china-policy/

46 Frederick Balfour and Tim Culpan, 'A look inside Foxconn – where iPhones are made', NBC News Online, 12 September 2010. https://www.nbcnews.com/id/wbna39099077

47 Mike Cormack, 'Dying for an iPhone: investigating Apple, Foxconn and the brutal exploitation of Chinese workers', *South China Morning Post*, 30 April 2020. https://www.scmp.com/magazines/post-magazine/books/article/3082307/dying-iphone-investigating-apple-foxconn-and-brutal

48 David Barbosa, 'How China Built "iPhone City" With Billions in Perks for Apple's Partner', *New York Times*, 29 December 2016. https://www.nytimes.com/2016/12/29/technology/apple-iphone-china-foxconn.html

49 'Direct flights between China and Taiwan begin', *New York Times*, 15 December 2008. https://www.nytimes.com/2008/12/15/world/asia/15iht-taiwan.1.18682000.html

50 Fell, p. 188.

51 'Taiwan, China sign historic trade deal', CNN, 29 June 2010. https://edition.cnn.com/2010/WORLD/asiapcf/06/29/china.taiwan.deal/index.html

52 Ben Bland, 'Xi Jinping and Ma Ying-jeou meet in Singapore', *Financial Times*, 7 November 2015. https://www.ft.com/content/630d83a4-853c-11e5-9f8c-a8d619fa707c

53 James Pomfret, Mathew Miller and Ben Blanchard, 'After vote, China tells Taiwan to abandon independence "hallucination"', Reuters, 17 January 2017. https://www.reuters.com/article/taiwan-election-idUSKCN0UV02I

54 Hu Xijin, 'Mainland stops importing two Taiwan fruits, and DPP authority is howling', *Global Times*, 20 September 2021. https://www.globaltimes.cn/page/202109/1234662.shtml

55 Richard Lloyd Parry, 'Japanese help Taiwanese run rings around pineapple ban', *The Times*, 20 March 2021. https://www.thetimes.co.uk/article/japanese-help-taiwan-run-rings-round-pineapple-ban-7dr8tv9p6

56 Reuters, 'China offers more access for Taiwan firms, Taiwan warns of a trap', 4 November 2019. https://www.reuters.com/article/us-china-taiwan-idUSKBN1XE0YV

57 Huang Tien-lin, 'Reiterating ECFA is a poison pill', *Taipei Times*, 11 September 2020. https://www.taipeitimes.com/News/editorials/archives/2020/09/11/2003743193

58 Samson Hill and Argin Chang, 'Tycoon targeted by China Speaks Out Against Taiwan Independence', Bloomberg, 30 November 2021. https://www.bloomberg.com/news/articles/2021-11-30/tycoon-targeted-by-china-speaks-out-against-taiwan-independence

59 Reuters, 'Choose a side, China tells Taiwan firms as it punishes conglomerate', 22 November 2021. https://www.reuters.com/markets/commodities/choose-side-china-tells-taiwan-firms-it-punishes-conglomerate-2021-11-22/

60 Berkeley Economic Review, 27 October 2020.

61 Bloomberg, 'World's Top Bicycle Maker Says the Era of "Made in China" Is Over', Industry Week, 18 June 2019. https://www.industryweek.com/supply-chain/article/22027768/worlds-top-bicycle-maker-says-the-era-of-made-in-china-is-over

62 Bonnie Glaser and Jeremy Mark, 'Taiwan and China are Locked in Economic Co-Dependence', *The Diplomat*, 14 April 2021. https://foreignpolicy.com/2021/04/14/taiwan-china-econonomic-codependence/

63 Reuters, 'Taiwan proposes tightening law to prevent China stealing technology', 29 November 2021. https://www.reuters.com/article/us-china-taiwan-idUSKBN1XE0YV

64 Cheng Ting-Fang and Lauly Li, 'China bans recruitment for jobs in China to combat brain drain', *Nikkei Asia*, 30 April 2021. https://asia.nikkei.com/Business/Tech/Semiconductors/Taiwan-bans-recruitment-for-jobs-in-China-to-combat-brain-drain?s=09

65 Philip Sherwell, 'China seeks microchip supremacy by any means possible,' *The Times*, 17 April 2022. https://www.thetimes.co.uk/article/2d9d6140-bdba-11ec-84c4-70cc6ae427fb?shareToken=7fe79bc8074792b3df1632b5e9b98eb8

## Chapter 12:
## Japan: Asia's Quiet Achiever Steps Out of the Shadows

1 John Feng, 'China Outraged After Japanese PM Calls Taiwan "Country"', *Newsweek*, 10 June 2021. https://www.newsweek.com/china-outraged-japanese-pm-calls-taiwan-country-1599276

2 Richard Lloyd Parry, 'Japanese minister's defence of Taiwan hints at shift in China policy', *The Times*, 29 June 2021. https://www.thetimes.co.uk/article/japanese-minister-s-defence-of-taiwan-hints-at-shift-in-china-policy-hq280nltx

3 Vincent Ni, 'China blasts Japanese minister's "sinister" remarks about Taiwan', *The Guardian*, 29 June 2021. https://www.theguardian.com/world/2021/jun/29/china-blasts-japanese-ministers-sinister-remarks-about-taiwan
4 Richard Lloyd Parry and Didi Tang, 'Japan would defend Taiwan if China invaded, says deputy PM', *The Times*, 7 July 2021. https://www.thetimes.co.uk/article/japan-would-defend-taiwan-if-china-invaded-says-deputy-pm-l7dnhdfn0
5 The references to Taiwan can be found on page 19 of the Japanese Defence Ministry's white paper, '2021 Defense of Japan', which can be accessed via the Ministry's website. https://www.mod.go.jp/en/publ/w_paper/wp2021/DOJ2021_Digest_EN.pdf
6 Ken Moriyasu, 'A tale of two covers: Japan's message on Taiwan draws US notice', *Nikkei Asia*, 21 July 2021. https://asia.nikkei.com/Politics/International-relations/Indo-Pacific/A-tale-of-two-covers-Japan-s-message-on-Taiwan-draws-US-notice
7 Robin Harding and Leo Lewis, 'Japan calls for greater attention to "survival of Taiwan"', *Financial Times*, 2 August 2021. https://www.ft.com/content/e82fe924-ba9b-4325-b8a4-0d5482ee1d24?shareType=nongift
8 Robert D. Kaplan, *Asia's Cauldron: The South China Sea and the End of a Stable Pacific* (New York: Random House, 2014), p.143.
9 Kyodo News, 'Japan bolstering defence of Nansei Islands as China puts pressure on Taiwan', *Japan Times*, 17 April 2021. https://www.japantimes.co.jp/news/2021/05/02/national/nansei-islands-defense/
10 Kyodo News, 'Chinese vessels sail near Senkakus for record 112 days in a row', 4 June 2021. https://english.kyodonews.net/news/2021/06/67d5c54a1cca-chinese-vessels-sail-near-senkakus-for-record-112-days-in-row.html
11 John Feng, 'China Ship Armed With Autocannon Enters Japanese Waters, Harasses Fishing Vessel', *Newsweek*, 16 February 2021. https://www.newsweek.com/china-ship-armed-autocannon-enters-japanese-waters-harasses-fishing-vessel-1569486
12 For a detailed overview of China's growing military activities in the East China Sea and Japan's response, see 'China's Military Activities in the East China Sea. Implications for Japan's Air Self-Defence Force', a 2018 Rand Corporation paper, written by Edmund J. Burke, Timothy R. Heath, Jeffrey W. Hornung, Logan

Ma, Lyle J. Morros and Michael S. Chase. https://www.rand.org/pubs/research_reports/RR2574.html

13 Felix K. Chang, 'The Ryukyu Defense Line: Japan's Response to China's Naval Push into the Pacific Ocean', Foreign Policy Research Institute, 8 February 2021. https://www.fpri.org/article/2021/02/the-ryukyu-defense-line-japans-response-to-chinas-naval-push-into-the-pacific-ocean/

14 Ibid.

15 Desmond Ball and Richard Tanter, *The Tools of Owatatsumi: Japan's Ocean Coastal Surveillance and Coastal Defence Capabilities* (Canberra: Australian National University Press, 2015), pp. 52–4. https://library.oapen.org/viewer/web/viewer.html?file=/bitstream/handle/20.500.12657/33253/515942.pdf?sequence=1&isAllowed=y

16 Demetri Sevastopulo, 'Joe Biden reaffirms commitment to defending Senkaku Islands', *Financial Times*, 28 January 2021. https://www.ft.com/content/5f142efe-4d4d-4d5a-b42e-eddcbd3a5df8

17 David Pilling, *Bending Adversity. Japan and the art of survival* (London: Allen Lane, 2014), p. 239.

18 'Japan's Self-Defence Forces are beginning to focus on China', *The Economist*, 20 April 2019. https://www.economist.com/asia/2019/04/17/japans-self-defence-forces-are-beginning-to-focus-on-china

19 Gavin Blair, 'Japan increases military budget over territorial threats', *The Times*, 20 August 2021. https://www.thetimes.co.uk/article/japan-increases-military-budget-over-territorial-threats-mkf2qsxw3

20 Yoshihiro Inaba, 'Japan's Helicopter Destroyer Modified to operate F-35B Fighters', *Naval News*, 20 July 2021. https://www.navalnews.com/naval-news/2021/07/japans-izumo-helicopter-destroyer-modified-to-operate-f-35b-fighters/

21 Steven Stashwick, 'In a First, US Jets Will Fly Off a Japanese Warship This Fall', *The Diplomat*, 4 September 2021. https://thediplomat.com/2021/09/in-a-first-us-jets-will-fly-off-a-japanese-warship-this-fall/

22 Mark Fitzpatrick, *Asia's Latent Nuclear Powers: Japan, South Korea and Taiwan* (Abingdon: Routledge, 2016), p. 65.

23 Mark Fitzpatrick, 'How Japan could go nuclear', International Institute for Strategic Studies expert commentary, 3 October 2019.

https://www.iiss.org/blogs/analysis/2019/10/how-japan-could-go-nuclear

24 *The Economist*, 20 April 2019.

25 Tim Kelly and Ju-min Park, 'Analysis: Japan's ruling party makes unprecedented defence spending pledge', Reuters, 13 October 2021. https://www.reuters.com/world/asia-pacific/with-an-eye-china-japans-ruling-party-makes-unprecedented-defence-spending-2021-10-13/

26 Kinling Lo, 'China, North Korea reaffirm ties on defence treaty anniversary', *South China Morning Post*, 11 July 2021. https://www.scmp.com/news/china/diplomacy/article/3140675/china-north-korea-reaffirm-ties-defence-treaty-anniversary

27 David Brunnstrom, 'US accuses China of "flagrant" N. Korea violations, offers $5 million reward', Reuters, 1 December 2020. https://www.reuters.com/article/usa-northkorea-china-idUSKBN28B540

28 Michael R. Gorden, 'Covert Chinese Trade With North Korea Moves Into the Open', *Wall Street Journal*, 7 December 2020. https://www.wsj.com/articles/covert-chinese-trade-with-north-korea-moves-into-the-open-11607345372

29 Christoph Koettl, 'How Illicit Oil Is Smuggled Into North Korea With China's Help', *New York Times*, 24 March 2021. https://www.nytimes.com/2021/03/24/world/asia/tankers-north-korea-china.html

30 Colum Lynch, '"It Was Like Having the Chinese Government in the Room With US"', *Foreign Policy*, 15 October 2021. https://foreignpolicy.com/2021/10/15/china-sanctions-north-korea-hardball/#

31 See page 56 of the 4 March 2021 report S2021/211 by the Panel of Experts on North Korean sanctions, drawn up for the UN Security Council. https://documents-dds-ny.un.org/doc/UNDOC/GEN/N21/034/37/PDF/N2103437.pdf?OpenElement

32 See pages 34 and 35 of the 8 September 2021 report S2021/777 by the Panel of Experts on North Korean sanctions, drawn up for the UN Security Council. https://documents-dds-ny.un.org/doc/UNDOC/GEN/N21/220/95/PDF/N2122095.pdf?OpenElement

33 David E. Sanger, William J. Broad and Choe Sang-Hun, 'Biden Is Facing an Uneasy Truth: North Korea Isn't Giving Up Its Nuclear Arsenal', *New York Times*, 20 May 2021. https://www.nytimes.com/2021/05/20/us/politics/biden-north-korea-nuclear-weapons.html

34 Reuters and Nandita Bose, 'Biden administration sets new North Korea policy of practical diplomacy', Reuters, 30 April 2021. https://www.reuters.com/world/asia-pacific/biden-administration-has-completed-north-korea-policy-review-white-house-2021-04-30/

35 Reuters, 'North Korea boasts of "shaking the world" by testing missile that can strike the US', CNN, 9 February 2022. https://edition.cnn.com/2022/02/08/asia/north-korea-missile-tests-united-states-intl-hnk/index.html

36 Edward White and Katrina Manson, 'Biden's tentative steps towards North Korea's Kim greeted with scepticism', *Financial Times*, 5 May 2021. https://www.ft.com/content/aceff9c7-5461-42f7-8761-15d4f7ad667a

37 Jack Detsch, 'Biden Team Fears North Korean Sanctions Aren't Working', *Foreign Policy*, 1 October 2021. https://foreignpolicy.com/2021/10/01/biden-north-korea-nuclear-weapons-kim-jong-un-sanctions/

38 Christian Shepherd, 'Americans vanquished, China triumphant: 2021's hit war epic doesn't fit Hollywood script', *Washington Post*, 14 October 2021. https://www.washingtonpost.com/world/2021/10/14/battle-lake-changjin-china-movies/

39 Liu Caiyu and Yu Jincui, 'Korean War film breaks records, has implications for today's China-US competition', *Global Times*, 1 October 2021. https://www.globaltimes.cn/page/202110/1235556.shtml?id=12

40 Steven Lee Myers and Amy Chang Chien, 'Chinese Journalist Detained After Criticising Government-Sponsored Blockbuster', *New York Times*, 8 October 2021. https://www.nytimes.com/2021/10/08/world/asia/luo-changping-china-battle-at-lake-changjin.html

41 Andrew Kuech, 'The Dangerous Reprise of Chinese Korean War Propaganda', *The Diplomat*, 14 June 2019. https://thediplomat.com/2019/06/the-dangerous-reprise-of-chinese-korean-war-propaganda/

42 *Xinhua* news agency, 'China Focus: "Be ready to Win Wars," China's Xi orders reshaped PLA', 1 July 2017. http://www.xinhuanet.com//english/2017-08/01/c_136491455.htm

43 BBC Online, 'Kimchi ferments cultural feud between South Korea and China', 30 November 2020. https://www.bbc.co.uk/news/world-asia-55129805

44 Choi Seong Hyeon, 'A Korean Poet Is the Latest Example of China's "Cultural Imperialism"', *The Diplomat*, 26 February 2021. https://thediplomat.com/2021/02/a-korean-poet-is-the-latest-example-of-chinas-cultural-imperialism/

45 Laura Silver, Kat Devlin and Christine Huang, 'Unfavourable Views of China Reach Historic Highs in Many Countries', Pew Research Center, 6 October 2020. https://www.pewresearch.org/global/2020/10/06/unfavorable-views-of-china-reach-historic-highs-in-many-countries/

46 Park Chan-kyong, 'South Korea cancels Korea-China Culture Town Project amid mounting anti-Chinese sentiment', *South China Morning Post*, 27 April 2021. https://www.scmp.com/week-asia/politics/article/3131255/south-korea-cancels-korea-china-culture-town-project-amid

47 'TV series "Joseon Exorcist" terminated over history controversy', *Korea Times*, 26 March 2021. https://w.koreatimes.co.kr/www/art/2021/09/688_306136.html

48 Christian Davies, 'Beijing Winter Olympics speed skating spat stokes anti-China hostility in South Korea', *Financial Times*, 15 February2022. https://www.ft.com/content/08474d92-cd25-4b68-a384-8e3cc8467b3a?shareType=nongift

49 Ibid.

50 The full joint statement at the end of the May 2021 summit meeting in Washington between presidents Joe Biden and Moon Jae-in can be accessed at the White House website. https://www.whitehouse.gov/briefing-room/statements-releases/2021/05/21/u-s-rok-leaders-joint-statement/

51 Jun Mai, 'Don't "play with fire", China tells US and South Korea over Taiwan concerns', *South China Morning Post*, 24 May 2021. https://www.scmp.com/print/news/china/diplomacy/article/3134670/dont-play-fire-china-tells-us-and-south-korea-over-taiwan

52 Mari Yamaguchi, 'Japan, S. Korea leaders look to deepen ties despite strains', Associated Press, 16 October 2021. https://apnews.com/article/business-china-japan-tokyo-seoul-209400e4a2dc4ee8b-3ba547f4877e3e3

53 Richard Lloyd Parry, 'Military exercises around Liancourt Rocks aggravate tension between Seoul and Tokyo', *The Times*, 15 June 2021. https://www.thetimes.co.uk/article/military-exercises-arou

nd-liancourt-rocks-aggravate-tensions-between-seoul-and-tokyo-b7nxndzcz

54 Shohei Kanaya and Tsubasa Ukishima, 'Cancel Xi Jinping's visit to Japan say 62% in Nikkei poll', *Nikkei Asia*, 20 July 2020. https://asia.nikkei.com/Politics/International-relations/Cancel-Xi-Jinping-s-visit-to-Japan-say-62-in-Nikkei-poll

55 William Sposato, 'Japan's Foreign Minister Faces Tough Calls on China', *Foreign Policy*, 11 November 2021. https://foreignpolicy.com/2021/11/11/yoshimasa-hayashi-japan-new-foreign-minister-qualified-china/

56 Sebastian Strangio, *In the Dragon's Shadow: Southeast Asia in the Chinese Century* (New Haven and London: Yale University Press, 2020), p. 258.

57 'A glimpse into Japan's understated financial heft in South-East Asia', *The Economist*, 14 August 2021. https://www.economist.com/finance-and-economics/2021/08/14/a-glimpse-into-japans-understated-financial-heft-in-south-east-asia

58 Strangio, p. 36.

59 Kripendra Amatya, 'Japan the Titan of Soft Power', *Modern Diplomacy*, 31 October 2020. https://moderndiplomacy.eu/2020/10/31/japan-the-titan-of-soft-power/

60 Brand Finance, 'Global Soft Power Index 2021: Japan is top-performing Asian nation, ranking 2nd overall', 26 February 2021. https://brandfinance.com/press-releases/global-soft-power-index-2021-japan-is-top-performing-asian-nation-ranking-2nd-overall

61 *The Economist*, 14 August 2021.

62 Strangio, p. 36.

## Chapter 13: The Muddled China Policy of 'Global Britain'

1 Dominic Nicholls, 'Royal Navy submarine jousts with Japanese in show of strength aimed at China', *The Telegraph*, 5 October 2021. https://www.telegraph.co.uk/news/2021/10/05/royal-navy-submarine-jousts-japanese-show-strength-aimed-china/

2 Royal Navy Forum, 'Pacific training for Carrier Strike Group as Japan visit comes to an end', 10 September 2021. https://www.royalnavy.mod.uk/news-and-latest-activity/news/2021/september/10/210910-carrier-strike-group-in-japan

3 See the Royal Navy factsheet with all the statistics about the HMS *Queen Elizabeth*. https://www.royalnavy.mod.uk/our-organisation/the-fighting-arms/surface-fleet/aircraft-carriers/hms-queen-elizabeth
4 Royal Navy press release, 26 April 2021. https://www.royalnavy.mod.uk/sitecore/content/home/news%20and%20latest%20activity/news/2021/april/26/210426%20csg21%20deployment
5 Ministry of Defence press release, 'Carrier Strike Group sets sail on seven-month maiden deployment', 22 May 2021. https://www.gov.uk/government/news/carrier-strike-group-sets-sail-on-seven-month-maiden-deployment--2
6 Will Self, 'The empty theatre of Boris Johnson', *The New European*, 4 June 2021. https://www.theneweuropean.co.uk/brexit-news-europe-news-will-self-boris-johnson-carrier-strike-group-8011654/
7 Jonathan Beale, 'HMS Queen Elizabeth: Why is a UK aircraft carrier going on a world tour?' BBC Online, 21 May 2021. https://www.bbc.co.uk/news/uk-57195317
8 Helen Warrell and George Parker, 'Challenging China: Brexit Britain experiments with battleship diplomacy', *Financial Times*, 19 May 2021. https://www.ft.com/content/3de612af-20cf-49c2-b8f3-7159dd0c7fae?shareType=nongift
9 Rajat Pandit, 'UK carrier group conducts exercise with India in strategic signal to China', *Times of India*, 22 July 2022. https://timesofindia.indiatimes.com/india/uk-carrier-group-conducts-. . .se-with-india-in-strategic-signal-to-china/articleshow/84656682.cms
10 Dewey Sim, 'Asia's oldest defence pact, the FPDA, is a "stabiliser for region", says Singapore defence minister', *South China Morning Post*, 18 October 2021. https://www.scmp.com/week-asia/politics/article/3152741/asias-oldest-defence-pact-fpda-marks-golden-jubilee
11 Reuters, 'China condemns Britain for Taiwan Strait warship mission', 27 September 2021. https://www.reuters.com/world/asia-pacific/british-frigate-sails-through-taiwan-strait-2021-09-27/
12 Wei Dongxu, 'Showing off its tier-2 naval power, Britain can hardly affect regional affairs in Asia', *Global Times*, 26 August 2021. https://www.globaltimes.cn/page/202108/1232563.shtml
13 'UK shouldn't tempt own fate in South China Sea', *Global*

*Times* editorial, 29 July 2021. https://www.globaltimes.cn/page/202107/1230053.shtml

14 See the Ministry of Defence press release of 19 July 2021, which also describes in more detail the exercises conducted by the carrier strike group. https://www.gov.uk/government/news/uk-carrier-strike-group-to-exercise-with-indo-pacific-partners

15 Reuters, 'UK's Johnson tells China: We believe in rule of the sea', 21 May 2021. https://www.reuters.com/world/china/uks-johnson-tells-china-we-believe-rule-sea-2021-05-21/

16 BBC Online, 'Aukus: UK, US and Australia launch pact to counter China', 16 September 2021. https://www.bbc.co.uk/news/world-58564837

17 A video of Boris Johnson in parliament making this point and expanding more widely on the Aukus pact on 16 September 2021 is available on *The Guardian* website. https://www.theguardian.com/politics/video/2021/sep/16/johnson-says-aukus-not-intended-to-be-adversarial-towards-china-video

18 HM Government, 'Global Britain in a competitive age. The Integrated Review of Security, Defence, Development and Foreign Policy', March 2021 https://assets.publishing.service.gov.uk/government/uploads/system/uploads/attachment_data/file/975077/Global_Britain_in_a_Competitive_Age-_the_Integrated_Review_of_Security__Defence__Development_and_Foreign_Policy.pdf

19 Warrell and Parker, *Financial Times*, 19 May 2021.

20 A video of the 18 October 2021 Bloomberg interview with Boris Johnson in which he talks about China and investment is available online at https://www.bloomberg.com/news/videos/2021-10-18/johnson-says-u-k-won-t-pitchfork-away-chinese-investment

21 George Parker and Daniel Thomas, 'UK says China is welcome to invest in non-strategic parts of the economy', *Financial Times*, 17 October 2021. https://www.ft.com/content/09e4cbf3-9cf0-4447-aa68-428ac2b4ba37

22 This investment was announced in a 19 October 2021 government press release, 'Investors pledge almost £10bn at UK Global Investment Summit'. https://www.gov.uk/government/news/investors-pledge-almost-10bn-at-uk-global-investment-summit

23 See the Shell 15 July 2021 press statement, released when the Minety facility began to trade, 'Shell starts trading power from Europe's largest battery'. https://www.shell.co.uk/media/2021-media-releases/shell-starts-trading-power-from-europes-largest-battery.html

24 Henry Sanderson and Eleanor Olcott, 'UK's first "gigafactory" set for huge expansion', *Financial Times*, 25 October 2021. https://www.ft.com/content/e02b9c29-85c7-4e61-ac18-49a64d7beb1d?shareType=nongift

25 A brief biography of Lei Zhang can be found among the speaker biographies for the Carbon Trust's 2020 Corporate Sustainability Summit, held on 14 October 2020, where he was keynote speaker. https://prod-drupal-files.storage.googleapis.com/documents/resource/public/Speaker-biographies.pdf

26 'China's Shenghe to acquire stake in Australian firm Peak Rare Earths', Mining Technology, 14 February 2022. https://www.mining-technology.com/news/shenghe-stake-peak-rare-earths/

27 Steven Swinford and Emily Gosden, 'British state could buy stake in Sizewell nuclear plant to keep China out', *The Times*, 27 July 2021. https://www.thetimes.co.uk/article/44733c38-ee02-11eb-8f01-2c678acbb979?shareToken=599f9066fe59d45b6e9b5eca2ead24dd

28 Jim Pickard and Nathalie Thomas, 'UK looks to remove China's CGN from nuclear power projects', *Financial Times*, 25 July 2021. https://www.ft.com/content/c4a3fe02-8535-45a4-aacf-0c4fbcc8409d

29 Jamie Nimmo and Robert Watts, 'How Beijing bought up Britain', *The Sunday Times*, 2 May 2021. https://www.thetimes.co.uk/article/how-beijing-bought-up-britain-hqll9tjtx

30 Patrick Wintour, 'Chinese threat prompts calls for UK to toughen company takeover laws', *The Guardian*, 14 May 2020. https://www.theguardian.com/business/2020/may/14/chinese-threat-prompts-calls-uk-toughen-company-takeover-laws

31 Ryan Gallagher, 'Cameras linked to Chinese government stir alarm in UK parliament', *The Intercept*, 9 April 2019. https://theintercept.com/2019/04/09/hikvision-cameras-uk-parliament/

32 Avi Asher-Schapiro, 'Exclusive: Half London councils found using Chinese surveillance tech linked to Uighur abuses', Reuters, 18 February 2021. https://www.reuters.com/article/us-britain-tech-china-idUSKBN2AI0QJ

33 Hilary Clarke, 'Matt Hancock kissing video leak sparks fears of bugged UK government offices', *South China Morning Post*, 1 July 2021, https://www.scmp.com/news/world/europe/article/3139457/matt-hancock-kissing-video-leak-sparks-fears-bugged-uk-government

34 Helen Warrell and Nic Fildes, 'UK spies warn local government over "smart city" tech risks', *Financial Times*, 7 May 2021.

https://www.ft.com/content/46d35d62-0307-41d8-96a8-de9b52bf0ec3?shareType=nongift

35 Ian Levy's 7 May 2021 blog post, 'Connected places: new NCSC security principles for "Smart Cities"', can be accessed via the website of the National Cyber Security Centre. https://www.ncsc.gov.uk/blog-post/connected-places-new-ncsc-security-principles-for-smart-cities

36 James Hurley, 'Foreign takeover rules on national security eased for fear of losing overseas investors', *The Times*, 12 April 2021. https://www.thetimes.co.uk/article/foreign-takeover-rules-on-national-security-eased-for-fear-of-losing-overseas-investors-ms5np2dgp

37 Charles Parton, 'How to counter China. Britain needs a proper strategy', *The Spectator*, 22 October 2021. https://www.spectator.co.uk/article/how-to-counter-china

38 Mark Sweney, 'Chinese-owned firm acquires UK's largest semiconductor manufacturer', *The Guardian*, 5 July 2021. https://www.theguardian.com/business/2021/jul/05/chinese-owned-firm-acquires-uks-largest-semiconductor-manufacturer

39 See the UK government press release, 'Dedicated government team to protect researchers' work from hostile activity', 25 May 2021. https://www.gov.uk/government/news/dedicated-government-team-to-protect-researchers-work-from-hostile-activity

40 Universities UK International, *International Facts and Figures 2019*, July 2019. https://www.universitiesuk.ac.uk/policy-and-analysis/reports/Pages/Intl-facts-figs-19.aspx

41 Radomir Tylecote and Robert Clarke, 'Inadvertently arming China? The Chinese military complex and its potential exploitation of scientific research at UK universities', Civitas, February 2021. https://www.civitas.org.uk/publications/inadvertently-arming-china/

42 George Greenwood, Fiona Hamilton and Charlie Parker, 'British research "could help China build superweapons"', *The Times*, 4 February 2022. https://www.thetimes.co.uk/article/cdbc1624-85d6-11ec-a9c8-2dfad00a5965?shareToken=18c835a40b3c9018104fe3c535900945

43 Bethan Staton, Helen Warrell and Jasmine Cameron-Chileshe, 'UK academics struggle with stricter security on China partnerships', *Financial Times*, 20 February 2021. https://www.ft.com/content/ce587d32-1c1e-4f03-93bd-846379ed993d

44 Oxford Economics, 'The Economic Impact of Huawei in the UK', May 2019. The highlights plus the full report commissioned by Huawei are available via the Huawei website. https://www.huawei.com/uk/press-events/news/uk/2019/huawei-investment-commitments-in-uk-leads-to-billions-in-benefits-to-the-economy

45 Nic Fildes, 'Huawei buys access to UK innovation with Oxford stake', *Financial Times*, 2 October 2019. https://www.ft.com/content/28892c04-e453-11e9-b112-9624ec9edc59

46 Bethan Staton and Laura Hughes, 'Cambridge sets guidelines to reduce overseas engagement risks', *Financial Times*, 1 October 2021. https://www.ft.com/content/96d1efb7-49fc-49bb-b432-56dbcc18919a

47 See the statement and photograph on the Chinese embassy website, 'Ambassador Liu Xiaoming Meets with Stephen Toope, the New Vice-Chancellor of the University of Cambridge', 23 November 2017. https://www.chinese-embassy.org.uk/eng/ambassador/t1516053.htm

48 Gu Zhenqui, Gui Tao and Peter Barker, 'Interview: Cambridge seeks closer ties with China', *Xinhua* news agency, 22 March 2018. http://www.xinhuanet.com/english/2018-03/22/c_137057021.htm

49 See the Cambridge University press release, 'Cambridge and Nanjing break ground on "smart cities" Centre', 16 September 2019. https://www.eng.cam.ac.uk/news/cambridge-and-nanjing-break-ground-smart-cities-centre

50 Luke May, 'Cambridge University received "generous gift" from Chinese software giant with links to country's spy agency to fund engineering fellowship', *Mail Online*, 11 February 2021. https://www.dailymail.co.uk/news/article-9245151/Cambridge-University-received-generous-gift-Chinese-software-giant-Tencent.html

51 See Cambridge University's Department of Engineering 10 September 2019 press statement announcing the 'generous gift' from Tencent, 'A new postgraduate research fellowship in the Department of Engineering to be funded by Tencent'. https://www.eng.cam.ac.uk/news/new-postdoctoral-research-fellowship-department-engineering-be-funded-tencent

52 There are many sources for information about the role of WeChat (Weixin in China) in censorship and control. A good primer is provided in a 7 May 2020 paper, 'WeChat surveillance explained'

by Miles Kenyon and published by Citizen Lab, a University of Toronto group studying internet censorship. https://citizenlab.ca/2020/05/wechat-surveillance-explained/

53 See Cambridge University's 9 March 2021 press statement, announcing the start of work on the new building and giving details of its funding, 'Cambridge Institute for Sustainability Leadership. World-first sustainable office retrofit begins at new University of Cambridge Institute for Sustainability Leadership headquarters'. https://www.cisl.cam.ac.uk/news/news-items/entopia-building

54 See the Huawei press release, 'Cambridge Wireless and Huawei to partner to build the first private 5G testbed in Cambridge Science Park', 11 November 2020. https://www.huawei.com/uk/news/uk/2020/cambridge%20wireless%20partnership

55 See Trinity College, Cambridge, press release, 'Landmark Joint Venture at Cambridge Science Park', 1 February 2018. https://www.trin.cam.ac.uk/news/landmark-joint-venture-at-cambridge-science-park/

56 BBC Online, 'Xu Zhangrun: Outspoken professor detained in China', 6 July 2020. https://www.bbc.co.uk/news/world-asia-china-53306280

57 Christian Shepherd, 'Fear and oppression in Xinjiang: China's war on Uighur culture', *Financial Times*, 12 September 2019. https://www.ft.com/content/48508182-d426-11e9-8367-807ebd53ab77

58 James Cook and Morgan Meaker, 'Why Cambridge's Silicon Fen is fast becoming Europe's answer to California', *The Telegraph*, 30 April 2021. https://www.telegraph.co.uk/technology/2021/04/30/cambridges-silicon-fen-fast-becoming-europes-answer-california/

59 BBC Online, 'Trump administration claims Huawei "backed by Chinese military"', 25 June 2020. https://www.bbc.co.uk/news/business-53172057

60 See the Huawei press release on the day that planning permission was granted, 'Huawei to Build an Optoelectronics RnD and Manufacturing Centre in Cambridge', 25 June 2020. https://www.huawei.com/uk/news/uk/2020/huawei%20to%20build%20an%20optoelectronics%20rnd%20and%20manufacturing%20centre%20in%20cambridge

61 Harry Goodwin, 'Stephen Toope: Blind to Tyranny', *The Cambridge Student*, 28 May 2020. https://www.tcs.cam.ac.uk/stephen-toope-blind-to-tyranny/

62 Sam Dunning, Martin Williams, Peter Geoghegan and Gabriel Pogrund, 'Cambridge professor whose role was "funded by China" cautioned against Uyghur debate', Open Democracy, 5 June 2021. https://www.opendemocracy.net/en/dark-money-investigations/cambridge-professor-role-funded-by-china-cautioned-uyghur-debate-peter-nolan/
63 See the website of the Chinese embassy in London, 'Ambassador Zheng Zeguang Meets with British Scholar Peter Nolan', 20 August 2021. http://uk.china-embassy.org/eng/ambassador/t1901770.htm
64 See the website of Jesus College, Cambridge, which gives details of the Chinese Executive Leadership Programme as part of a biography of Professor Peter Nolan, the programme's director. https://www.jesus.cam.ac.uk/people/peter-nolan
65 Sasi Valaiyapathi, 'Protesters take to street over Carrie Lam's Wolfson Fellowship', *Varsity*, 16 November 2019. https://www.varsity.co.uk/news/18287
66 Christy Leung, 'National security law: Hong Kong leader Carrie Lam cuts ties with University of Cambridge's Wolfson College', *South China Morning Post*, 16 August 2020. https://www.scmp.com/print/news/hong-kong/politics/article/3097527/national-security-law-hong-kong-leader-carrie-lam-cuts-ties
67 Laura Mannering, 'Hong Kong students in UK call for action over pro-China threats and harassment', *Hong Kong Free Press*, 26 November 2019. https://hongkongfp.com/2019/11/26/hong-kong-students-uk-call-action-pro-china-threats-harassment/
68 Christopher Dorrell, 'Cambridge University attempts to navigate new era of China relations', *Varsity*, 12 March 2021. https://www.varsity.co.uk/news/21016
69 Dan Sabbagh, 'MI5 accuses lawyer of trying to influence politicians on behalf of China', *The Guardian*, 13 January 2022. https://www.theguardian.com/uk-news/2022/jan/13/chinese-national-trying-to-improperly-influence-politicians-says-mi5
70 A full transcript of Richard Moore's 30 November 2021 speech to the International Institute for Strategic Studies can be accessed via the UK government website. https://www.gov.uk/government/speeches/cs-speech-to-the-international-institute-for-strategic-studies
71 House of Lords International Relations and Defence Committee, 'The UK and China's security and trade relationship: A strategic

void', 10 September 2021. https://publications.parliament.uk/pa/ld5802/ldselect/ldintrel/62/62.pdf

72 Ibid., p. 5.

73 Patrick Wintour, 'Seven former foreign secretaries urge UK to take lead on Hong Kong', *The Guardian*, 1 June 2020. https://www.theguardian.com/world/2020/jun/01/seven-former-foreign-secretaries-urge-uk-to-take-lead-on-hong-kong

74 Hong Kong Watch, 'MPs and Hong Kong Student Leaders call for UK to extend visa rights and to consider Magnitsky sanctions of Hong Kong officials at Parliamentary event', 9 September 2019. https://www.hongkongwatch.org/all-posts/2019/9/9/mps-and-hong-kong-student-leaders-call-for-uk-to-extend-visa-rights-and-to-consider-magnitsky-sanctions-of-hong-kong-officials-at-parliamentary-event

75 These remarks were made during a parliamentary debate on the Aukus defence partnership on 16 September 2021, and the full debate can be accessed via Hansard at the UK parliament website. https://hansard.parliament.uk/commons/2021-09-16/debates/4835BC3D-E0BF-43E0-9A3B-9BCC5B77DF7F/AUKUS

76 BBC Online, 'Uighurs: China bans UK MPs after abuse sanctions', 26 March 2021. https://www.bbc.com/news/uk-56532569

77 Reuters, 'UK parliament declares genocide in China's Xinjiang; Beijing condemns move', 22 April 2021. https://www.reuters.com/world/uk/uk-parliament-declares-genocide-chinas-xinjiang-raises-pressure-johnson-2021-04-22/

78 Matt Dathan, 'Liz Truss pulls no punches about "genocide" of Uighurs by China', *The Times*, 1 November 2021. https://www.thetimes.co.uk/article/0d292eb6-3a8a-11ec-9bef-aa3112940013?shareToken=644e66d29384f91e6ab370baa5fd6e3b

79 Ben Riley-Smith, 'Liz Truss: "Thatcher's devotion to democracy inspires me to tackle today's global challenges"', *The Telegraph*, 22 October 2021. https://www.telegraph.co.uk/politics/2021/10/22/liz-truss-thatchers-devotion-democracy-inspires-tackle-todays/

80 Helen Cahill, 'Rishi Sunak bids to reset China relations to boost trade', *Sunday Telegraph*, 30 January 2022. https://www.telegraph.co.uk/business/2022/01/29/rishi-sunak-bids-reset-china-relations-boost-trade/

81 Jim Pickard, 'Boris Johnson seeks to forge closer economic ties with China', *Financial Times*, 11 February 2022. https://www.

ft.com/content/321ffeaf-58b7-4ed5-a367-4d175edbab8a?shareType=nongift

82 Louise Watt, 'China hits out at irresponsible Liz Truss over remarks on Hong Kong rights', *The Telegraph*, 25 October 2021. https://www.telegraph.co.uk/world-news/2021/10/25/china-hits-irresponsible-liz-truss-remarks-hong-kong-rights/

83 'New kids on the cell block', *The Economist*, 13 November 2021. https://www.economist.com/china/2021/11/11/behind-bars-hong-kongs-democrats-remain-popular

84 Jonathan White, 'Hong Kong marathon, first event of its kind since pandemic hit, marred by injuries, allegations of censorship', *South China Morning Post*, 24 October 2021. https://www.scmp.com/news/hong-kong/society/article/3153499/hong-kong-marathon-first-event-its-kind-pandemic-hit-marred

85 Peter Simpson, 'London's new Chinese embassy attracts controversy and protests as Sino-British relations worsen', *South China Morning Post*, 29 November 2020. https://www.scmp.com/magazines/post-magazine/long-reads/article/3111447/londons-new-chinese-embassy-attracts-controversy

86 Gabriel Pogrund and Emanuele Midolo, 'Revealed: Johnson's aide Edward Lister linked to both sides in Chinese embassy deal', *The Sunday Times*, 7 February 2021. https://www.thetimes.co.uk/article/revealed-johnsons-aide-edward-lister-linked-to-both-sides-in-chinese-embassy-deal-tswqbpz62

87 See the 6 July 2018 statement on the Chinese embassy website, 'Ambassador Liu Xiaoming Meets with Sir Edward Lister, Non-Executive Director at the Foreign & Commonwealth Office'. http://www.chinese-embassy.org.uk/eng/ambassador/t1575365.htm

88 Jim Pickard and George Hammond, 'Double life of Johnson's ally raises awkward conflict of interest questions', *Financial Times*, 30 April 2021. https://www.ft.com/content/4382aa0f-4784-4b21-a775-c87091f9ba31

89 Ibid.

90 Jim Dunton, 'Former No. 10 chief of staff cleared to work at HSBC', *Civil Service World*, 22 September 2021. https://www.civilserviceworld.com/news/article/former-no10-chief-of-staff-cleared-to-work-at-hsbc

91 Mike Brooke, 'Pressure on China's Royal Mint embassy plans at Tower Hill over plight of its Uighur Muslims', *East London*

*Advertiser*, 30 September 2020. https://www.eastlondonadvertiser.co.uk/news/local-council/china-royal-mint-embassy-3673428

92 Louisa Clarence-Smith, 'Tower Hamlets objects to New Chinese embassy after Uighur crackdown', *The Times*, 16 November 2020. https://www.thetimes.co.uk/article/tower-hamlets-objects-to-new-china-embassy-after-uighur-crackdown-x8h7m9dgr

93 Haroon Siddique, 'Tiananmen Square, Uyghur Court: Tower Hamlets plans name changes in solidarity', *The Guardian*, 19 March 2021. https://www.theguardian.com/uk-news/2021/mar/19/uyghur-court-hong-kong-road-tower-hamlets-plans-name-changes-in-solidarity

94 Sophia Yan, 'Chinese state broadcaster hires former Ofcom director amid investigation', *The Telegraph*, 11 July 2019. https://www.telegraph.co.uk/news/2019/07/11/chinese-state-broadcaster-hires-former-ofcom-director-amid-investigation/

95 Charlotte Tobitt, 'Ofcom to investigate claim Chinese broadcaster aired forced confessions on UK TV', *Press Gazette*, 9 May 2019. https://www.pressgazette.co.uk/ofcom-to-investigate-claim-chinese-state-broadcaster-aired-forced-confession-on-uk-tv/

96 See Ofcom's press release, 'Ofcom revokes CGTN's licence to broadcast in the UK', 4 February 2021. https://www.ofcom.org.uk/about-ofcom/latest/media/media-releases/2021/ofcom-revokes-cgtn-licence-to-broadcast-in-uk

97 Patrick Wintour, 'China bans BBC World News in retaliation for UK licence blow', *The Guardian*, 11 February 2021. https://www.theguardian.com/world/2021/feb/11/china-bans-bbc-world-news

98 See the statement from Safeguard Defenders, 'No, CGTN is not really back on the air in the UK', 24 August 2021. https://safeguarddefenders.com/en/blog/no-cgtn-not-really-back-air-uk

99 Ben Woods, 'How China's propaganda station CGTN made a surprise return to British screens', *The Telegraph*, 23 August 2021. https://www.telegraph.co.uk/business/2021/08/23/chinas-propaganda-station-cgtn-made-surprise-return-british/

100 Latika Bourke, 'I wouldn't sign a China trade deal now: Tony Abbott', *The Sydney Morning Herald*, 28 July 2021. https://www.smh.com.au/world/europe/i-wouldn-t-sign-a-china-trade-deal-now-tony-abbott-20210728-p58dif.html

101 The full transcript of Tony Abbott's 21 July 2021 keynote speech is available on the Policy Exchange website: https://policyexchange.org.uk/pxevents/strategic-trade/

## Chapter 14:
## Standing up to China: Lessons from Aussie 'Scumbags' and 'Tiny, Crazy' Lithuanians

1 Frank Chung, 'Senior diplomat labels Australians who criticise China "scumbags", embassy omits insult in English', news.com.au, 4 March 2021. https://www.news.com.au/technology/innovation/military/senior-diplomat-warns-australians-who-make-enemies-of-china-will-be-cast-aside-in-history/news-story/d2f7f25cc5723a2873cc929e889e9814

2 'GT Voice: Australia in over its head with provocative action', *Global Times*, 22 April 2021. https://www.globaltimes.cn/page/202104/1221840.shtml

3 Chen Qingqing and Liu Xin, 'Australia gets "slap to the face" as global community welcomes China-sponsored resolution of COVID-19', *Global Times*, 19 May 2020. https://www.globaltimes.cn/content/1188817.shtml

4 Lily Kuo, 'Australia called "gum stuck to China's shoe" by state media in coronavirus investigation stoush', *The Guardian*, 28 April 2020. https://www.theguardian.com/world/2020/apr/28/australia-called-gum-stuck-to-chinas-shoe-by-state-media-in-coronavirus-investigation-stoush

5 Richard McGregor, 'Australia can teach the UK a lesson in Chinese wrath', *Financial Times*, 19 March 2021. https://www.ft.com/content/b3b77c27-329e-41ac-be6b-f7cc1436177d?shareType=nongift

6 Daniel Hurst, 'How much is China's trade war really costing Australia?' *The Guardian*, 28 October 2020. https://www.theguardian.com/australia-news/2020/oct/28/how-much-is-chinas-trade-war-really-costing-australia

7 *Global Times*, 22 April 2021.

8 Daniel Hurst, 'Cyber-attack Australia: sophisticated attacks from "state-backed actor", says PM', *The Guardian*, 19 June 2020. https://www.theguardian.com/australia-news/2020/jun/19/australia-cyber-attack-attacks-hack-state-based-actor-says-australian-prime-minister-scott-morrison

9 Jamie Tarabay, 'How Hackers Hammered Australia After China Ties Turned Sour', Bloomberg, 30 August 2021. https://www.bloomberg.com/news/features/2021-08-30/covid-origin-probe-calls-australian-government-businesses-universities-hacked

10 Jamie Seidel, 'China's "major" Australian miscalculation', news.

com.au, 21 November 2020. https://www.news.com.au/world/asia/chinas-major-australian-miscalculation/news-story/95a402febde3b2842d2dfd101019e28d

11 'Australia should firmly face crux of current setback: Chinese FM', *Global Times*, 19 November 2020. https://www.globaltimes.cn/content/1207410.shtml

12 Jason Scott, 'Australia PM Defiant After China Airs 14 Grievances', Bloomberg, 19 November 2020. https://www.bloombergquint.com/politics/morrison-defiant-after-china-airs-14-grievances-with-australia

13 Erin Handley, 'Pretty Woman or Godzilla? Two former PMs weigh in on Australia's frosty relationship with China', ABC News, 11 August 2021. https://www.abc.net.au/news/2021-08-11/rudd-and-turnbull-on-china-australia-relationship/100368978

14 McGregor, *Financial Times*, 19 March 2021.

15 Laurie Oakes, 'US fury over Darwin port lease to Chinese is no surprise', news.com.au, 20 November 2015. https://www.news.com.au/us-fury-over-darwin-port-lease-to-chinese-is-no-surprise/news-story/a4bf7a3385e4c077757d626dd4659a3a

16 Angus Grigg, 'China's "invisible billionaire" – the Port of Darwin's new owner', *Australian Financial Review*, 23 November 2015. https://www.afr.com/world/chinas-invisible-billionaire--the-port-of-darwins-new-owner-20151122-gl4rtn

17 Philip Wen, 'New Darwin port group's militia links to China's military', *The Sydney Morning Herald*, 17 November 2015. https://www.smh.com.au/business/new-darwin-port-owners-militia-links-to-chinas-military-20151117-gl1b4y.html

18 Geoff Wade, 'Landbridge, Darwin and the PRC', *The Strategist*, 9 November 2015. https://www.aspistrategist.org.au/landbridge-darwin-and-the-prc/

19 ABC News, 'Darwin Port deal with Chinese company could be reviewed as think-tank claims of a "Communist Party front" slammed by NT chief minister', 13 November 2015. https://www.abc.net.au/news/2015-11-13/treasurer-signals-possible-review-of-chinese-port-deal/6939958

20 News Corp Australia Network, 'Chinese president Xi Jinping signs free-trade deal with Australia after addressing parliament', 17 November 2014. https://www.news.com.au/national/chinese-president-xi-jinping-signs-freetrade-deal-with-australia-after-

addressing-parliament/news-story/f22f2856fbac5ca573aec2c33 85bf3d0

21 Daniel Hurst, 'China lambasts Tony Abbott for "despicable and insane performance in Taiwan"', *The Guardian*, 10 October 2021. https://www.theguardian.com/australia-news/2021/oct/10/china-lambasts-tony-abbott-for-despicable-and-insane-performance-in-taiwan

22 Reuters, 'Australia reviewing lease of Darwin port to Chinese firm – source', 3 May 2021. https://www.reuters.com/world/asia-pacific/australia-review-lease-port-chinese-firm-media-report-2021-05-02/

23 Daniel Hurst, 'Darwin port's Chinese owner says it will cooperate with Australian defence review', *The Guardian*, 3 May 2021. https://www.theguardian.com/australia-news/2021/may/03/darwin-ports-chinese-owner-says-it-will-cooperate-with-australi an-defence-review

24 Hugh White, 'America or China? Australia is fooling itself that it doesn't have to choose', *The Guardian*, 26 November 2017. https://www.theguardian.com/australia-news/2017/nov/27/america-or-china-were-fooling-ourselves-that-we-dont-have-to-choose

25 Paul Karp, 'Coalition bill to ban foreign political donations passes senate', *The Guardian*, 15 November 2018. https://www.theguardian.com/australia-news/2018/nov/15/coalition-bill-to-ban-foreign-political-donations-passes-senate

26 'How China's sharp power is muting criticism abroad', *The Economist*, 14 December 2017. https://www.economist.com/briefing/2017/12/14/how-chinas-sharp-power-is-muting-criticism-abroad

27 Katharine Murphy, 'Sam Dastyari told to resign from Senate position after China revelations', *The Guardian*, 29 November 2017. https://www.theguardian.com/australia-news/2017/nov/30/sam-dastyari-told-to-resign-from-senate-positions-after-china-revelation

28 Taken from Prime Minister Malcom Turnbull's speech introducing the National Security Legislation Amendment (Espionage and Foreign Interference) Bill 2017, 7 December 2017. Full text is available on Turnbull's website. https://www.malcolmturnbull.com.au/media/speech-introducing-the-national-security-legisla tion-amendment-espionage-an

29 Colin Packman, 'Australian spy chief warns of "unprecedented" foreign espionage threat', Reuters, 24 February 2020. https://www.reuters.com/article/us-australia-security/australia-spy-chief-warns-of-unprecedented-foreign-espionage-threat-idUSKCN20I1CY

30 Salvatore Babones, 'The China Student Boom and the Risks It Poses to Australian Universities', The Centre for Independent Studies, August 2019. https://www.cis.org.au/app/uploads/2019/08/ap5.pdf

31 Sophie McNeil, 'They Don't Understand the Fear We Have: How China's Long Reach of Repression Undermines Academic Freedom at Australia's Universities', Human Rights Watch, 30 June 2021. https://www.hrw.org/report/2021/06/30/they-dont-understand-fear-we-have/how-chinas-long-reach-repression-undermines

32 Sophie Williams, 'The students calling out China on Australia's campuses', BBC Online, 25 June 2021. https://www.bbc.com/news/world-australia-56478621

33 Alex Joske, Lin Li, Alexandra Pascoe and Nathan Attrill, 'The influence environment. A survey of Chinese language media in Australia', Australian Strategic Policy Institute, December 2020. https://s3-ap-southeast-2.amazonaws.com/ad-aspi/2020-12/The%20influence%20environment.pdf

34 Helen Chan and Wei Wang, '"Trapped in an information vortex": Why banning WeChat in Australia may not be as easy as it sounds', SBS, 25 August 2020. https://www.sbs.com.au/chinese/english/trapped-in-an-information-vortex-why-banning-wechat-in-australia-may-not-be-as-easy-as-it-sounds

35 Jack Norton, 'Australian call for Covid-19 inquiry like Brutus knifing Caesar: China's deputy ambassador', *The Strategist*, 26 August 2020. https://www.aspistrategist.org.au/australian-call-for-covid-19-inquiry-like-brutus-knifing-caesar-chinas-deputy-ambassador/

36 Frances Mao, 'How reliant is Australia on China?' BBC Online, 17 July 2020. https://www.bbc.co.uk/news/world-australia-52915879

37 Ji Siqi and Su-Lin Tan, 'China–Australia relations: how smuggled lobsters take "grey channels" to Chinese plates via Hong Kong', *South China Morning Post*, 7 July 2021. https://www.scmp.com/print/economy/china-economy/article/3140019/china-australia-relations-how-smuggled-lobsters-take-grey

38 Bernard Lagan, 'Australia gets around wine war with China via soaring exports to Hong Kong', *The Times*, 22 July 2021. https://www.thetimes.co.uk/article/australian-wine-gets-around-tariff-war-with-china-with-soaring-exports-to-hong-kong-6wwnr7h75

39 Jamie Smyth, 'Australia shrugs off China trade dispute and opens new markets', *Financial Times*, 26 May 2021. https://www.ft.com/content/95ad03ce-f012-49e9-a0c2-6e9e95353dd1

40 Brianna McKee, 'Australian exports to China set new records in first half of 2021', Sky News, 15 July 2021. https://www.skynews.com.au/world-news/china/australian-exports-to-china-set-new-records-in-first-half-of-2021/news-story/28be306f765a69fc42dbd20c13d7d80d

41 Reuters, 'Australian files WTO complaint against China over wine duties', 28 June 2021. https://www.reuters.com/world/americas/australia-files-wto-complaint-against-china-over-wine-duties-2021-06-28/

42 Eryk Bagshaw and Anthony Galloway, '"Firmly and forcefully": China threatens Australia over Belt and Road decision', *The Sydney Morning Herald*, 22 April 2021. https://www.smh.com.au/politics/federal/firmly-and-forcefully-china-threatens-australian-over-belt-and-road-decision-20210422-p57lia.html

43 Kirsty Needham, 'Australia faces down China in high stakes strategy', Reuters, 4 September 2020. https://www.reuters.com/investigates/special-report/australia-china-relations/

44 Julia Hollingsworth and Ben Westcott, 'A Pacific nation's Covid-19 crisis has become a political power play between China and Australia', CNN, 19 July 2021. https://edition.cnn.com/2021/07/18/asia/papua-new-guinea-china-vaccines-intl-hnk-dst/index.html

45 Jonathan Pearlman, 'Australia moves to block China from buying Pacific telco', *Straits Times*, 31 July 2021. https://www.straitstimes.com/asia/australianz/australia-moves-to-block-china-from-buying-pacific-telco

46 See Lowy Institute 2021 poll, 'Trust in global powers', available at https://poll.lowyinstitute.org/charts/trust-in-global-powers

47 See Lowy Institute 2021 poll, 'China: economic partner or security threat?' available at https://poll.lowyinstitute.org/charts/china-economic-partner-or-security-threat

48 'China condemns opening of Taiwan office in Lithuania as

"egregious act"', *The Guardian*, 19 November 2019. https://www.theguardian.com/world/2021/nov/19/china-condemns-opening-of-taiwan-office-in-lithuania-as-egregious-act

49 Hu Xijin, 'Lithuania will pay the price for making radical moves over the Taiwan question', *Global Times*, 10 August 2021. https://www.globaltimes.cn/page/202108/1231087.shtml

50 'China would rather be feared than defied', *The Economist*, 28 August 2021. https://www.economist.com/china/2021/08/26/china-would-rather-be-feared-than-defied

51 Kathrin Hille, Richard Milne and Demetri Sevastopulo, 'Lithuania pulls diplomats from China as row deepens over Taiwan ties', *Financial Times*, 15 December 2021. https://www.ft.com/content/587cff8f-3a7f-45c3-b4c7-8ac6f3e0aa9c?shareType=nongift

52 Stuart Lau, 'Lithuania sends jabs to Taiwan amid pressure from Beijing', *Politico*, 22 June 2021. https://www.politico.eu/article/lithuania-sends-jabs-to-taiwan-amid-pressure-from-beijing/

53 Stuart Lau, 'Lithuania pulls out of China's "17+1" bloc in Eastern Europe', *Politico*, 21 May 2021. https://www.politico.eu/article/lithuania-pulls-out-china-17-1-bloc-eastern-central-europe-foreign-minister-gabrielius-landsbergis/

54 BBC Online, 'Lithuania urges people to throw away Chinese phones', 22 September 2021. https://www.bbc.com/news/technology-58652249

55 Baltic News Service, 'Lithuania blocks Chinese tech at airports over security concerns', LRT, 17 February 2021. https://www.lrt.lt/en/news-in-english/19/1346778/lithuania-blocks-chinese-tech-at-airports-over-security-concerns

56 'China's push for Lithuanian port poses risk to NATO', LRT, 26 November 2019. https://www.lrt.lt/en/news-in-english/19/1119707/china-s-push-for-lithuanian-port-poses-risk-to-nato

57 Andrius Sytas, 'Lithuanian parliament latest to call China's treatment of Uyghurs "genocide"', Reuters, 20 May 2021. https://www.reuters.com/world/china/lithuanian-parliament-latest-call-chinas-treatment-uyghurs-genocide-2021-05-20/

58 Andrius Sytas, 'Lithuania raps Chinese diplomats for role at pro-Hong Kong protest', Reuters, 2 September 2019. https://www.reuters.com/article/us-lithuania-china-idUSKCN1VN1GV

59 Liudas Dapkus, 'Lithuania outraged by Chinese tourist's removal

of HK cross', Associated Press, 30 December 2019. https://apnews.com/article/7ee8dc0ea88df720118048e1b1732738

60 Andrew Higgins, 'Lithuania vs. China: A Baltic Minnow Defies a Rising Superpower', *New York Times*, 2 October 2021. https://www.nytimes.com/2021/09/30/world/europe/lithuania-china-disputes.html?referringSource=articleShare

61 Ibid.

62 John O'Donnell and Andrius Sytas, 'Exclusive: Lithuania braces itself for China-led corporate boycott', Reuters, 9 December 2021. https://www.reuters.com/world/china/exclusive-lithuania-braces-china-led-corporate-boycott-2021-12-09/

63 Ibid.

64 Robbie Gramer, 'Pressured by China, Lithuania won't back down over Taiwan', *Foreign Policy*, 7 September 2021. https://foreignpolicy.com/2021/09/07/lithuania-taiwan-china-dispute-geopolitics-europe-landsbergis/

65 Keith Johnson and Jack Detsch, 'Australia Draws a Line on China', *Foreign Affairs*, 4 May 2021. https://foreignpolicy.com/2021/05/04/australia-china-defense-tariffs-policy-taiwan-us/

66 Peter Hartcher, 'Australia leads world on standing up to China, Blinken says', *The Sydney Morning Herald*, 10 February 2022. https://www.smh.com.au/national/australia-leads-world-on-standing-up-to-china-blinken-says-20220210-p59vhd.html

67 Georgi Kantchev and Stu Woo, 'Taiwan Gains Favor in Europe's East, Angering China', *Wall Street Journal*, 26 October 2021. https://www.wsj.com/articles/taiwan-gains-favor-in-europes-east-angering-china-11635248811

68 Stuart Lau, 'Slovenia to bolster trade ties with Taiwan, wading into row with China', *Politico*, 18 January 2022. https://www.politico.eu/article/jansa-slovenia-to-follow-lithuania-for-new-office-in-taiwan/

69 Eleni Varvitsioti, 'Piraeus port deal intensifies Greece's unease over China links', *Financial Times*, 19 October 2021. https://www.ft.com/content/3e91c6d2-c3ff-496a-91e8-b9c81aed6eb8

70 Vincent Ni, 'EU parliament "freezes" China trade deal over sanctions', *The Guardian*, 20 May 2021. https://www.theguardian.com/world/2021/may/20/eu-parliament-freezes-china-trade-deal-over-sanctions

71 Reuters, 'EU plan for anti-coercion trade measures faces scepticism',

7 December 2021. https://www.reuters.com/business/eu-plan-anti-coercion-trade-measure-faces-scepticism-2021-12-07/

72 Reuters, 'China pressuring German car parts giant Continental to cut links with Lithuania, sources say', *South China Morning Post*, 17 December 2021. https://www.scmp.com/news/china/diplomacy/article/3160174/china-pressuring-german-car-parts-giant-continental-cut-links

73 Andrius Sytas and John O'Donnell, 'Analysis: German big business piles pressure on Lithuania in China row', Reuters, 21 January 2021. https://www.reuters.com/world/europe/german-big-business-piles-pressure-lithuania-china-row-2022-01-21/

74 Peter Martin, *China's Civilian Army: The making of wolf warrior diplomacy* (New York: Oxford University Press, 2021), p. 137.

75 'Lithuania, Australia won't be only victims if China not stopped – Landsbergis', *The Baltic Times*, 9 February 2022. https://www.baltictimes.com/lithuania__australia_won_t_be_only_victims__if_china_s_not_stropped___landsbergis/

76 Erin Handley, 'Pretty Woman or Godzilla? Two former PMs weigh in on Australia's frosty relationship with China', ABC News, 11 August 2021. https://www.abc.net.au/news/2021-08-11/rudd-and-turnbull-on-china-australia-relationship/100368978

77 Reuters, 'Lithuania says its rocky ties with China are a "wake-up call" for Europe', 4 November 2021. https://www.reuters.com/world/europe/lithuania-says-its-rocky-ties-with-china-are-wake-up-call-europe-2021-11-03/

## Chapter 15: Peak China: The Future of the Chinese Communist Party

1 Cissy Zhou, 'China power crisis: thermal coal inventory nears record low as country suffers worst outages in a decade', *South China Morning Post*, 29 September 2021. https://www.scmp.com/economy/china-economy/article/3150457/china-power-crisis-thermal-coal-inventory-nears-record-low

2 Lauri Myllyvirta, 'The Real Reasons Behind China's Energy Crisis', *Foreign Policy*, 7 October 2021. https://foreignpolicy.com/2021/10/07/china-energy-crisis-electricity-coal-pricing-renewables/

3 Reuters, 'China coal prices plunge from record high as government

considers intervention', 19 October 2021. https://www.reuters.com/business/energy/china-coal-prices-drop-record-high-govt-weighs-intervention-2021-10-19/

4 Eamon Barrett, 'China burned over half the world's coal last year, in spite of Xi Jinping's net-zero pledge', *Fortune*, 29 March 2021. https://fortune.com/2021/03/29/china-coal-energy-electricity-xi-jinping-2020-ember/

5 Ben Webster, 'China's coal use offsets global cuts', *The Times*, 7 April 2021. https://www.thetimes.co.uk/article/c1902b48-96fc-11eb-934d-93ce24b2a1c4?shareToken=4b563292951bb5c12e0f2c88557ce069

6 Vincent Ni and Helen Sullivan, '"Big line in the sand": China promises no new coal-fired power projects abroad', *The Guardian*, 22 September 2021. https://www.theguardian.com/world/2021/sep/22/china-climate-no-new-coal-fired-power-projects-abroad-xi-jinping

7 Vasuki Shastry, 'China's Electricity Crisis – Don't Blame It On Renewables', *Forbes*, 15 October 2021. https://www.forbes.com/sites/vasukishastry/2021/10/15/chinas-electricity-crisis-dont-blame-it-on-renewables/?sh=4e7805e33ca4

8 Shi Jiangtao, 'Climate crisis: China's all or nothing stand on talks leaves John Kerry cornered', *South China Morning Post*, 7 September 2021. https://www.scmp.com/news/china/diplomacy/article/3147854/climate-crisis-chinas-all-or-nothing-stand-talks-leaves-john

9 'GT Voice: Glasgow climate conference can't be highjacked by the US', *Global Times*, 6 September 2021. https://www.globaltimes.cn/page/202109/1233495.shtml

10 Leslie Hook, Camilla Hodgson and Jim Pickard, 'India and China weaken pledge to phase out coal as COP26 ends', *Financial Times*, 13 November 2021. https://www.ft.com/content/471c7db9-925f-479e-ad57-09162310a21a

11 BBC Online, 'China floods: 12 dead in Zhengzhou train and thousands evacuated in Henan', 21 July 2021. https://www.bbc.com/news/world-asia-china-57861067

12 Steven Lee Myers and Chris Buckley, 'Xi hasn't left China in 21 months. Covid May Be Only Part of the Reason', *New York Times*, 30 October 2021. https://www.nytimes.com/2021/10/30/world/asia/china-xi-jinping-g20.html

13 Agence France-Presse, 'China locks down city of 4m people after six Covid cases detected', *The Guardian*, 26 October 2021. https://www.theguardian.com/world/2021/oct/26/china-locks-down-city-lanzhou-gansu-covid

14 Natasha Khan and Erich Schwartzel, 'China Locks 30,000 Visitors Inside Shanghai Disneyland After One Guest Gets Covid-19', *Wall Street Journal*, 1 November 2021. https://www.wsj.com/articles/shanghai-disneyland-suspends-operations-as-visitors-queue-for-covid-19-tests-before-exiting-11635755117

15 BBC Online, 'Public shaming returns amid Covid fears', 29 December 2021. https://www.bbc.co.uk/news/world-asia-china-59818971

16 Li Yuan, 'The Army of Millions Who Enforce China's Zero-Covid Policy at All Costs', *New York Times*, 13 January 2022. https://www.nytimes.com/2022/01/12/business/china-zero-covid-policy-xian.html?referringSource=articleShare

17 Nectar Gan, 'Xi's China is closing to the world. And it isn't just about borders', CNN, 16 November 2021. https://edition.cnn.com/2021/11/14/china/china-border-closure-inward-turn-dst-intl-hnk/index.html

18 Orange Wang, 'China sparks fear about Taiwan tensions, food shortages, after families urged to stockpile "daily necessities"', *South China Morning Post*, 2 November 2021. https://www.scmp.com/print/economy/china-economy/article/3154603/china-sparks-fear-about-taiwan-tensions-food-shortages-after

19 Martin Farrer, 'China property market rocked as Evergrande struggles to repay $300bn debts', *The Guardian*, 9 September 2021. https://www.theguardian.com/world/2021/sep/09/china-property-market-evergrande-300bn-debt-share-slump

20 Alexander Stevenson and Cao Li, 'Evergrande Gave Workers a Choice: Lend Us Cash or Lose Your Bonus', *New York Times*, 19 September 2021. https://www.nytimes.com/2021/09/19/business/china-evergrande-debt-protests.html?referringSource=articleShare

21 Venus Feng, 'Evergrande Bondholders Eye Founders Megayacht, Planes, Mansions', Bloomberg, 4 November 2021. https://www.bloomberg.com/news/articles/2021-11-04/evergrande-bondholders-eye-founder-s-megayacht-planes-mansions

22 Ibid.

23 Lina Batarags, 'China has at least 65 million empty homes – at least enough to house the population of France. It offers a glimpse into the country's housing market problem', *Business Insider*, 14 October 2021. https://www.businessinsider.com/china-empty-homes-real-estate-evergrande-housing-market-problem-2021-10?op=1&r=US&IR=T

24 Logan Wright, 'China's Property Sector Has Bigger Problems Than Evergrande', *Foreign Policy*, 29 September 2021. https://foreignpolicy.com/2021/09/29/chinas-property-sector-evergrande/

25 Reuters, 'China banking regulator says property market is biggest "grey rhino"', 30 November 2020. https://www.reuters.com/article/us-china-banking-idUSKBN28A1SY

26 Thomas Hale and Sun Yu, 'China's property slowdown sends chill through the economy', *Financial Times*, 21 September 2021. https://www.ft.com/content/4b179ceb-bdd4-4d0a-b009-aea7c9ec0d8d

27 Amanda Lee, 'Explainer: Is China's local government debt a concern and what role do LGFVs play in infrastructure spending', *South China Morning Post*, 2 November 2021. https://www.scmp.com/economy/china-economy/article/3154549/chinas-local-government-debt-concern-and-what-role-do-lgfvs

28 Ryan McMorrow, 'ByteDance's Zhang Yiming steps down as chair of Chinese social media group', *Financial Times*, 3 November 2021. https://www.ft.com/content/2f7becaf-defe-457d-9191-1f87152bf618?shareType=nongift

29 Kevin Yao, 'Explainer: What is China's "common prosperity" drive and why does it matter?', Reuters, 2 September 2021. https://www.reuters.com/world/china/what-is-chinas-common-prosperity-drive-why-does-it-matter-2021-09-02/

30 William Zheng, 'China's Communist Party expels ex-chief of e-commerce hub Hangzhou in corruption probe', *South China Morning Post*, 27 January 2022. https://www.scmp.com/print/news/china/politics/article/3161821/chinas-communist-party-expels-ex-chief-e-commerce-hub-hangzhou

31 Hal Brands, 'The Dangers of China's Decline,' *Foreign Policy*, 14 April 2022. https://foreignpolicy.com/2022/04/14/china-decline-dangers/?ut...Editors%20Picks%20OC&utm_term=41360&tpcc=Editors%20Picks%20OC

32 Farah Elbahrawy, 'Goldman Clients Are Asking If China's Stocks Are Uninvestable', Bloomberg, 29 July 2021. https://www.

bloomberg.com/news/articles/2021-07-29/goldman-clients-are-asking-if-china-s-stocks-are-uninvestable

33 BBC Online, 'Microsoft shutting down LinkedIn in China', 14 October 2021. https://www.bbc.com/news/technology-58911297

34 Vincent Ni, 'Yahoo withdraws from China as Beijing's grip on tech firms tightens', *The Guardian*, 2 November 2021. https://www.theguardian.com/technology/2021/nov/02/yahoo-withdraws-from-china-as-beijings-grip-on-tech-firms-tightens

35 Ker Gibbs, 'Expat exodus is bad for China, bad for the US and bad for the world', *South China Morning Post*, 19 November 2021. https://www.scmp.com/comment/opinion/article/3156404/expat-exodus-bad-china-bad-us-and-bad-world

36 Cliff Buddle, 'An expat exodus is looming fast as Hong Kong's allure fades', *South China Morning Post*, 16 May 2021. https://www.scmp.com/comment/opinion/article/3133636/expat-exodus-looming-fast-allure-fades

37 Didi Tang, 'Mother of all problems for China as birth rate plummets', *The Times*, 24 October 2021. https://www.thetimes.co.uk/article/11738d4c-4d1b-11ec-a89c-4bee41baeb9c?shareToken=6f1cceb46ce117eea017d7553a8fcfce

38 China File, 'What Should China Do about Its Aging Population?' 6 May 2021. https://www.chinafile.com/conversation/what-should-china-do-about-its-aging-population

39 Wang Xiangwei, 'TV parades of corrupt officials snared in Xi Jinping's anti-graft campaign raise more questions than answers', *South China Morning Post*, 22 January 2022. https://www.scmp.com/print/week-asia/opinion/article/3164226/tv-parades-corrupt-officials-snared-xi-jinpings-anti-graft

40 Laura Silver, Kat Devlin and Christine Huang, 'Large Majorities Say China Does Not Respect the Personal Freedoms of Its People', Pew Research Center, 30 June 2021. https://www.pewresearch.org/global/2021/06/30/large-majorities-say-china-does-not-respect-the-personal-freedoms-of-its-people/

41 Muhammed Akbar Notezai, 'Gwadar Protests Highlight CPEC's Achilles' Heel', *The Diplomat*, 9 December 2021. https://thediplomat.com/2021/12/gwadar-protests-highlight-cpecs-achilles-heel/

42 Shah Meer Baloch, 'Protests in Pakistan erupt against China's belt and road plan', *The Guardian*, 20 August 2021. https://www.

theguardian.com/environment/2021/aug/20/water-protests-in-pakistan-erupt-against-chinas-belt-and-road-plan

43 See the Gwadar Port Authority website. http://www.gwadarport.gov.pk/home.aspx

44 Eleni Varvitsioti, 'Piraeus port deal intensifies Greece's unease over China links', *Financial Times*, 19 October 2021. https://www.ft.com/content/3e91c6d2-c3ff-496a-91e8-b9c81aed6eb8?shareType=nongift

45 John Hurley, Scott Morris and Gailyn Portelance, 'Examining the Debt Implications of the Belt and Road Initiative from a Policy Perspective', Center for Global Development, March 2018. https://www.cgdev.org/sites/default/files/examining-debt-implications-belt-and-road-initiative-policy-perspective.pdf

46 David Pilling and Kathrin Hille, 'China cuts finance pledge to Africa amid growing debt concerns', *Financial Times*, 30 November 2021. https://www.ft.com/content/b7bd253a-766d-41b0-923e-9f6701176916

47 'The pandemic is hurting China's Belt and Road Initiative', *The Economist*, 6 June 2020. https://www.economist.com/china/2020/06/04/the-pandemic-is-hurting-chinas-belt-and-road-initiative

48 Ammar A. Malik, Bradley Parks, Brooke Russell, Joyce Jiahui Lin, Katherine Walsh, Kyra Solomon, Sheng Zhang, Thai-Binh Elston and Seth Goodman, 'Banking on the Belt and Road: Insights from a new global dataset of 13,427 Chinese Development Projects', AidData, a Research Lab at William and May, September 2021. https://docs.aiddata.org/ad4/pdfs/Banking_on_the_Belt_and_Road__Insights_from_a_new_global_dataset_of_13427_Chinese_development_projects.pdf

49 Douglas Bulloch, 'China's Xi Jinping Isn't Adolf Hitler, But He Might Be Kaiser Wilhelm', *The National Interest*, 18 August 2020. https://nationalinterest.org/feature/chinas-xi-jinping-isn't-adolf-hitler-he-might-be-kaiser-wilhelm-167122

50 William Safire, *Safire's Political Dictionary* (Oxford and New York: Oxford University Press, 2008), p. 543.

51 Kristin Huang, '"Prepare for war", Xi Jinping tells military region that monitors South China Sea', *South China Morning Post*, 26 October 2018. https://www.scmp.com/news/china/military/article/2170452/prepare-war-xi-jinping-tells-military-region-monitors-south

52 Julian Berger and Helen Davidson, 'Secret group of US military trainers has been in Taiwan for at least a year', *The Guardian*, 7 October 2021. https://www.theguardian.com/world/2021/oct/07/taiwan-us-military-trainers-china

53 Lee Hsi-min and Eric Lee, 'Taiwan's Overall Defense Concept, Explained', *The Diplomat*, 3 November 2020. https://thediplomat.com/2020/11/taiwans-overall-defense-concept-explained/

54 Gideon Rachman, 'Why Aukus is welcome in the Asia-Pacific', *Financial Times*, 20 September 2021. https://www.ft.com/content/cac4b3b0-faec-4648-a49d-8dbcd96eac02?shareType=nongift

55 Roula Khalaf and Henry Foy, 'Nato to expand focus to counter rising China', *Financial Times*, 18 October 2021. https://www.ft.com/content/0202ed6e-62d1-44b6-a61c-8b1278fcf31b?shareType=nongift

56 'The Quad is finding its purpose at last', *The Economist*, 12 June 2021. https://www.economist.com/asia/2021/06/12/the-quad-is-finding-its-purpose-at-last?frsc=dg%7Ce

57 Alex Vivona, 'Water Wars: No One in the Mood for Compromise in the South China Sea', Lawfare, 7 July 2021. https://www.lawfareblog.com/water-wars-no-one-mood-compromise-south-china-sea

58 A 12 June 2021 factsheet, giving details of the Build Back Better Partnership can be accessed via the White House website. https://www.whitehouse.gov/briefing-room/statements-releases/2021/06/12/fact-sheet-president-biden-and-g7-leaders-launch-build-back-better-world-b3w-partnership/

59 Laura Hughes and Sebastian Payne, 'UK seeks to counter China's influence with development investment arm', *Financial Times*, 24 November 2021. https://www.ft.com/content/93de6cc1-451a-465d-8233-8c9b903cedd4?shareType=nongift

60 'WTA boss "willing to pull business out of China" as pressure mounts over missing Peng Shuai', Tennis 365, 19 November 2021. https://www.tennis365.com/wta-tour/wta-steve-simon-withdraw-business-china-missing-peng-shuai/

61 BBC Online, 'Peng Shuai: Doubt cast on email from Chinese tennis star', 18 November 2021. https://www.bbc.co.uk/news/world-asia-china-59325399

62 Ryan Haas, 'China Is Not Ten Feet Tall', *Foreign Affairs*, 3 March 2021. https://www.foreignaffairs.com/articles/china/2021-03-03/china-not-ten-feet-tall

63 Katsuji Nakazawa, 'Analysis: China's ex-Washington envoy surfaces with an important message', *Nikkei Asia*, 13 January 2022. https://asia.nikkei.com/Editor-s-Picks/China-up-close/Analysis-China-s-ex-Washington-envoy-resurfaces-with-an-important-message

## Epilogue

1 These figures are from Janes, an open-source intelligence group, whose website is a respected source of data on comparative military spending. https://www.janes.com/defence-news/news-detail/china-increases-2022-defence-budget-by-71 and https://www.janes.com/defence-news/news-detail/taiwan-proposes-defence-budget-increase-for-2022

2 Evelyn Cheng, 'China's Covid lockdowns are hitting more than just Shanghai and Beijing', CNBC, 5 May 2022. https://www.cnbc.com/2022/05/06/chinas-covid-lockdowns-hit-more-of-the-country-beyond-shanghai-beijing.html

3 Jesse Yeung, 'China tightens ban on "non-essential" overseas travel as lockdown anger rises,' CNN, 13 May 2022. https://edition.cnn.com/2022/05/13/china/china-covid-outbound-travel-restriction-intl-hnk-mic/index.html

4 Vincent Ni, 'Beijing orders 'stress test' as fears of Russia-style sanctions mount', *The Guardian*, 4 May 2022. https://www.theguardian.com/world/2022/may/04/beijing-orders-stress-test-as-fears-of-russia-style-sanctions-mount

5 Chun Han Wong, 'China Insists Party Elites Shed Overseas Assets, eyeing Western Sanctions on Russia,' *The Wall Street Journal*, 19 May 2022. https://www.wsj.com/articles/china-insists-party-elites-shed-overseas-assets-eyeing-western-sanctions-on-russia-11652956787

6 Emma Farge, 'UN to set up inquiry into possible Russian war crimes in Ukraine', Reuters, 13 May 2022. https://www.reuters.com/world/europe/un-rights-chief-says-many-ukraine-abuses-may-amount-war-crimes-2022-05-12/

7 Zhong Sheng, 'U.S. has inescapable responsibilities for Ukrainian crisis', *People's Daily*, 30 March 2022. http://en.people.cn/n3/2022/0330/c90000-10077602.html

8 Jun Mai, 'China hammers home its message of US blame for

Ukraine war to domestic audience,' *South China Morning Post*, 29 March 2022. https://www.scmp.com/news/china/diplomacy/article/3172228/china-hammers-home-its-message-us-blame-ukraine-war-domestic

9 Chris Buckley, 'Bristling Against the West, China Rallies Domestic Sympathy for Russia', *The New York Times*, 4 April 2022. https://www.nytimes.com/2022/04/04/world/asia/china-russia-ukraine.html

10 Derek Saul, 'Russia and China Are Leading a "New World Order", Russian Foreign Minister says', Forbes, 30 March 2022. https://www.forbes.com/sites/dereksaul/2022/03/30/russia-and-china-are-leading-a-new-world-order-russian-foreign-minister-says/

11 Demetri Sevastopulo, Kathrin Hille and Kana Inagaki, 'Chinese and Russian nuclear bombers fly over Sea of Japan as Biden visits Tokyo,' *Financial Times*, 24 May 2022. https://www.ft.com/content/2b77473c-44d8-4b27-98f8-07c096f5302c

12 Andy Bounds, Sam Fleming, Tome Mitchell and Eleanor Olcott, 'China calls on EU to act independently of US foreign policy', *Financial Times*, 1 April 2022. https://www.ft.com/content/5aff68f9-af65-4aa4-9c47-f4fbb35df48f?shareType=nongift

13 'What Taiwan can learn from Russia's invasion of Ukraine,' *The Economist*, 23 April 2022. https://www.economist.com/briefing/what-taiwan-can-learn-from-russias-invasion-of-ukraine/21808850

14 Trever Hunnicutt and Sakura Murakami, 'Biden says he would be willing to use force to defend Taiwan against China', Reuters, 23 May 2022. https://www.reuters.com/world/biden-meets-japanese-emperor-start-visit-launch-regional-economic-plan-2022-05-23/

15 Finbarr Bermingham, 'EU-China summit was a "dialogue of the deaf", says top Brussels diplomat'. *South China Morning Post*, 6 April 2022. https://www.scmp.com/news/china/article/3173188/eu-china-summit-was-dialogue-deaf-says-top-brussels-diplomat

16 James Politi, 'CIA director says China 'unsettled; by Ukraine war', *Financial Times*, 7 May 2022. https://www.ft.com/content/a4e8de3b-a2aa-4f10-a820-a910274175a8

17 Patrick Wintour, 'Japanese premier warns of Ukraine-style invasion by "autocratic powers"', *The Guardian*, 5 May 2022. https://www.theguardian.com/world/2022/may/05/japanese-premier-warns-of-ukraine-style-invasion-by-autocratic-powers

18 See 5 May 2022 statement from the UK Prime Minister's office,

'UK and Japan set to rapidly accelerate defence and security ties with landmark agreement'. https://www.gov.uk/government/news/uk-and-japan-set-to-rapidly-accelerate-defence-and-security-ties-with-landmark-agreement

19 Gavin Blair, David Charter and Michael Evans, 'Japan doubles arms spending to counter threat from China', *The Times*, 28 April 2022. https://www.thetimes.co.uk/article/japan-looks-to-double-defence-budget-as-threats-intensify-m8nkg7dgl

20 See Hu Xijin's 5 May 2022 tweet: https://twitter.com/HuXijin_GT/status/1522062382666682369

21 Demetri Sevastopulo and Kathrin Hille, 'US holds high level talks with UK over China threat to Taiwan', Financial Times, 1 May 2022. https://www.ft.com/content/b0991186-d511-45c2-b5f0-9bd5b8ceee40?shareType=nongift

22 Cristina Gallardo, 'UK's Liz Truss: NATO should protect Taiwan too', Politico, 27 April 2022. https://www.politico.eu/article/liz-truss-nato-taiwan-protect/?aid=app_feed

23 Sam Fleming, Javier Espinoza and Andy Bounds, 'EU warns of €195bn cost to free bloc from Russian energy', *Financial Times* 12 May 2022. https://www.ft.com/content/2aef066b-3cdb-49c2-9258-38575b4ad799?shareType=nongift

24 Jim Pickard, 'UK to consider Chinese takeover of semiconductor plant', Financial Times, 25 May 2022. https://www.ft.com/content/3a3f7c22-138f-4dd5-a3c4-e3ac1f3cca61

25 Dan Sabbagh, 'Foreign agent scheme omitted from UK national security bill', The Guardian, 11 May 2022. https://www.theguardian.com/uk-news/2022/may/11/foreign-agent-scheme-omitted-from-uk-national-security-bill

26 Keoni Everington, '30% more Taiwanese willing to fight for country after Russian invasion of Ukraine', Taiwan News, 17 March 2022. https://www.taiwannews.com.tw/en/news/4476140

# Index